2023 Document Supplement to
Contract Law and Theory

2023 Document Supplement to
Contract Law and Theory

*Selected Provisions: Restatement of Contracts,
Uniform Commercial Code, and CISG*

SIXTH EDITION

2023

Robert E. Scott
ALFRED MCCORMACK PROFESSOR OF LAW EMERITUS
COLUMBIA LAW SCHOOL

Jody P. Kraus
ALFRED MCCORMACK PROFESSOR OF LAW
COLUMBIA LAW SCHOOL

CAROLINA ACADEMIC PRESS
Durham, North Carolina

ISBN 978-1-5310-2398-0
eISBN 978-1-5310-2399-7

Carolina Academic Press, LLC
700 Kent Street
Durham, North Carolina 27701
(919) 489-7486
www.cap-press.com

Printed in the United States of America

Table of Contents

UNIFORM COMMERCIAL CODE

2023 Document Supplement to

Contract Law and Theory

RESTATEMENT (SECOND) OF CONTRACTS*

Chapter 1

MEANING OF TERMS

§ 1. Contract Defined

A contract is a promise or a set of promises for the breach of which the law gives a remedy, or the performance of which the law in some way recognizes as a duty.

§ 2. Promise; Promisor; Promisee; Beneficiary

(1) A promise is a manifestation of intention to act or refrain from acting in a specified way, so made as to justify a promisee in understanding that a commitment has been made.

(2) The person manifesting the intention is the promisor.

(3) The person to whom the manifestation is addressed is the promisee.

(4) Where performance will benefit a person other than the promisee, that person is a beneficiary.

Comment

b. Manifestation of intention. Many contract disputes arise because different people attach different meanings to the same words and conduct. The phrase "manifestation of intention" adopts an external or objective standard for interpreting conduct; it means the external expression of intention as distinguished from undisclosed intention. A promisor manifests an intention if he believes or has reason to believe that the promisee will infer that intention from his words or conduct. Rules governing cases where the promisee could reasonably draw more than one inference as to the promisor's intention are stated in connection with the acceptance of offers (see § 20), and the scope of contractual obligations (see § 201).

§ 4. How a Promise May Be Made

A promise may be stated in words either oral or written, or may be inferred wholly or partly from conduct.

Chapter 2

FORMATION OF CONTRACTS—
PARTIES AND CAPACITY

§ 12. Capacity to Contract

(1) No one can be bound by contract who has not legal capacity to incur at least voidable contractual duties. Capacity to contract may be partial and its existence in respect of a particular transaction may depend upon the nature of the transaction or upon other circumstances.

(2) A natural person who manifests assent to a transaction has full legal capacity to incur contractual duties thereby unless he is
  (a) under guardianship, or
  (b) an infant, or
  (c) mentally ill or defective, or
  (d) intoxicated.

§ 13. Persons Affected by Guardianship

A person has no capacity to incur contractual duties if his property is under guardianship by reason of an adjudication of mental illness or defect.

§ 14. Infants

Unless a statute provides otherwise, a natural person has the capacity to incur only voidable contractual duties until the beginning of the day before the person's eighteenth birthday.

§ 15. Mental Illness or Defect

(1) A person incurs only voidable contractual duties by entering into a transaction if by reason of mental illness or defect
  (a) he is unable to understand in a reasonable manner the nature and consequences of the transaction, or
  (b) he is unable to act in a reasonable manner in relation to the transaction and the other party has reason to know of his condition.

(2) Where the contract is made on fair terms and the other party is without knowledge of the mental illness or defect, the power of avoidance under Subsection(1) terminates to the extent that the contract has been so performed in whole or in part or the circumstances have so changed that avoidance would be unjust. In such a case a court may grant relief as justice requires.

§ 16. Intoxicated Persons

A person incurs only voidable contractual duties by entering into a transaction if the other party has reason to know that by reason of intoxication

(a) he is unable to understand in a reasonable manner the nature and consequences of the transaction, or

(b) he is unable to act in a reasonable manner in relation to the transaction.

Chapter 3

FORMATION OF CONTRACTS — MUTUAL ASSENT

In General

§ 17. Requirement of a Bargain

(1) Except as stated in Subsection (2), the formation of a contract requires a bargain in which there is a manifestation of mutual assent to the exchange and a consideration.

(2) Whether or not there is a bargain a contract may be formed under special rules applicable to formal contracts or under the rules stated in §§ 82-94.

Manifestation of Assent in General

§ 18. Manifestation of Mutual Assent

Manifestation of mutual assent to an exchange requires that each party either make a promise or begin or render a performance.

[The predecessor of § 18 is § 20 of the First Restatement. It read as follows:

§ 20. Requirement of Manifestation of Mutual Assent

A manifestation of mutual assent by the parties to an informal contract is essential to its formation and the acts by which such assent is manifested must be done with the intent to do those acts; but, except as qualified by §§ 55, 71 and 72, neither mental assent to the promises in the contract nor real or apparent intent that the promises shall be legally binding is essential.]

§ 19. Conduct as Manifestation of Assent

(1) The manifestation of assent may be made wholly or partly by written or spoken words or by other acts or by failure to act.

(2) The conduct of a party is not effective as a manifestation of his assent unless he intends to engage in the conduct and knows or has reason to know that the other party may infer from his conduct that he assents.

(3) The conduct of a party may manifest assent even though he does not in fact assent. In such cases a resulting contract may be voidable because of fraud, duress, mistake, or other invalidating cause.

§ 20. Effect of Misunderstanding

(1) There is no manifestation of mutual assent to an exchange if the parties attach materially different meanings to their manifestations and
  (a) neither party knows or has reason to know the meaning attached by the other; or
  (b) each party knows or each party has reason to know the meaning attached by the other.

(2) The manifestations of the parties are operative in accordance with the meaning attached to them by one of the parties if
  (a) that party does not know of any different meaning attached by the other, and the other knows the meaning attached by the first party; or
  (b) that party has no reason to know of any different meaning attached by the other, and the other has reason to know the meaning attached by the first party.

§ 21. Intention to Be Legally Bound

Neither real nor apparent intention that a promise be legally binding is essential to the formation of a contract, but a manifestation of intention that a promise shall not affect legal relations may prevent the formation of a contract.

§ 22. Mode of Assent: Offer and Acceptance

(1) The manifestation of mutual assent to an exchange ordinarily takes the form of an offer or proposal by one party followed by an acceptance by the other party or parties.

(2) A manifestation of mutual assent may be made even though neither offer nor acceptance can be identified and even though the moment of formation cannot be determined.

Comment

b. Assent by course of conduct. Problems of offer and acceptance are important primarily in cases where advance commitment serves to shift a risk from one party to the other, as in sales of goods which are subject to rapid price fluctuations, in sales of land, and in insurance contracts. Controversies as to whether and when the commitment is made are less likely to be important even in such cases once performance is well under way. Offer and acceptance become still less important after there have been repeated occasions for performance by one party where the other knows the nature of the performance and has an opportunity for objection to it. See Uniform Commercial Code § 2-208(1). In such cases it is unnecessary to determine the moment of making of the contract, or which party made the offer and which the acceptance. Thus, Uniform Commercial Code §§ 2-204 and 2-207(3), relating to contracts for the sale of goods, provide that conduct by both parties which recognizes the existence of a contract is sufficient to establish it although the writings of the parties do not otherwise establish a contract. The principle has also been applied in non-sales contexts.

Making of Offers

§ 24. Offer Defined

An offer is the manifestation of willingness to enter into a bargain, so made as to justify another person in understanding that his assent to that bargain is invited and will conclude it.

§ 25. Option Contracts

An option contract is a promise which meets the requirements for the formation of a contract and limits the promisor's power to revoke an offer.

§ 26. Preliminary Negotiations

A manifestation of willingness to enter into a bargain is not an offer if the person to whom it is addressed knows or has reason to know that the person making it does not intend to conclude a bargain until he has made a further manifestation of assent.

[The predecessor of § 26 is § 25 of the First Restatement. It read as follows:

§ 25. When a Manifestation of Intention Is Not an Offer

If from a promise, or manifestation of intention, or from the circumstances existing at the time, the person to whom the promise or manifestation is addressed knows or has reason to know that the person making it does not intend it as an expression of his fixed purpose until he has given a further expression of assent, he has not made an offer.]

§ 27. Existence of Contract Where Written Memorial Is Contemplated

Manifestations of assent that are in themselves sufficient to conclude a contract will not be prevented from so operating by the fact that the parties also manifest an intention to prepare and adopt a written memorial thereof; but the circumstances may show that the agreements are preliminary negotiations.

§ 30. Form of Acceptance Invited

(1) An offer may invite or require acceptance to be made by an affirmative answer
     in words, or by performing or refraining from performing a specified act, or
     may empower the offeree to make a selection of terms in his acceptance.

(2) Unless otherwise indicated by the language or the circumstances, an offer in-
     vites acceptance in any manner and by any medium reasonable in the circum-
     stances.

§ 32. Invitation of Promise or Performance

In case of doubt an offer is interpreted as inviting the offeree to accept either by prom-
ising to perform what the offer requests or by rendering the performance, as the offeree
chooses.

§ 33. Certainty

(1) Even though a manifestation of intention is intended to be understood as an
     offer, it cannot be accepted so as to form a contract unless the terms of the con-
     tract are reasonably certain.

(2) The terms of a contract are reasonably certain if they provide a basis for deter-
     mining the existence of a breach and for giving an appropriate remedy.

(3) The fact that one or more terms of a proposed bargain are left open or uncertain
     may show that a manifestation of intention is not intended to be understood as
     an offer or as an acceptance.

§ 34. Certainty and Choice of Terms; Effect of Performance or Reliance

(1) The terms of a contract may be reasonably certain even though it empowers one
     or both parties to make a selection of terms in the course of performance.

(2) Part performance under an agreement may remove uncertainty and establish
     that a contract enforceable as a bargain has been formed.

(3) Action in reliance on an agreement may make a contractual remedy appropriate
     even though uncertainty is not removed.

Duration of the Offeree's Power of Acceptance

§ 35. The Offeree's Power of Acceptance

(1) An offer gives to the offeree a continuing power to complete the manifestation
     of mutual assent by acceptance of the offer.

(2) A contract cannot be created by acceptance of an offer after the power of accep-
     tance has been terminated in one of the ways listed in § 36.

§ 36. Methods of Termination of the Power of Acceptance

(1) An offeree's power of acceptance may be terminated by

    (a) rejection or counter-offer by the offeree, or

    (b) lapse of time, or

    (c) revocation by the offeror, or

    (d) death or incapacity of the offeror or offeree.

(2) In addition, an offeree's power of acceptance is terminated by the non-occurrence of any condition of acceptance under the terms of the offer.

§ 38. Rejection

(1) An offeree's power of acceptance is terminated by his rejection of the offer, unless the offeror has manifested a contrary intention.

(2) A manifestation of intention not to accept an offer is a rejection unless the offeree manifests an intention to take it under further advisement.

§ 39. Counter-Offers

(1) A counter-offer is an offer made by an offeree to his offeror relating to the same matter as the original offer and proposing a substituted bargain differing from that proposed by the original offer.

(2) An offeree's power of acceptance is terminated by his making of a counter-offer, unless the offeror has manifested a contrary intention or unless the counter-offer manifests a contrary intention of the offeree.

[The predecessor of § 39 was § 38 of the First Restatement. It read as follows:

§ 38. Rejection of Offer by Counter-Offer

A counter-offer by the offeree, relating to the same matter as the original offer, is a rejection of the original offer, unless the offeror in his offer, or the offeree in his counter-offer states that in spite of the counter-offer the original offer shall not be terminated.]

§ 40. Time When Rejection or Counter-Offer Terminates the Power of Acceptance

Rejection or counter-offer by mail or telegram does not terminate the power of acceptance until received by the offeror, but limits the power so that a letter or telegram of acceptance started after the sending of an otherwise effective rejection or counter-offer is only a counter-offer unless the acceptance is received by the offeror before he receives the rejection or counter-offer.

§ 41. Lapse of Time

(1) An offeree's power of acceptance is terminated at the time specified in the offer, or, if no time is specified, at the end of a reasonable time.

(2) What is a reasonable time is a question of fact, depending on all the circumstances existing when the offer and attempted acceptance are made.

(3) Unless otherwise indicated by the language or the circumstances, and subject to the rule stated in § 49, an offer sent by mail is seasonably accepted if an acceptance is mailed at any time before midnight on the day on which the offer is received.

§ 42. Revocation by Communication From Offeror Received by Offeree

An offeree's power of acceptance is terminated when the offeree receives from the offeror a manifestation of an intention not to enter into the proposed contract.

§ 43. Indirect Communication of Revocation

An offeree's power of acceptance is terminated when the offeror takes definite action inconsistent with an intention to enter into the proposed contract and the offeree acquires reliable information to that effect.

§ 45. Option Contract Created by Part Performance or Tender

(1) Where an offer invites an offeree to accept by rendering a performance and does not invite a promissory acceptance, an option contract is created when the offeree tenders or begins the invited performance or tenders a beginning of it.

(2) The offeror's duty of performance under any option contract so created is conditional on completion or tender of the invited performance in accordance with the terms of the offer.

§ 46. Revocation of General Offer

Where an offer is made by advertisement in a newspaper or other general notification to the public or to a number of persons whose identity is unknown to the offeror, the offeree's power of acceptance is terminated when a notice of termination is given publicity by advertisement or other general notification equal to that given to the offer and no better means of notification is reasonably available.

Acceptance of Offers

§ 48. Death or Incapacity of Offeror or Offeree

An offeree's power of acceptance is terminated when the offeree or offeror dies or is deprived of legal capacity to enter into the proposed contract.

§ 50. Acceptance of Offer Defined; Acceptance by Performance; Acceptance by Promise

(1) Acceptance of an offer is a manifestation of assent to the terms thereof made by the offeree in a manner invited or required by the offer.

(2) Acceptance by performance requires that at least part of what the offer requests be performed or tendered and includes acceptance by a performance which operates as a return promise.

(3) Acceptance by a promise requires that the offeree complete every act essential to the making of the promise.

Comment

b. Acceptance by performance. Where the offer requires acceptance by performance and does not invite a return promise, as in the ordinary case of an offer of a reward, a contract can be created only by the offeree's performance. See Comment b to § 32. In such cases the act requested and performed as consideration for the offeror's promise ordinarily also constitutes acceptance; under § 45 the beginning of performance or the tender of part performance of what is requested may both indicate assent and furnish consideration for an option contract. In some other cases the offeree may choose to create a contract either by making a promise or by rendering or tendering performance; in most such cases the beginning of performance or a tender of part performance operates as a promise to render complete performance. See §§ 32, 62. Mere preparation to perform, however, is not acceptance, although in some cases preparation may make the offeror's promise binding under § 87(2).

c. Acceptance by promise. The typical contract consists of mutual promises and is formed by an acceptance constituting a return promise by the offeree. A promissory acceptance may be explicitly required by the offer, or may be the only type of acceptance which is reasonable under the circumstances, or the offeree may choose to accept by promise an offer which invites acceptance either by promise or by performance. See §§ 30, 32. The promise may be made in words or other symbols of assent, or it may be implied from conduct, other than acts of performance, provided only that it is in a form invited or required by the offer. An act of performance may also operate as a return promise, but the acceptance in such a case is treated as an acceptance by performance rather than an acceptance by promise; thus the requirement of notification is governed by § 54 rather than by § 56. As appears from § 63, acceptance by promise may be effective when a written promise is started on its way, but the offeree must complete the acts necessary on his part to constitute a promise by him. Similarly, in cases where communication to the offeror is unnecessary under § 69, the acts constituting the promise must be complete.

§ 51. Effect of Part Performance Without Knowledge of Offer

Unless the offeror manifests a contrary intention, an offeree who learns of an offer after he has rendered part of the performance requested by the offer may accept by completing the requested performance.

§ 52. Who May Accept an Offer

An offer can be accepted only by a person whom it invites to furnish the consideration.

§ 53. Acceptance by Performance; Manifestation of Intention Not to Accept

(1) An offer can be accepted by the rendering of a performance only if the offer invites such an acceptance.

(2) Except as stated in § 69, the rendering of a performance does not constitute an acceptance if within a reasonable time the offeree exercises reasonable diligence to notify the offeror of non-acceptance.

(3) Where an offer of a promise invites acceptance by performance and does not invite a promissory acceptance, the rendering of the invited performance does not constitute an acceptance if before the offeror performs his promise the offeree manifests an intention not to accept.

§ 54. Acceptance by Performance; Necessity of Notification to Offeror

(1) Where an offer invites an offeree to accept by rendering a performance, no notification is necessary to make such an acceptance effective unless the offer requests such a notification.

(2) If an offeree who accepts by rendering a performance has reason to know that the offeror has no adequate means of learning of the performance with reasonable promptness and certainty, the contractual duty of the offeror is discharged unless

    (a) the offeree exercises reasonable diligence to notify the offeror of acceptance, or

    (b) the offeror learns of the performance within a reasonable time, or

    (c) the offer indicates that notification of acceptance is not required.

§ 55. Acceptance of Non-Promissory Offers

Acceptance by promise may create a contract in which the offeror's performance is completed when the offeree's promise is made.

§ 56. Acceptance by Promise; Necessity of Notification to Offeror

Except as stated in § 69 or where the offer manifests a contrary intention, it is essential to an acceptance by promise either that the offeree exercise reasonable diligence to notify the offeror of acceptance or that the offeror receive the acceptance seasonably.

§ 58. Necessity of Acceptance Complying with Terms of Offer

An acceptance must comply with the requirements of the offer as to the promise to be made or the performance to be rendered.

§ 59. Purported Acceptance Which Adds Qualifications

A reply to an offer which purports to accept it but is conditional on the offeror's assent to terms additional to or different from those offered is not an acceptance but is a counter-offer.

§ 60. Acceptance of Offer Which States Place, Time or Manner of Acceptance

If an offer prescribes the place, time or manner of acceptance its terms in this respect must be complied with in order to create a contract. If an offer merely suggests a permitted place, time or manner of acceptance, another method of acceptance is not precluded.

§ 61. Acceptance Which Requests Change of Terms

An acceptance which requests a change or addition to the terms of the offer is not thereby invalidated unless the acceptance is made to depend on an assent to the changed or added terms.

§ 62. Effect of Performance by Offeree Where Offer Invites Either Performance or Promise

(1) Where an offer invites an offeree to choose between acceptance by promise and acceptance by performance, the tender or beginning of the invited performance or a tender of a beginning of it is an acceptance by performance.

(2) Such an acceptance operates as a promise to render complete performance.

§ 63. Time When Acceptance Takes Effect

Unless the offer provides otherwise,
  (a) an acceptance made in a manner and by a medium invited by an offer is operative and completes the manifestation of mutual assent as soon as put out of the offeree's possession, without regard to whether it ever reaches the offeror; but
  (b) an acceptance under an option contract is not operative until received by the offeror.

§ 66. Acceptance Must Be Properly Dispatched

An acceptance sent by mail or otherwise from a distance is not operative when dispatched, unless it is properly addressed and such other precautions taken as are ordinarily observed to insure safe transmission of similar messages.

§ 69. Acceptance by Silence or Exercise of Dominion

(1) Where an offeree fails to reply to an offer, his silence and inaction operate as an acceptance in the following cases only:

    (a) Where an offeree takes the benefit of offered services with reasonable opportunity to reject them and reason to know that they were offered with the expectation of compensation.

    (b) Where the offeror has stated or given the offeree reason to understand that assent may be manifested by silence or inaction, and the offeree in remaining silent and inactive intends to accept the offer.

    (c) Where because of previous dealings or otherwise, it is reasonable that the offeree should notify the offeror if he does not intend to accept.

(2) An offeree who does any act inconsistent with the offeror's ownership of offered property is bound in accordance with the offered terms unless they are manifestly unreasonable. But if the act is wrongful as against the offeror it is an acceptance only if ratified by him.

Chapter 4

FORMATION OF CONTRACTS — CONSIDERATION

The Requirement of Consideration

§ 71. Requirement of Exchange; Types of Exchange

(1) To constitute consideration, a performance or a return promise must be bargained for.

(2) A performance or return promise is bargained for if it is sought by the promisor in exchange for his promise and is given by the promisee in exchange for that promise.

(3) The performance may consist of

    (a) an act other than a promise, or

    (b) a forbearance, or

    (c) the creation, modification, or destruction of a legal relation.

(4) The performance or return promise may be given to the promisor or to some other person. It may be given by the promisee or by some other person.

§ 73. Performance of Legal Duty

Performance of a legal duty owed to a promisor which is neither doubtful nor the subject of honest dispute is not consideration; but a similar performance is consideration if it differs from what was required by the duty in a way which reflects more than a pretense of bargain.

§ 74. Settlement of Claims

(1) Forbearance to assert or the surrender of a claim or defense which proves to be invalid is not consideration unless
    (a) the claim or defense is in fact doubtful because of uncertainty as to the facts or the law, or
    (b) the forbearing or surrendering party believes that the claim or defense may be fairly determined to be valid.

(2) The execution of a written instrument surrendering a claim or defense by one who is under no duty to execute it is consideration if the execution of the written instrument is bargained for even though he is not asserting the claim or defense and believes that no valid claim or defense exists.

§ 77. Illusory and Alternative Promises

A promise or apparent promise is not consideration if by its terms the promisor or purported promisor reserves a choice of alternative performances unless
    (a) each of the alternative performances would have been consideration if it alone had been bargained for; or
    (b) one of the alternative performances would have been consideration and there is or appears to the parties to be a substantial possibility that before the promisor exercises his choice events may eliminate the alternatives which would not have been consideration.

§ 79. Adequacy of Consideration; Mutuality of Obligation

If the requirement of consideration is met, there is no additional requirement of
    (a) a gain, advantage, or benefit to the promisor or a loss, disadvantage, or detriment to the promisee; or
    (b) equivalence in the values exchanged; or
    (c) "mutuality of obligation."

§ 81. Consideration as Motive or Inducing Cause

(1) The fact that what is bargained for does not of itself induce the making of a promise does not prevent it from being consideration for the promise.

(2) The fact that a promise does not of itself induce a performance or return promise does not prevent the performance or return promise from being consideration for the promise.

Comment

a. "Bargained for." Consideration requires that a performance or return promise be "bargained for" in exchange for a promise; this means that the promisor must manifest an intention to induce the performance or return promise and to be induced by it, and that the promisee must manifest an intention to induce the making of the promise and to be induced by it. In most commercial bargains the consideration is the object of the promisor's desire and that desire is a material motive or cause inducing the making of the promise, and the reciprocal desire of the promisee for the making of the promise similarly induces the furnishing of the consideration.

b. Immateriality of motive or cause. This Section makes explicit a limitation on the requirement that consideration be bargained for. Even in the typical commercial bargain, the promisor may have more than one motive, and the person furnishing the consideration need not inquire into the promisor's motives. Unless both parties know that the purported consideration is mere pretense, it is immaterial that the promisor's desire for the consideration is incidental to other objectives and even that the other party knows this to be so.

Contracts Without Consideration

§ 82. Promise to Pay Indebtedness; Effect on the Statute of Limitations

(1) A promise to pay all or part of an antecedent contractual or quasi-contractual indebtedness owed by the promisor is binding if the indebtedness is still enforceable or would be except for the effect of a statute of limitations.

(2) The following facts operate as such a promise unless other facts indicate a different intention:
  (a) A voluntary acknowledgment to the obligee, admitting the present existence of the antecedent indebtedness; or
  (b) A voluntary transfer of money, a negotiable instrument, or other thing by the obligor to the obligee, made as interest on or part payment of or collateral security for the antecedent indebtedness; or
  (c) A statement to the obligee that the statute of limitations will not be pleaded as a defense.

§ 83. Promise to Pay Indebtedness Discharged in Bankruptcy

An express promise to pay all or part of an indebtedness of the promisor, discharged or dischargeable in bankruptcy proceedings begun before the promise is made, is binding.

§ 84. Promise to Perform a Duty in Spite of Non-Occurrence Of a Condition

(1) Except as stated in Subsection (2), a promise to perform all or part of a conditional duty under an antecedent contract in spite of the non-occurrence of the condition is binding, whether the promise is made before or after the time for the condition to occur, unless

    (a) occurrence of the condition was a material part of the agreed exchange for the performance of the duty and the promisee was under no duty that it occur; or

    (b) uncertainty of the occurrence of the condition was an element of the risk assumed by the promisor.

(2) If such a promise is made before the time for the occurrence of the condition has expired and the condition is within the control of the promisee or a beneficiary, the promisor can make his duty again subject to the condition by notifying the promisee or beneficiary of his intention to do so if

    (a) the notification is received while there is still a reasonable time to cause the condition to occur under the antecedent terms or an extension given by the promisor; and

    (b) reinstatement of the requirement of the condition is not unjust because of a material change of position by the promisee or beneficiary; and

    (c) the promise is not binding apart from the rule stated in Subsection (1).

§ 86. Promise for Benefit Received

(1) A promise made in recognition of a benefit previously received by the promisor from the promisee is binding to the extent necessary to prevent injustice.

(2) A promise is not binding under Subsection (1)

    (a) if the promisee conferred the benefit as a gift or for other reasons the promisor has not been unjustly enriched; or

    (b) to the extent that its value is disproportionate to the benefit.

§ 87. Option Contract

(1) An offer is binding as an option contract if it

    (a) is in writing and signed by the offeror, recites a purported consideration for the making of the offer, and proposes an exchange on fair terms within a reasonable time; or

    (b) is made irrevocable by statute.

(2) An offer which the offeror should reasonably expect to induce action or forbearance of a substantial character on the part of the offeree before acceptance and which does induce such action or forbearance is binding as an option contract to the extent necessary to avoid injustice.

§ 89. Modification of Executory Contract

A promise modifying a duty under a contract not fully performed on either side is binding
  (a) if the modification is fair and equitable in view of circumstances not anticipated by the parties when the contract was made; or
  (b) to the extent provided by statute; or
  (c) to the extent that justice requires enforcement in view of material change of position in reliance on the promise.

§ 90. Promise Reasonably Inducing Action or Forbearance

(1) A promise which the promisor should reasonably expect to induce action or forbearance on the part of the promisee or a third person and which does induce such action or forbearance is binding if injustice can be avoided only by enforcement of the promise. The remedy granted for breach may be limited as justice requires.

(2) A charitable subscription or a marriage settlement is binding under Subsection (1) without proof that the promise induced action or forbearance.

[The predecessor of § 90, in the First Restatement, read as follows:

§ 90. Promise Reasonably Inducing Definite and Substantial Action

A promise which the promisor should reasonably expect to induce action or forbearance of definite and substantial character on the part of the promisee and which does induce such action or forbearance is binding if injustice can be avoided only by enforcement of the promise.]

Contracts Under Seal: Writing as a Statutory Substitute for the Seal

[The Introduction to this topic notes that the effect of a seal is governed by statute in most states.]

§ 95. Requirements for Sealed Contract or Written Contract or Instrument

(1) In the absence of statute a promise is binding without consideration if
  (a) it is in writing and sealed; and
  (b) the document containing the promise is delivered; and
  (c) the promisor and promisee are named in the document or so described as to be capable of identification when it is delivered.

(2) When a statute provides in effect that a written contract or instrument is binding without consideration or that lack of consideration is an affirmative defense to an action on a written contract or instrument, in order to be subject to the statute a promise must either

(a) be expressed in a document signed or otherwise assented to by the promisor and delivered; or

(b) be expressed in a writing or writings to which both promisor and promisee manifest assent.

Chapter 5

THE STATUTE OF FRAUDS

§ 110. Classes of Contracts Covered

(1) The following classes of contracts are subject to a statute, commonly called the Statute of Frauds, forbidding enforcement unless there is a written memorandum or an applicable exception:

(a) a contract of an executor or administrator to answer for a duty of his decedent (the executor administrator provision);

(b) a contract to answer for the duty of another (the suretyship provision);

(c) a contract made upon consideration of marriage (the marriage provision);

(d) a contract for the sale of an interest in land (the land contract provision);

(e) a contract that is not to be performed within one year from the making thereof (the one-year provision).

(2) The following classes of contracts, which were traditionally subject to the Statute of Frauds, are now governed by Statute of Frauds provisions of the Uniform Commercial Code:

(a) a contract for the sale of goods for the price of $ 500 or more (Uniform Commercial Code § 2-201);

(b) a contract for the sale of securities (Uniform Commercial Code § 8-319);

(c) a contract for the sale of personal property not otherwise covered, to the extent of enforcement by way of action or defense beyond $ 5,000 in amount or value of remedy (Uniform Commercial Code § 1-206).

(3) In addition the Uniform Commercial Code requires a writing signed by the debtor for an agreement which creates or provides for a security interest in personal property or fixtures not in the possession of the secured party.

(4) Statutes in most states provide that no acknowledgment or promise is sufficient evidence of a new or continuing contract to take a case out of the operation of a statute of limitations unless made in some writing signed by the party to be charged, but that the statute does not alter the effect of any payment of principal or interest.

(5) In many states other classes of contracts are subject to a requirement of a writing.

The Land Contract Provision

§ 125. Contract to Transfer, Buy, or Pay for an Interest in Land

(1) A promise to transfer to any person any interest in land is within the Statute of Frauds.

(2) A promise to buy any interest in land is within the Statute of Frauds, irrespective of the person to whom the transfer is to be made.

(3) When a transfer of an interest in land has been made, a promise to pay the price, if originally within the Statute of Frauds, ceases to be within it unless the promised price is itself in whole or in part an interest in land.

(4) Statutes in most states except from the land contract and one-year provisions of the Statute of Frauds short-term leases and contracts to lease, usually for a term not longer than one year.

§ 129. Action in Reliance; Specific Performance

A contract for the transfer of an interest in land may be specifically enforced notwithstanding failure to comply with the Statute of Frauds if it is established that the party seeking enforcement, in reasonable reliance on the contract and on the continuing assent of the party against whom enforcement is sought, has so changed his position that injustice can be avoided only by specific enforcement.

The One-Year Provision

§ 130. Contract Not to Be Performed Within a Year

(1) Where any promise in a contract cannot be fully performed within a year from the time the contract is made, all promises in the contract are within the Statute of Frauds until one party to the contract completes his performance.

(2) When one party to a contract has completed his performance, the one-year provision of the Statute does not prevent enforcement of the promises of other parties.

Satisfaction of the Statute by a Memorandum

§ 131. General Requisites of a Memorandum

Unless additional requirements are prescribed by the particular statute, a contract within the Statute of Frauds is enforceable if it is evidenced by any writing, signed by or on behalf of the party to be charged, which
  (a) reasonably identifies the subject matter of the contract,
  (b) is sufficient to indicate that a contract with respect thereto has been made between the parties or offered by the signer to the other party, and
  (c) states with reasonable certainty the essential terms of the unperformed promises in the contract.

§ 132. Several Writings

The memorandum may consist of several writings if one of the writings is signed and the writings in the circumstances clearly indicate that they relate to the same transaction.

§ 134. Signature

The signature to a memorandum may be any symbol made or adopted with an intention, actual or apparent, to authenticate the writing as that of the signer.

Consequences of Non-Compliance

§ 139. Enforcement by Virtue of Action in Reliance

(1) A promise which the promisor should reasonably expect to induce action or forbearance on the part of the promisee or a third person and which does induce the action or forbearance is enforceable notwithstanding the Statute of Frauds if injustice can be avoided only by enforcement of the promise. The remedy granted for breach is to be limited as justice requires.

(2) In determining whether injustice can be avoided only by enforcement of the promise, the following circumstances are significant:
   (a) the availability and adequacy of other remedies, particularly cancellation and restitution;
   (b) the definite and substantial character of the action or forbearance in relation to the remedy sought;
   (c) the extent to which the action or forbearance corroborates evidence of the making and terms of the promise, or the making and terms are otherwise established by clear and convincing evidence;
   (d) the reasonableness of the action or forbearance;
   (e) the extent to which the action or forbearance was foreseeable by the promisor.

Chapter 6

MISTAKE

§ 151. Mistake Defined

A mistake is a belief that is not in accord with the facts.

Comment

a. Belief as to facts. In this Restatement the word "mistake" is used to refer to an erroneous belief. A party's erroneous belief is therefore said to be a "mistake" of that party. The belief need not be an articulated one, and a party may have a belief as to a fact when he merely makes an assumption with respect to it, without being aware of alternatives.

The word "mistake" is not used here, as it is sometimes used in common speech, to refer to an improvident act, including the making of a contract, that is the result of such an erroneous belief. This usage is avoided here for the sake of clarity and consistency. Furthermore, the erroneous belief must relate to the facts as they exist at the time of the making of the contract. A party's prediction or judgment as to events to occur in the future, even if erroneous, is not a "mistake" as that word is defined here. An erroneous belief as to the contents or effect of a writing that expresses the agreement is, however, a mistake. Mistake alone, in the sense in which the word is used here, has no legal consequences. The legal consequences of mistake in connection with the creation of contractual liability are determined by the rules stated in the rest of this Chapter.

Illustration

1. A contracts with B to raise and float B's boat which has run aground on a reef. At the time of making the contract, A believes that the sea will remain calm until the work is completed. Several days later, during a sudden storm, the boat slips into deep water and fills with mud, making it more difficult for A to raise it. Although A may have shown poor judgment in making the contract, there was no mistake of either A or B, and the rules stated in this Chapter do not apply. Whether A is discharged by supervening impracticability is governed by the rules stated in Chapter 11. See Illustration 5 to § 261. If, however, the boat had already slipped into deep water at the time the contract was made, although they both believed that it was still on the reef, there would have been a mistake of both A and B. Its legal consequences, if any, would be governed by the rule stated in § 152.

§ 152. When Mistake of Both Parties Makes a Contract Voidable

(1) Where a mistake of both parties at the time a contract was made as to a basic assumption on which the contract was made has a material effect on the agreed exchange of performances, the contract is voidable by the adversely affected party unless he bears the risk of the mistake under the rule stated in § 154.

(2) In determining whether the mistake has a material effect on the agreed exchange of performances, account is taken of any relief by way of reformation, restitution, or otherwise.

Comment

b. Basic assumption. A mistake of both parties does not make the contract voidable unless it is one as to a basic assumption on which both parties made the contract. The term "basic assumption" has the same meaning here as it does in Chapter 11 in connection with impracticability (§§ 261, 266(1)) and frustration (§§ 265, 266(2)). See Uniform Commercial Code § 2-615(a). For example, market conditions and the financial situation of the parties are ordinarily not such assumptions, and, generally, just as shifts in market conditions or financial ability do not effect discharge under the rules governing impracticability, mistakes as to market conditions or financial ability do not justify avoidance under the rules governing mistake. The parties may have had such a "basic assumption," even though they were not conscious of alternatives. See Introductory Note to Chapter 11. Where, for example, a party purchases an annuity on the life of another person, it can be said that it was a basic assumption that the other person was alive at the time, even though the parties never consciously addressed themselves to the possibility that he was dead.

Illustrations

1. A contracts to sell and B to buy a tract of land, the value of which has depended mainly on the timber on it. Both A and B believe that the timber is still there, but in fact it has been destroyed by fire. The contract is voidable by B.

2. A contracts to sell and B to buy a tract of land, on the basis of the report of a surveyor whom A has employed to determine the acreage. The price is, however, a lump sum not calculated from the acreage. Because of an error in computation by the surveyor, the tract contains ten per cent more acreage than he reports. The contract is voidable by A. Compare Illustrations 8 and 11 to this Section and Illustration 2 to § 158.

3. A contracts to sell and B to buy a tract of land. B agrees to pay A $ 100,000 in cash and to assume a mortgage that C holds on the tract. Both A and B believe that the amount of the mortgage is $ 50,000, but in fact it is only $ 10,000. The contract is voidable by A, unless the court supplies a term under which B is entitled to enforce the contract if he agrees to pay an appropriate additional sum, and B does so.

Comment

c. Material effect on agreed exchange. A party cannot avoid a contract merely because both parties were mistaken as to a basic assumption on which it was made. He must, in addition, show that the mistake has a material effect on the agreed exchange of performances. It is not enough for him to prove that he would not have made the contract had it not been for the mistake. He must show that the resulting imbalance in the agreed exchange is so severe that he can not fairly be required to carry it out. Ordinarily he will be able to do this by showing that the exchange is not only less desirable to him but is also more advantageous to the other party. Sometimes this is so because the adversely affected party will give, and the other party will receive, something more than they supposed. Sometimes it is so because the other party will give, and the adversely affected party will receive, something less than they supposed. In such cases the materiality of the effect on the agreed exchange will be determined by the overall impact on both parties. In exceptional cases the adversely affected party may be able to show that the effect on the agreed exchange has been material simply on the ground that the exchange has become less desirable for him, even though there has been no effect on the other party. Cases of hardship that result in no advantage to the other party are, however, ordinarily appropriately left to the rules on impracticability and frustration. The standard of materiality here, as elsewhere in this Restatement (e.g., § 237), is a flexible one to be applied in the light of all the circumstances.

§ 153. When Mistake of One Party Makes a Contract Voidable

Where a mistake of one party at the time a contract was made as to a basic assumption on which he made the contract has a material effect on the agreed exchange of performances that is adverse to him, the contract is voidable by him if he does not bear the risk of the mistake under the rule stated in § 154, and

> (a) the effect of the mistake is such that enforcement of the contract would be unconscionable, or
>
> (b) the other party had reason to know of the mistake or his fault caused the mistake.

§ 154. When a Party Bears the Risk of a Mistake

A party bears the risk of a mistake when

> (a) the risk is allocated to him by agreement of the parties, or
>
> (b) he is aware, at the time the contract is made, that he has only limited knowledge with respect to the facts to which the mistake relates but treats his limited knowledge as sufficient, or
>
> (c) the risk is allocated to him by the court on the ground that it is reasonable in the circumstances to do so.

§ 155. When Mistake of Both Parties as to Written Expression Justifies Reformation

Where a writing that evidences or embodies an agreement in whole or in part fails to express the agreement because of a mistake of both parties as to the contents or effect of the writing, the court may at the request of a party reform the writing to express the agreement, except to the extent that rights of third parties such as good faith purchasers for value will be unfairly affected.

§ 157. Effect of Fault of Party Seeking Relief

A mistaken party's fault in failing to know or discover the facts before making the contract does not bar him from avoidance or reformation under the rules stated in this Chapter, unless his fault amounts to a failure to act in good faith and in accordance with reasonable standards of fair dealing.

§ 158. Relief Including Restitution

(1) In any case governed by the rules stated in this Chapter, either party may have a claim for relief including restitution under the rules stated in §§ 240 and 376.

(2) In any case governed by the rules stated in this Chapter, if those rules together with the rules stated in Chapter 16 will not avoid injustice, the court may grant relief on such terms as justice requires including protection of the parties' reliance interests.

Chapter 7

MISREPRESENTATION, DURESS AND UNDUE INFLUENCE

Misrepresentation

§ 159. Misrepresentation Defined

A misrepresentation is an assertion that is not in accord with the facts.

Comment

a. Nature of the assertion. A misrepresentation, being a false assertion of fact, commonly takes the form of spoken or written words. Whether a statement is false depends on the meaning of the words in all the circumstances, including what may fairly be inferred from them. An assertion may also be inferred from conduct other than words. Concealment or even non-disclosure may have the effect of a misrepresentation under the rules stated in §§ 160 and 161. Whether a misrepresentation is fraudulent is determined by the rule stated in § 162(1). However, an assertion need not be fraudulent to be a misrepresentation. Thus a statement intended to be truthful may be a misrepresentation because of ignorance or carelessness, as when the word "not" is inadvertently omitted or when inaccurate language is used. But a misrepresentation that is not fraudulent has no consequences under this Chapter unless it is material. Whether an assertion is material is determined by the rule stated in § 162(2). The consequences of a misrepresentation are dealt with in §§ 163, 164 and 166.

§ 160. When Action is Equivalent to an Assertion (Concealment)

Action intended or known to be likely to prevent another from learning a fact is equivalent to an assertion that the fact does not exist.

Comment

b. Common situations. The rule stated in this Section is commonly applied in two situations, although it is not limited to them. In the first, a party actively hides something from the other, as when the seller of a building paints over a defect. See Illustration 1. In such a case his conduct has the same effect as an assertion that the defect does not exist, and it is therefore a misrepresentation. Similarly, if the offeror reads a written offer to the offeree and omits a portion of it, his conduct has the same effect as an assertion that the omitted portion is not contained in the writing and is therefore a misrepresentation. In the second situation, a party prevents the other from making an investigation that would have disclosed a defect. An analogous situation arises where a party frustrates an investigation made by the other, for example by sending him in search of information where it cannot be found. Even a false denial of knowledge by a party who has possession of the facts may amount to a misrepresentation as to the facts that he knows, just as if he had actually misstated them, if its effect on the other is to lead him to believe that the facts do not exist or cannot be discovered. Action may be considered as likely to prevent another from learning of a fact even though it does not make it impossible to learn of it.

§ 161. When Non-Disclosure Is Equivalent to an Assertion

A person's non-disclosure of a fact known to him is equivalent to an assertion that the fact does not exist in the following cases only:

(a) where he knows that disclosure of the fact is necessary to prevent some previous assertion from being a misrepresentation or from being fraudulent or material.

(b) where he knows that disclosure of the fact would correct a mistake of the other party as to a basic assumption on which that party is making the contract and if non-disclosure of the fact amounts to a failure to act in good faith and in accordance with reasonable standards of fair dealing.

(c) where he knows that disclosure of the fact would correct a mistake of the other party as to the contents or effect of a writing, evidencing or embodying an agreement in whole or in part.

(d) where the other person is entitled to know the fact because of a relation of trust and confidence between them.

§ 162. When a Misrepresentation Is Fraudulent or Material

(1) A misrepresentation is fraudulent if the maker intends his assertion to induce a party to manifest his assent and the maker

(a) knows or believes that the assertion is not in accord with the facts, or

(b) does not have the confidence that he states or implies in the truth of the assertion, or

(c) knows that he does not have the basis that he states or implies for the assertion.

(2) A misrepresentation is material if it would be likely to induce a reasonable person to manifest his assent, or if the maker knows that it would be likely to induce the recipient to do so.

Comment

b. *"Scienter."* The word "scienter" is often used by courts to refer to the requirement that the maker know of the untrue character of his assertion. Subsection (1) states three ways in which this requirement can be met. First, it is clearly met if the maker knows the fact to be otherwise than as stated. However, knowledge of falsity is not essential, and it is sufficient under the rule stated in Clause (a) if he believes the assertion to be false. It will not suffice merely to show that the misrepresentation is one that a person of ordinary care and intelligence would have recognized as false, although this is evidence from which his belief in its falsity may be inferred. Second, the requirement is met under the rule stated in Clause (b), if the maker, lacking confidence in the truth of his assertion that he states or implies, nevertheless chooses to make it as one of his own knowledge rather than one merely of his opinion. This is so when he is conscious that he has only a belief in its truth and recognizes that there is some chance that it may not be true. This conclusion is often expressed by saying that the misrepresentation has been made without belief in its truth or that it has been made recklessly, without regard to whether it is true or false. Third, the requirement is met under the rule stated in Clause (c), if the maker has said or implied that the assertion is made on some particular basis, such as his personal knowledge or his personal investigation, when it is not so made. This is so even though the maker is honestly convinced of its truth from hearsay or other source that he believes is reliable.

§ 164. When a Misrepresentation Makes a Contract Voidable

(1) If a party's manifestation of assent is induced by either a fraudulent or a material misrepresentation by the other party upon which the recipient is justified in relying, the contract is voidable by the recipient.

(2) If a party's manifestation of assent is induced by either a fraudulent or a material misrepresentation by one who is not a party to the transaction upon which the recipient is justified in relying, the contract is voidable by the recipient, unless the other party to the transaction in good faith and without reason to know of the misrepresentation either gives value or relies materially on the transaction.

§ 167. When a Misrepresentation Is an Inducing Cause

A misrepresentation induces a party's manifestation of assent if it substantially contributes to his decision to manifest his assent.

§ 168. Reliance on Assertions of Opinion

(1) An assertion is one of opinion if it expresses only a belief, without certainty, as to the existence of a fact or expresses only a judgment as to quality, value, authenticity, or similar matters.

(2) If it is reasonable to do so, the recipient of an assertion of a person's opinion as to facts not disclosed and not otherwise known to the recipient may properly interpret it as an assertion
   (a) that the facts known to that person are not incompatible with his opinion, or
   (b) that he knows facts sufficient to justify him in forming it.

§ 169. When Reliance on an Assertion of Opinion Is Not Justified

To the extent that an assertion is one of opinion only, the recipient is not justified in relying on it unless the recipient
   (a) stands in such a relation of trust and confidence to the person whose opinion is asserted that the recipient is reasonable in relying on it, or

(b) reasonably believes that, as compared with himself, the person whose opinion is asserted has special skill, judgment or objectivity with respect to the subject matter, or

(c) is for some other special reason particularly susceptible to a misrepresentation of the type involved.

Duress and Undue Influence

§ 174. When Duress by Physical Compulsion Prevents Formation of a Contract

If conduct that appears to be a manifestation of assent by a party who does not intend to engage in that conduct is physically compelled by duress, the conduct is not effective as a manifestation of assent.

§ 175. When Duress by Threat Makes a Contract Voidable

(1) If a party's manifestation of assent is induced by an improper threat by the other party that leaves the victim no reasonable alternative, the contract is voidable by the victim.

(2) If a party's manifestation of assent is induced by one who is not a party to the transaction, the contract is voidable by the victim unless the other party to the transaction in good faith and without reason to know of the duress either gives value or relies materially on the transaction.

§ 176. When a Threat Is Improper

(1) A threat is improper if
    (a) what is threatened is a crime or a tort, or the threat itself would be a crime or a tort if it resulted in obtaining property,
    (b) what is threatened is a criminal prosecution,
    (c) what is threatened is the use of civil process and the threat is made in bad faith, or
    (d) the threat is a breach of the duty of good faith and fair dealing under a contract with the recipient.

(2) A threat is improper if the resulting exchange is not on fair terms, and
    (a) the threatened act would harm the recipient and would not significantly benefit the party making the threat,
    (b) the effectiveness of the threat in inducing the manifestation of assent is significantly increased by prior unfair dealing by the party making the threat, or
    (c) what is threatened is otherwise a use of power for illegitimate ends.

§ 177. When Undue Influence Makes a Contract Voidable

(1) Undue influence is unfair persuasion of a party who is under the domination of the person exercising the persuasion or who by virtue of the relation between them is justified in assuming that that person will not act in a manner inconsistent with his welfare.

(2) If a party's manifestation of assent is induced by undue influence by the other party, the contract is voidable by the victim.

(3) If a party's manifestation of assent is induced by one who is not a party to the transaction, the contract is voidable by the victim unless the other party to the transaction in good faith and without reason to know of the undue influence either gives value or relies materially on the transaction.

Chapter 8

UNENFORCEABILITY ON GROUNDS OF PUBLIC POLICY

Unenforceability in General

§ 178. When a Term Is Unenforceable on Grounds of Public Policy

(1) A promise or other term of an agreement is unenforceable on grounds of public policy if legislation provides that it is unenforceable or the interest in its enforcement is clearly outweighed in the circumstances by a public policy against the enforcement of such terms.

(2) In weighing the interest in the enforcement of a term, account is taken of
    (a) the parties' justified expectations,
    (b) any forfeiture that would result if enforcement were denied, and
    (c) any special public interest in the enforcement of the particular term.

(3) In weighing a public policy against enforcement of a term, account is taken of
    (a) the strength of that policy as manifested by legislation or judicial decisions,
    (b) the likelihood that a refusal to enforce the term will further that policy,
    (c) the seriousness of any misconduct involved and the extent to which it was deliberate, and
    (d) the directness of the connection between that misconduct and the term.

§ 181. Effect of Failure to Comply with Licensing or Similar Requirement

If a party is prohibited from doing an act because of his failure to comply with a licensing, registration or similar requirement, a promise in consideration of his doing that act or of his promise to do it is unenforceable on grounds of public policy if

    (a) the requirement has a regulatory purpose, and

    (b) the interest in the enforcement of the promise is clearly outweighed by the public policy behind the requirement.

§ 182. Effect of Performance if Intended Use Is Improper

If the promisee has substantially performed, enforcement of a promise is not precluded on grounds of public policy because of some improper use that the promisor intends to make of what he obtains unless the promisee

    (a) acted for the purpose of furthering the improper use, or

    (b) knew of the use and the use involves grave social harm.

Restraint of Trade

§ 187. Non-Ancillary Restraints on Competition

A promise to refrain from competition that imposes a restraint that is not ancillary to an otherwise valid transaction or relationship is unreasonably in restraint of trade.

§ 188. Ancillary Restraints on Competition

(1) A promise to refrain from competition that imposes a restraint that is ancillary to an otherwise valid transaction or relationship is unreasonably in restraint of trade if

    (a) the restraint is greater than is needed to protect the promisee's legitimate interest, or

    (b) the promisee's need is outweighed by the hardship to the promisor and the likely injury to the public.

(2) Promises imposing restraints that are ancillary to a valid transaction or relationship include the following:

    (a) a promise by the seller of a business not to compete with the buyer in such a way as to injure the value of the business sold;

    (b) a promise by an employee or other agent not to compete with his employer or other principal;

    (c) a promise by a partner not to compete with the partnership.

Comment

a. Rule of reason. Manifestation of intention. The rules stated in this Section apply to promises not to compete that, because they impose ancillary restraints, are not necessarily invalid. Subsection (1) restates in more detail the general rule of reason of §186 as it applies to such promises. Under this formulation the restraint may be unreasonable in either of two situations. The first occurs when the restraint is greater than necessary to protect the legitimate interests of the promisee. The second occurs when, even though the restraint is not greater than necessary to protect those interests, the promisee's need for protection is outweighed by the hardship to the promisor and the likely injury to the public. In the second situation the court may be faced with a particularly difficult task of balancing competing interests. No mathematical formula can be offered for this process.

h. Promise by partner. A rule similar to that applicable to an employee or agent applies to a partner who makes a promise not to compete that is ancillary to the partnership agreement or to an agreement by which he disposes of his partnership interest. The same is true of joint adventurers, who are treated as partners in this respect.

Interference with Other Protected Interests

§ 194. Promise Interfering with Contract with Another

A promise that tortiously interferes with performance of a contract with a third person or a tortiously induced promise to commit a breach of contract is unenforceable on grounds of public policy.

§ 195. Term Exempting From Liability for Harm Caused Intentionally, Recklessly or Negligently

(1) A term exempting a party from tort liability for harm caused intentionally or recklessly is unenforceable on grounds of public policy.

(2) A term exempting a party from tort liability for harm caused negligently is unenforceable on grounds of public policy if
   (a) the term exempts an employer from liability to an employee for injury in the course of his employment;
   (b) the term exempts one charged with a duty of public service from liability to one to whom that duty is owed for compensation for breach of that duty, or
   (c) the other party is similarly a member of a class protected against the class to which the first party belongs.

(3) A term exempting a seller of a product from his special tort liability for physical harm to a user or consumer is unenforceable on grounds of public policy unless the term is fairly bargained for and is consistent with the policy underlying that liability.

Restitution

§ 198. Restitution in Favor of Party Who Is Excusably Ignorant or Is Not Equally in the Wrong

A party has a claim in restitution for performance that he has rendered under or in return for a promise that is unenforceable on grounds of public policy if
   (a) he was excusably ignorant of the facts or of legislation of a minor character, in the absence of which the promise would be enforceable, or
   (b) he was not equally in the wrong with the promisor.

Chapter 9

THE SCOPE OF CONTRACTUAL OBLIGATIONS

The Meaning of Agreements

§ 201. Whose Meaning Prevails

(1) Where the parties have attached the same meaning to a promise or agreement or a term thereof, it is interpreted in accordance with that meaning.

(2) Where the parties have attached different meanings to a promise or agreement or a term thereof, it is interpreted in accordance with the meaning attached by one of them if at the time the agreement was made

    (a) that party did not know of any different meaning attached by the other, and the other knew the meaning attached by the first party; or

    (b) that party had no reason to know of any different meaning attached by the other, and the other had reason to know the meaning attached by the first party.

(3) Except as stated in this Section, neither party is bound by the meaning attached by the other, even though the result may be a failure of mutual assent.

§ 202. Rules in Aid of Interpretation

(1) Words and other conduct are interpreted in the light of all the circumstances, and if the principal purpose of the parties is ascertainable it is given great weight.

(2) A writing is interpreted as a whole, and all writings that are part of the same transaction are interpreted together.

(3) Unless a different intention is manifested,

    (a) where language has a generally prevailing meaning, it is interpreted in accordance with that meaning;

    (b) technical terms and words of art are given their technical meaning when used in a transaction within their technical field.

(4) Where an agreement involves repeated occasions for performance by either party with knowledge of the nature of the performance and opportunity for objection to it by the other, any course of performance accepted or acquiesced in without objection is given great weight in the interpretation of the agreement.

(5) Wherever reasonable, the manifestations of intention of the parties to a promise or agreement are interpreted as consistent with each other and with any relevant course of performance, course of dealing, or usage of trade.

§ 203. Standards of Preference in Interpretation

In the interpretation of a promise or agreement or a term thereof, the following standards of preference are generally applicable:

(a) an interpretation which gives a reasonable, lawful, and effective meaning to all the terms is preferred to an interpretation which leaves a part unreasonable, unlawful, or of no effect;

(b) express terms are given greater weight than course of performance, course of dealing, and usage of trade, course of performance is given greater weight than course of dealing or usage of trade, and course of dealing is given greater weight than usage of trade;

(c) specific terms and exact terms are given greater weight than general language;

(d) separately negotiated or added terms are given greater weight than standardized terms or other terms not separately negotiated.

§ 204. Supplying an Omitted Essential Term

When the parties to a bargain sufficiently defined to be a contract have not agreed with respect to a term which is essential to a determination of their rights and duties, a term which is reasonable in the circumstances is supplied by the court.

Considerations of Fairness and the Public Interest

§ 205. Duty of Good Faith and Fair Dealing

Every contract imposes upon each party a duty of good faith and fair dealing in its performance and its enforcement.

Comments

a. Meanings of "good faith." Good faith is defined in Uniform Commercial Code § 1-201(19) as "honesty in fact in the conduct or transaction concerned." "In the case of a merchant" Uniform Commercial Code § 2-103(1)(b) provides that good faith means "honesty in fact and the observance of reasonable commercial standards of fair dealing in the trade." The phrase "good faith" is used in a variety of contexts, and its meaning varies somewhat with the context. Good faith performance or enforcement of a contract emphasizes faithfulness to an agreed common purpose and consistency with the justified expectations of the other party; it excludes a variety of types of conduct characterized as involving "bad faith" because they violate community standards of decency, fairness or reasonableness. The appropriate remedy for a breach of the duty of good faith also varies with the circumstances.

d. Good faith performance. Subterfuges and evasions violate the obligation of good faith in performance even though the actor believes his conduct to be justified. But the obligation goes further: bad faith may be overt or may consist of inaction, and fair dealing may require more than honesty. A complete catalogue of types of bad faith is impossible, but the following types are among those which have been recognized in judicial decisions: evasion of the spirit of the bargain, lack of diligence and slacking off, willful rendering of imperfect performance, abuse of a power to specify terms, and interference with or failure to cooperate in the other party's performance.

§ 206. Interpretation Against the Draftsman

In choosing among the reasonable meanings of a promise or agreement or a term thereof, that meaning is generally preferred which operates against the party who supplies the words or from whom a writing otherwise proceeds.

§ 208. Unconscionable Contract or Term

If a contract or term thereof is unconscionable at the time the contract is made a court may refuse to enforce the contract, or may enforce the remainder of the contract without the unconscionable term, or may so limit the application of any unconscionable term as to avoid any unconscionable result.

Effect of Adoption of a Writing

§ 209. Integrated Agreements

(1) An integrated agreement is a writing or writings constituting a final expression of one or more terms of an agreement.

(2) Whether there is an integrated agreement is to be determined by the court as a question preliminary to determination of a question of interpretation or to application of the parol evidence rule.

(3) Where the parties reduce an agreement to a writing which in view of its completeness and specificity reasonably appears to be a complete agreement, it is taken to be an integrated agreement unless it is established by other evidence that the writing did not constitute a final expression.

§ 210. Completely and Partially Integrated Agreements

(1) A completely integrated agreement is an integrated agreement adopted by the parties as a complete and exclusive statement of the terms of the agreement.

(2) A partially integrated agreement is an integrated agreement other than a completely integrated agreement.

(3) Whether an agreement is completely or partially integrated is to be determined by the court as a question preliminary to determination of a question of interpretation or to application of the parol evidence rule.

Comment

b. Proof of complete integration. That a writing was or was not adopted as a completely integrated agreement may be proved by any relevant evidence. A document in the form of a written contract, signed by both parties and apparently complete on its face, may be decisive of the issue in the absence of credible contrary evidence. But a writing cannot of itself prove its own completeness, and wide latitude must be allowed for inquiry into circumstances bearing on the intention of the parties.

§ 211. Standardized Agreements

(1) Except as stated in Subsection (3), where a party to an agreement signs or otherwise manifests assent to a writing and has reason to believe that like writings are regularly used to embody terms of agreements of the same type, he adopts the writing as an integrated agreement with respect to the terms included in the writing.

(2) Such a writing is interpreted wherever reasonable as treating alike all those similarly situated, without regard to their knowledge or understanding of the standard terms of the writing.

(3) Where the other party has reason to believe that the party manifesting such assent would not do so if he knew that the writing contained a particular term, the term is not part of the agreement.

§ 212. Interpretation of Integrated Agreement

(1) The interpretation of an integrated agreement is directed to the meaning of the terms of the writing or writings in the light of the circumstances, in accordance with the rules stated in this Chapter.

(2) A question of interpretation of an integrated agreement is to be determined by the trier of fact if it depends on the credibility of extrinsic evidence or on a choice among reasonable inferences to be drawn from extrinsic evidence. Otherwise a question of interpretation of an integrated agreement is to be determined as a question of law.

Comment

a. "Objective" and "subjective" meaning. Interpretation of contracts deals with the meaning given to language and other conduct by the parties rather than with meanings established by law. But the relevant intention of a party is that manifested by him rather than any different undisclosed intention. In cases of misunderstanding, there may be a contract in accordance with the meaning of one party if the other knows or has reason to know of the misunderstanding and the first party does not. See § 201. The meaning of one party may prevail as to one term and the meaning of the other as to another term; thus the contract as a whole may not be entirely in accordance with the understanding of either. When a party is thus held to a meaning of which he had reason to know, it is sometimes said that the "objective" meaning of his language or other conduct prevails over his "subjective" meaning. Even so, the operative meaning is found in the transaction and its context rather than in the law or in the usages of people other than the parties.

b. Plain meaning and extrinsic evidence. It is sometimes said that extrinsic evidence cannot change the plain meaning of a writing, but meaning can almost never be plain except in a context. Accordingly, the rule stated in Subsection (1) is not limited to cases where it is determined that the language used is ambiguous. Any determination of meaning or ambiguity should only be made in the light of the relevant evidence of the situation and relations of the parties, the subject matter of the transaction, preliminary negotiations and statements made therein, usages of trade, and the course of dealing between the parties. See §§ 202, 219–23. But after the transaction has been shown in all its length and breadth, the words of an integrated agreement remain the most important evidence of intention. Standards of preference among reasonable meanings are stated in §§ 203, 206.

§ 213. Effect of Integrated Agreement on Prior Agreements (Parol Evidence Rule)

(1) A binding integrated agreement discharges prior agreements to the extent that it is inconsistent with them.

(2) A binding completely integrated agreement discharges prior agreements to the extent that they are within its scope.

(3) An integrated agreement that is not binding or that is voidable and avoided does not discharge a prior agreement. But an integrated agreement, even though not binding, may be effective to render inoperative a term which would have been part of the agreement if it had not been integrated.

§ 214. Evidence of Prior or Contemporaneous Agreements and Negotiations

Agreements and negotiations prior to or contemporaneous with the adoption of a writing are admissible in evidence to establish

    (a) that the writing is or is not an integrated agreement;

    (b) that the integrated agreement, if any, is completely or partially integrated;

    (c) the meaning of the writing, whether or not integrated;

    (d) illegality, fraud, duress, mistake, lack of consideration, or other invalidating cause.

§ 215. Contradiction of Integrated Terms

Except as stated in the preceding Section, where there is a binding agreement, either completely or partially integrated, evidence of prior or contemporaneous agreements or negotiations is not admissible in evidence to contradict a term of the writing.

§ 216. Consistent Additional Terms

(1) Evidence of a consistent additional term is admissible to supplement an integrated agreement unless the court finds that the agreement was completely integrated.

(2) An agreement is not completely integrated if the writing omits a consistent additional agreed term which is
    (a) agreed to for separate consideration, or
    (b) such a term as in the circumstances might naturally be omitted from the writing.

§ 217. Integrated Agreement Subject to Oral Requirement of a Condition

Where the parties to a written agreement agree orally that performance of the agreement is subject to the occurrence of a stated condition, the agreement is not integrated with respect to the oral condition.

Comment

b. Requirement of a condition inconsistent with a written term. The rule of this Section may be regarded as a particular application of the rule of § 216(2)(b), giving effect to consistent additional terms omitted naturally from a writing. So regarded, it has sometimes been limited to requirements of conditions consistent with the written terms. But an oral requirement of a condition is never completely consistent with a signed written agreement which is complete on its face; in such cases evidence of the oral requirement bears directly on the issues whether the writing was adopted as an integrated agreement and if so whether the agreement was completely integrated or partially integrated. Inconsistency is merely one factor in the preliminary determination of those issues. If the parties orally agreed that performance of the written agreement was subject to a condition, either the writing is not an integrated agreement or the agreement is only partially integrated until the condition occurs. Even a "merger" clause in the writing, explicitly negating oral terms, does not control the question whether there is an integrated agreement or the scope of the writing.

Scope as Affected by Usage

§ 220. Usage Relevant to Interpretation

(1) An agreement is interpreted in accordance with a relevant usage if each party knew or had reason to know of the usage and neither party knew or had reason to know that the meaning attached by the other was inconsistent with the usage.

(2) When the meaning attached by one party accorded with a relevant usage and the other knew or had reason to know of the usage, the other is treated as having known or had reason to know the meaning attached by the first party.

§ 221. Usage Supplementing an Agreement

An agreement is supplemented or qualified by a reasonable usage with respect to agreements of the same type if each party knows or has reason to know of the usage and neither party knows or has reason to know that the other party has an intention inconsistent with the usage.

§ 222. Usage of Trade

(1) A usage of trade is a usage having such regularity of observance in a place, vocation, or trade as to justify an expectation that it will be observed with respect to a particular agreement. It may include a system of rules regularly observed even though particular rules are changed from time to time.

(2) The existence and scope of a usage of trade are to be determined as questions of fact. If a usage is embodied in a written trade code or similar writing the interpretation of the writing is to be determined by the court as a question of law.

(3) Unless otherwise agreed, a usage of trade in the vocation or trade in which the parties are engaged or a usage of trade of which they know or have reason to know gives meaning to or supplements or qualifies their agreement.

§ 223. Course of Dealing

(1) A course of dealing is a sequence of previous conduct between the parties to an agreement which is fairly to be regarded as establishing a common basis of understanding for interpreting their expressions and other conduct.

(2) Unless otherwise agreed, a course of dealing between the parties gives meaning to or supplements or qualifies their agreement.

Conditions and Similar Events

§ 224. Condition Defined

A condition is an event, not certain to occur, which must occur, unless its non-occurrence is excused, before performance under a contract becomes due.

§ 225. Effects of the Non-Occurrence Of a Condition

(1) Performance of a duty subject to a condition cannot become due unless the condition occurs or its non-occurrence is excused.

(2) Unless it has been excused, the non-occurrence of a condition discharges the duty when the condition can no longer occur.

(3) Non-occurrence of a condition is not a breach by a party unless he is under a duty that the condition occur.

§ 226. How an Event May Be Made a Condition

An event may be made a condition either by the agreement of the parties or by a term supplied by the court.

§ 227. Standards of Preference with Regard to Conditions

(1) In resolving doubts as to whether an event is made a condition of an obligor's duty, and as to the nature of such an event, an interpretation is preferred that will reduce the obligee's risk of forfeiture, unless the event is within the obligee's control or the circumstances indicate that he has assumed the risk.

(2) Unless the contract is of a type under which only one party generally undertakes duties, when it is doubtful whether
  (a) a duty is imposed on an obligee that an event occur, or
  (b) the event is made a condition of the obligor's duty, or
  (c) the event is made a condition of the obligor's duty and a duty is imposed on the obligee that the event occur, the first interpretation is preferred if the event is within the obligee's control.

(3) In case of doubt, an interpretation under which an event is a condition of an obligor's duty is preferred over an interpretation under which the non-occurrence of the event is a ground for discharge of that duty after it has become a duty to perform.

§ 228. Satisfaction of the Obligor as a Condition

When it is a condition of an obligor's duty that he be satisfied with respect to the obligee's performance or with respect to something else, and it is practicable to determine whether a reasonable person in the position of the obligor would be satisfied, an interpretation is preferred under which the condition occurs if such a reasonable person in the position of the obligor would be satisfied.

§ 229. Excuse of a Condition to Avoid Forfeiture

To the extent that the non-occurrence of a condition would cause disproportionate forfeiture, a court may excuse the non-occurrence of that condition unless its occurrence was a material part of the agreed exchange.

§ 230. Event That Terminates a Duty

(1) Except as stated in Subsection (2), if under the terms of the contract the occurrence of an event is to terminate an obligor's duty of immediate performance or one to pay damages for breach, that duty is discharged if the event occurs.

(2) The obligor's duty is not discharged if occurrence of the event
   (a) is the result of a breach by the obligor of his duty of good faith and fair dealing, or
   (b) could not have been prevented because of impracticability and continuance of the duty does not subject the obligor to a materially increased burden.

(3) The obligor's duty is not discharged if, before the event occurs, the obligor promises to perform the duty even if the event occurs and does not revoke his promise before the obligee materially changes his position in reliance on it.

Chapter 10

PERFORMANCE AND NON-PERFORMANCE

Performances to Be Exchanged Under an Exchange of Promises

§ 234. Order of Performances

(1) Where all or part of the performances to be exchanged under an exchange of promises can be rendered simultaneously, they are to that extent due simultaneously, unless the language or the circumstances indicate the contrary.

(2) Except to the extent stated in Subsection (1), where the performance of only one party under such an exchange requires a period of time, his performance is due at an earlier time than that of the other party, unless the language or the circumstances indicate the contrary.

Comment

a. Advantages of simultaneous performance. A requirement that the parties perform simultaneously where their performances are to be exchanged under an exchange of promises is fair for two reasons. First, it offers both parties maximum security against disappointment of their expectations of a subsequent exchange of performances by allowing each party to defer his own performance until he has been assured that the other will perform. This advantage is implemented by the rule stated in § 238, which deals with offers to perform. Second, it avoids placing on either party the burden of financing the other before the latter has performed. Subsection (1) therefore imposes a requirement of simultaneous performance whenever this is feasible under the contract, in the absence of language or circumstances indicating a contrary intention. A notable example of such a requirement is that laid down for contracts for the sale of goods by Uniform Commercial Code §§ 2-507 and 2-511. The requirement is subject to the agreement of the parties, as by an express provision extending credit to the buyer, or one requiring him to pay against documents or to furnish a letter of credit. Even absent an express provision, a contrary intention may be shown by circumstances including usage of trade and course of dealing (§§ 221, 223; Uniform Commercial Code § 1-205).

Effect of Performance and Non-Performance

§ 235. Effect of Performance as Discharge and of Non-Performance As Breach

(1) Full performance of a duty under a contract discharges the duty.

(2) When performance of a duty under a contract is due any non-performance is a breach.

§ 236. Claims for Damages for Total and for Partial Breach

(1) A claim for damages for total breach is one for damages based on all of the injured party's remaining rights to performance.

(2) A claim for damages for partial breach is one for damages based on only part of the injured party's remaining rights to performance.

§ 237. Effect on Other Party's Duties of a Failure to Render Performance

Except as stated in § 240, it is a condition of each party's remaining duties to render performances to be exchanged under an exchange of promises that there be no uncured material failure by the other party to render any such performance due at an earlier time.

§ 238. Effect on Other Party's Duties of a Failure to Offer Performance

Where all or part of the performances to be exchanged under an exchange of promises are due simultaneously, it is a condition of each party's duties to render such performance that the other party either render or, with manifested present ability to do so, offer performance of his part of the simultaneous exchange.

§ 240. Part Performances as Agreed Equivalents

If the performances to be exchanged under an exchange of promises can be apportioned into corresponding pairs of part performances so that the parts of each pair are properly regarded as agreed equivalents, a party's performance of his part of such a pair has the same effect on the other's duties to render performance of the agreed equivalent as it would have if only that pair of performances had been promised.

§ 241. Circumstances Significant in Determining Whether a Failure Is Material

In determining whether a failure to render or to offer performance is material, the following circumstances are significant:

(a) the extent to which the injured party will be deprived of the benefit which he reasonably expected;

(b) the extent to which the injured party can be adequately compensated for the part of that benefit of which he will be deprived;

(c) the extent to which the party failing to perform or to offer to perform will suffer forfeiture;

(d) the likelihood that the party failing to perform or to offer to perform will cure his failure, taking account of all the circumstances including any reasonable assurances;

(e) the extent to which the behavior of the party failing to perform or to offer to perform comports with standards of good faith and fair dealing.

Comment

b. Loss of benefit to injured party. Since the purpose of the rules stated in §§ 237 and 238 is to secure the parties' expectation of an exchange of performances, an important circumstance in determining whether a failure is material is the extent to which the injured party will be deprived of the benefit which he reasonably expected from the exchange (Subsection (a)). If the consideration given by either party consists partly of some performance and only partly of a promise, regard must be had to the entire exchange, including that performance, in applying this criterion. Although the relationship between the monetary loss to the injured party as a result of the failure and the contract price may be significant, no simple rule based on the ratio of the one to the other can be laid down, and here, as elsewhere under this Section, all relevant circumstances must be considered. In construction contracts, for example, defects affecting structural soundness are ordinarily regarded as particularly significant. In the sale of goods a particularly exacting standard has evolved. There it has long been established that, in the absence of a showing of a contrary intention, a buyer is entitled to expect strict performance of the contract, and Uniform Commercial Code § 2-601 carries forward this expectation by allowing the buyer to reject "if the goods or the tender of delivery fail in any respect to conform to the contract." The Code, however, compensates to some extent for the severity of this standard by extending the seller's right to cure beyond the point when the time for performance has expired in some instances (§ 2-508(2)), by allowing revocation of acceptance only if a nonconformity "substantially impairs" the value of the goods to the buyer (§ 2-608(1)), and by allowing the injured party to treat a nonconformity or default as to one installment under an installment contract as a breach of the whole only if it "substantially impairs" the value of the whole (§ 2-612(3)).

§ 242. Circumstances Significant in Determining When Remaining Duties Are Discharged

In determining the time after which a party's uncured material failure to render or to offer performance discharges the other party's remaining duties to render performance under the rules stated in §§ 237 and 238, the following circumstances are significant:

(a) those stated in § 241;

(b) the extent to which it reasonably appears to the injured party that delay may prevent or hinder him in making reasonable substitute arrangements;

(c) the extent to which the agreement provides for performance without delay, but a material failure to perform or to offer to perform on a stated day does not of itself discharge the other party's remaining duties unless the circumstances, including the language of the agreement, indicate that performance or an offer to perform by that day is important.

§ 243. Effect of a Breach by Non-Performance As Giving Rise to a Claim for Damages for Total Breach

(1) With respect to performances to be exchanged under an exchange of promises, a breach by non-performance gives rise to a claim for damages for total breach only if it discharges the injured party's remaining duties to render such performance, other than a duty to render an agreed equivalent under § 240.

(2) Except as stated in Subsection (3), a breach by non-performance accompanied or followed by a repudiation gives rise to a claim for damages for total breach.

(3) Where at the time of the breach the only remaining duties of performance are those of the party in breach and are for the payment of money in installments not related to one another, his breach by non-performance as to less than the whole, whether or not accompanied or followed by a repudiation, does not give rise to a claim for damages for total breach.

(4) In any case other than those stated in the preceding subsections, a breach by non-performance gives rise to a claim for total breach only if it so substantially impairs the value of the contract to the injured party at the time of the breach that it is just in the circumstances to allow him to recover damages based on all his remaining rights to performance.

Effect of Prospective Non-Performance

§ 250. When a Statement or an Act Is a Repudiation

A repudiation is
    (a) a statement by the obligor to the obligee indicating that the obligor will commit a breach that would of itself give the obligee a claim for damages for total breach under § 243, or
    (b) a voluntary affirmative act which renders the obligor unable or apparently unable to perform without such a breach.

§ 251. When a Failure to Give Assurance May Be Treated as a Repudiation

(1) Where reasonable grounds arise to believe that the obligor will commit a breach by non-performance that would of itself give the obligee a claim for damages for total breach under § 243, the obligee may demand adequate assurance of due performance and may, if reasonable, suspend any performance for which he has not already received the agreed exchange until he receives such assurance.

(2) The obligee may treat as a repudiation the obligor's failure to provide within a reasonable time such assurance of due performance as is adequate in the circumstances of the particular case.

§ 252. Effect of Insolvency

(1) Where the obligor's insolvency gives the obligee reasonable grounds to believe that the obligor will commit a breach under the rule stated in § 251, the obligee may suspend any performance for which he has not already received the agreed exchange until he receives assurance in the form of performance itself, an offer of performance, or adequate security.

(2) A person is insolvent who either has ceased to pay his debts in the ordinary course of business or cannot pay his debts as they become due or is insolvent within the meaning of the federal bankruptcy law.

§ 253. Effect of a Repudiation as a Breach and on Other Party's Duties

(1) Where an obligor repudiates a duty before he has committed a breach by non-performance and before he has received all of the agreed exchange for it, his repudiation alone gives rise to a claim for damages for total breach.

(2) Where performances are to be exchanged under an exchange of promises, one party's repudiation of a duty to render performance discharges the other party's remaining duties to render performance.

§ 256. Nullification of Repudiation or Basis for Repudiation

(1) The effect of a statement as constituting a repudiation under § 250 or the basis for a repudiation under § 251 is nullified by a retraction of the statement if notification of the retraction comes to the attention of the injured party before he materially changes his position in reliance on the repudiation or indicates to the other party that he considers the repudiation to be final.

(2) The effect of events other than a statement as constituting a repudiation under § 250 or the basis for a repudiation under § 251 is nullified if, to the knowledge of the injured party, those events have ceased to exist before he materially changes his position in reliance on the repudiation or indicates to the other party that he considers the repudiation to be final.

§ 257. Effect of Urging Performance in Spite of Repudiation

The injured party does not change the effect of a repudiation by urging the repudiator to perform in spite of his repudiation or to retract his repudiation.

Chapter 11

IMPRACTICABILITY OF PERFORMANCE AND FRUSTRATION OF PURPOSE

Introductory Note

The rationale behind the doctrines of impracticability and frustration is sometimes said to be that there is an "implied term" of the contract that such extraordinary circumstances will not occur. This Restatement rejects this analysis in favor of that of Uniform Commercial Code § 2-615, under which the central inquiry is whether the non-occurrence of the circumstance was a "basic assumption on which the contract was made." See Comment f to § 2. In order for the parties to have had such a "basic assumption" it is not necessary for them to have been conscious of alternatives. Where, for example, an artist contracts to paint a painting, it can be said that the death of the artist is an event the non-occurrence of which was a basic assumption on which the contract was made, even though the parties never consciously addressed themselves to that possibility.

Determining whether the non-occurrence of a particular event was or was not a basic assumption involves a judgment as to which party assumed the risk of its occurrence. In contracting for the manufacture and delivery of goods at a price fixed in the contract, for example, the seller assumes the risk of increased costs within the normal range. If, however, a disaster results in an abrupt tenfold increase in cost to the seller, a court might determine that the seller did not assume this risk by concluding that the non-occurrence of the disaster was a "basic assumption" on which the contract was made. In making such determinations, a court will look at all circumstances, including the terms of the contract. The fact that the event was unforeseeable is significant as suggesting that its non-occurrence was a basic assumption. However, the fact that it was foreseeable, or even foreseen, does not, of itself, argue for a contrary conclusion, since the parties may not have thought it sufficiently important a risk to have made it a subject of their bargaining. Another significant factor may be the relative bargaining positions of the parties and the relative ease with which either party could have included a clause. Another may be the effectiveness of the market in spreading such risks as, for example, where the obligor is a middleman who has an opportunity to adjust his prices to cover them.

Under the rationale of this Restatement, the obligor is relieved of his duty because the contract, having been made on a different "basic assumption," is regarded as not covering the case that has arisen. It is an omitted case, falling within a "gap" in the contract. Ordinarily, the just way to deal with the omitted case is to hold that the obligor's duty is discharged, in the case of changed circumstances, or has never arisen, in the case of existing circumstances, and to shift the risk to the obligee.

§ 261. Discharge by Supervening Impracticability

Where, after a contract is made, a party's performance is made impracticable without his fault by the occurrence of an event the non-occurrence of which was a basic assumption on which the contract was made, his duty to render that performance is discharged, unless the language or the circumstances indicate the contrary.

Comment

b. Basic assumption. In order for a supervening event to discharge a duty under this Section, the non-occurrence of that event must have been a "basic assumption" on which both parties made the contract. This is the criterion used by Uniform Commercial Code § 2-615(a). Its application is simple enough in the cases of the death of a person or destruction of a specific thing necessary for performance. The continued existence of the person or thing (the non-occurrence of the death or destruction) is ordinarily a basic assumption on which the contract was made, so that death or destruction effects a discharge. Its application is also simple enough in the cases of market shifts or the financial inability of one of the parties. The continuation of existing market conditions and of the financial situation of the parties are ordinarily not such assumptions, so that mere market shifts or financial inability do not usually effect discharge under the rule stated in this Section. In borderline cases this criterion is sufficiently flexible to take account of factors that bear on a just allocation of risk. The fact that the event was foreseeable, or even foreseen, does not necessarily compel a conclusion that its non-occurrence was not a basic assumption.

Illustrations

1. On June 1, A agrees to sell and B to buy goods to be delivered in October at a designated port. The port is subsequently closed by quarantine regulations during the entire month of October, no commercially reasonable substitute performance is available (see Uniform Commercial Code § 2-614(1)), and A fails to deliver the goods. A's duty to deliver the goods is discharged, and A is not liable to B for breach of contract.

2. A contracts to produce a movie for B. As B knows, A's only source of funds is a $100,000 deposit in C bank. C bank fails, and A does not produce the movie. A's duty to produce the movie is not discharged, and A is liable to B for breach of contract.

§ 262. Death or Incapacity of Person Necessary for Performance

If the existence of a particular person is necessary for the performance of a duty, his death or such incapacity as makes performance impracticable is an event the non-occurrence of which was a basic assumption on which the contract was made.

§ 263. Destruction, Deterioration or Failure to Come Into Existence of Thing Necessary for Performance

If the existence of a specific thing is necessary for the performance of a duty, its failure to come into existence, destruction, or such deterioration as makes performance impracticable is an event the non-occurrence of which was a basic assumption on which the contract was made.

§ 265. Discharge by Supervening Frustration

Where, after a contract is made, a party's principal purpose is substantially frustrated without his fault by the occurrence of an event the non-occurrence of which was a basic assumption on which the contract was made, his remaining duties to render performance are discharged, unless the language or the circumstances indicate the contrary.

Comment

a. Rationale. This Section deals with the problem that arises when a change in circumstances makes one party's performance virtually worthless to the other, frustrating his purpose in making the contract. It is distinct from the problem of impracticability dealt with in the four preceding sections because there is no impediment to performance by either party. Although there has been no true failure of performance in the sense required for the application of the rule stated in § 237, the impact on the party adversely affected will be similar. The rule stated in this Section sets out the requirements for the discharge of that party's duty. First, the purpose that is frustrated must have been a principal purpose of that party in making the contract. It is not enough that he had in mind some specific object without which he would not have made the contract. The object must be so completely the basis of the contract that, as both parties understand, without it the transaction would make little sense. Second, the frustration must be substantial. It is not enough that the transaction has become less profitable for the affected party or even that he will sustain a loss. The frustration must be so severe that it is not fairly to be regarded as within the risks that he assumed under the contract. Third, the non-occurrence of the frustrating event must have been a basic assumption on which the contract was made. This involves essentially the same sorts of determinations that are involved under the general rule on impracticability. See Comment b to § 261. The foreseeability of the event is here, as it is there, a factor in that determination, but the mere fact that the event was foreseeable does not compel the conclusion that its non-occurrence was not such a basic assumption.

Illustrations

1. A and B make a contract under which B is to pay A $ 1,000 and is to have the use of A's window on January 10 to view a parade that has been scheduled for that day. Because of the illness of an important official, the parade is cancelled. B refuses to use the window or pay the $ 1,000. B's duty to pay $ 1,000 is discharged, and B is not liable to A for breach of contract.

2. A contracts with B to print an advertisement in a souvenir program of an international yacht race, which has been scheduled by a yacht club, for a price of $ 10,000. The yacht club cancels the race because of the outbreak of war. A has already printed the programs, but B refuses to pay the $ 10,000. B's duty to pay $ 10,000 is discharged, and B is not liable to A for breach of contract. A may have a claim under the rule stated in § 272(1).

§ 266. Existing Impracticability or Frustration

(1) Where, at the time a contract is made, a party's performance under it is impracticable without his fault because of a fact of which he has no reason to know and the non-existence of which is a basic assumption on which the contract is made, no duty to render that performance arises, unless the language or circumstances indicate the contrary.

(2) Where, at the time a contract is made, a party's principal purpose is substantially frustrated without his fault by a fact of which he has no reason to know and the non-existence of which is a basic assumption on which the contract is made, no duty of that party to render performance arises, unless the language or circumstances indicate the contrary.

§ 272. Relief Including Restitution

(1) In any case governed by the rules stated in this Chapter, either party may have a claim for relief including restitution under the rules stated in §§ 240 and 377.

(2) In any case governed by the rules stated in this Chapter, if those rules together with the rules stated in Chapter 16 will not avoid injustice, the court may grant relief on such terms as justice requires including protection of the parties' reliance interests.

Chapter 12

DISCHARGE BY ASSENT OR ALTERATION

Substituted Performance, Substituted Contract, Accord and Account Stated

§ 281. Accord and Satisfaction

(1) An accord is a contract under which an obligee promises to accept a stated performance in satisfaction of the obligor's existing duty. Performance of the accord discharges the original duty.

(2) Until performance of the accord, the original duty is suspended unless there is such a breach of the accord by the obligor as discharges the new duty of the

obligee to accept the performance in satisfaction. If there is such a breach, the obligee may enforce either the original duty or any duty under the accord.

(3) Breach of the accord by the obligee does not discharge the original duty, but the obligor may maintain a suit for specific performance of the accord, in addition to any claim for damages for partial breach.

Agreement of Rescission, Release and Contract Not to Sue

§ 285. Contract Not to Sue

(1) A contract not to sue is a contract under which the obligee of a duty promises never to sue the obligor or a third person to enforce the duty or not to do so for a limited time.

(2) Except as stated in Subsection (3), a contract never to sue discharges the duty and a contract not to sue for a limited time bars an action to enforce the duty during that time.

(3) A contract not to sue one co-obligor bars levy of execution on the property of the promisee during the agreed time but does not bar an action or the recovery of judgment against any co-obligor.

Alteration

§ 286. Alteration of Writing

(1) If one to whom a duty is owed under a contract alters a writing that is an integrated agreement or that satisfies the Statute of Frauds with respect to that contract, the duty is discharged if the alteration is fraudulent and material.

(2) An alteration is material if it would, if effective, vary any party's legal relations with the maker of the alteration or adversely affect that party's legal relations with a third person. The unauthorized insertion in a blank space in a writing is an alteration.

Chapter 13

JOINT AND SEVERAL PROMISORS AND PROMISEES

Joint and Several Promisors

§ 288. Promises of the Same Performance

(1) Where two or more parties to a contract make a promise or promises to the same promisee, the manifested intention of the parties determines whether they promise that the same performance or separate performances shall be given.

(2) Unless a contrary intention is manifested, a promise by two or more promisors is a promise that the same performance shall be given.

§ 293. Effect of Performance or Satisfaction on Co-Promisors

Full or partial performance or other satisfaction of the contractual duty of a promisor discharges the duty to the obligee of each other promisor of the same performance to the extent of the amount or value applied to the discharge of the duty of the promisor who renders it.

§ 294. Effect of Discharge on Co-Promisors

(1) Except as stated in § 295, where the obligee of promises of the same performance discharges one promisor by release, rescission or accord and satisfaction,

    (a) co-promisors who are bound only by a joint duty are discharged unless the discharged promisor is a surety for the co-promisor;

    (b) co-promisors who are bound by joint and several duties or by several duties are not discharged except to the extent required by the law of suretyship.

(2) By statute in many states a discharge of one promisor does not discharge other promisors of the same performance except to the extent required by the law of suretyship.

(3) Any consideration received by the obligee for discharge of one promisor discharges the duty of each other promisor of the same performance to the extent of the amount or value received. An agreement to the contrary is not effective unless it is made with a surety and expressly preserves the duty of his principal.

Chapter 14

CONTRACT BENEFICIARIES

§ 302. Intended and Incidental Beneficiaries

(1) Unless otherwise agreed between promisor and promisee, a beneficiary of a promise is an intended beneficiary if recognition of a right to performance in the beneficiary is appropriate to effectuate the intention of the parties and either

    (a) the performance of the promise will satisfy an obligation of the promisee to pay money to the beneficiary; or

    (b) the circumstances indicate that the promisee intends to give the beneficiary the benefit of the promised performance.

(2) An incidental beneficiary is a beneficiary who is not an intended beneficiary.

Comment

a. Promisee and beneficiary. This Section distinguishes an "intended" beneficiary, who acquires a right by virtue of a promise, from an "incidental" beneficiary, who does not. Section 2 defines "promisee" as the person to whom a promise is addressed, and "beneficiary" as a person other than the promisee who will be benefitted by performance of the promise. Both terms are neutral with respect to rights and duties: either or both or neither may have a legal right to performance. Either promisee or beneficiary may but need not be connected with the transaction in other ways: neither promisee nor beneficiary is necessarily the person to whom performance is to be rendered, the person who will receive economic benefit, or the person who furnished the consideration.

Illustrations

1. A owes C a debt of $ 100. The debt is barred by the statute of limitations or by a discharge in bankruptcy, or is unenforceable because of the Statute of Frauds. B promises A to pay the barred or unenforceable debt. C is an intended beneficiary under Subsection (1)(a).

2. B promises A to furnish support for A's minor child C, whom A is bound by law to support. C is an intended beneficiary under Subsection (1)(a).

3. B promises A to pay whatever debts A may incur in a certain undertaking. A incurs in the undertaking debts to C, D and E. If the promise is interpreted as a promise that B will pay C, D and E, they are intended beneficiaries under Subsection (1)(a); if the money is to be paid to A in order that he may be provided with money to pay C, D and E, they are at most incidental beneficiaries.

Comment

e. Incidental beneficiaries. Performance of a contract will often benefit a third person. But unless the third person is an intended beneficiary as here defined, no duty to him is created.

Illustrations

16. B contracts with A to erect an expensive building on A's land. C's adjoining land would be enhanced in value by the performance of the contract. C is an incidental beneficiary.

17. B contracts with A to buy a new car manufactured by C. C is an incidental beneficiary, even though the promise can only be performed if money is paid to C.

18. A, a labor union, promises B, a trade association, not to strike against any member of B during a certain period. One of the members of B charters a ship from C on terms under which such a strike would cause financial loss to C. C is an incidental beneficiary of A's promise.

§ 309. Defenses Against the Beneficiary

(1) A promise creates no duty to a beneficiary unless a contract is formed between the promisor and the promisee; and if a contract is voidable or unenforceable at the time of its formation the right of any beneficiary is subject to the infirmity.

(2) If a contract ceases to be binding in whole or in part because of impracticability, public policy, nonoccurrence of a condition, or present or prospective failure of performance, the right of any beneficiary is to that extent discharged or modified.

(3) Except as stated in Subsections (1) and (2) and in § 311 or as provided by the contract, the right of any beneficiary against the promisor is not subject to the promisor's claims or defenses against the promisee or to the promisee's claims or defenses against the beneficiary.

(4) A beneficiary's right against the promisor is subject to any claim or defense arising from his own conduct or agreement.

§ 311. Variation of a Duty to a Beneficiary

(1) Discharge or modification of a duty to an intended beneficiary by conduct of the promisee or by a subsequent agreement between promisor and promisee is ineffective if a term of the promise creating the duty so provides.

(2) In the absence of such a term, the promisor and promisee retain power to discharge or modify the duty by subsequent agreement.

(3) Such a power terminates when the beneficiary, before he receives notification of the discharge or modification, materially changes his position in justifiable reliance on the promise or brings suit on it or manifests assent to it at the request of the promisor or promisee.

(4) If the promisee receives consideration for an attempted discharge or modification of the promisor's duty which is ineffective against the beneficiary, the beneficiary can assert a right to the consideration so received. The promisor's duty is discharged to the extent of the amount received by the beneficiary.

Comment

a. The power to create an irrevocable duty. The parties to a contract cannot by agreement preclude themselves from varying their duties to each other by subsequent agreement. Nor can they force a right on an unwilling beneficiary, or prevent the beneficiary from joining with them in an agreement varying the duty to him. Compare Restatement, Second, Trusts § 338. But they can by agreement create a duty to a beneficiary which cannot be varied without the beneficiary's consent. Compare § 104; Restatement, Second, Trusts §§ 330, 331.

§ 313. Government Contracts

(1) The rules stated in this Chapter apply to contracts with a government or governmental agency except to the extent that application would contravene the policy of the law authorizing the contract or prescribing remedies for its breach.

(2) In particular, a promisor who contracts with a government or governmental agency to do an act for or render a service to the public is not subject to contractual liability to a member of the public for consequential damages resulting from performance or failure to perform unless
    (a) the terms of the promise provide for such liability; or
    (b) the promisee is subject to liability to the member of the public for the damages and a direct action against the promisor is consistent with the terms

of the contract and with the policy of the law authorizing the contract and prescribing remedies for its breach.

Chapter 15

ASSIGNMENT AND DELEGATION

What Can Be Assigned or Delegated

§ 317. Assignment of a Right

(1) An assignment of a right is a manifestation of the assignor's intention to transfer it by virtue of which the assignor's right to performance by the obligor is extinguished in whole or in part and the assignee acquires a right to such performance.

(2) A contractual right can be assigned unless

    (a) the substitution of a right of the assignee for the right of the assignor would materially change the duty of the obligor, or materially increase the burden or risk imposed on him by his contract, or materially impair his chance of obtaining return performance, or materially reduce its value to him, or

    (b) the assignment is forbidden by statute or is otherwise inoperative on grounds of public policy, or

    (c) assignment is validly precluded by contract.

§ 318. Delegation of Performance of Duty

(1) An obligor can properly delegate the performance of his duty to another unless the delegation is contrary to public policy or the terms of his promise.

(2) Unless otherwise agreed, a promise requires performance by a particular person only to the extent that the obligee has a substantial interest in having that person perform or control the acts promised.

(3) Unless the obligee agrees otherwise, neither delegation of performance nor a contract to assume the duty made with the obligor by the person delegated discharges any duty or liability of the delegating obligor.

§ 319. Delegation of Performance of Condition

(1) Where a performance by a person is made a condition of a duty, performance by a person delegated by him satisfies that requirement unless the delegation is contrary to public policy or the terms of the agreement.

(2) Unless otherwise agreed, an agreement requires performance of a condition by a particular person only to the extent that the obligor has a substantial interest in having that person perform or control the acts required.

§ 321. Assignment of Future Rights

(1) Except as otherwise provided by statute, an assignment of a right to payment expected to arise out of an existing employment or other continuing business relationship is effective in the same way as an assignment of an existing right.

(2) Except as otherwise provided by statute and as stated in Subsection (1), a purported assignment of a right expected to arise under a contract not in existence operates only as a promise to assign the right when it arises and as a power to enforce it.

§ 322. Contractual Prohibition of Assignment

(1) Unless the circumstances indicate the contrary, a contract term prohibiting assignment of "the contract" bars only the delegation to an assignee of the performance by the assignor of a duty or condition.

(2) A contract term prohibiting assignment of rights under the contract, unless a different intention is manifested,
   (a) does not forbid assignment of a right to damages for breach of the whole contract or a right arising out of the assignor's due performance of his entire obligation;
   (b) gives the obligor a right to damages for breach of the terms forbidding assignment but does not render the assignment ineffective;
   (c) is for the benefit of the obligor, and does not prevent the assignee from acquiring rights against the assignor or the obligor from discharging his duty as if there were no such prohibition.

Mode of Assignment or Delegation

§ 328. Interpretation of Words of Assignment; Effect of Acceptance of Assignment

(1) Unless the language or the circumstances indicate the contrary, as in an assignment for security, an assignment of "the contract" or of "all my rights under the contract" or an assignment in similar general terms is an assignment of the assignor's rights and a delegation of his unperformed duties under the contract.

(2) Unless the language or the circumstances indicate the contrary, the acceptance by an assignee of such an assignment operates as a promise to the assignor to perform the assignor's unperformed duties, and the obligor of the assigned rights is an intended beneficiary of the promise.

Effect Between Assignor and Assignee

§ 331. Partially Effective Assignments

An assignment may be conditional, revocable, or voidable by the assignor, or unenforceable by virtue of a Statute of Frauds.

§ 332. Revocability of Gratuitous Assignments

(1) Unless a contrary intention is manifested, a gratuitous assignment is irrevocable if
  (a) the assignment is in a writing either signed or under seal that is delivered by the assignor; or
  (b) the assignment is accompanied by delivery of a writing of a type customarily accepted as a symbol or as evidence of the right assigned.

(2) Except as stated in this Section, a gratuitous assignment is revocable and the right of the assignee is terminated by the assignor's death or incapacity, by a subsequent assignment by the assignor, or by notification from the assignor received by the assignee or by the obligor.

(3) A gratuitous assignment ceases to be revocable to the extent that before the assignee's right is terminated he obtains
  (a) payment or satisfaction of the obligation, or
  (b) judgment against the obligor, or
  (c) a new contract of the obligor by novation.

(4) A gratuitous assignment is irrevocable to the extent necessary to avoid injustice where the assignor should reasonably expect the assignment to induce action or forbearance by the assignee or a subassignee and the assignment does induce such action or forbearance.

(5) An assignment is gratuitous unless it is given or taken
  (a) in exchange for a performance or return promise that would be consideration for a promise; or
  (b) as security for or in total or partial satisfaction of a pre-existing debt or other obligation.

Effect on the Obligor's Duty

§ 336. Defenses Against an Assignee

(1) By an assignment the assignee acquires a right against the obligor only to the extent that the obligor is under a duty to the assignor; and if the right of the assignor would be voidable by the obligor or unenforceable against him if no assignment had been made, the right of the assignee is subject to the infirmity.

(2) The right of an assignee is subject to any defense or claim of the obligor which accrues before the obligor receives notification of the assignment, but not to defenses or claims which accrue thereafter except as stated in this Section or as provided by statute.

(3) Where the right of an assignor is subject to discharge or modification in whole or in part by impracticability, public policy, non-occurrence of a condition, or present or prospective failure of performance by an obligee, the right of the assignee is to that extent subject to discharge or modification even after the obligor receives notification of the assignment.

(4) An assignee's right against the obligor is subject to any defense or claim arising from his conduct or to which he was subject as a party or a prior assignee because he had notice.

Chapter 16

REMEDIES

In General

§ 344. Purposes of Remedies

Judicial remedies under the rules stated in this Restatement serve to protect one or more of the following interests of a promisee:

    (a) his "expectation interest," which is his interest in having the benefit of his bargain by being put in as good a position as he would have been in had the contract been performed,

    (b) his "reliance interest," which is his interest in being reimbursed for loss caused by reliance on the contract by being put in as good a position as he would have been in had the contract not been made, or

    (c) his "restitution interest," which is his interest in having restored to him any benefit that he has conferred on the other party.

Comment

a. Three interests. The law of contract remedies implements the policy in favor of allowing individuals to order their own affairs by making legally enforceable promises. Ordinarily, when a court concludes that there has been a breach of contract, it enforces the broken promise by protecting the expectation that the injured party had when he made the contract. It does this by attempting to put him in as good a position as he would have been in had the contract been performed, that is, had there been no breach. The interest protected in this way is called the "expectation interest." It is sometimes said to give the injured party the "benefit of the bargain." This is not, however, the only interest that may be protected.

The promisee may have changed his position in reliance on the contract by, for example, incurring expenses in preparing to perform, in performing, or in foregoing opportunities to make other contracts. In that case, the court may recognize a claim based on his reliance rather than on his expectation. It does this by attempting to put him back in the position in which he would have been had the contract not been made. The interest protected in this way is called "reliance interest." Although it may be equal to the expectation interest, it is ordinarily smaller because it does not include the injured party's lost profit.

In some situations a court will recognize yet a third interest and grant relief to prevent unjust enrichment. This may be done if a party has not only changed his own position in reliance on the contract but has also conferred a benefit on the other party by, for example, making a part payment or furnishing services under the contract. The court may then require the other party to disgorge the benefit that he has received by returning it to the party who conferred it. The interest of the claimant protected in this way is called the "restitution interest." Although it may be equal to the expectation or reliance interest, it is ordinarily smaller because it includes neither the injured party's lost profit nor that part of his expenditures in reliance that resulted in no benefit to the other party.

The interests described in this Section are not inflexible limits on relief and in situations in which a court grants such relief as justice requires, the relief may not correspond precisely to any of these interests. See §§ 15, 87, 89, 90, 139, 158 and 272.

Illustrations

1. A contracts to build a building for B on B's land for $ 100,000. B repudiates the contract before either party has done anything in reliance on it. It would have cost A $ 90,000 to build the building. A has an expectation interest of $ 10,000, the difference between the $ 100,000 price and his savings of $ 90,000 in not having to do the work. Since A has done nothing in reliance, A's reliance interest is zero. Since A has conferred no benefit on B, A's restitution interest is zero.

2. The facts being otherwise as stated in Illustration 1, B does not repudiate until A has spent $ 60,000 of the $ 90,000. A has been paid nothing and can salvage nothing from the $ 60,000 that he has spent. A now has an expectation interest of $ 70,000, the difference between the $ 100,000 price and his saving of $ 30,000 in not having to do the work. A also has a reliance interest of $ 60,000, the amount that he has spent. If the benefit to B of the partly finished building is $ 40,000, A has a restitution interest of $ 40,000.

Comment

b. Expectation interest. In principle, at least, a party's expectation interest represents the actual worth of the contract to him rather than to some reasonable third person. Damages based on the expectation interest therefore take account of any special circumstances that are peculiar to the situation of the injured party, including his personal values and even his idiosyncracies, as well as his own needs and opportunities. See Illustration 3. In practice, however, the injured party is often held to a more objective valuation of his expectation interest because he may be barred from recovering for loss resulting from such special circumstances on the ground that it was not foreseeable or cannot be shown with sufficient certainty. See §§ 351 and 352. Furthermore, since he cannot recover for loss that he could have avoided by arranging a substitute transaction on the market, his recovery is often limited by the objective standard of market price.

The expectation interest is not based on the injured party's hopes when he made the contract but on the actual value that the contract would have had to him had it been performed. See Illustration 5. It is therefore based on the circumstances at the time for performance and not those at the time of the making of the contract.

Illustrations

5. A makes a contract with B under which A is to pay B for drilling an oil well on B's land, adjacent to that of A, for development and exploration purposes. Both A and B believe that the well will be productive and will substantially enhance the value of A's land in an amount that they estimate to be $ 1,000,000. Before A has paid anything, B breaks the contract by refusing to drill the well. Other exploration then proves that there is no oil in the region. A's expectation interest is zero.

Enforcement by Award of Damages

§ 346. Availability of Damages

(1) The injured party has a right to damages for any breach by a party against whom the contract is enforceable unless the claim for damages has been suspended or discharged.

(2) If the breach caused no loss or if the amount of the loss is not proved under the rules stated in this Chapter, a small sum fixed without regard to the amount of loss will be awarded as nominal damages.

§ 347. Measure of Damages in General

Subject to the limitations stated in §§ 350–53, the injured party has a right to damages based on his expectation interest as measured by
   (a) the loss in the value to him of the other party's performance caused by its failure or deficiency, plus
   (b) any other loss, including incidental or consequential loss, caused by the breach, less
   (c) any cost or other loss that he has avoided by not having to perform.

§ 348. Alternatives to Loss in Value of Performance

(1) If a breach delays the use of property and the loss in value to the injured party is not proved with reasonable certainty, he may recover damages based on the rental value of the property or on interest on the value of the property.

(2) If a breach results in defective or unfinished construction and the loss in value to the injured party is not proved with sufficient certainty, he may recover damages based on
   (a) the diminution in the market price of the property caused by the breach, or
   (b) the reasonable cost of completing performance or of remedying the defects if that cost is not clearly disproportionate to the probable loss in value to him.

(3) If a breach is of a promise conditioned on a fortuitous event and it is uncertain whether the event would have occurred had there been no breach, the injured party may recover damages based on the value of the conditional right at the time of breach.

§ 349. Damages Based on Reliance Interest

As an alternative to the measure of damages stated in § 347, the injured party has a right to damages based on his reliance interest, including expenditures made in preparation for performance or in performance, less any loss that the party in breach can prove with reasonable certainty the injured party would have suffered had the contract been performed.

Comment

a. Reliance interest where profit uncertain. Loss in value and cost or other loss avoided are key components of contract damages. See § 347. If the injured party was to supply services such as erecting a building, for example, the difference between loss in value of the other party's performance and the cost or other loss avoided by the injured party will be equal to the cost of the injured party's expenditures in reliance, up to the time of breach, plus the profit that would have been made had the contract been fully performed. To the extent that "overhead" costs are fixed costs, they are not included in the cost of expenditures in reliance for this purpose. Under the rule stated in this Section, the injured party may, if he chooses, ignore the element of profit and recover as damages his expenditures in reliance. He may choose to do this if he cannot prove his profit with reasonable certainty. He may also choose to do this in the case of a losing contract, one under which he would have had a loss rather than a profit. In that case, however, it is open to the party in breach to prove the amount of the loss, to the extent that he can do so with reasonable certainty under the standard stated in § 352, and have it subtracted from the injured party's damages. The resulting damages will then be the same as those under the rule stated in § 347. If the injured party's expenditures exceed the contract price, it is clear that at least to the extent of the excess, there would have been a loss. For this reason, recovery for expenditures under the rule stated in this section may not exceed the full contract price. As to the possibility of restitution in such a case, see § 373. Often the reliance consists of preparation for performance or actual performance of the contract, and this is sometimes called "essential reliance." It may, however, also consist of preparation for collateral transactions that a party plans to carry out when the contract in question is performed, and this is sometimes called "incidental" reliance.

b. Reliance interest in other cases. There are other instances in which damages may be based on the reliance interest. Under the rules stated in §§ 87, 89, 90 and 139, if a promise is enforceable because it has induced action or forbearance, the remedy granted for breach may be limited as justice requires. Under these rules, relief may be limited to damages measured by the extent of the promisee's reliance rather than by the terms of the promise. Furthermore, even when the contract is enforceable because of consideration, a court may, under the rule stated in § 353, conclude that the circumstances require that damages be limited to losses incurred in reliance.

§ 350. Avoidability as a Limitation on Damages

(1) Except as stated in Subsection (2), damages are not recoverable for loss that the injured party could have avoided without undue risk, burden or humiliation.

(2) The injured party is not precluded from recovery by the rule stated in Subsection (1) to the extent that he has made reasonable but unsuccessful efforts to avoid loss.

§ 351. Unforeseeability and Related Limitations on Damages

(1) Damages are not recoverable for loss that the party in breach did not have reason to foresee as a probable result of the breach when the contract was made.

(2) Loss may be foreseeable as a probable result of a breach because it follows from the breach
    (a) in the ordinary course of events, or
    (b) as a result of special circumstances, beyond the ordinary course of events, that the party in breach had reason to know.

(3) A court may limit damages for foreseeable loss by excluding recovery for loss of profits, by allowing recovery only for loss incurred in reliance, or otherwise if it concludes that in the circumstances justice so requires in order to avoid disproportionate compensation.

§ 352. Uncertainty as a Limitation on Damages

Damages are not recoverable for loss beyond an amount that the evidence permits to be established with reasonable certainty.

§ 353. Loss Due to Emotional Disturbance

Recovery for emotional disturbance will be excluded unless the breach also caused bodily harm or the contract or the breach is of such a kind that serious emotional disturbance was a particularly likely result.

§ 354. Interest as Damages

(1) If the breach consists of a failure to pay a definite sum in money or to render a performance with fixed or ascertainable monetary value, interest is recoverable from the time for performance on the amount due less all deductions to which the party in breach is entitled.

(2) In any other case, such interest may be allowed as justice requires on the amount that would have been just compensation had it been paid when performance was due.

§ 355. Punitive Damages

Punitive damages are not recoverable for a breach of contract unless the conduct constituting the breach is also a tort for which punitive damages are recoverable.

§ 356. Liquidated Damages and Penalties

(1) Damages for breach by either party may be liquidated in the agreement but only at an amount that is reasonable in the light of the anticipated or actual loss caused by the breach and the difficulties of proof of loss. A term fixing unreasonably large liquidated damages is unenforceable on grounds of public policy as a penalty.

(2) A term in a bond providing for an amount of money as a penalty for non-occurrence of the condition of the bond is unenforceable on grounds of public policy to the extent that the amount exceeds the loss caused by such non-occurrence.

Enforcement by Specific Performance and Injunction

§ 359. Effect of Adequacy of Damages

(1) Specific performance or an injunction will not be ordered if damages would be adequate to protect the expectation interest of the injured party.

(2) The adequacy of the damage remedy for failure to render one part of the performance due does not preclude specific performance or injunction as to the contract as a whole.

(3) Specific performance or an injunction will not be refused merely because there is a remedy for breach other than damages, but such a remedy may be considered in exercising discretion under the rule stated in § 357.

§ 360. Factors Affecting Adequacy of Damages

In determining whether the remedy in damages would be adequate, the following circumstances are significant:
   (a) the difficulty of proving damages with reasonable certainty,
   (b) the difficulty of procuring a suitable substitute performance by means of money awarded as damages, and
   (c) the likelihood that an award of damages could not be collected.

Restitution

§ 370. Requirement That Benefit Be Conferred

A party is entitled to restitution under the rules stated in this Restatement only to the extent that he has conferred a benefit on the other party by way of part performance or reliance.

§ 371. Measure of Restitution Interest

If a sum of money is awarded to protect a party's restitution interest, it may as justice requires be measured by either

    (a) the reasonable value to the other party of what he received in terms of what it would have cost him to obtain it from a person in the claimant's position, or

    (b) the extent to which the other party's property has been increased in value or his other interests advanced.

§ 373. Restitution When Other Party Is in Breach

(1) Subject to the rule stated in Subsection (2), on a breach by non-performance that gives rise to a claim for damages for total breach or on a repudiation, the injured party is entitled to restitution for any benefit that he has conferred on the other party by way of part performance or reliance.

(2) The injured party has no right to restitution if he has performed all of his duties under the contract and no performance by the other party remains due other than payment of a definite sum of money for that performance.

§ 374. Restitution in Favor of Party in Breach

(1) Subject to the rule stated in Subsection (2), if a party justifiably refuses to perform on the ground that his remaining duties of performance have been discharged by the other party's breach, the party in breach is entitled to restitution for any benefit that he has conferred by way of part performance or reliance in excess of the loss that he has caused by his own breach.

(2) To the extent that, under the manifested assent of the parties, a party's performance is to be retained in the case of breach, that party is not entitled to restitution if the value of the performance as liquidated damages is reasonable in the light of the anticipated or actual loss caused by the breach and the difficulties of proof of loss.

Comment

a. Restitution in spite of breach. The rule stated in this Section applies where a party, after having rendered part performance, commits a breach by either non-performance or repudiation that justifies the other party in refusing further performance. It is often unjust to allow the injured party to retain the entire benefit of the part performance rendered by the party in breach without paying anything in return. The party in breach is, in any case, liable for the loss caused by his breach. If the benefit received by the injured party does not exceed that loss, he owes nothing to the party in breach. If the benefit received exceeds that loss, the rule stated in this Section generally gives the party in breach the right to recover the excess in restitution. If the injured party has a right to specific performance and remains willing and able to perform, he may keep what he has received and sue for specific performance of the balance.

The rule stated in this Section is of particular importance in connection with breach by the buyer under a land sale contract and breach by the builder under a construction contract. It is less important in the case of the defaulting employee, who has the protection afforded by statutes that require salary payments at relatively short intervals. The case of defaulting buyer of goods is governed by Uniform Commercial Code § 2-718(2), which generally allows restitution of all but an amount fixed by that section. Furthermore, to the extent that the contract is "divisible" so that pairs of part performances on each side are agreed equivalents (§ 240), the party in breach can recover under the terms of the contract and does not need restitution to obtain relief.

b. Measurement of benefit. If the party in breach seeks restitution of money that he has paid, no problem arises in measuring the benefit to the other party. If, however, he seeks to recover a sum of money that represents the benefit of services rendered to the other party, measurement of the benefit is more difficult. Since the party seeking restitution is responsible for posing the problem of measurement of benefit, doubts will be resolved against him and his recovery will not exceed the less generous of the two measures stated in § 370, that of the other party's increase in wealth. If no value can be put on this, he cannot recover. Although the contract price is evidence of the benefit, it is not conclusive. However, in no case will the party in breach be allowed to recover more than a ratable portion of the total contract price where such a portion can be determined.

A party who intentionally furnishes services or builds a building that is materially different from what he promised is properly regarded as having acted officiously and not in part performance of his promise and will be denied recovery on that ground even if his performance was of some benefit to the other party. This is not the case, however, if the other party has accepted or agreed to accept the substitute performance.

§ 375. Restitution When Contract Is Within Statute of Frauds

A party who would otherwise have a claim in restitution under a contract is not barred from restitution for the reason that the contract is unenforceable by him because of the Statute of Frauds unless the Statute provides otherwise or its purpose would be frustrated by allowing restitution.

Comment

a. Restitution generally available. Parties to a contract that is unenforceable under the Statute of Frauds frequently act in reliance on it before discovering that it is unenforceable. A party may, for example, render services under the contract or may make improvements on land that is the subject of the contract. The rule stated in this Section allows restitution in such cases. If the party claiming restitution is in breach, the right to restitution is subject to the rule stated in § 374. If the other party is in breach it is subject to the rule stated in § 373. Since allowing restitution does not amount to enforcement of the contract, it ordinarily does not contravene the policy behind the Statute. Restitution will not be allowed, however, if the Statute so provides or if restitution would frustrate the purpose of the Statute. However, the mere fact that the particular wording of the Statute makes the contract "void" is not controlling in this respect.

For the purposes of this Section, the measure of the benefit conferred is generally the same as that applicable to similar situations under enforceable contracts. See Comment b to § 374. The agreement, although unenforceable, may be evidence of this benefit. As to the possibility of recovery based on the reliance interest, see § 139.

§ 376. Restitution When Contract Is Voidable

A party who has avoided a contract on the ground of lack of capacity, mistake, misrepresentation, duress, undue influence or abuse of a fiduciary relation is entitled to restitution for any benefit that he has conferred on the other party by way of part performance or reliance.

§ 377. Restitution in Cases of Impracticability, Frustration, Non-Occurrence of Condition or Disclaimer by Beneficiary

A party whose duty of performance does not arise or is discharged as a result of impracticability of performance, frustration of purpose, non-occurrence of a condition or disclaimer by a beneficiary is entitled to restitution for any benefit that he has conferred on the other party by way of part performance or reliance.

UNIFORM COMMERCIAL CODE
ARTICLES 1 and 2 *
ARTICLE 1 — GENERAL PROVISIONS

[Editors' Note: All fifty states have adopted the revised version of Article 1. However, none of the enacting states have adopted Revised 1-301, the choice of law provision of the UCC.]

PART 1 GENERAL PROVISIONS

PART 2 GENERAL DEFINITIONS AND PRINCIPLES OF INTERPRETATION

PART 3 TERRITORIAL APPLICABILITY AND GENERAL RULES

PART 1 GENERAL PROVISIONS

SECTION 1-101. SHORT TITLES

(a) This [Act] may be cited as the Uniform Commercial Code.

(b) This article may be cited as Uniform Commercial Code — General Provisions.

Official Comments

Source: Former Section 1-101.

Changes from former law: Subsection (b) is new. It is added in order to make the structure of Article 1 parallel with that of the other articles of the Uniform Commercial Code.

1. Each other article of the Uniform Commercial Code (except Articles 10 and 11) may also be cited by its own short title. See Sections 2-101, 2A-101, 3-101, 4-101, 4A-101, 5-101, 6-101, 7-101, 8-101, and 9-101.

SECTION 1-102. SCOPE OF ARTICLE.

This article applies to a transaction to the extent that it is governed by another article of [the Uniform Commercial Code].

Official Comments

Source: New.

1. This section is intended to resolve confusion that has occasionally arisen as to the applicability of the substantive rules in this article. This section makes clear what has always been the case — the rules in Article 1 apply to transactions to the extent that those transactions are governed by one of the other articles of the Uniform Commercial Code. See also Comment 1 to Section 1-301.

SECTION 1-103. CONSTRUCTION OF [UNIFORM COMMERCIAL CODE] TO PROMOTE ITS PURPOSES AND POLICIES; APPLICABILITY OF SUPPLEMENTAL PRINCIPLES OF LAW.

(a) [The Uniform Commercial Code] must be liberally construed and applied to promote its underlying purposes and policies, which are:

    (1) to simplify, clarify, and modernize the law governing commercial transactions;

    (2) to permit the continued expansion of commercial practices through custom, usage, and agreement of the parties; and

    (3) to make uniform the law among the various jurisdictions.

(b) Unless displaced by the particular provisions of [the Uniform Commercial Code], the principles of law and equity, including the law merchant and the law relative to capacity to contract, principal and agent, estoppel, fraud, misrepresentation, duress, coercion, mistake, bankruptcy, and other validating or invalidating cause supplement its provisions.

Official Comments

Source: Former Section 1-102 (1)-(2); Former Section 1-103.

Changes from former law: This section is derived from subsections (1) and (2) of former Section 1-102 and from former Section 1-103. Subsection (a) of this section combines subsections (1) and (2) of former Section 1-102. Except for changing the form of reference to the Uniform Commercial Code and minor stylistic changes, its language is the same as subsections (1) and (2) of former Section 1-102. Except for changing the form of reference to the Uniform Commercial Code and minor stylistic changes, subsection (b) of this section is identical to former Section 1-103. The provisions have been combined in this section to reflect the interrelationship between them.

1. The Uniform Commercial Code is drawn to provide flexibility so that, since it is intended to be a semi-permanent and infrequently-amended piece of legislation, it will provide its own machinery for expansion of commercial practices. It is intended to make it possible for the law embodied in the Uniform Commercial Code to be applied by the courts in the light of unforeseen and new circumstances and practices. The proper construction of the Uniform Commercial Code requires, of course, that its interpretation and application be limited to its reason.

Even prior to the enactment of the Uniform Commercial Code, courts were careful to keep broad acts from being hampered in their effects by later acts of limited scope. See *Pacific Wool Growers v. Draper & Co.*, 158 Or. 1, 73 P.2d 1391 (1937), and compare Section 1-104. The courts have often recognized that the policies embodied in an act are applicable in reason to subject-matter that was not expressly included in the language of the act, *Commercial Nat. Bank of New Orleans v. Canal-Louisiana Bank & Trust Co.*, 239 U.S. 520, 36 S.Ct. 194, 60 L.Ed. 417 (1916) (bona fide purchase policy of Uniform Warehouse Receipts Act extended to case not covered but of equivalent nature), and did the same where reason and policy so required, even where the subject-matter had been intentionally excluded from the act in general. *Agar v. Orda*, 264 N.Y. 248, 190 N.E. 479 (1934) (Uniform Sales Act change in seller's remedies applied to contract for sale of choses in action even though the general coverage of that Act was intentionally limited to goods "other than things in action.") They implemented a statutory policy with liberal and useful remedies not provided in the statutory text. They disregarded a statutory limitation of remedy where the reason of the limitation did not apply. *Fiterman v. J. N. Johnson & Co.*, 156 Minn. 201, 194 N.W. 399 (1923) (requirement of return of the goods as a condition to rescission for breach of warranty; also, partial rescission allowed). Nothing in the Uniform Commercial Code stands in the way of the continuance of such action by the courts.

The Uniform Commercial Code should be construed in accordance with its underlying purposes and policies. The text of each section should be read in the light of the purpose and policy of the rule or principle in question, as also of the Uniform Commercial Code as a whole, and the application of the language should be construed narrowly or broadly, as the case may be, in conformity with the purposes and policies involved.

2. Applicability of supplemental principles of law. Subsection (b) states the basic relationship of the Uniform Commercial Code to supplemental bodies of law. The Uniform Commercial Code was drafted against the backdrop of existing bodies of law, including the common law and equity, and relies on those bodies of law to supplement it provisions in many important ways. At the same time, the Uniform Commercial Code is the primary source of commercial law rules in areas that it governs, and its rules represent choices made by its drafters and the enacting legislatures about the appropriate policies to be furthered in the transactions it covers. Therefore, while principles of common law and equity may *supplement* provisions of the Uniform Commercial Code, they may not be used to *supplant* its provisions, or the purposes and policies those provisions reflect, unless a specific provision of the Uniform Commercial Code provides otherwise. In the absence of such a provision, the Uniform Commercial Code preempts principles of common law and equity that are inconsistent with either its provisions or its purposes and policies.

The language of subsection (b) is intended to reflect both the concept of supplementation and the concept of preemption. Some courts, however, had difficulty in applying the identical language of former Section 1-103 to determine when other law appropriately may be applied to supplement the Uniform Commercial Code, and when that law has been displaced by the Code. Some decisions applied other law in situations in which that application, while not inconsistent with the text of any particular provision of the Uniform Commercial Code, clearly was inconsistent with the underlying purposes and policies reflected in the relevant provisions of the Code. *See, e.g., Sheerbonnet, Ltd. v. American Express Bank, Ltd.*, 951 F. Supp. 403 (S.D.N.Y. 1995). In part, this difficulty arose from Comment 1 to former Section 1-103, which stated that "this section indicates the continued applicability to commercial contracts of all supplemental bodies of law except insofar as they are explicitly displaced by this Act." The "explicitly displaced" language of that Comment did not accurately reflect the proper scope of Uniform Commercial Code preemption, which extends to displacement of other law that is inconsistent with the purposes and policies of the Uniform Commercial Code, as well as with its text.

3. Application of subsection (b) to statutes. The primary focus of Section 1-103 is on the relationship between the Uniform Commercial Code and principles of common law and equity as developed by the courts. State law, however, increasingly is statutory. Not only are there a growing number of state statutes addressing specific issues that come within the scope of the Uniform Commercial Code, but in some States many general principles of common law and equity have been codified. When the other law relating to a matter within the scope of the Uniform Commercial Code is a statute, the principles of subsection (b) remain relevant to the court's analysis of the relationship between that statute and the Uniform Commercial Code, but other principles of statutory interpretation that specifically address the interrelationship between statutes will be relevant as well. In some situations, the principles of subsection (b) still will be determinative. For example, the mere fact that an equitable principle is stated in statutory form rather than in judicial decisions should not change the court's analysis of whether the principle can be used to supplement the Uniform Commercial Code — under subsection (b), equitable principles may supplement provisions of the Uniform Commercial Code only if they are consistent with the purposes and policies of the Uniform Commercial Code as well as its text. In other situations, however, other interpretive principles addressing the interrelationship between statutes may lead the court to conclude that the other statute is controlling, even though it conflicts with the Uniform Commercial Code. This, for example, would be the result in a situation where the other statute was specifically intended to provide additional protection to a class of individuals engaging in transactions covered by the Uniform Commercial Code.

4. Listing not exclusive. The list of sources of supplemental law in subsection (b) is intended to be merely illustrative of the other law that may supplement the Uniform Commercial Code, and is not exclusive. No listing could be exhaustive. Further, the fact that a particular section of the Uniform Commercial Code makes express reference to other law is not intended to suggest the negation of the general application of the principles of subsection (b). Note also that the word "bankruptcy" in subsection (b), continuing the use of that word from former Section 1-103, should be understood not as a specific reference to federal bankruptcy law but, rather as a reference to general principles of insolvency, whether under federal or state law.

SECTION 1-104. CONSTRUCTION AGAINST IMPLIED REPEAL.

[The Uniform Commercial Code] being a general act intended as a unified coverage of its subject matter, no part of it shall be deemed to be impliedly repealed by subsequent legislation if such construction can reasonably be avoided.

Official Comments

Source: Former Section 1-104.

Changes from former law: Except for changing the form of reference to the Uniform Commercial Code, this section is identical to former Section 1-104.

1. This section embodies the policy that an act that bears evidence of carefully considered permanent regulative intention should not lightly be regarded as impliedly repealed by subsequent legislation. The Uniform Commercial Code, carefully integrated and intended as a uniform codification of permanent character covering an entire "field" of law, is to be regarded as particularly resistant to implied repeal.

SECTION 1-105. SEVERABILITY.

If any provision or clause of [the Uniform Commercial Code] or its application to any person or circumstance is held invalid, the invalidity does not affect other provisions or applications of [the Uniform Commercial Code] which can be given effect without the invalid provision or application, and to this end the provisions of [the Uniform Commercial Code] are severable.

Official Comments

Source: Former Section 1-108.

Changes from former law: Except for changing the form of reference to the Uniform Commercial Code, this section is identical to former Section 1-108.

1. This is the model severability section recommended by the National Conference of Commissioners on Uniform State Laws for inclusion in all acts of extensive scope.

SECTION 1-106. USE OF SINGULAR AND PLURAL; GENDER.

In [the Uniform Commercial Code], unless the statutory context otherwise requires:

(1) words in the singular number include the plural, and those in the plural include the singular; and

(2) words of any gender also refer to any other gender.

Official Comments

Source: Former Section 1-102(5). See also 1 U.S.C. Section 1.

Changes from former law: Other than minor stylistic changes, this section is identical to former Section 1-102(5).

1. This section makes it clear that the use of singular or plural in the text of the Uniform Commercial Code is generally only a matter of drafting style — singular words may be applied in the plural, and plural words may be applied in the singular. Only when it is clear from the statutory context that the use of the singular or plural does not include the other is this rule inapplicable. *See, e.g.,* Section 9-322.

SECTION 1-107. SECTION CAPTIONS.

Section captions are part of [the Uniform Commercial Code].

Official Comments

Source: Former Section 1-109.

Changes from former law: None.

1. Section captions are a part of the text of the Uniform Commercial Code, and not mere surplusage. This is not the case, however, with respect to subsection headings appearing in Article 9. See Comment 3 to Section 9-101 ("subsection headings are not a part of the official text itself and have not been approved by the sponsors.").

SECTION 1-108. RELATION TO ELECTRONIC SIGNATURES IN GLOBAL AND NATIONAL COMMERCE ACT.

This [Act] modifies, limits, and supersedes the federal Electronic Signatures in Global and National Commerce Act, (15 U.S.C. Section 7001, et. seq.) but does not modify, limit, or supersede Section 101(c) of that act (15 U.S.C. Section 7001(c)) or authorize electronic delivery of any of the notices described in Section 103(b) of that act (15 U.S.C. Section 103(b)).

Official Comments

Source: New

1. The federal Electronic Signatures in Global and National Commerce Act, 15 U.S.C. Section 7001 *et seq* became effective in 2000. Section 102(a) of that Act provides that a State statute may modify, limit, or supersede the provisions of section 101 of that Act with respect to state law if such statute, *inter alia*, specifies the alternative procedures or requirements for the use or acceptance (or both) of electronic records or electronic signatures to establish the legal effect, validity, or enforceability of contracts or other records, and (i) such alternative procedures or requirements are consistent with Titles I and II of that Act, (ii) such alternative procedures or requirements do not require, or accord greater legal status or effect to, the implementation or application of a specific technology or technical specification for performing the functions of creating, storing, generating, receiving, communicating, or authenticating electronic records or electronic signatures; and (iii) if enacted or adopted after the date of the enactment of that Act, makes specific reference to that Act. Article 1 fulfills the first two of those three criteria; this Section fulfills the third criterion listed above.

2. As stated in this section, however, Article 1 does not modify, limit, or supersede Section 101(c) of the Electronic Signatures in Global and National Commerce Act (requiring affirmative consent from a consumer to electronic delivery of transactional disclosures that are required by state law to be in writing); nor does it authorize electronic delivery of any of the notices described in Section 103(b) of that Act.

PART 2 GENERAL DEFINITIONS AND PRINCIPLES OF INTERPRETATION

SECTION 1-201. GENERAL DEFINITIONS.

(a) Unless the context otherwise requires, words or phrases defined in this section, or in the additional definitions contained in other articles of [the Uniform Commercial Code] that apply to particular articles or parts thereof, have the meanings stated.

(b) Subject to definitions contained in other articles of [the Uniform Commercial Code] that apply to particular articles or parts thereof:

    (1) "Action", in the sense of a judicial proceeding, includes recoupment, counterclaim, set-off, suit in equity, and any other proceeding in which rights are determined.

    (2) "Aggrieved party" means a party entitled to pursue a remedy.

    (3) "Agreement", as distinguished from "contract", means the bargain of the parties in fact, as found in their language or inferred from other circumstances, including course of performance, course of dealing, or usage of trade as provided in Section 1-303.

    (4) "Bank" means a person engaged in the business of banking and includes a savings bank, savings and loan association, credit union, and trust company.

    (5) "Bearer" means a person in possession of a negotiable instrument, document of title, or certificated security that is payable to bearer or indorsed in blank.

    (6) "Bill of lading" means a document evidencing the receipt of goods for shipment issued by a person engaged in the business of transporting or forwarding goods.

    (7) "Branch" includes a separately incorporated foreign branch of a bank.

    (8) "Burden of establishing" a fact means the burden of persuading the trier of fact that the existence of the fact is more probable than its nonexistence.

    (9) "Buyer in ordinary course of business" means a person that buys goods in good faith, without knowledge that the sale violates the rights of another person in the goods, and in the ordinary course from a person, other than a pawnbroker, in the business of selling goods of that kind. A person buys goods in the ordinary course if the sale to the person comports with the usual or customary practices in the kind of business in which the seller is engaged or with the seller's own usual or customary practices. A person that sells oil, gas, or other minerals at the wellhead or minehead is a person in the business of selling goods of that kind. A buyer in ordinary course of business may buy for cash, by exchange of other property, or on secured or unsecured credit, and may acquire goods or documents of title under a preexisting contract for sale. Only a buyer that takes possession of the goods or has a right to recover the goods from the seller under Article 2 may be a buyer in

ordinary course of business. "Buyer in ordinary course of business" does not include a person that acquires goods in a transfer in bulk or as security for or in total or partial satisfaction of a money debt.

(10) "Conspicuous", with reference to a term, means so written, displayed, or presented that a reasonable person against which it is to operate ought to have noticed it. Whether a term is "conspicuous" or not is a decision for the court. Conspicuous terms include the following:

    (A) a heading in capitals equal to or greater in size than the surrounding text, or in contrasting type, font, or color to the surrounding text of the same or lesser size; and

    (B) language in the body of a record or display in larger type than the surrounding text, or in contrasting type, font, or color to the surrounding text of the same size, or set off from surrounding text of the same size by symbols or other marks that call attention to the language.

(11) "Consumer" means an individual who enters into a transaction primarily for personal, family, or household purposes

(12) "Contract", as distinguished from "agreement", means the total legal obligation that results from the parties' agreement as determined by [the Uniform Commercial Code] as supplemented by any other applicable laws.

(13) "Creditor" includes a general creditor, a secured creditor, a lien creditor, and any representative of creditors, including an assignee for the benefit of creditors, a trustee in bankruptcy, a receiver in equity, and an executor or administrator of an insolvent debtor's or assignor's estate.

(14) "Defendant" includes a person in the position of defendant in a counterclaim, cross-claim, or third-party claim.

(15) "Delivery", with respect to an instrument, document of title, or chattel paper, means voluntary transfer of possession.

(16) "Document of title" includes bill of lading, dock warrant, dock receipt, warehouse receipt or order for the delivery of goods, and also any other document which in the regular course of business or financing is treated as adequately evidencing that the person in possession of it is entitled to receive, hold, and dispose of the document and the goods it covers. To be a document of title, a document must purport to be issued by or addressed to a bailee and purport to cover goods in the bailee's possession which are either identified or are fungible portions of an identified mass.

(17) "Fault" means a default, breach, or wrongful act or omission.

(18) "Fungible goods" means:

    (A) goods of which any unit, by nature or usage of trade, is the equivalent of any other like unit; or

    (B) goods that by agreement are treated as equivalent.

(19) "Genuine" means free of forgery or counterfeiting.

(20) "Good faith," except as otherwise provided in Article 5, means honesty in fact and the observance of reasonable commercial standards of fair dealing.

(21) "Holder" means:

  (A) the person in possession of a negotiable instrument that is payable either to bearer or to an identified person that is the person in possession; or

  (B) the person in possession of a document of title if the goods are deliverable either to bearer or to the order of the person in possession.

(22) "Insolvency proceeding" includes an assignment for the benefit of creditors or other proceeding intended to liquidate or rehabilitate the estate of the person involved.

(23) "Insolvent" means:

  (A) having generally ceased to pay debts in the ordinary course of business other than as a result of bona fide dispute;

  (B) being unable to pay debts as they become due; or

  (C) being insolvent within the meaning of federal bankruptcy law.

(24) "Money" means a medium of exchange currently authorized or adopted by a domestic or foreign government. The term includes a monetary unit of account established by an intergovernmental organization or by agreement between two or more countries.

(25) "Organization" means a person other than an individual.

(26) "Party", as distinguished from "third party", means a person that has engaged in a transaction or made an agreement subject to [the Uniform Commercial Code].

(27) "Person" means an individual, corporation, business trust, estate, trust, partnership, limited liability company, association, joint venture, government, governmental subdivision, agency, or instrumentality, public corporation, or any other legal or commercial entity.

(28) "Present value" means the amount as of a date certain of one or more sums payable in the future, discounted to the date certain by use of either an interest rate specified by the parties if that rate is not manifestly unreasonable at the time the transaction is entered into or, if an interest rate is not so specified, a commercially reasonable rate that takes into account the facts and circumstances at the time the transaction is entered into.

(29) "Purchase" means taking by sale, lease, discount, negotiation, mortgage, pledge, lien, security interest, issue or reissue, gift, or any other voluntary transaction creating an interest in property.

(30) "Purchaser" means a person that takes by purchase.

(31) "Record" means information that is inscribed on a tangible medium or that is stored in an electronic or other medium and is retrievable in perceivable form.

(32) "Remedy" means any remedial right to which an aggrieved party is entitled with or without resort to a tribunal.

(33) "Representative" means a person empowered to act for another, including an agent, an officer of a corporation or association, and a trustee, executor, or administrator of an estate.

(34) "Right" includes remedy.

(35) "Security interest" means an interest in personal property or fixtures which secures payment or performance of an obligation. "Security interest" includes any interest of a consignor and a buyer of accounts, chattel paper, a payment intangible, or a promissory note in a transaction that is subject to Article 9. "Security interest" does not include the special property interest of a buyer of goods on identification of those goods to a contract for sale under Section 2-401, but a buyer may also acquire a "security interest" by complying with Article 9. Except as otherwise provided in Section 2-505, the right of a seller or lessor of goods under Article 2 or 2A to retain or acquire possession of the goods is not a "security interest", but a seller or lessor may also acquire a "security interest" by complying with Article 9. The retention or reservation of title by a seller of goods notwithstanding shipment or delivery to the buyer under Section 2-401 is limited in effect to a reservation of a "security interest." Whether a transaction in the form of a lease creates a "security interest" is determined pursuant to Section 1-203.

(36) "Send" in connection with a writing, record, or notice means:

(A) to deposit in the mail or deliver for transmission by any other usual means of communication with postage or cost of transmission provided for and properly addressed and, in the case of an instrument, to an address specified thereon or otherwise agreed, or if there be none to any address reasonable under the circumstances; or

(B) in any other way to cause to be received any record or notice within the time it would have arrived if properly sent.

(37) "Signed" includes using any symbol executed or adopted with present intention to adopt or accept a writing.

(38) "State" means a State of the United States, the District of Columbia, Puerto Rico, the United States Virgin Islands, or any territory or insular possession subject to the jurisdiction of the United States.

(39) "Surety" includes a guarantor or other secondary obligor.

(40) "Term" means a portion of an agreement that relates to a particular matter.

(41) "Unauthorized signature" means a signature made without actual, implied, or apparent authority. The term includes a forgery.

(42) "Warehouse receipt" means a receipt issued by a person engaged in the business of storing goods for hire.

(43) "Writing" includes printing, typewriting, or any other intentional reduction to tangible form. "Written" has a corresponding meaning.

Official Comments

Source: Former Section 1-201.

Changes from former law: In order to make it clear that all definitions in the Uniform Commercial Code (not just those appearing in Article 1, as stated in former Section 1-201, but also those appearing in other Articles) do not apply if the context otherwise requires, a new subsection (a) to that effect has been added, and the definitions now appear in subsection (b). The reference in subsection (a) to the "context" is intended to refer to the context in which the defined term is used in the Uniform Commercial Code. In other words, the definition applies whenever the defined term is used unless the context in which the defined term is used in the statute indicates that the term was not used in its defined sense. Consider, for example, Sections 3-103(a)(9) (defining "promise," in relevant part, as "a written undertaking to pay money signed by the person undertaking to pay") and 3-303(a)(1) (indicating that an instrument is issued or transferred for value if "the instrument is issued or transferred for a promise of performance, to the extent that the promise has been performed"). It is clear from the statutory context of the use of the word "promise" in Section 3-303(a)(1) that the term was not used in the sense of its definition in Section 3-103(a)(9). Thus, the Section 3-103(a)(9) definition should not be used to give meaning to the word "promise" in Section 3-303(a).

Some definitions in former Section 1-201 have been reformulated as substantive provisions and have been moved to other sections. See Sections 1-202 (explicating concepts of notice and knowledge formerly addressed in Sections 1-201(25)-(27)), 1-204 (determining when a person gives value for rights, replacing the definition of "value" in former Section 1-201(44)), and 1-206 (addressing the meaning of presumptions, replacing the definitions of "presumption" and "presumed" in former Section 1-201(31)). Similarly, the portion of the definition of "security interest" in former Section 1-201(37) which explained the difference between a security interest and a lease has been relocated to Section 1-203.

Two definitions in former Section 1-201 have been deleted. The definition of "honor" in former Section 1-201(21) has been moved to Section 2-103(1)(b), inasmuch as the definition only applies to the use of the word in Article 2. The definition of "telegram" in former Section 1-201(41) has been deleted because that word no longer appears in the definition of "conspicuous."

Other than minor stylistic changes and renumbering, the remaining definitions in this section are as in former Article 1 except as noted below.

1. "Action." Unchanged from former Section 1-201, which was derived from similar definitions in Section 191, Uniform Negotiable Instruments Law; Section 76, Uniform Sales Act; Section 58, Uniform Warehouse Receipts Act; Section 53, Uniform Bills of Lading Act.

2. "Aggrieved party." Unchanged from former Section 1-201.

3. "Agreement." Derived from former Section 1-201. As used in the Uniform Commercial Code the word is intended to include full recognition of usage of trade, course of dealing, course of performance and the surrounding circumstances as effective parts thereof, and of any agreement permitted under the provisions of the Uniform Commercial Code to displace a stated rule of law. Whether an agreement has legal consequences is determined by applicable provisions of the Uniform Commercial Code and, to the extent provided in Section 1-103, by the law of contracts.

4. "Bank." Derived from Section 4A-104.

5. "Bearer." Unchanged from former Section 1-201, which was derived from Section 191, Uniform Negotiable Instruments Law.

6. "Bill of Lading." Derived from former Section 1-201. The reference to, and definition of, an "airbill" has been deleted as no longer necessary.

7. "Branch." Unchanged from former Section 1-201.

8. "Burden of establishing a fact." Unchanged from former Section 1-201.

9. "Buyer in ordinary course of business." Except for minor stylistic changes, identical to former Section 1-201 (as amended in conjunction with the 1999 revisions to Article 9). The major significance of the phrase lies in Section 2-403 and in the Article on Secured Transactions (Article 9).

The first sentence of paragraph (9) makes clear that a buyer from a pawnbroker cannot be a buyer in ordinary course of business. The second sentence explains what it means to buy "in the ordinary course." The penultimate sentence prevents a buyer that does not have the right to possession as against the seller from being a buyer in ordinary course of business. Concerning when a buyer obtains possessory rights, see Sections 2-502 and 2-716. However, the penultimate sentence is not intended to affect a buyer's status as a buyer in ordinary course of business in cases (such as a "drop shipment") involving delivery by the seller to a person buying from the buyer or a donee from the buyer. The requirement relates to whether *as against the seller* the buyer or one taking through the buyer has possessory rights.

10. "Conspicuous." Derived from former Section 1-201(10). This definition states the general standard that to be conspicuous a term ought to be noticed by a reasonable person. Whether a term is conspicuous is an issue for the court. Subparagraphs (A) and (B) set out several methods for making a term conspicuous. Requiring that a term be conspicuous blends a notice function (the term ought to be noticed) and a planning function (giving guidance to the party relying on the term regarding how that result can be achieved). Although these paragraphs indicate some of the methods for making a term attention-calling, the test is whether attention can reasonably be expected to be called to it. The statutory language should not be construed to permit a result that is inconsistent with that test.

11. "Consumer." Derived from Section 9-102(a)(25).

12. "Contract." Except for minor stylistic changes, identical to former Section 1-201.

13. "Creditor." Unchanged from former Section 1-201.

14. "Defendant." Except for minor stylistic changes, identical to former Section 1-201, which was derived from Section 76, Uniform Sales Act.

15. "Delivery." Derived from former Section 1-201. The reference to certificated securities has been deleted in light of the more specific treatment of the matter in Section 8-301.

16. "Document of title." Unchanged from former Section 1-201, which was derived from Section 76, Uniform Sales Act. By making it explicit that the obligation or designation of a third party as "bailee" is essential to a document of title, this definition clearly rejects any such result as obtained in *Hixson v. Ward*, 254 Ill.App. 505 (1929), which treated a conditional sales contract as a document of title. Also the definition is left open so that new types of documents may be included. It is unforeseeable what documents may one day serve the essential purpose now filled by warehouse receipts and bills of lading. Truck transport has already opened up problems which do not fit the patterns of practice resting upon the assumption that a draft can move through banking channels faster than the goods themselves can reach their destination. There lie ahead air transport and such probabilities as teletype transmission of what may some day be regarded commercially as "Documents of Title." The definition is stated in terms of the function of the documents with the intention that any document which gains commercial recognition as accomplishing the desired result shall be included within its scope. Fungible goods are adequately identified within the language of the definition by identification of the mass of which they are a part.

Dock warrants were within the Sales Act definition of document of title apparently for the purpose of recognizing a valid tender by means of such paper. In current commercial practice a dock warrant or receipt is a kind of interim certificate issued by steamship companies upon delivery of the goods at the dock, entitling a designated person to have issued to him at the company's office a bill of lading. The receipt itself is invariably nonnegotiable in form although it may indicate that a negotiable bill is to be forthcoming. Such a document is not within the general compass of the definition, although trade usage may in some cases entitle such paper to be treated as a document of title. If the dock receipt actually represents a storage obligation undertaken by the shipping company, then it is a warehouse receipt within this section regardless of the name given to the instrument.

The goods must be "described," but the description may be by marks or labels and may be qualified in such a way as to disclaim personal knowledge of the issuer regarding contents or condition. However, baggage and parcel checks and similar "tokens" of storage which identify stored goods only as those received in exchange for the token are not covered by this Article.

The definition is broad enough to include an airway bill.

17. "Fault." Derived from former Section 1-201. "Default" has been added to the list of events constituting fault.

18. "Fungible goods." Derived from former Section 1-201. References to securities have been deleted because Article 8 no longer uses the term "fungible" to describe securities. Accordingly, this provision now defines the concept only in the context of goods.

19. "Genuine." Unchanged from former Section 1-201.

20. "Good faith." Former Section 1-201(19) defined "good faith" simply as honesty in fact; the definition contained no element of commercial reasonableness. Initially, that definition applied throughout the Code with only one exception. Former Section 2-103(1)(b) provided that "*in this Article* . . . good faith in the case of a merchant means honesty in fact and the observance of reasonable commercial standards of fair dealing in the trade." This alternative definition was limited in applicability in three ways. First, it applied only to transactions within the scope of Article 2. Second, it applied only to merchants. Third, strictly construed it applied only to uses of the phrase "good faith" *in Article 2*; thus, so construed it would not define "good faith" for its most important use — the obligation of good faith imposed by former Section 1-203.

Over time, however, amendments to the Uniform Commercial Code brought the Article 2 merchant concept of good faith (subjective honesty and objective commercial reasonableness) into other Articles. First, Article 2A explicitly incorporated the Article 2 standard. See Section 2A-103(7). Then, other Articles broadened the applicability of that standard by adopting it for all parties rather than just for merchants. See, e.g., Sections 3-103(a)(4), 4A-105(a)(6), 8-102(a)(10), and 9-102(a)(43). All of these definitions are comprised of two elements — honesty in fact *and* the observance of reasonable commercial standards of fair dealing. Only revised Article 5 defines "good faith" solely in terms of subjective honesty, and only Article 6 and Article 7 are without definitions of good faith. (It should be noted that, while revised Article 6 did not define good faith, Comment 2 to revised Section 6-102 states that "this Article adopts the definition of 'good faith' in Article 1 in all cases, even when the buyer is a merchant.") Given these developments, it is appropriate to move the broader definition of "good faith" to Article 1. Of course, this definition is subject to the applicability of the narrower definition in revised Article 5.

21. "Holder." Derived from former Section 1-201. The definition has been reorganized for clarity.

22. "Insolvency proceedings." Unchanged from former Section 1-201.

23. "Insolvent." Derived from former Section 1-201. The three tests of insolvency — "generally ceased to pay debts in the ordinary course of business other than as a result of a bona fide dispute as to them," "unable to pay debts as they become due," and "insolvent within the meaning of the federal bankruptcy law" — are expressly set up as alternative tests and must be approached from a commercial standpoint.

24. "Money." Substantively identical to former Section 1-201. The test is that of sanction of government, whether by authorization before issue or adoption afterward, which recognizes the circulating medium as a part of the official currency of that government. The narrow view that money is limited to legal tender is rejected.

25. "Organization." The former definition of this word has been replaced with the standard definition used in acts prepared by the National Conference of Commissioners on Uniform State Laws.

26. "Party." Substantively identical to former Section 1-201. Mention of a party includes, of course, a person acting through an agent. However, where an agent comes into opposition or contrast to the principal, particular account is taken of that situation.

27. "Person." The former definition of this word has been replaced with the standard definition used in acts prepared by the National Conference of Commissioners on Uniform State Laws.

28. "Present value." This definition was formerly contained within the definition of "security interest" in former Section 1-201(37).

29. "Purchase." Derived from former Section 1-201. The form of definition has been changed from "includes" to "means."

30. "Purchaser." Unchanged from former Section 1-201.

31. "Record." Derived from Section 9-102(a)(69).

32. "Remedy." Unchanged from former Section 1-201. The purpose is to make it clear that both remedy and right (as defined) include those remedial rights of "self help" which are among the most important bodies of rights under the Uniform Commercial Code, remedial rights being those to which an aggrieved party may resort on its own.

33. "Representative." Derived from former Section 1-201. Reorganized, and form changed from "includes" to "means."

34. "Right." Except for minor stylistic changes, identical to former Section 1-201.

35. "Security Interest." The definition is the first paragraph of the definition of "security interest" in former Section 1-201, with minor stylistic changes. The remaining portion of that definition has been moved to Section 1-203. Note that, because of the scope of Article 9, the term includes the interest of certain outright buyers of certain kinds of property.

36. "Send." Derived from former Section 1-201. Compare "notifies".

37. "Signed." Derived from former Section 1-201. Former Section 1-201 referred to "intention to authenticate"; because other articles now use the term "authenticate," the language has been changed to "intention to adopt or accept." The latter formulation is derived from the definition of "authenticate" in Section 9-102(a)(7). This provision refers only to writings, because the term "signed," as used in some articles, refers only to writings. This provision also makes it clear that, as the term "signed" is used in the Uniform Commercial Code, a complete signature is not necessary. The symbol may be printed, stamped or written; it may be by initials or by thumbprint. It may be on any part of the document and in appropriate cases may be found in a billhead or letterhead. No catalog of possible situations can be complete and the court must use common sense and commercial experience in passing upon these matters. The question always

is whether the symbol was executed or adopted by the party with present intention to adopt or accept the writing.

38. "State." This is the standard definition of the term used in acts prepared by the National Conference of Commissioners on Uniform State Laws.

39. "Surety." This definition makes it clear that "surety" includes all secondary obligors, not just those whose obligation refers to the person obligated as a surety. As to the nature of secondary obligations generally, see Restatement (Third), Suretyship and Guaranty Section 1 (1996).

40. "Term." Unchanged from former Section 1-201.

41. "Unauthorized signature." Unchanged from former Section 1-201.

42. "Warehouse receipt." Unchanged from former Section 1-201, which was derived from Section 76(1), Uniform Sales Act; Section 1, Uniform Warehouse Receipts Act. Receipts issued by a field warehouse are included, provided the warehouseman and the depositor of the goods are different persons.

43. "Written" or "writing." Unchanged from former Section 1-201.

SECTION 1-202. NOTICE; KNOWLEDGE.

(a) Subject to subsection (f), a person has "notice" of a fact if the person:
   (1) has actual knowledge of it;
   (2) has received a notice or notification of it; or
   (3) from all the facts and circumstances known to the person at the time in question, has reason to know that it exists.

   (b) "Knowledge" means actual knowledge. "Knows" has a corresponding meaning.

   (c) "Discover", "learn", or words of similar import refer to knowledge rather than to reason to know.

   (d) A person "notifies" or "gives" a notice or notification to another person by taking such steps as may be reasonably required to inform the other person in ordinary course, whether or not the other person actually comes to know of it.

   (e) Subject to subsection (f), a person "receives" a notice or notification when:
   (1) it comes to that person's attention; or
   (2) it is duly delivered in a form reasonable under the circumstances at the place of business through which the contract was made or at another location held out by that person as the place for receipt of such communications.

   (f) Notice, knowledge, or a notice or notification received by an organization is effective for a particular transaction from the time it is brought to the attention of the individual conducting that transaction and, in any event, from the time it would have been brought to the individual's attention if the organization had exercised due diligence. An organization exercises due diligence if it maintains reasonable routines for communicating significant information to the person conducting the transaction and there is reasonable compliance with the routines. Due diligence does not require an individual acting for the organization to communicate information unless the communication is part of the individual's regular duties or the individual has reason to know of the transaction and that the transaction would be materially affected by the information.

Official Comments

Source: Derived from former Section 1-201(25)-(27).

Changes from former law: These provisions are substantive rather than purely definitional. Accordingly, they have been relocated from Section 1-201 to this section. The reference to the "forgotten notice" doctrine has been deleted.

1. Under subsection (a), a person has notice of a fact when, *inter alia*, the person has received a notification of the fact in question.

2. As provided in subsection (d), the word "notifies" is used when the essential fact is the proper dispatch of the notice, not its receipt. Compare "Send." When the essential fact is the other party's receipt of the notice, that is stated. Subsection (e) states when a notification is received.

3. Subsection (f) makes clear that notice, knowledge, or a notification, although "received," for instance, by a clerk in Department A of an organization, is effective for a transaction conducted in Department B only from the time when it was or should have been communicated to the individual conducting that transaction.

SECTION 1-203. LEASE DISTINGUISHED FROM SECURITY INTEREST.

(a) Whether a transaction in the form of a lease creates a lease or security interest is determined by the facts of each case.

(b) A transaction in the form of a lease creates a security interest if the consideration that the lessee is to pay the lessor for the right to possession and use of the goods is an obligation for the term of the lease and is not subject to termination by the lessee, and:

(1) the original term of the lease is equal to or greater than the remaining economic life of the goods;

(2) the lessee is bound to renew the lease for the remaining economic life of the goods or is bound to become the owner of the goods;

(3) the lessee has an option to renew the lease for the remaining economic life of the goods for no additional consideration or for nominal additional consideration upon compliance with the lease agreement; or

(4) the lessee has an option to become the owner of the goods for no additional consideration or for nominal additional consideration upon compliance with the lease agreement.

(c) A transaction in the form of a lease does not create a security interest merely because:

(1) the present value of the consideration the lessee is obligated to pay the lessor for the right to possession and use of the goods is substantially equal to or is greater than the fair market value of the goods at the time the lease is entered into;

(2) the lessee assumes risk of loss of the goods;

(3) the lessee agrees to pay, with respect to the goods, taxes, insurance, filing, recording, or registration fees, or service or maintenance costs;

(4) the lessee has an option to renew the lease or to become the owner of the goods;

(5) the lessee has an option to renew the lease for a fixed rent that is equal to or greater than the reasonably predictable fair market rent for the use of the goods for the term of the renewal at the time the option is to be performed; or

(6) the lessee has an option to become the owner of the goods for a fixed price that is equal to or greater than the reasonably predictable fair market value of the goods at the time the option is to be performed.

(d) Additional consideration is nominal if it is less than the lessee's reasonably predictable cost of performing under the lease agreement if the option is not exercised. Additional consideration is not nominal if:

(1) when the option to renew the lease is granted to the lessee, the rent is stated to be the fair market rent for the use of the goods for the term of the renewal determined at the time the option is to be performed; or

(2) when the option to become the owner of the goods is granted to the lessee, the price is stated to be the fair market value of the goods determined at the time the option is to be performed.

(e) The "remaining economic life of the goods" and "reasonably predictable" fair market rent, fair market value, or cost of performing under the lease agreement must be determined with reference to the facts and circumstances at the time the transaction is entered into.

Official Comments

Source: Former Section 1-201(37).

Changes from former law: This section is substantively identical to those portions of former Section 1-201(37) that distinguished "true" leases from security interests, except that the definition of "present value" formerly embedded in Section 1-201(37) has been placed in Section 1-201(28).

1. An interest in personal property or fixtures which secures payment or performance of an obligation is a "security interest." See Section 1-201(37). Security interests are sometimes created by transactions in the form of leases. Because it can be difficult to distinguish leases that create security interests from those that do not, this section provides rules that govern the determination of whether a transaction in the form of a lease creates a security interest.

2. One of the reasons it was decided to codify the law with respect to leases was to resolve an issue that created considerable confusion in the courts: what is a lease? The confusion existed, in part, due to the last two sentences of the definition of security interest in the 1978 Official Text of the Act, Section 1-201(37). The confusion was compounded by the rather considerable change in the federal, state and local tax laws and accounting rules as they relate to leases of goods. The answer is important because the definition of lease determines not only the rights and remedies of the parties to the lease but also those of third parties. If a transaction creates a lease and not a security interest, the lessee's interest in the goods is limited to its leasehold estate; the residual interest in the goods belongs to the lessor. This has significant implications to the lessee's creditors. "On common law theory, the lessor, since he has not parted with title, is entitled to full protection against the lessee's creditors and trustee in bankruptcy ...." 1 G. Gilmore, *Security Interests in Personal Property* Section 3.6, at 76 (1965).

Under pre-UCC chattel security law there was generally no requirement that the lessor file the lease, a financing statement, or the like, to enforce the lease agreement against the lessee or any third party; the Article on Secured Transactions (Article 9) did not change the common law in that respect. Coogan, Leasing and the Uniform Commercial Code, in *Equipment Leasing — Leveraged Leasing* 681, 700 n.25, 729 n.80 (2d ed.1980). The Article on Leases (Article 2A) did not change the law in that respect, except for leases of fixtures. Section 2A-309. An examination of the common law will not provide an adequate answer to the question of what is a lease. The definition of security interest in Section 1-201(37) of the 1978 Official Text of the Act provided that the Article on Secured Transactions (Article 9) governs security interests disguised as leases, *i.e.*, leases intended as security; however, the definition became vague and outmoded.

Lease is defined in Article 2A as a transfer of the right to possession and use of goods for a term, in return for consideration. Section 2A-103(1)(j). The definition continues by stating that the retention or creation of a security interest is not a lease. Thus, the task of sharpening the line between true leases and security interests disguised as leases continues to be a function of this Article.

This section begins where Section 1-201(35) leaves off. It draws a sharper line between leases and security interests disguised as leases to create greater certainty in commercial transactions.

Prior to enactment of the rules now codified in this section, the 1978 Official Text of Section 1-201(37) provided that whether a lease was intended as security (*i.e.*, a security interest disguised as a lease) was to be determined from the facts of each case;

however, (a) the inclusion of an option to purchase did not itself make the lease one intended for security, and (b) an agreement that upon compliance with the terms of the lease the lessee would become, or had the option to become, the owner of the property for no additional consideration, or for a nominal consideration, did make the lease one intended for security.

Reference to the intent of the parties to create a lease or security interest led to unfortunate results. In discovering intent, courts relied upon factors that were thought to be more consistent with sales or loans than leases. Most of these criteria, however, were as applicable to true leases as to security interests. Examples include the typical net lease provisions, a purported lessor's lack of storage facilities or its character as a financing party rather than a dealer in goods. Accordingly, this section contains no reference to the parties' intent.

Subsections (a) and (b) were originally taken from Section 1(2) of the Uniform Conditional Sales Act (act withdrawn 1943), modified to reflect current leasing practice. Thus, reference to the case law prior to the incorporation of those concepts in this article will provide a useful source of precedent. Gilmore, *Security Law, Formalism and Article 9*, 47 Neb.L.Rev. 659, 671 (1968). Whether a transaction creates a lease or a security interest continues to be determined by the facts of each case. Subsection (b) further provides that a transaction creates a security interest if the lessee has an obligation to continue paying consideration for the term of the lease, if the obligation is not terminable by the lessee (thus correcting early statutory gloss, e.g., *In re Royer's Bakery, Inc.*, 1 U.C.C. Rep.Serv. (Callaghan) 342 (Bankr.E.D.Pa.1963)) and if one of four additional tests is met. The first of these four tests, subparagraph (1), is that the original lease term is equal to or greater than the remaining economic life of the goods. The second of these tests, subparagraph (2), is that the lessee is either bound to renew the lease for the remaining economic life of the goods or to become the owner of the goods. *In re Gehrke Enters.*, 1 Bankr. 647, 651-52 (Bankr.W.D.Wis.1979). The third of these tests, subparagraph (3), is whether the lessee has an option to renew the lease for the remaining economic life of the goods for no additional consideration or for nominal additional consideration, which is defined later in this section. *In re Celeryvale Transp.*, 44 Bankr. 1007, 1014–15 (Bankr.E.D.Tenn.1984). The fourth of these tests, subparagraph (4), is whether the lessee has an option to become the owner of the goods for no additional consideration or for nominal additional consideration. All of these tests focus on economics, not the intent of the parties. *In re Berge*, 32 Bankr. 370, 371–73 (Bankr.W.D.Wis.1983).

The focus on economics is reinforced by subsection (c). It states that a transaction does not create a security interest merely because the transaction has certain characteristics listed therein. Subparagraph (1) has no statutory derivative; it states that a full payout lease does not *per se* create a security interest. *Rushton v. Shea*, 419 F.Supp. 1349, 1365 (D.Del.1976). Subparagraphs (2) and (3) provide the same regarding the provisions of the typical net lease. *Compare All-States Leasing Co. v. Ochs*, 42 Or.App. 319, 600 P.2d 899 (Ct.App.1979), *with In re Tillery*, 571 F.2d 1361 (5th Cir.1978). Subparagraph (4) restates and expands the provisions of the 1978 Official Text of Section 1-201(37) to make clear that the option can be to buy or renew. Subparagraphs (5) and (6) treat fixed price options and provide that fair market value must be determined at the time the transaction is entered into. *Compare Arnold Mach. Co. v. Balls*, 624 P.2d 678 (Utah 1981), *with Aoki v. Shepherd Mach. Co.*, 665 F.2d 941 (9th Cir.1982).

The relationship of subsection (b) to subsection (c) deserves to be explored. The fixed price purchase option provides a useful example. A fixed price purchase option in a lease does not of itself create a security interest. This is particularly true if the fixed price is equal to or greater than the reasonably predictable fair market value of the goods at the time the option is to be performed. A security interest is created only if the option price is nominal and the conditions stated in the introduction to the second paragraph of this subsection are met. There is a set of purchase options whose fixed price is less than fair market value but greater than nominal that must be determined on the facts of each case to ascertain whether the transaction in which the option is included creates a lease or a security interest.

It was possible to provide for various other permutations and combinations with respect to options to purchase and renew. For example, this section could have stated a rule to govern the facts of *In re Marhoefer Packing Co.*, 674 F.2d 1139 (7th Cir.1982). This was not done because it would unnecessarily complicate the definition. Further development of this rule is left to the courts.

Subsections (d) and (e) provide definitions and rules of construction.

SECTION 1-204. VALUE.

Except as otherwise provided in Articles 3, 4, [and] 5, [and 6], a person gives value for rights if the person acquires them:

(1) in return for a binding commitment to extend credit or for the extension of immediately available credit, whether or not drawn upon and whether or not a charge-back is provided for in the event of difficulties in collection;

(2) as security for, or in total or partial satisfaction of, a preexisting claim;

(3) by accepting delivery under a preexisting contract for purchase; or

(4) in return for any consideration sufficient to support a simple contract.

Official Comments

Source: Former Section 1-201(44).

Changes from former law: Unchanged from former Section 1-201, which was derived from Sections 25, 26, 27, 191, Uniform Negotiable Instruments Law; Section 76, Uniform Sales Act; Section 53, Uniform Bills of Lading Act; Section 58, Uniform Warehouse Receipts Act; Section 22(1), Uniform Stock Transfer Act; Section 1, Uniform

Trust Receipts Act. These provisions are substantive rather than purely definitional. Accordingly, they have been relocated from former Section 1-201 to this section.

1. All the Uniform Acts in the commercial law field (except the Uniform Conditional Sales Act) have carried definitions of "value." All those definitions provided that value was any consideration sufficient to support a simple contract, including the taking of property in satisfaction of or as security for a pre-existing claim. Subsections (1), (2), and (4) in substance continue the definitions of "value" in the earlier acts. Subsection (3) makes explicit that "value" is also given in a third situation: where a buyer by taking delivery under a pre-existing contract converts a contingent into a fixed obligation.

This definition is not applicable to Articles 3 and 4, but the express inclusion of immediately available credit as value follows the separate definitions in those Articles. See Sections 4-208, 4-209, 3-303. A bank or other financing agency which in good faith makes advances against property held as collateral becomes a bona fide purchaser of that property even though provision may be made for charge-back in case of trouble. Checking credit is "immediately available" within the meaning of this section if the bank would be subject to an action for slander of credit in case checks drawn against the credit were dishonored, and when a charge-back is not discretionary with the bank, but may only be made when difficulties in collection arise in connection with the specific transaction involved.

SECTION 1-205. REASONABLE TIME; SEASONABLENESS.

(a) Whether a time for taking an action required by [the Uniform Commercial Code] is reasonable depends on the nature, purpose, and circumstances of the action.

(b) An action is taken seasonably if it is taken at or within the time agreed or, if no time is agreed, at or within a reasonable time.

Official Comments

Source: Former Section 1-204(2)-(3).

Changes from former law: This section is derived from subsections (2) and (3) of former Section 1-204. Subsection (1) of that section is now incorporated in Section 1-302(b).

1. Subsection (a) makes it clear that requirements that actions be taken within a "reasonable" time are to be applied in the transactional context of the particular action.

2. Under subsection (b), the agreement that fixes the time need not be part of the main agreement, but may occur separately. Notice also that under the definition of "agreement" (Section 1-201) the circumstances of the transaction, including course of dealing or usages of trade or course of performance may be material. On the question what is a reasonable time these matters will often be important.

SECTION 1-206. PRESUMPTIONS.

Whenever [the Uniform Commercial Code] creates a "presumption" with respect to a fact, or provides that a fact is "presumed," the trier of fact must find the existence of the fact unless and until evidence is introduced that supports a finding of its non-existence.

Legislative Note: Former Section 1-206, a Statute of Frauds for sales of "kinds of personal property not otherwise covered," has been deleted. The other articles of the Uniform Commercial Code make individual determinations as to requirements for memorializing transactions within their scope, so that the primary effect of former Section 1-206 was to impose a writing requirement on sales transactions not otherwise governed by the UCC. Deletion of former Section 1-206 does not constitute a recommendation to legislatures as to whether such sales transactions should be covered by a Statute of Frauds; rather, it reflects a determination that there is no need for uniform commercial law to resolve that issue.

Official Comments

Source: Former Section 1-201(31).

Changes from former law. None, other than stylistic changes.

1. Several sections of the Uniform Commercial Code state that there is a "presumption" as to a certain fact, or that the fact is "presumed." This section, derived from the definition appearing in former Section 1-201(31), indicates the effect of those provisions on the proof process.

PART 3 TERRITORIAL APPLICABILITY AND GENERAL RULES

SECTION 1-301. TERRITORIAL APPLICABILITY; PARTIES' POWER TO CHOOSE APPLICABLE LAW.

(a) In this section:
    (1) "Domestic transaction" means a transaction other than an international transaction.
    (2) "International transaction" means a transaction that bears a reasonable relation to a country other than the United States.

(b) This section applies to a transaction to the extent that it is governed by another article of the [Uniform Commercial Code].

(c) Except as otherwise provided in this section:
    (1) an agreement by parties to a domestic transaction that any or all of their rights and obligations are to be determined by the law of this State or of another State is effective, whether or not the transaction bears a relation to the State designated; and
    (2) an agreement by parties to an international transaction that any or all of their rights and obligations are to be determined by the law of this State or of

another State or country is effective, whether or not the transaction bears a relation to the State or country designated.

(d) In the absence of an agreement effective under subsection (c), and except as provided in subsections (e) and (g), the rights and obligations of the parties are determined by the law that would be selected by application of this State's conflict of laws principles.

(e) If one of the parties to a transaction is a consumer, the following rules apply:

    (1) An agreement referred to in subsection (c) is not effective unless the transaction bears a reasonable relation to the State or country designated.

    (2) Application of the law of the State or country determined pursuant to subsection (c) or (d) may not deprive the consumer of the protection of any rule of law governing a matter within the scope of this section, which both is protective of consumers and may not be varied by agreement:

        (A) of the State or country in which the consumer principally resides, unless subparagraph (B) applies; or

        (B) if the transaction is a sale of goods, of the State or country in which the consumer both makes the contract and takes delivery of those goods, if such State or country is not the State or country in which the consumer principally resides.

(f) An agreement otherwise effective under subsection (c) is not effective to the extent that application of the law of the State or country designated would be contrary to a fundamental policy of the State or country whose law would govern in the absence of agreement under subsection (d).

(g) To the extent that [the Uniform Commercial Code] governs a transaction, if one of the following provisions of [the Uniform Commercial Code] specifies the applicable law, that provision governs and a contrary agreement is effective only to the extent permitted by the law so specified:

    (1) Section 2-402;

    (2) Sections 2A-105 and 2A-106;

    (3) Section 4-102;

    (4) Section 4A-507;

    (5) Section 5-116;

    (6) [Section 6-103;]

    (7) Section 8-110;

    (8) Sections 9-301 through 9-307.

Official Comments

Source: Former Section 1-105.

Summary of changes from former law: Section 1-301, which replaces former Section 1-105, represents a significant rethinking of choice of law issues addressed in that section. The new section reexamines both the power of parties to select the jurisdiction whose law will govern their transaction and the determination of the governing law in the absence of such selection by the parties. With respect to the power to select governing law, the draft affords greater party autonomy than former Section 1-105, but with important safeguards protecting consumer interests and fundamental policies.

Section 1-301 addresses contractual designation of governing law somewhat differently than does former Section 1-105. Former law allowed the parties to any transaction to designate a jurisdiction whose law governs if the transaction bears a "reasonable relation" to that jurisdiction. Section 1-301 deviates from this approach by providing different rules for transactions involving a consumer than for non-consumer transactions, such as "business to business" transactions.

In the context of consumer transactions, the language of Section 1-301, unlike that of former Section 1-105, protects consumers against the possibility of losing the protection of consumer protection rules applicable to the aspects of the transaction governed by the Uniform Commercial Code. In most situations, the relevant consumer protection rules will be those of the consumer's home jurisdiction. A special rule, however, is provided for certain face-to-face sales transactions. (See Comment 3.)

In the context of business-to-business transactions, Section 1-301 generally provides the parties with greater autonomy to designate a jurisdiction whose law will govern than did former Section 1-105, but also provides safeguards against abuse that did not appear in former Section 1-105. In the non-consumer context, following emerging international norms, greater autonomy is provided in subsections (c)(1) and (c)(2) by deleting the former requirement that the transaction bear a "reasonable relation" to the jurisdiction. In the case of wholly domestic transactions, however, the jurisdiction designated must be a State. (See Comment 4.)

An important safeguard not present in former Section 1-105 is found in subsection (f). Subsection (f) provides that the designation of a jurisdiction's law is not effective (even if the transaction bears a reasonable relation to that jurisdiction) to the extent that application of that law would be contrary to a fundamental policy of the jurisdiction whose law would govern in the absence of contractual designation. Application of the law designated may be contrary to a fundamental policy of the State or country whose law would otherwise govern either because of the nature of the law designated or because of the "mandatory" nature of the law that would otherwise apply. (See Comment 6.)

In the absence of an effective contractual designation of governing law, former Section 1-105(1) directed the forum to apply its own law if the transaction bore "an appropriate relation to this state." This direction, however, was frequently ignored by courts. Section 1-301(d) provides that, in the absence of an effective contractual designation, the forum should apply the forum's general choice of law principles, subject to certain special rules in consumer transactions. (See Comments 3 and 7).

1. *Applicability of section.* This section is neither a complete restatement of choice of law principles nor a free-standing choice of law statute. Rather, it is a provision of Article 1 of the Uniform Commercial Code. As such, the scope of its application is limited in two significant ways.

First, this section is subject to Section 1-102, which states the scope of Article 1. As that section indicates, Article 1, and the rules contained therein, apply to transactions to the extent that they are governed by one of the other Articles of the Uniform Commercial Code. Thus, this section does not apply to matters outside the scope of the Uniform Commercial Code, such as a services contract, a credit card agreement, or a contract for the sale of real estate. This limitation was implicit in former Section 1-105, and is made explicit in Section 1-301(b).

Second, subsection (g) provides that this section is subject to the specific choice of law provisions contained in other Articles of the Uniform Commercial Code. Thus, to the extent that a transaction otherwise within the scope of this section also is within the scope of one of those provisions, the rules of that specific provision, rather than of this section, apply.

The following cases illustrate these two limitations on the scope of Section 1-301:

> **Example 1:** A, a resident of Indiana, enters into an agreement with Credit Card Company, a Delaware corporation with its chief executive office located in New York, pursuant to which A agrees to pay Credit Card Company for purchases charged to A's credit card. The agreement contains a provision stating that it is governed by the law of South Dakota. The choice of law rules in Section 1-301 do not apply to this agreement because the agreement is not governed by any of the other Articles of the Uniform Commercial Code.

> **Example 2:** A, a resident of Indiana, maintains a checking account with Bank B, an Ohio banking corporation located in Ohio. At the time that the account was established, Bank B and A entered into a "Bank-Customer Agreement" governing their relationship with respect to the account. The Bank-Customer Agreement contains some provisions that purport to limit the liability of Bank B with respect to its decisions whether to honor or dishonor checks purporting to be drawn on A's account. The Bank-Customer Agreement also contains a provision stating that it is governed by the law of Ohio. The provisions purporting to limit the liability of Bank B deal with issues governed by Article 4. Therefore, determination of the law applicable to those issues (including determination of the effectiveness of the choice of law clause as it applies to those issues) is within the scope of Section 1-301 as provided in subsection (b). Nonetheless, the rules of Section 1-301 would not apply to that determination because of subsection (g), which states that the choice of law rules in Section 4-102 govern instead.

2. *Contractual choice of law.* This section allows parties broad autonomy, subject to several important limitations, to select the law governing their transaction, even if the transaction does not bear a relation to the State or country whose law is selected. This recognition of party autonomy with respect to governing law has already been established in several Articles of the Uniform Commercial Code (see Sections 4A-507, 5-116, and 8-110) and is consistent with international norms. See, e.g., Inter-American Convention on the Law Applicable to International Contracts, Article 7 (Mexico

City 1994); Convention on the Law Applicable to Contracts for the International Sale of Goods, Article 7(1) (The Hague 1986); EC Convention on the Law Applicable to Contractual Obligations, Article 3(1) (Rome 1980).

There are three important limitations on this party autonomy to select governing law. First, a different, and more protective, rule applies in the context of consumer transactions. (See Comment 3). Second, in an entirely domestic transaction, this section does not validate the selection of foreign law. (See Comment 4.) Third, contractual choice of law will not be given effect to the extent that application of the law designated would be contrary to a fundamental policy of the State or country whose law would be applied in the absence of such contractual designation. (See Comment 6).

This Section does not address the ability of parties to designate non-legal codes such as trade codes as the set of rules governing their transaction. The power of parties to make such a designation as part of their agreement is found in the principles of Section 1-302. That Section, allowing parties broad freedom of contract to structure their relations, is adequate for this purpose. This is also the case with respect to the ability of the parties to designate recognized bodies of rules or principles applicable to commercial transactions that are promulgated by intergovernmental organizations such as UNCITRAL or Unidroit. See, e.g., Unidroit Principles of International Commercial Contracts.

3. *Consumer transactions*. If one of the parties is a consumer (as defined in Section 1-201(b)(11)), subsection (e) provides the parties less autonomy to designate the State or country whose law will govern.

First, in the case of a consumer transaction, subsection (e)(1) provides that the transaction must bear a reasonable relation to the State or country designated. Thus, the rules of subsection (c) allowing the parties to choose the law of a jurisdiction to which the transaction bears no relation do not apply to consumer transactions.

Second, subsection (e)(2) provides that application of the law of the State or country determined by the rules of this section (whether or not that State or country was designated by the parties) cannot deprive the consumer of the protection of rules of law which govern matters within the scope of Section 1-301, are protective of consumers, and are not variable by agreement. The phrase "rule of law" is intended to refer to case law as well as statutes and administrative regulations. The requirement that the rule of law be one "governing a matter within the scope of this section" means that, consistent with the scope of Section 1-301, which governs choice of law only with regard to the aspects of a transaction governed by the Uniform Commercial Code, the relevant consumer rules are those that govern those aspects of the transaction. Such rules may be found in the Uniform Commercial Code itself, as are the consumer-protective rules in Part 6 of Article 9, or in other law if that other law governs the UCC aspects of the transaction. See, for example, the rule in Section 2.403 of the Uniform Consumer Credit Code which prohibits certain sellers and lessors from taking negotiable instruments other than checks and provides that a holder is not in good faith if the holder takes a negotiable instrument with notice that it is issued in violation of that section.

With one exception (explained in the next paragraph), the rules of law the protection of which the consumer may not be deprived are those of the jurisdiction in which the consumer principally resides. The jurisdiction in which the consumer principally resides is determined at the time relevant to the particular issue involved. Thus, for example, if the issue is one related to formation of a contract, the relevant consumer protective rules are rules of the jurisdiction in which the consumer principally resided at the time the facts relevant to contract formation occurred, even if the consumer no longer principally resides in that jurisdiction at the time the dispute arises or is litigated. If, on the other hand, the issue is one relating to enforcement of obligations, then the relevant consumer protective rules are those of the jurisdiction in which the consumer principally resides at the time enforcement is sought, even if the consumer did not principally reside in that jurisdiction at the time the transaction was entered into.

In the case of a sale of goods to a consumer, in which the consumer both makes the contract and takes possession of the goods in the same jurisdiction and that jurisdiction is not the consumer's principal residence, the rule in subsection (e)(2)(B) applies. In that situation, the relevant consumer protective rules, the protection of which the consumer may not be deprived by the choice of law rules of subsections (c) and (d), are those of the State or country in which both the contract is made and the consumer takes delivery of the goods. This rule, adapted from Section 2A-106 and Article 5 of the EC Convention on the Law Applicable to Contractual Obligations, enables a seller of goods engaging in face-to-face transactions to ascertain the consumer protection rules to which those sales are subject, without the necessity of determining the principal residence of each buyer. The reference in subsection (e)(2)(B) to the State or country in which the consumer makes the contract should not be read to incorporate formalistic concepts of where the last event necessary to conclude the contract took place; rather, the intent is to identify the state in which all material steps necessary to enter into the contract were taken by the consumer.

The following examples illustrate the application of Section 1-301(e)(2) in the context of a contractual choice of law provision:

> **Example 3:** Seller, located in State A, agrees to sell goods to Consumer, whose principal residence is in State B. The parties agree that the law of State A would govern this transaction. Seller ships the goods to Consumer in State B. An issue related to contract formation subsequently arises. Under the law of State A, that issue is governed by State A's uniform version of Article 2. Under the law of State B, that issue is governed by a non-uniform rule, protective of consumers and not variable by agreement, that brings about a different result than would occur under the uniform version of Article 2. Under Section 1-301(e)(2)(A), the parties' agreement that the law of State A would govern their transaction cannot deprive Consumer of the protection of State B's consumer protective rule. This is the case whether State B's rule is codified in Article 2 of its Uniform Commercial Code or is found elsewhere in the law of State B.

Example 4: Same facts as Example 3, except that (i) Consumer takes all material steps necessary to enter into the agreement to purchase the goods from Seller, and takes delivery of those goods, while on vacation in State A and (ii) the parties agree that the law of State C (in which Seller's chief executive office is located) would govern their transaction. Under subsections (c)(1) and (e)(1), the designation of the law of State C as governing will be effective so long as the transaction is found to bear a reasonable relation to State C (assuming that the relevant law of State C is not contrary to a fundamental policy of the State whose law would govern in the absence of agreement), but that designation cannot deprive Consumer of the protection of any rule of State A that is within the scope of this section and is both protective of consumers and not variable by agreement. State B's consumer protective rule is not relevant because, under Section 1-301(e)(2)(B), the relevant consumer protective rules are those of the jurisdiction in which the consumer both made the contract and took delivery of the goods — here, State A — rather than those of the jurisdiction in which the consumer principally resides.

It is important to note that subsection (e)(2) applies to all determinations of applicable law in transactions in which one party is a consumer, whether that determination is made under subsection (c) (in cases in which the parties have designated the governing law in their agreement) or subsection (d) (in cases in which the parties have not made such a designation). In the latter situation, application of the otherwise-applicable conflict of laws principles of the forum might lead to application of the laws of a State or country other than that of the consumer's principal residence. In such a case, however, subsection (e)(2) applies to preserve the applicability of consumer protection rules for the benefit of the consumer as described above.

4. *Wholly domestic transactions.* While this Section provides parties broad autonomy to select governing law, that autonomy is limited in the case of wholly domestic transactions. In a "domestic transaction," subsection (c)(1) validates only the designation of the law of a State. A "domestic transaction" is a transaction that does not bear a reasonable relation to a country other than the United States. (See subsection (a)). Thus, in a wholly domestic non-consumer transaction, parties may (subject to the limitations set out in subsections (f) and (g)) designate the law of any State but not the law of a foreign country.

5. *International transactions.* This section provides greater autonomy in the context of international transactions. As defined in subsection (a)(2), a transaction is an "international transaction" if it bears a reasonable relation to a country other than the United States. In a non-consumer international transaction, subsection (c)(2) provides that a designation of the law of any State or country is effective (subject, of course, to the limitations set out in subsections (f) and (g)). It is important to note that the transaction need not bear a relation to the State or country designated if the transaction is international. Thus, for example, in a non-consumer lease of goods in which the lessor is located in Mexico and the lessee is located in Louisiana, a designation of the law of Ireland to govern the transaction would be given effect under this section even though the transaction bears no relation to Ireland. The ability to designate the law of any country in non-consumer international transactions is important in light of the common practice in many commercial contexts of designating the law of a "neutral" jurisdiction or of a jurisdiction whose law is well-developed. If a country has two or more territorial units in which different systems of law relating to matters within the scope of this section are applicable (as is the case, for example, in Canada and the United Kingdom), subsection (c)(2) should be applied to designation by the parties of the law of one of those territorial units. Thus, for example, subsection (c)(2) should be applied if the parties to a non-consumer international transaction designate the laws of Ontario or Scotland as governing their transaction.

6. *Fundamental policy.* Subsection (f) provides that an agreement designating the governing law will not be given effect to the extent that application of the designated law would be contrary to a fundamental policy of the State or country whose law would otherwise govern. This rule provides a narrow exception to the broad autonomy afforded to parties in subsection (c). One of the prime objectives of contract law is to protect the justified expectations of the parties and to make it possible for them to foretell with accuracy what will be their rights and liabilities under the contract. In this way, certainty and predictability of result are most likely to be secured. See Restatement (Second) Conflict of Laws, Section 187, comment *e*.

Under the fundamental policy doctrine, a court should not refrain from applying the designated law merely because application of that law would lead to a result different than would be obtained under the local law of the State or country whose law would otherwise govern. Rather, the difference must be contrary to a public policy of that jurisdiction that is so substantial that it justifies overriding the concerns for certainty and predictability underlying modern commercial law as well as concerns for judicial economy generally. Thus, application of the designated law will rarely be found to be contrary to a fundamental policy of the State or country whose law would otherwise govern when the difference between the two concerns a requirement, such as a statute of frauds, that relates to formalities, or general rules of contract law, such as those concerned with the need for consideration.

The opinion of Judge Cardozo in *Loucks v. Standard Oil Co. of New York*, 120 N.E. 198 (1918), regarding the related issue of when a state court may decline to apply the law of another state, is a helpful touchstone here:

> Our own scheme of legislation may be different. We may even have no legislation on the subject. That is not enough to show that public policy forbids us to enforce the foreign right. A right of action is property. If a foreign statute gives the right, the mere fact that we do not give a like right is no reason for refusing to help the plaintiff in getting what belongs to him. We are not so provincial as to say that every solution of a problem is wrong because we deal with it otherwise at home. Similarity of legislation has indeed this importance; its presence shows beyond question that the foreign statute does not offend the

local policy. But its absence does not prove the contrary. It is not to be exalted into an indispensable condition. The misleading word 'comity' has been responsible for much of the trouble. It has been fertile in suggesting a discretion unregulated by general principles.

The courts are not free to refuse to enforce a foreign right at the pleasure of the judges, to suit the individual notion of expediency or fairness. They do not close their doors, unless help would violate some fundamental principle of justice, some prevalent conception of good morals, some deep-rooted tradition of the common weal.

120 N.E. at 201–02 (citations to authorities omitted).

Application of the designated law may be contrary to a fundamental policy of the State or country whose law would otherwise govern either (i) because the substance of the designated law violates a fundamental principle of justice of that State or country or (ii) because it differs from a rule of that State or country that is "mandatory" in that it *must* be applied in the courts of that State or country without regard to otherwise-applicable choice of law rules of that State or country and without regard to whether the designated law is otherwise offensive. The mandatory rules concept appears in international conventions in this field, *e.g.*, EC Convention on the Law Applicable to Contractual Obligations, although in some cases the concept is applied to authorize the *forum* state to apply *its* mandatory rules, rather than those of the State or country whose law would otherwise govern. The latter situation is not addressed by this section. (See Comment 9.)

It is obvious that a rule that is freely changeable by agreement of the parties under the law of the State or country whose law would otherwise govern cannot be construed as a mandatory rule of that State or country. This does not mean, however, that rules that cannot be changed by agreement under that law are, for that reason alone, mandatory rules. Otherwise, contractual choice of law in the context of the Uniform Commercial Code would be illusory and redundant; the parties would be able to accomplish by choice of law no more than can be accomplished under Section 1-302, which allows variation of otherwise applicable rules by agreement. (Under Section 1-302, the parties could agree to vary the rules that would otherwise govern their transaction by substituting for those rules the rules that would apply if the transaction were governed by the law of the designated State or country without designation of governing law.) Indeed, other than cases in which a mandatory choice of law rule is established by statute (see, *e.g.*, Sections 9-301 through 9-307, explicitly preserved in subsection (g)), cases in which courts have declined to follow the designated law solely because a rule of the State or country whose law would otherwise govern is mandatory are rare.

7. *Choice of law in the absence of contractual designation.* Subsection (d), which replaces the second sentence of former Section 1-105(1), determines which jurisdiction's law governs a transaction in the absence of an effective contractual choice by

the parties. Former Section 1-105(1) provided that the law of the forum (*i.e.*, the Uniform Commercial Code) applied if the transaction bore "an appropriate relation to this state." By using an "appropriate relation" test, rather than, for example, a "most significant relationship" test, Section 1-105(1) expressed a bias in favor of applying the forum's law. This bias, while not universally respected by the courts, was justifiable in light of the uncertainty that existed at the time of drafting as to whether the Uniform Commercial Code would be adopted by all the states; the pro-forum bias would assure that the Uniform Commercial Code would be applied so long as the transaction bore an "appropriate" relation to the forum. Inasmuch as the Uniform Commercial Code has been adopted, at least in part, in all U.S. jurisdictions, the vitality of this point is minimal in the domestic context, and international comity concerns militate against continuing the pro-forum, pro-UCC bias in transnational transactions. Whether the choice is between the law of two jurisdictions that have adopted the Uniform Commercial Code, but whose law differs (because of differences in enacted language or differing judicial interpretations), or between the Uniform Commercial Code and the law of another country, there is no strong justification for directing a court to apply different choice of law principles to that determination than it would apply if the matter were not governed by the Uniform Commercial Code. Similarly, given the variety of choice of law principles applied by the states, it would not be prudent to designate only one such principle as the proper one for transactions governed by the Uniform Commercial Code. Accordingly, in cases in which the parties have not made an effective choice of law, Section 1-301(d) simply directs the forum to apply its ordinary choice of law principles to determine which jurisdiction's law governs, subject to the special rules of Section 1-301(e)(2) with regard to consumer transactions.

8. *Primacy of other Uniform Commercial Code choice of law rules.* Subsection (g), which is essentially identical to former Section 1-105(2), indicates that choice of law rules provided in the other Articles govern when applicable.

9. *Matters not addressed by this section.* As noted in Comment 1, this section is not a complete statement of conflict of laws doctrines applicable in commercial cases. Among the issues this section does not address, and leaves to other law, three in particular deserve mention. First, a forum will occasionally decline to apply the law of a different jurisdiction selected by the parties when application of that law would be contrary to a fundamental policy of the forum jurisdiction, even if it would not be contrary to a fundamental policy of the State or country whose law would govern in the absence of contractual designation. Standards for application of this doctrine relate primarily to concepts of sovereignty rather than commercial law and are thus left to the courts. Second, in determining whether to give effect to the parties' agreement that the law of a particular State or country will govern their relationship, courts must, of necessity, address some issues as to the basic validity of that agreement. These issues might relate, for example, to capacity to contract and absence of duress. This section does not address these issues. Third, this section leaves to other choice of law principles of the forum the issues of whether, and to what extent, the forum will apply the same law to the non-UCC aspects of a transaction that it applies to the aspects of the transaction governed by the Uniform Commercial Code.

SECTION 1-302. VARIATION BY AGREEMENT.

(a) Except as otherwise provided in subsection (b) or elsewhere in [the Uniform Commercial Code], the effect of provisions of [the Uniform Commercial Code] may be varied by agreement.

(b) The obligations of good faith, diligence, reasonableness, and care prescribed by [the Uniform Commercial Code] may not be disclaimed by agreement. The parties, by agreement, may determine the standards by which the performance of those obligations is to be measured if those standards are not manifestly unreasonable. Whenever [the Uniform Commercial Code] requires an action to be taken within a reasonable time, a time that is not manifestly unreasonable may be fixed by agreement.

(c) The presence in certain provisions of [the Uniform Commercial Code] of the phrase "unless otherwise agreed", or words of similar import, does not imply that the effect of other provisions may not be varied by agreement under this section.

Official Comments

Source: Former Sections 1-102(3)-(4) and 1-204(1).

Changes: This section combines the rules from subsections (3) and (4) of former Section 1-102 and subsection (1) of former Section 1-204. No substantive changes are made.

1. Subsection (a) states affirmatively at the outset that freedom of contract is a principle of the Uniform Commercial Code: "the effect" of its provisions may be varied by "agreement." The meaning of the statute itself must be found in its text, including its definitions, and in appropriate extrinsic aids; it cannot be varied by agreement. But the Uniform Commercial Code seeks to avoid the type of interference with evolutionary growth found in pre-Code cases such as *Manhattan Co. v. Morgan*, 242 N.Y. 38, 150 N.E. 594 (1926). Thus, private parties cannot make an instrument negotiable within the meaning of Article 3 except as provided in Section 3-104; nor can they change the meaning of such terms as "bona fide purchaser," "holder in due course," or "due negotiation," as used in the Uniform Commercial Code. But an agreement can change the legal consequences that would otherwise flow from the provisions of the Uniform Commercial Code. "Agreement" here includes the effect given to course of dealing, usage of trade and course of performance by Sections 1-201 and 1-303; the effect of an agreement on the rights of third parties is left to specific provisions of the Uniform Commercial Code and to supplementary principles applicable under Section 1-103. The rights of third parties under Section 9-317 when a security interest is unperfected, for example, cannot be destroyed by a clause in the security agreement.

This principle of freedom of contract is subject to specific exceptions found elsewhere in the Uniform Commercial Code and to the general exception stated here. The specific exceptions vary in explicitness: the statute of frauds found in Section 2-201, for example, does not explicitly preclude oral waiver of the requirement of a writing, but a fair reading denies enforcement to such a waiver as part of the "contract" made unenforceable; Section 9-602, on the other hand, is a quite explicit limitation on freedom of contract. Under the exception for "the obligations of good faith, diligence, reasonableness and care prescribed by [the Uniform Commercial Code]," provisions of the Uniform Commercial Code prescribing such obligations are not to be disclaimed. However, the section also recognizes the prevailing practice of having agreements set forth standards by which due diligence is measured and explicitly provides that, in the absence of a showing that the standards manifestly are unreasonable, the agreement controls. In this connection, Section 1-303 incorporating into the agreement prior course of dealing and usages of trade is of particular importance.

Subsection (b) also recognizes that nothing is stronger evidence of a reasonable time than the fixing of such time by a fair agreement between the parties. However, provision is made for disregarding a clause which whether by inadvertence or overreaching fixes a time so unreasonable that it amounts to eliminating all remedy under the contract. The parties are not required to fix the most reasonable time but may fix any time which is not obviously unfair as judged by the time of contracting.

2. An agreement that varies the effect of provisions of the Uniform Commercial Code may do so by stating the rules that will govern in lieu of the provisions varied. Alternatively, the parties may vary the effect of such provisions by stating that their relationship will be governed by recognized bodies of rules or principles applicable to commercial transactions. Such bodies of rules or principles may include, for example, those that are promulgated by intergovernmental authorities such as UNCITRAL or Unidroit (*see, e.g.,* Unidroit Principles of International Commercial Contracts), or non-legal codes such as trade codes.

3. Subsection (c) is intended to make it clear that, as a matter of drafting, phrases such as "unless otherwise agreed" have been used to avoid controversy as to whether the subject matter of a particular section does or does not fall within the exceptions to subsection (b), but absence of such words contains no negative implication since under subsection (b) the general and residual rule is that the effect of all provisions of the Uniform Commercial Code may be varied by agreement.

SECTION 1-303. COURSE OF PERFORMANCE, COURSE OF DEALING, AND USAGE OF TRADE.

(a) A "course of performance" is a sequence of conduct between the parties to a particular transaction that exists if:

    (1) the agreement of the parties with respect to the transaction involves repeated occasions for performance by a party; and

    (2) the other party, with knowledge of the nature of the performance and

opportunity for objection to it, accepts the performance or acquiesces in it without objection.

(b) A "course of dealing" is a sequence of conduct concerning previous transactions between the parties to a particular transaction that is fairly to be regarded as establishing a common basis of understanding for interpreting their expressions and other conduct.

(c) A "usage of trade" is any practice or method of dealing having such regularity of observance in a place, vocation, or trade as to justify an expectation that it will be observed with respect to the transaction in question. The existence and scope of such a usage must be proved as facts. If it is established that such a usage is embodied in a trade code or similar record, the interpretation of the record is a question of law.

(d) A course of performance or course of dealing between the parties or usage of trade in the vocation or trade in which they are engaged or of which they are or should be aware is relevant in ascertaining the meaning of the parties' agreement, may give particular meaning to specific terms of the agreement, and may supplement or qualify the terms of the agreement. A usage of trade applicable in the place in which part of the performance under the agreement is to occur may be so utilized as to that part of the performance.

(e) Except as otherwise provided in subsection (f), the express terms of an agreement and any applicable course of performance, course of dealing, or usage of trade must be construed whenever reasonable as consistent with each other. If such a construction is unreasonable:
   (1) express terms prevail over course of performance, course of dealing, and usage of trade;
   (2) course of performance prevails over course of dealing and usage of trade; and
   (3) course of dealing prevails over usage of trade.

(f) Subject to Section 2-209, a course of performance is relevant to show a waiver or modification of any term inconsistent with the course of performance.

(g) Evidence of a relevant usage of trade offered by one party is not admissible unless that party has given the other party notice that the court finds sufficient to prevent unfair surprise to the other party.

Official Comments

Source: Former Sections 1-205, 2-208, and Section 2A-207.

Changes from former law: This section integrates the "course of performance" concept from Articles 2 and 2A into the principles of former Section 1-205, which deals with course of dealing and usage of trade. In so doing, the section slightly modifies the articulation of the course of performance rules to fit more comfortably with the approach and structure of former Section 1-205. There are also slight modifications to be more consistent with the definition of "agreement" in former Section 1-201(3). It should be noted that a course of performance that might otherwise establish a defense to the obligation of a party to a negotiable instrument is not available as a defense against a holder in due course who took the instrument without notice of that course of performance.

1. The Uniform Commercial Code rejects both the "lay-dictionary" and the "conveyancer's" reading of a commercial agreement. Instead the meaning of the agreement of the parties is to be determined by the language used by them and by their action, read and interpreted in the light of commercial practices and other surrounding circumstances. The measure and background for interpretation are set by the commercial context, which may explain and supplement even the language of a formal or final writing.

2. "Course of dealing," as defined in subsection (b), is restricted, literally, to a sequence of conduct between the parties previous to the agreement. A sequence of conduct after or under the agreement, however, is a "course of performance." "Course of dealing" may enter the agreement either by explicit provisions of the agreement or by tacit recognition.

3. The Uniform Commercial Code deals with "usage of trade" as a factor in reaching the commercial meaning of the agreement that the parties have made. The language used is to be interpreted as meaning what it may fairly be expected to mean to parties involved in the particular commercial transaction in a given locality or in a given vocation or trade. By adopting in this context the term "usage of trade," the Uniform Commercial Code expresses its intent to reject those cases which see evidence of "custom" as representing an effort to displace or negate "established rules of law." A distinction is to be drawn between mandatory rules of law such as the Statute of Frauds provisions of Article 2 on Sales whose very office is to control and restrict the actions of the parties, and which cannot be abrogated by agreement, or by a usage of trade, and those rules of law (such as those in Part 3 of Article 2 on Sales) which fill in points which the parties have not considered and in fact agreed upon. The latter rules hold "unless otherwise agreed" but yield to the contrary agreement of the parties. Part of the agreement of the parties to which such rules yield is to be sought for in the usages of trade which furnish the background and give particular meaning to the language used, and are the framework of common understanding controlling any general rules of law which hold only when there is no such understanding.

4. A usage of trade under subsection (c) must have the "regularity of observance" specified. The ancient English tests for "custom" are abandoned in this connection. Therefore, it is not required that a usage of trade be "ancient or immemorial," "universal," or the like. Under the requirement of subsection (c) full recognition is thus available for new usages and for usages currently observed by the great majority of decent dealers, even though dissidents ready to cut corners do not agree. There is room also for proper recognition of usage agreed upon by merchants in trade codes.

5. The policies of the Uniform Commercial Code controlling explicit unconsciona-ble contracts and clauses (Sections 1-304, 2-302) apply to implicit clauses that rest on usage of trade and carry forward the policy underlying the ancient requirement that a custom or usage must be "reasonable." However, the emphasis is shifted. The very fact of commercial acceptance makes out a *prima facie* case that the usage is reasonable, and the burden is no longer on the usage to establish itself as being reasonable. But the anciently established policing of usage by the courts is continued to the extent necessary to cope with the situation arising if an unconscionable or dishonest practice should become standard.

6. Subsection (d), giving the prescribed effect to usages of which the parties "are or should be aware," reinforces the provision of subsection (c) requiring not universal-ity but only the described "regularity of observance" of the practice or method. This subsection also reinforces the point of subsection (c) that such usages may be either general to trade or particular to a special branch of trade.

7. Although the definition of "agreement" in Section 1-201 includes the elements of course of performance, course of dealing, and usage of trade, the fact that express reference is made in some sections to those elements is not to be construed as carrying a contrary intent or implication elsewhere. Compare Section 1-302(c).

8. In cases of a well-established line of usage varying from the general rules of the Uniform Commercial Code where the precise amount of the variation has not been worked out into a single standard, the party relying on the usage is entitled, in any event, to the minimum variation demonstrated. The whole is not to be disregarded because no particular line of detail has been established. In case a dominant pattern has been fairly evidenced, the party relying on the usage is entitled under this section to go to the trier of fact on the question of whether such dominant pattern has been incorporated into the agreement.

9. Subsection (g) is intended to insure that this Act's liberal recognition of the needs of commerce in regard to usage of trade shall not be made into an instrument of abuse.

SECTION 1-304. OBLIGATION OF GOOD FAITH.

Every contract or duty within [the Uniform Commercial Code] imposes an obliga-tion of good faith in its performance and enforcement.

Official Comments

Source: Former Section 1-203.

Changes from former law: Except for changing the form of reference to the Uni-form Commercial Code, this section is identical to former Section 1-203.

1. This section sets forth a basic principle running throughout the Uniform Com-mercial Code. The principle is that in commercial transactions good faith is required in the performance and enforcement of all agreements or duties. While this duty is explicitly stated in some provisions of the Uniform Commercial Code, the applicability of the duty is broader than merely these situations and applies generally, as stated in this section, to the performance or enforcement of every contract or duty within this Act. It is further implemented by Section 1-303 on course of dealing, course of performance, and usage of trade. This section does not support an independent cause of action for failure to perform or enforce in good faith. Rather, this section means that a failure to perform or enforce, in good faith, a specific duty or obligation under the contract, constitutes a breach of that contract or makes unavailable, under the particular circumstances, a remedial right or power. This distinction makes it clear that the doctrine of good faith merely directs a court towards interpreting contracts within the commercial context in which they are created, performed, and enforced, and does not create a separate duty of fairness and reasonableness which can be independently breached.

2. "Performance and enforcement" of contracts and duties within the Uniform Commercial Code include the exercise of rights created by the Uniform Commercial Code.

SECTION 1-305. REMEDIES TO BE LIBERALLY ADMINISTERED.

(a) The remedies provided by [the Uniform Commercial Code] must be liberally administered to the end that the aggrieved party may be put in as good a position as if the other party had fully performed but neither consequential or special damages nor penal damages may be had except as specifically provided in [the Uniform Commercial Code] or by other rule of law.

(b) Any right or obligation declared by [the Uniform Commercial Code] is enforceable by action unless the provision declaring it specifies a different and limited effect.

Official Comments

Source: Former Section 1-106.

Changes from former law: Other than changes in the form of reference to the Uniform Commercial Code, this section is identical to former Section 1-106.

1. Subsection (a) is intended to effect three propositions. The first is to negate the possibility of unduly narrow or technical interpretation of remedial provisions by providing that the remedies in the Uniform Commercial Code are to be liberally administered to the end stated in this section. The second is to make it clear that compensatory damages are limited to compensation. They do not include consequential or special damages, or penal damages; and the Uniform Commercial Code elsewhere makes it clear that damages must be minimized. Cf. Sections 1-304, 2-706(1), and 2-712(2). The third purpose of subsection (a) is to reject any doctrine that damages must be calculable with mathematical accuracy. Compensatory damages are often at best approximate: they have to be proved with whatever definiteness and accuracy the facts permit, but no more. Cf. Section 2-204(3).

2. Under subsection (b), any right or obligation described in the Uniform Commercial Code is enforceable by action, even though no remedy may be expressly provided, unless a particular provision specifies a different and limited effect. Whether specific performance or other equitable relief is available is determined not by this section but by specific provisions and by supplementary principles. Cf. Sections 1-103, 2-716.

3. "Consequential" or "special" damages and "penal" damages are not defined in the Uniform Commercial Code; rather, these terms are used in the sense in which they are used outside the Uniform Commercial Code.

SECTION 1-306. WAIVER OR RENUNCIATION OF CLAIM OR RIGHT AFTER BREACH.

A claim or right arising out of an alleged breach may be discharged in whole or in part without consideration by agreement of the aggrieved party in an authenticated record.

Official Comments

Source: Former Section 1-107.

Changes from former law: This section changes former law in two respects. First, former Section 1-107, requiring the "delivery" of a "written waiver or renunciation" merges the separate concepts of the aggrieved party's agreement to forego rights and the manifestation of that agreement. This section separates those concepts, and explicitly requires *agreement* of the aggrieved party. Second, the revised section reflects developments in electronic commerce by providing for memorialization in an authenticated record. In this context, a party may "authenticate" a record by (i) signing a record that is a writing or (ii) attaching to or logically associating with a record that is not a writing an electronic sound, symbol or process with the present intent to adopt or accept the record. See Sections 1-201(b)(37) and 9-102(a)(7).

1. This section makes consideration unnecessary to the effective renunciation or waiver of rights or claims arising out of an alleged breach of a commercial contract where the agreement effecting such renunciation is memorialized in a record authenticated by the aggrieved party. Its provisions, however, must be read in conjunction with the section imposing an obligation of good faith. (Section 1-304).

SECTION 1-307. PRIMA FACIE EVIDENCE BY THIRD-PARTY DOCUMENTS.

A document in due form purporting to be a bill of lading, policy or certificate of insurance, official weigher's or inspector's certificate, consular invoice, or any other document authorized or required by the contract to be issued by a third party is prima facie evidence of its own authenticity and genuineness and of the facts stated in the document by the third party.

Official Comments

Source: Former Section 1-202.

Changes from former law: Except for minor stylistic changes, this Section is identical to former Section 1-202.

1. This section supplies judicial recognition for documents that are relied upon as trustworthy by commercial parties.

2. This section is concerned only with documents that have been given a preferred status by the parties themselves who have required their procurement in the agreement, and for this reason the applicability of the section is limited to actions arising out of the contract that authorized or required the document. The list of documents is intended to be illustrative and not exclusive.

3. The provisions of this section go no further than establishing the documents in question as prima facie evidence and leave to the court the ultimate determination of the facts where the accuracy or authenticity of the documents is questioned. In this connection the section calls for a commercially reasonable interpretation.

4. Documents governed by this section need not be writings if records in another medium are generally relied upon in the context.

SECTION 1-308. PERFORMANCE OR ACCEPTANCE UNDER RESERVATION OF RIGHTS.

(a) A party that with explicit reservation of rights performs or promises performance or assents to performance in a manner demanded or offered by the other party does not thereby prejudice the rights reserved. Such words as "without prejudice," "under protest," or the like are sufficient.

(b) Subsection (a) does not apply to an accord and satisfaction.

Official Comments

Source: Former Section 1-207.

Changes from former law: This section is identical to former Section 1-207.

1. This section provides machinery for the continuation of performance along the lines contemplated by the contract despite a pending dispute, by adopting the mercantile device of going ahead with delivery, acceptance, or payment "without prejudice," "under protest," "under reserve," "with reservation of all our rights," and the like. All of these phrases completely reserve all rights within the meaning of this section. The section therefore contemplates that limited as well as general reservations and acceptance by a party may be made "subject to satisfaction of our purchaser," "subject to acceptance by our customers," or the like.

2. This section does not add any new requirement of language of reservation where not already required by law, but merely provides a specific measure on which a party

can rely as that party makes or concurs in any interim adjustment in the course of performance. It does not affect or impair the provisions of this Act such as those under which the buyer's remedies for defect survive acceptance without being expressly claimed if notice of the defects is given within a reasonable time. Nor does it disturb the policy of those cases which restrict the effect of a waiver of a defect to reasonable limits under the circumstances, even though no such reservation is expressed.

The section is not addressed to the creation or loss of remedies in the ordinary course of performance but rather to a method of procedure where one party is claiming as of right something which the other believes to be unwarranted.

3. Subsection (b) states that this section does not apply to an accord and satisfaction. Section 3-311 governs if an accord and satisfaction is attempted by tender of a negotiable instrument as stated in that section. If Section 3-311 does not apply, the issue of whether an accord and satisfaction has been effected is determined by the law of contract. Whether or not Section 3-311 applies, this section has no application to an accord and satisfaction.

SECTION 1-309. OPTION TO ACCELERATE AT WILL.

A term providing that one party or that party's successor in interest may accelerate payment or performance or require collateral or additional collateral "at will" or when the party "deems itself insecure," or words of similar import, means that the party has power to do so only if that party in good faith believes that the prospect of payment or performance is impaired. The burden of establishing lack of good faith is on the party against which the power has been exercised.

Official Comments

Source: Former Section 1-208.

Changes from former law: Except for minor stylistic changes, this section is identical to former Section 1-208.

1. The common use of acceleration clauses in many transactions governed by the Uniform Commercial Code, including sales of goods on credit, notes payable at a definite time, and secured transactions, raises an issue as to the effect to be given to a clause that seemingly grants the power to accelerate at the whim and caprice of one party. This section is intended to make clear that despite language that might be so construed and which further might be held to make the agreement void as against public policy or to make the contract illusory or too indefinite for enforcement, the option is to be exercised only in the good faith belief that the prospect of payment or performance is impaired.

Obviously this section has no application to demand instruments or obligations whose very nature permits call at any time with or without reason. This section applies only to an obligation of payment or performance which in the first instance is due at a future date.

SECTION 1-310. SUBORDINATED OBLIGATIONS.

An obligation may be issued as subordinated to performance of another obligation of the person obligated, or a creditor may subordinate its right to performance of an obligation by agreement with either the person obligated or another creditor of the person obligated. Subordination does not create a security interest as against either the common debtor or a subordinated creditor.

Official Comments

Source: Former Section 1-209.

Changes from former law: This section is substantively identical to former Section 1-209. The language in that section stating that it "shall be construed as declaring the law as it existed prior to the enactment of this section and not as modifying it" has been deleted.

1. Billions of dollars of subordinated debt are held by the public and by institutional investors. Commonly, the subordinated debt is subordinated on issue or acquisition and is evidenced by an investment security or by a negotiable or non-negotiable note. Debt is also sometimes subordinated after it arises, either by agreement between the subordinating creditor and the debtor, by agreement between two creditors of the same debtor, or by agreement of all three parties. The subordinated creditor may be a stockholder or other "insider" interested in the common debtor; the subordinated debt may consist of accounts or other rights to payment not evidenced by any instrument. All such cases are included in the terms "subordinated obligation," "subordination," and "subordinated creditor."

2. Subordination agreements are enforceable between the parties as contracts; and in the bankruptcy of the common debtor dividends otherwise payable to the subordinated creditor are turned over to the superior creditor. This "turn-over" practice has on occasion been explained in terms of "equitable lien," "equitable assignment," or "constructive trust," but whatever the label the practice is essentially an equitable remedy and does not mean that there is a transaction "that creates a security interest in personal property...by contract" or a "sale of accounts, chattel paper, payment intangibles, or promissory notes" within the meaning of Section 9-109. On the other hand, nothing in this section prevents one creditor from assigning his rights to another creditor of the same debtor in such a way as to create a security interest within Article 9, where the parties so intend.

3. The enforcement of subordination agreements is largely left to supplementary principles under Section 1-103. If the subordinated debt is evidenced by a certificated security, Section 8-202(a) authorizes enforcement against purchasers on terms stated or referred to on the security certificate. If the fact of subordination is noted on a negotiable instrument, a holder under Sections 3-302 and 3-306 is subject to the term because notice precludes him from taking free of the subordination. Sections 3-302(3)(a), 3-306, and 8-317 severely limit the rights of levying creditors of a subordinated creditor in such cases.

ARTICLE 2 — SALES

[Editors' Note: In 2003, the American Law Institute and the National Conference of Commissioners on Uniform State Laws approved Proposed Amendments to Article 2. No states adopted the Proposed Amendments, and their sponsors ultimately withdrew them in 2011.]

PART 1. SHORT TITLE, GENERAL CONSTRUCTION AND SUBJECT MATTER

PART 2. FORM, FORMATION AND READJUSTMENT OF CONTRACT

PART 3. GENERAL OBLIGATION AND CONSTRUCTION OF CONTRACT

PART 4. TITLE, CREDITORS AND GOOD FAITH PURCHASERS

PART 5. PERFORMANCE

PART 6. BREACH, REPUDIATION AND EXCUSE

PART 7. REMEDIES

PART 1. SHORT TITLE, GENERAL CONSTRUCTION AND SUBJECT MATTER

§ 2-101. Short Title

This Article shall be known and may be cited as Uniform Commercial Code-Sales.

This Article is a complete revision and modernization of the Uniform Sales Act which was promulgated by the National Conference of Commissioners on Uniform

State Laws in 1906 and has been adopted in 34 states and Alaska, the District of Columbia and Hawaii.

The coverage of the present Article is much more extensive than that of the old Sales Act and extends to the various bodies of case law which have been developed both outside of and under the latter.

The arrangement of the present Article is in terms of contract for sale and the various steps of its performance. The legal consequences are stated as following directly from the contract and action taken under it without resorting to the idea of when property or title passed or was to pass as being the determining factor. The purpose is to avoid making practical issues between practical men turn upon the location of an intangible something, the passing of which no man can prove by evidence and to substitute for such abstractions proof of words and actions of a tangible character.

§ 2-102. Scope; Certain Security and Other Transactions Excluded From This Article

Unless the context otherwise requires, this Article applies to transactions in goods; it does not apply to any transaction which although in the form of an unconditional contract to sell or present sale is intended to operate only as a security transaction nor does this Article impair or repeal any statute regulating sales to consumers, farmers or other specified classes of buyers.

Official Comments

Prior Uniform Statutory Provision: Section 75, Uniform Sales Act.

Changes: Section 75 has been rephrased.

Purposes of Changes and New Matter: To make it clear that:

The Article leaves substantially unaffected the law relating to purchase money security such as conditional sale or chattel mortgage though it regulates the general sales aspects of such transactions. "Security transaction" is used in the same sense as in the Article on Secured Transactions (Article 9).

Cross Reference:

Article 9.

Definitional Cross References:

"Contract". Section 1-201.

"Contract for sale". Section 2-106.

"Present sale". Section 2-106.

"Sale". Section 2-106.

§ 2-103. Definitions and Index of Definitions

(1) In this Article unless the context otherwise requires
    (a) "Buyer" means a person who buys or contracts to buy goods.
    (b) "Good faith" in the case of a merchant means honesty in fact and the observance of reasonable commercial standards of fair dealing in the trade.
    (c) "Receipt" of goods means taking physical possession of them.
    (d) "Seller" means a person who sells or contracts to sell goods.

(2) Other definitions applying to this Article or to specified Parts thereof, and the sections in which they appear are:
"Acceptance". Section 2-606.
"Banker's credit". Section 2-325.
"Between merchants". Section 2-104.
"Cancellation". Section 2-106(4).
"Commercial unit". Section 2-105.
"Confirmed credit". Section 2-325.
"Conforming to contract". Section 2-106.
"Contract for sale". Section 2-106.
"Cover". Section 2-712.
"Entrusting". Section 2-403.
"Financing agency". Section 2-104.
"Future goods". Section 2-105.
"Goods". Section 2-105.
"Identification". Section 2-501.
"Installment contract". Section 2-612.
"Letter of Credit". Section 2-325.
"Lot". Section 2-105.
"Merchant". Section 2-104.
"Overseas". Section 2-323.
"Person in position of seller". Section 2-707.
"Present sale". Section 2-106.
"Sale". Section 2-106.
"Sale on approval". Section 2-326.
"Sale or return". Section 2-326.
"Termination". Section 2-106.

(3) The following definitions in other Articles apply to this Article:
"Check". Section 3-104.
"Consignee". Section 7-102.
"Consignor". Section 7-102.
"Consumer goods". Section 9-109.
"Dishonor". Section 3-502.
"Draft". Section 3-104.

(4) In addition Article 1 contains general definitions and principles of construction and interpretation applicable throughout this Article.
As amended in 1994.

Official Comments

Prior Uniform Statutory Provision: Subsection (1): Section 76, Uniform Sales Act.

Changes:

The definitions of "buyer" and "seller" have been slightly rephrased, the reference in Section 76 of the prior Act to "any legal successor in interest of such person" being omitted. The definition of "receipt" is new.

Purposes of Changes and New Matter:

1. The phrase "any legal successor in interest of such person" has been eliminated since Section 2-210 of this Article, which limits some types of delegation of performance on assignment of a sales contract, makes it clear that not every such successor can be safely included in the definition. In every ordinary case, however, such successors are as of course included.

2. "Receipt" must be distinguished from delivery particularly in regard to the problems arising out of shipment of goods, whether or not the contract calls for making delivery by way of documents of title, since the seller may frequently fulfill his obligations to "deliver" even though the buyer may never "receive" the goods. Delivery with respect to documents of title is defined in Article 1 and requires transfer of physical delivery. Otherwise the many divergent incidents of delivery are handled incident by incident.

Cross References:

Point 1: See Section 2-210 and Comment thereon.

Point 2: Section 1-201.

Definitional Cross Reference:

"Person". Section 1-201.

§ 2-104. Definitions: "Merchant"; "Between Merchants"; "Financing Agency"

(1) "Merchant" means a person who deals in goods of the kind or otherwise by his occupation holds himself out as having knowledge or skill peculiar to the practices or goods involved in the transaction or to whom such knowledge or skill may be attributed by his employment of an agent or broker or other intermediary who by his occupation holds himself out as having such knowledge or skill.

(2) "Financing agency" means a bank, finance company or other person who in the ordinary course of business makes advances against goods or documents of title or who by arrangement with either the seller or the buyer intervenes in ordinary

course to make or collect payment due or claimed under the contract for sale, as by purchasing or paying the seller's draft or making advances against it or by merely taking it for collection whether or not documents of title accompany the draft. "Financing agency" includes also a bank or other person who similarly intervenes between persons who are in the position of seller and buyer in respect to the goods (Section 2-707).

(3) "Between merchants" means in any transaction with respect to which both parties are chargeable with the knowledge or skill of merchants.

Official Comments

Prior Uniform Statutory Provision: None. But see Sections 15(2), (5), 16(c), 45(2) and 71, Uniform Sales Act, and Sections 35 and 37, Uniform Bills of Lading Act for examples of the policy expressly provided for in this Article.

Purposes:

1. This Article assumes that transactions between professionals in a given field require special and clear rules which may not apply to a casual or inexperienced seller or buyer. It thus adopts a policy of expressly stating rules applicable "between merchants" and "as against a merchant", wherever they are needed instead of making them depend upon the circumstances of each case as in the statutes cited above. This section lays the foundation of this policy by defining those who are to be regarded as professionals or "merchants" and by stating when a transaction is deemed to be "between merchants".

2. The term "merchant" as defined here roots in the "law merchant" concept of a professional in business. The professional status under the definition may be based upon specialized knowledge as to the goods, specialized knowledge as to business practices, or specialized knowledge as to both and which kind of specialized knowledge may be sufficient to establish the merchant status is indicated by the nature of the provisions.

The special provisions as to merchants appear only in this Article and they are of three kinds. Sections 2-201(2), 2-205, 2-207 and 2-209 dealing with the statute of frauds, firm offers, confirmatory memoranda and modification rest on normal business practices which are or ought to be typical of and familiar to any person in business. For purposes of these sections almost every person in business would, therefore, be deemed to be a "merchant" under the language "who...by his occupation holds himself out as having knowledge or skill peculiar to the practices...involved in the transaction..." since the practices involved in the transaction are non-specialized business practices such as answering mail. In this type of provision, banks or even universities, for example, well may be "merchants." But even these sections only apply to a merchant in his mercantile capacity; a lawyer or bank president buying fishing tackle for his own use is not a merchant.

On the other hand, in Section 2-314 on the warranty of merchantability, such warranty is implied only "if the seller is a merchant with respect to goods of that kind." Obviously this qualification restricts the implied warranty to a much smaller group than everyone who is engaged in business and requires a professional status as to particular kinds of goods. The exception in Section 2-402(2) for retention of possession by a merchant-seller falls in the same class; as does Section 2-403(2) on entrusting of possession to a merchant "who deals in goods of that kind".

A third group of sections includes 2-103(1)(b), which provides that in the case of a merchant "good faith" includes observance of reasonable commercial standards of fair dealing in the trade; 2-327(1)(c), 2-603 and 2-605, dealing with responsibilities of merchant buyers to follow seller's instructions, etc.; 2-509 on risk of loss, and 2-609 on adequate assurance of performance. This group of sections applies to persons who are merchants under either the "practices" or the "goods" aspect of the definition of merchant.

3. The "or to whom such knowledge or skill may be attributed by his employment of an agent or broker ..." clause of the definition of merchant means that even persons such as universities, for example, can come within the definition of merchant if they have regular purchasing departments or business personnel who are familiar with business practices and who are equipped to take any action required.

Cross References:

Point 1: See Sections 1-102 and 1-203.

Point 2: See Sections 2-314, 2-315 and 2-320 to 2-325, of this Article, and Article 9.

Definitional Cross References:

"Bank". Section 1-201.

"Buyer". Section 2-103.

"Contract for sale". Section 2-106.

"Document of title". Section 1-201.

"Draft". Section 3-104.

"Goods". Section 2-105.

"Person". Section 1-201.

"Purchase". Section 1-201.

"Seller". Section 2-103.

§ 2-105. Definitions: Transferability; "Goods"; "Future" Goods; "Lot"; "Commercial Unit"

(1) "Goods" means all things (including specially manufactured goods) which are movable at the time of identification to the contract for sale other than the money in which the price is to be paid, investment securities (Article 8) and things in action. "Goods" also includes the unborn young of animals and growing crops and other identified things attached to realty as described in the section on goods to be severed from realty (Section 2-107).

(2) Goods must be both existing and identified before any interest in them can pass. Goods which are not both existing and identified are "future" goods. A purported present sale of future goods or of any interest therein operates as a contract to sell.

(3) There may be a sale of a part interest in existing identified goods.

(4) An undivided share in an identified bulk of fungible goods is sufficiently identified to be sold although the quantity of the bulk is not determined. Any agreed proportion of such a bulk or any quantity thereof agreed upon by number, weight or other measure may to the extent of the seller's interest in the bulk be sold to the buyer who then becomes an owner in common.

(5) "Lot" means a parcel or a single article which is the subject matter of a separate sale or delivery, whether or not it is sufficient to perform the contract.

(6) "Commercial unit" means such a unit of goods as by commercial usage is a single whole for purposes of sale and division of which materially impairs its character or value on the market or in use. A commercial unit may be a single article (as a machine) or a set of articles (as a suite of furniture or an assortment of sizes) or a quantity (as a bale, gross, or carload) or any other unit treated in use or in the relevant market as a single whole.

Official Comments

Prior Uniform Statutory Provision: Subsections (1), (2), (3) and (4) — Sections 5, 6 and 76, Uniform Sales Act; Subsections (5) and (6) — none.

Changes: Rewritten.

Purposes of Changes and New Matter:

1. Subsection (1) on "goods": The phraseology of the prior uniform statutory provision has been changed so that:

The definition of goods is based on the concept of movability and the term "chattels personal" is not used. It is not intended to deal with things which are not fairly identifiable as movables before the contract is performed.

Growing crops are included within the definition of goods since they are frequently intended for sale. The concept of "industrial" growing crops has been abandoned, for under modern practices fruit, perennial hay, nursery stock and the like must be brought within the scope of this Article. The young of animals are also included expressly in this definition since they, too, are frequently intended for sale and may be contracted for before birth. The period of gestation of domestic animals is such that the provisions of the section on identification can apply as in the case of crops to be planted.

The reason of this definition also leads to the inclusion of a wool crop or the like as "goods" subject to identification under this Article.

The exclusion of "money in which the price is to be paid" from the definition of goods does not mean that foreign currency which is included in the definition of money may not be the subject matter of a sales transaction. Goods is intended to cover the sale of money when money is being treated as a commodity but not to include it when money is the medium of payment.

As to contracts to sell timber, minerals, or structures to be removed from the land Section 2-107(1) (Goods to be severed from Realty: recording) controls.

The use of the word "fixtures" is avoided in view of the diversity of definitions of that term. This Article in including within its scope "things attached to realty" adds the further test that they must be capable of severance without material harm thereto. As between the parties any identified things which fall within that definition become "goods" upon the making of the contract for sale.

"Investment securities" are expressly excluded from the coverage of this Article. It is not intended by this exclusion, however, to prevent the application of a particular section of this Article by analogy to securities (as was done with the Original Sales Act in Agar v. Orda, 264 N.Y. 248, 190 N.E. 479, 99 A.L.R. 269 (1934)) when the reason of that section makes such application sensible and the situation involved is not covered by the Article of this Act dealing specifically with such securities (Article 8).

2. References to the fact that a contract for sale can extend to future or contingent goods and that ownership in common follows the sale of a part interest have been omitted here as obvious without need for expression; hence no inference to negate these principles should be drawn from their omission.

3. Subsection (4) does not touch the question of how far an appropriation of a bulk of fungible goods may or may not satisfy the contract for sale.

4. Subsections (5) and (6) on "lot" and "commercial unit" are introduced to aid in the phrasing of later sections.

5. The question of when an identification of goods takes place is determined by the provisions of Section 2-501 and all that this section says is what kinds of goods may be the subject of a sale.

Cross References:

Point 1: Sections 2-107, 2-201, 2-501 and Article 8.

Point 5: Section 2-501.

See also Section 1-201.

Definitional Cross References:

"Buyer". Section 2-103.

"Contract". Section 1-201.

"Contract for sale". Section 2-106.

"Fungible". Section 1-201.

"Money". Section 1-201.

"Present sale". Section 2-106.

"Sale". Section 2-106.

"Seller". Section 2-103.

§ 2-106. Definitions: "Contract"; "Agreement"; "Contract for Sale"; "Sale"; "Present Sale"; "Conforming" to Contract; "Termination"; "Cancellation"

(1) In this Article unless the context otherwise requires "contract" and "agreement" are limited to those relating to the present or future sale of goods. "Contract for sale" includes both a present sale of goods and a contract to sell goods at a future time. A "sale" consists in the passing of title from the seller to the buyer for a price (Section 2-401). A "present sale" means a sale which is accomplished by the making of the contract.

(2) Goods or conduct including any part of a performance are "conforming" or conform to the contract when they are in accordance with the obligations under the contract.

(3) "Termination" occurs when either party pursuant to a power created by agreement or law puts an end to the contract otherwise than for its breach. On "termination" all obligations which are still executory on both sides are discharged but any right based on prior breach or performance survives.

(4) "Cancellation" occurs when either party puts an end to the contract for breach by the other and its effect is the same as that of "termination" except that the cancelling party also retains any remedy for breach of the whole contract or any unperformed balance.

Official Comments

Prior Uniform Statutory Provision: Subsection (1) — Section 1(1) and (2), Uniform Sales Act; Subsection (2) — none, but subsection generally continues policy of Sections 11, 44 and 69, Uniform Sales Act; Subsections (3) and (4) — none.

Changes: Completely rewritten.

Purposes of Changes and New Matter:

1. Subsection (1): "Contract for sale" is used as a general concept throughout this Article, but the rights of the parties do not vary according to whether the transaction is a present sale or a contract to sell unless the Article expressly so provides.

2. Subsection (2): It is in general intended to continue the policy of requiring exact performance by the seller of his obligations as a condition to his right to require acceptance. However, the seller is in part safeguarded against surprise as a result of sudden technicality on the buyer's part by the provisions of Section 2-508 on seller's cure of improper tender or delivery. Moreover usage of trade frequently permits commercial leeways in performance and the language of the agreement itself must be read in the

light of such custom or usage and also, prior course of dealing, and in a long term contract, the course of performance.

3. Subsections (3) and (4): These subsections are intended to make clear the distinction carried forward throughout this Article between termination and cancellation.

Cross References:

Point 2: Sections 1-203, 1-205, 2-208 and 2-508.

Definitional Cross References:

"Agreement". Section 1-201.

"Buyer". Section 2-103.

"Contract". Section 1-201.

"Goods". Section 2-105.

"Party". Section 1-201.

"Remedy". Section 1-201.

"Rights". Section 1-201.

"Seller". Section 2-103.

§ 2-107. Goods to Be Severed From Realty: Recording

(1) A contract for the sale of minerals or the like (including oil and gas) or a structure or its materials to be removed from realty is a contract for the sale of goods within this Article if they are to be severed by the seller but until severance a purported present sale thereof which is not effective as a transfer of an interest in land is effective only as a contract to sell.

(2) A contract for the sale apart from the land of growing crops or other things attached to realty and capable of severance without material harm thereto but not described in subsection (1) or of timber to be cut is a contract for the sale of goods within this Article whether the subject matter is to be severed by the buyer or by the seller even though it forms part of the realty at the time of contracting, and the parties can by identification effect a present sale before severance.

(3) The provisions of this section are subject to any third party rights provided by the law relating to realty records, and the contract for sale may be executed and recorded as a document transferring an interest in land and shall then constitute notice to third parties of the buyer's rights under the contract for sale.

As amended in 1972.

Official Comments

Prior Uniform Statutory Provision: See Section 76, Uniform Sales Act on prior policy; Section 7, Uniform Conditional Sales Act.

Purposes:

1. Subsection (1). Notice that this subsection applies only if the minerals or structures "are to be severed by the seller". If the buyer is to sever, such transactions are considered contracts affecting land and all problems of the Statute of Frauds and of the recording of land rights apply to them. Therefore, the Statute of Frauds section of this Article does not apply to such contracts though they must conform to the Statute of Frauds affecting the transfer of interests in land.

2. Subsection (2). "Things attached" to the realty which can be severed without material harm are goods within this Article regardless of who is to effect the severance. The word "fixtures" has been avoided because of the diverse definitions of this term, the test of "severance without material harm" being substituted.

The provision in subsection (3) for recording such contracts is within the purview of this Article since it is a means of preserving the buyer's rights under the contract of sale.

3. The security phases of things attached to or to become attached to realty are dealt with in the Article on Secured Transactions (Article 9) and it is to be noted that the definition of goods in that Article differs from the definition of goods in this Article.

However, both Articles treat as goods growing crops and also timber to be cut under a contract of severance.

Cross References:

Point 1: Section 2-201.

Point 2: Section 2-105.

Point 3: Articles 9 and 9-105.

Definitional Cross References:

"Buyer". Section 2-103.

"Contract". Section 1-201.

"Contract for sale". Section 2-106.

"Goods". Section 2-105.

"Party". Section 1-201.

"Present sale". Section 2-106.

"Rights". Section 1-201.

"Seller". Section 2-103.

PART 2. FORM, FORMATION AND READJUSTMENT OF CONTRACT

§ 2-201. Formal Requirements; Statute of Frauds

(1) Except as otherwise provided in this section a contract for the sale of goods for the price of $500 or more is not enforceable by way of action or defense unless there is some writing sufficient to indicate that a contract for sale has been made between the parties and signed by the party against whom enforcement is sought or by his authorized agent or broker. A writing is not insufficient because it omits or incorrectly states a term agreed upon but the contract is not enforceable under this paragraph beyond the quantity of goods shown in such writing.

(2) Between merchants if within a reasonable time a writing in confirmation of the contract and sufficient against the sender is received and the party receiving it has reason to know its contents, it satisfies the requirements of subsection (1) against such party unless written notice of objection to its contents is given within 10 days after it is received.

(3) A contract which does not satisfy the requirements of subsection (1) but which is valid in other respects is enforceable

(a) if the goods are to be specially manufactured for the buyer and are not suitable for sale to others in the ordinary course of the seller's business and the seller, before notice of repudiation is received and under circumstances which reasonably indicate that the goods are for the buyer, has made either a substantial beginning of their manufacture or commitments for their procurement; or

(b) if the party against whom enforcement is sought admits in his pleading, testimony or otherwise in court that a contract for sale was made, but the contract is not enforceable under this provision beyond the quantity of goods admitted; or

(c) with respect to goods for which payment has been made and accepted or which have been received and accepted (Sec. 2-606).

Official Comments

Prior Uniform Statutory Provision: Section 4, Uniform Sales Act (which was based on Section 17 of the Statute of 29 Charles II).

Changes: Completely rephrased; restricted to sale of goods. See also Sections 1-206, 8-319 and 9-203.

Purposes of Changes: The changed phraseology of this section is intended to make it clear that:

1. The required writing need not contain all the material terms of the contract and such material terms as are stated need not be precisely stated. All that is required is that the writing afford a basis for believing that the offered oral evidence rests on a

real transaction. It may be written in lead pencil on a scratch pad. It need not indicate which party is the buyer and which the seller. The only term which must appear is the quantity term which need not be accurately stated but recovery is limited to the amount stated. The price, time and place of payment or delivery, the general quality of the goods, or any particular warranties may all be omitted.

Special emphasis must be placed on the permissibility of omitting the price term in view of the insistence of some courts on the express inclusion of this term even where the parties have contracted on the basis of a published price list. In many valid contracts for sale the parties do not mention the price in express terms, the buyer being bound to pay and the seller to accept a reasonable price which the trier of the fact may well be trusted to determine. Again, frequently the price is not mentioned since the parties have based their agreement on a price list or catalogue known to both of them and this list serves as an efficient safeguard against perjury. Finally, "market" prices and valuations that are current in the vicinity constitute a similar check. Thus if the price is not stated in the memorandum it can normally be supplied without danger of fraud. Of course if the "price" consists of goods rather than money the quantity of goods must be stated.

Only three definite and invariable requirements as to the memorandum are made by this subsection. First, it must evidence a contract for the sale of goods; second, it must be "signed", a word which includes any authentication which identifies the party to be charged; and third, it must specify a quantity.

2. "Partial performance" as a substitute for the required memorandum can validate the contract only for the goods which have been accepted or for which payment has been made and accepted.

Receipt and acceptance either of goods or of the price constitutes an unambiguous overt admission by both parties that a contract actually exists. If the court can make a just apportionment, therefore, the agreed price of any goods actually delivered can be recovered without a writing or, if the price has been paid, the seller can be forced to deliver an apportionable part of the goods. The overt actions of the parties make admissible evidence of the other terms of the contract necessary to a just apportionment. This is true even though the actions of the parties are not in themselves inconsistent with a different transaction such as a consignment for resale or a mere loan of money.

Part performance by the buyer requires the delivery of something by him that is accepted by the seller as such performance. Thus, part payment may be made by money or check, accepted by the seller. If the agreed price consists of goods or services, then they must also have been delivered and accepted.

3. Between merchants, failure to answer a written confirmation of a contract within ten days of receipt is tantamount to a writing under subsection (2) and is sufficient against both parties under subsection (1). The only effect, however, is to take away from the party who fails to answer the defense of the Statute of Frauds; the burden of persuading the trier of fact that a contract was in fact made orally prior to the written confirmation is unaffected. Compare the effect of a failure to reply under Section 2-207.

4. Failure to satisfy the requirements of this section does not render the contract void for all purposes, but merely prevents it from being judicially enforced in favor of a party to the contract. For example, a buyer who takes possession of goods as provided in an oral contract which the seller has not meanwhile repudiated, is not a trespasser. Nor would the Statute of Frauds provisions of this section be a defense to a third person who wrongfully induces a party to refuse to perform an oral contract, even though the injured party cannot maintain an action for damages against the party so refusing to perform.

5. The requirement of "signing" is discussed in the comment to Section 1-201.

6. It is not necessary that the writing be delivered to anybody. It need not be signed or authenticated by both parties but it is, of course, not sufficient against one who has not signed it. Prior to a dispute no one can determine which party's signing of the memorandum may be necessary but from the time of contracting each party should be aware that to him it is signing by the other which is important.

7. If the making of a contract is admitted in court, either in a written pleading, by stipulation or by oral statement before the court, no additional writing is necessary for protection against fraud. Under this section it is no longer possible to admit the contract in court and still treat the Statute as a defense. However, the contract is not thus conclusively established. The admission so made by a party is itself evidential against him of the truth of the facts so admitted and of nothing more; as against the other party, it is not evidential at all.

Cross References:

See Sections 1-201, 2-202, 2-207, 2-209 and 2-304.

Definitional Cross References:

"Action". Section 1-201.

"Between merchants". Section 2-104.

"Buyer". Section 2-103.

"Contract". Section 1-201.

"Contract for sale". Section 2-106.

"Goods". Section 2-105.

"Notice". Section 1-201.

"Party". Section 1-201.

"Reasonable time". Section 1-204.

"Sale". Section 2-106.

"Seller". Section 2-103.

§ 2-202. Final Written Expression: Parol or Extrinsic Evidence

Terms with respect to which the confirmatory memoranda of the parties agree or which are otherwise set forth in a writing intended by the parties as a final expression of their agreement with respect to such terms as are included therein may not be contradicted by evidence of any prior agreement or of a contemporaneous oral agreement but may be explained or supplemented

    (a) by course of dealing or usage of trade (Section 1-205) or by course of performance (Section 2-208); and

    (b) by evidence of consistent additional terms unless the court finds the writing to have been intended also as a complete and exclusive statement of the terms of the agreement.

Official Comments

Prior Uniform Statutory Provisions: None.

Purposes:

1. This section definitely rejects:

    (a) Any assumption that because a writing has been worked out which is final on some matters, it is to be taken as including all the matters agreed upon;

    (b) The premise that the language used has the meaning attributable to such language by rules of construction existing in the law rather than the meaning which arises out of the commercial context in which it was used; and

    (c) The requirement that a condition precedent to the admissibility of the type of evidence specified in paragraph (a) is an original determination by the court that the language used is ambiguous.

2. Paragraph (a) makes admissible evidence of course of dealing, usage of trade and course of performance to explain or supplement the terms of any writing stating the agreement of the parties in order that the true understanding of the parties as to the agreement may be reached. Such writings are to be read on the assumption that the course of prior dealings between the parties and the usages of trade were taken for granted when the document was phrased. Unless carefully negated they have become an element of the meaning of the words used. Similarly, the course of actual performance by the parties is considered the best indication of what they intended the writing to mean.

3. Under paragraph (b) consistent additional terms, not reduced to writing, may be proved unless the court finds that the writing was intended by both parties as a complete and exclusive statement of all the terms. If the additional terms are such that, if agreed upon, they would certainly have been included in the document in the view of the court, then evidence of their alleged making must be kept from the trier of fact.

Cross References:

Point 3: Sections 1-205, 2-207, 2-302 and 2-316.

Definitional Cross References:

"Agreed" and "agreement". Section 1-201.

"Course of dealing". Section 1-205.

"Parties". Section 1-201.

"Term". Section 1-201.

"Usage of trade". Section 1-205.

"Written" and "writing". Section 1-201.

§ 2-203. Seals Inoperative

The affixing of a seal to a writing evidencing a contract for sale or an offer to buy or sell goods does not constitute the writing a sealed instrument and the law with respect to sealed instruments does not apply to such a contract or offer.

Official Comments

Prior Uniform Statutory Provision: Section 3, Uniform Sales Act.

Changes: Portion pertaining to "seals" rewritten.

Purposes of Changes:

1. This section makes it clear that every effect of the seal which relates to "sealed instruments" as such is wiped out insofar as contracts for sale are concerned. However, the substantial effects of a seal, except extension of the period of limitations, may be had by appropriate drafting as in the case of firm offers (see Section 2-205).

2. This section leaves untouched any aspects of a seal which relate merely to signatures or to authentication of execution and the like. Thus, a statute providing that a purported signature gives prima facie evidence of its own authenticity or that a signature gives prima facie evidence of consideration is still applicable to sales transactions even though a seal may be held to be a signature within the meaning of such a statute. Similarly, the authorized affixing of a corporate seal bearing the corporate name to a contractual writing purporting to be made by the corporation may have effect as a signature without any reference to the law of sealed instruments.

Cross Reference:

Point 1: Section 2-205.

Definitional Cross References:

"Contract for sale". Section 2-106.

"Goods". Section 2-105.

"Writing". Section 1-201.

§ 2-204. Formation in General

(1) A contract for sale of goods may be made in any manner sufficient to show agreement, including conduct by both parties which recognizes the existence of such a contract.

(2) An agreement sufficient to constitute a contract for sale may be found even though the moment of its making is undetermined.

(3) Even though one or more terms are left open a contract for sale does not fail for indefiniteness if the parties have intended to make a contract and there is a reasonably certain basis for giving an appropriate remedy.

Official Comments

Prior Uniform Statutory Provision: Sections 1 and 3, Uniform Sales Act.

Changes: Completely rewritten by this and other sections of this Article.

Purposes of Changes:

Subsection (1) continues without change the basic policy of recognizing any manner of expression of agreement, oral, written or otherwise. The legal effect of such an agreement is, of course, qualified by other provisions of this Article.

Under subsection (1) appropriate conduct by the parties may be sufficient to establish an agreement. Subsection (2) is directed primarily to the situation where the interchanged correspondence does not disclose the exact point at which the deal was closed, but the actions of the parties indicate that a binding obligation has been undertaken.

Subsection (3) states the principle as to "open terms" underlying later sections of the Article. If the parties intend to enter into a binding agreement, this subsection recognizes that agreement as valid in law, despite missing terms, if there is any reasonably certain basis for granting a remedy. The test is not certainty as to what the parties were to do nor as to the exact amount of damages due the plaintiff. Nor is the fact that one or more terms are left to be agreed upon enough of itself to defeat an otherwise adequate agreement. Rather, commercial standards on the point of "indefiniteness" are intended to be applied, this Act making provision elsewhere for missing terms needed for performance, open price, remedies and the like.

The more terms the parties leave open, the less likely it is that they have intended to conclude a binding agreement, but their actions may be frequently conclusive on the matter despite the omissions.

Cross References:

Subsection (1): Sections 1-103, 2-201 and 2-302.

Subsection (2): Sections 2-205 through 2-209.

Subsection (3): See Part 3.

Definitional Cross References:

"Agreement". Section 1-201.

"Contract". Section 1-201.

"Contract for sale". Section 2-106.

"Goods". Section 2-105.

"Party". Section 1-201.

"Remedy". Section 1-201.

"Term". Section 1-201.

§ 2-205. Firm Offers

An offer by a merchant to buy or sell goods in a signed writing which by its terms gives assurance that it will be held open is not revocable, for lack of consideration, during the time stated or if no time is stated for a reasonable time, but in no event may such period of irrevocability exceed three months; but any such term of assurance on a form supplied by the offeree must be separately signed by the offeror.

Official Comments

Prior Uniform Statutory Provision: Sections 1 and 3, Uniform Sales Act.

Changes: Completely rewritten by this and other sections of this Article.

Purposes of Changes:

1. This section is intended to modify the former rule which required that "firm offers" be sustained by consideration in order to bind, and to require instead that they must merely be characterized as such and expressed in signed writings.

2. The primary purpose of this section is to give effect to the deliberate intention of a merchant to make a current firm offer binding. The deliberation is shown in the case of an individualized document by the merchant's signature to the offer, and in the case of an offer included on a form supplied by the other party to the transaction by the separate signing of the particular clause which contains the offer. "Signed" here also includes authentication but the reasonableness of the authentication herein allowed must be determined in the light of the purpose of the section. The circumstances surrounding the signing may justify something less than a formal signature or initialing but typically the kind of authentication involved here would consist of a minimum of initialing of the clause involved. A handwritten memorandum on the writer's letterhead purporting in its terms to "confirm" a firm offer already made would be enough to satisfy this section, although not subscribed, since under the circumstances it could not be considered a memorandum of mere negotiation and it would adequately show its own authenticity. Similarly, an authorized telegram will suffice, and this is true even though the original draft contained only a typewritten signature. However, despite settled courses of dealing or usages of the trade whereby firm offers are made by oral

communication and relied upon without more evidence, such offers remain revocable under this Article since authentication by a writing is the essence of this section.

3. This section is intended to apply to current "firm" offers and not to long term options, and an outside time limit of three months during which such offers remain irrevocable has been set. The three month period during which firm offers remain irrevocable under this section need not be stated by days or by date. If the offer states that it is "guaranteed" or "firm" until the happening of a contingency which will occur within the three month period, it will remain irrevocable until that event. A promise made for a longer period will operate under this section to bind the offeror only for the first three months of the period but may of course be renewed. If supported by consideration it may continue for as long as the parties specify. This section deals only with the offer which is not supported by consideration.

4. Protection is afforded against the inadvertent signing of a firm offer when contained in a form prepared by the offeree by requiring that such a clause be separately authenticated. If the offer clause is called to the offeror's attention and he separately authenticates it, he will be bound; Section 2-302 may operate, however, to prevent an unconscionable result which otherwise would flow from other terms appearing in the form.

5. Safeguards are provided to offer relief in the case of material mistake by virtue of the requirement of good faith and the general law of mistake.

Cross References:

Point 1: Section 1-102.

Point 2: Section 1-102.

Point 3: Section 2-201.

Point 5: Section 2-302.

Definitional Cross References:

"Goods". Section 2-105.

"Merchant". Section 2-104.

"Signed". Section 1-201.

"Writing". Section 1-201.

§ 2-206. Offer and Acceptance in Formation of Contract

(1) Unless otherwise unambiguously indicated by the language or circumstances
  (a) an offer to make a contract shall be construed as inviting acceptance in any manner and by any medium reasonable in the circumstances;
  (b) an order or other offer to buy goods for prompt or current shipment shall be construed as inviting acceptance either by a prompt promise to ship or by the prompt or current shipment of conforming or non-conforming goods, but such a shipment of non-conforming goods does not constitute an accep-

tance if the seller seasonably notifies the buyer that the shipment is offered only as an accommodation to the buyer.

(2) Where the beginning of a requested performance is a reasonable mode of acceptance an offeror who is not notified of acceptance within a reasonable time may treat the offer as having lapsed before acceptance.

Official Comments

Prior Uniform Statutory Provision: Sections 1 and 3, Uniform Sales Act.

Changes: Completely rewritten in this and other sections of this Article.

Purposes of Changes: To make it clear that:

1. Any reasonable manner of acceptance is intended to be regarded as available unless the offeror has made quite clear that it will not be acceptable. Former technical rules as to acceptance, such as requiring that telegraphic offers be accepted by telegraphed acceptance, etc., are rejected and a criterion that the acceptance be "in any manner and by any medium reasonable under the circumstances," is substituted. This section is intended to remain flexible and its applicability to be enlarged as new media of communication develop or as the more time-saving present day media come into general use.

2. Either shipment or a prompt promise to ship is made a proper means of acceptance of an offer looking to current shipment. In accordance with ordinary commercial understanding the section interprets an order looking to current shipment as allowing acceptance either by actual shipment or by a prompt promise to ship and rejects the artificial theory that only a single mode of acceptance is normally envisaged by an offer. This is true even though the language of the offer happens to be "ship at once" or the like. "Shipment" is here used in the same sense as in Section 2-504; it does not include the beginning of delivery by the seller's own truck or by messenger. But loading on the seller's own truck might be a beginning of performance under subsection (2).

3. The beginning of performance by an offeree can be effective as acceptance so as to bind the offeror only if followed within a reasonable time by notice to the offeror. Such a beginning of performance must unambiguously express the offeree's intention to engage himself. For the protection of both parties it is essential that notice follow in due course to constitute acceptance. Nothing in this section however bars the possibility that under the common law performance begun may have an intermediate effect of temporarily barring revocation of the offer, or at the offeror's option, final effect in constituting acceptance.

4. Subsection (1)(b) deals with the situation where a shipment made following an order is shown by a notification of shipment to be referable to that order but has a defect. Such a non-conforming shipment is normally to be understood as intended to close the bargain, even though it proves to have been at the same time a breach. However, the seller by stating that the shipment is non-conforming and is offered only as an accommodation to the buyer keeps the shipment or notification from operating as an acceptance.

Definitional Cross References:

"Buyer". Section 2-103.

"Conforming". Section 2-106.

"Contract". Section 1-201.

"Goods". Section 2-105.

"Notifies". Section 1-201.

"Reasonable time". Section 1-204.

§ 2-207. Additional Terms in Acceptance or Confirmation

(1) A definite and seasonable expression of acceptance or a written confirmation which is sent within a reasonable time operates as an acceptance even though it states terms additional to or different from those offered or agreed upon, unless acceptance is expressly made conditional on assent to the additional or different terms.

(2) The additional terms are to be construed as proposals for addition to the contract. Between merchants such terms become part of the contract unless:
    (a) the offer expressly limits acceptance to the terms of the offer;
    (b) they materially alter it; or
    (c) notification of objection to them has already been given or is given within a reasonable time after notice of them is received.

(3) Conduct by both parties which recognizes the existence of a contract is sufficient to establish a contract for sale although the writings of the parties do not otherwise establish a contract. In such case the terms of the particular contract consist of those terms on which the writings of the parties agree, together with any supplementary terms incorporated under any other provisions of this Act.

Official Comments

Prior Uniform Statutory Provision: Sections 1 and 3, Uniform Sales Act.

Changes: Completely rewritten by this and other sections of this Article.

Purposes of Changes:

1. This section is intended to deal with two typical situations. The one is the written confirmation, where an agreement has been reached either orally or by informal correspondence between the parties and is followed by one or both of the parties sending formal memoranda embodying the terms so far as agreed upon and adding terms not discussed. The other situation is offer and acceptance, in which a wire or letter expressed and intended as an acceptance or the closing of an agreement adds further minor suggestions or proposals such as "ship by Tuesday," "rush," "ship draft against bill of lading inspection allowed," or the like. A frequent example of the second situation is the exchange of printed purchase order and acceptance (sometimes called "acknowledgment") forms. Because the forms are oriented to the thinking of the re-

spective drafting parties, the terms contained in them often do not correspond. Often the seller's form contains terms different from or additional to those set forth in the buyer's form. Nevertheless, the parties proceed with the transaction. [Comment 1 was amended in 1966.]

2. Under this Article a proposed deal which in commercial understanding has in fact been closed is recognized as a contract. Therefore, any additional matter contained in the confirmation or in the acceptance falls within subsection (2) and must be regarded as a proposal for an added term unless the acceptance is made conditional on the acceptance of the additional or different terms. [Comment 2 was amended in 1966.]

3. Whether or not additional or different terms will become part of the agreement depends upon the provisions of subsection (2). If they are such as materially to alter the original bargain, they will not be included unless expressly agreed to by the other party. If, however, they are terms which would not so change the bargain they will be incorporated unless notice of objection to them has already been given or is given within a reasonable time.

4. Examples of typical clauses which would normally "materially alter" the contract and so result in surprise or hardship if incorporated without express awareness by the other party are: a clause negating such standard warranties as that of merchantability or fitness for a particular purpose in circumstances in which either warranty normally attaches; a clause requiring a guaranty of 90% or 100% deliveries in a case such as a contract by cannery, where the usage of the trade allows greater quantity leeways; a clause reserving to the seller the power to cancel upon the buyer's failure to meet any invoice when due; a clause requiring that complaints be made in a time materially shorter than customary or reasonable.

5. Examples of clauses which involve no element of unreasonable surprise and which therefore are to be incorporated in the contract unless notice of objection is seasonably given are: a clause setting forth and perhaps enlarging slightly upon the seller's exemption due to supervening causes beyond his control, similar to those covered by the provision of this Article on merchant's excuse by failure of presupposed conditions or a clause fixing in advance any reasonable formula of proration under such circumstances; a clause fixing a reasonable time for complaints within customary limits, or in the case of a purchase for sub-sale, providing for inspection by the sub-purchaser; a clause providing for interest on overdue invoices or fixing the seller's standard credit terms where they are within the range of trade practice and do not limit any credit bargained for; a clause limiting the right of rejection for defects which fall within the customary trade tolerances for acceptance "with adjustment" or otherwise limiting remedy in a reasonable manner (see Sections 2-718 and 2-719).

6. If no answer is received within a reasonable time after additional terms are proposed, it is both fair and commercially sound to assume that their inclusion has been assented to. Where clauses on confirming forms sent by both parties conflict each party must be assumed to object to a clause of the other conflicting with one on the confirmation sent by himself. As a result the requirement that there be notice of objection

which is found in subsection (2) is satisfied and the conflicting terms do not become a part of the contract. The contract then consists of the terms originally expressly agreed to, terms on which the confirmations agree, and terms supplied by this Act, including subsection (2). The written confirmation is also subject to Section 2-201. Under that section a failure to respond permits enforcement of a prior oral agreement; under this section a failure to respond permits additional terms to become part of the agreement. [Comment 6 was amended in 1966.]

7. In many cases, as where goods are shipped, accepted and paid for before any dispute arises, there is no question whether a contract has been made. In such cases, where the writings of the parties do not establish a contract, it is not necessary to determine which act or document constituted the offer and which the acceptance. See Section 2-204. The only question is what terms are included in the contract, and subsection (3) furnishes the governing rule. [Comment 7 was added in 1966.]

Cross References:

See generally Section 2-302.

Point 5: Sections 2-513, 2-602, 2-607, 2-609, 2-612, 2-614, 2-615, 2-616, 2-718 and 2-719.

Point 6: Sections 1-102 and 2-104.

Definitional Cross References:

"Between merchants". Section 2-104.

"Contract". Section 1-201.

"Notification". Section 1-201.

"Reasonable time". Section 1-204.

"Seasonably". Section 1-204.

"Send". Section 1-201.

"Term". Section 1-201.

"Written". Section 1-201.

§ 2-208. Course of Performance or Practical Construction

(1) Where the contract for sale involves repeated occasions for performance by either party with knowledge of the nature of the performance and opportunity for objection to it by the other, any course of performance accepted or acquiesced in without objection shall be relevant to determine the meaning of the agreement.

(2) The express terms of the agreement and any such course of performance, as well as any course of dealing and usage of trade, shall be construed whenever reasonable as consistent with each other; but when such construction is unreasonable, express terms shall control course of performance and course of performance shall control both course of dealing and usage of trade (Section 1-205).

(3) Subject to the provisions of the next section on modification and waiver, such course of performance shall be relevant to show a waiver or modification of any term inconsistent with such course of performance.

Official Comments

Prior Uniform Statutory Provision: No such general provision but concept of this section recognized by terms such as "course of dealing", "the circumstances of the case", "the conduct of the parties," etc., in Uniform Sales Act.

Purposes:

1. The parties themselves know best what they have meant by their words of agreement and their action under that agreement is the best indication of what that meaning was. This section thus rounds out the set of factors which determines the meaning of the "agreement" and therefore also of the "unless otherwise agreed" qualification to various provisions of this Article.

2. Under this section a course of performance is always relevant to determine the meaning of the agreement. Express mention of course of performance elsewhere in this Article carries no contrary implication when there is a failure to refer to it in other sections.

3. Where it is difficult to determine whether a particular act merely sheds light on the meaning of the agreement or represents a waiver of a term of the agreement, the preference is in favor of "waiver" whenever such construction, plus the application of the provisions on the reinstatement of rights waived (see Section 2-209), is needed to preserve the flexible character of commercial contracts and to prevent surprise or other hardship.

4. A single occasion of conduct does not fall within the language of this section but other sections such as the ones on silence after acceptance and failure to specify particular defects can affect the parties' rights on a single occasion (see Sections 2-605 and 2-607).

Cross References:

Point 1: Section 1-201.

Point 2: Section 2-202.

Point 3: Sections 2-209, 2-601 and 2-607.

Point 4: Sections 2-605 and 2-607.

§ 2-209. Modification, Rescission and Waiver

(1) An agreement modifying a contract within this Article needs no consideration to be binding.

(2) A signed agreement which excludes modification or rescission except by a signed writing cannot be otherwise modified or rescinded, but except as be-

tween merchants such a requirement on a form supplied by the merchant must be separately signed by the other party.

(3) The requirements of the statute of frauds section of this Article (Section 2-201) must be satisfied if the contract as modified is within its provisions.

(4) Although an attempt at modification or rescission does not satisfy the requirements of subsection (2) or (3) it can operate as a waiver.

(5) A party who has made a waiver affecting an executory portion of the contract may retract the waiver by reasonable notification received by the other party that strict performance will be required of any term waived, unless the retraction would be unjust in view of a material change of position in reliance on the waiver.

Official Comments

Prior Uniform Statutory Provision: Subsection (1) — Compare Section 1, Uniform Written Obligations Act; Subsections (2) to (5) — none.

Purposes of Changes and New Matter:

1. This section seeks to protect and make effective all necessary and desirable modifications of sales contracts without regard to the technicalities which at present hamper such adjustments.

2. Subsection (1) provides that an agreement modifying a sales contract needs no consideration to be binding.

However, modifications made thereunder must meet the test of good faith imposed by this Act. The effective use of bad faith to escape performance on the original contract terms is barred, and the extortion of a "modification" without legitimate commercial reason is ineffective as a violation of the duty of good faith. Nor can a mere technical consideration support a modification made in bad faith.

The test of "good faith" between merchants or as against merchants includes "observance of reasonable commercial standards of fair dealing in the trade" (Section 2-103), and may in some situations require an objectively demonstrable reason for seeking a modification. But such matters as a market shift which makes performance come to involve a loss may provide such a reason even though there is no such unforeseen difficulty as would make out a legal excuse from performance under Sections 2-615 and 2-616.

3. Subsections (2) and (3) are intended to protect against false allegations of oral modifications. "Modification or rescission" includes abandonment or other change by mutual consent, contrary to the decision in *Green v. Doniger*, 300 N.Y. 238, 90 N.E.2d 56 (1949); it does not include unilateral "termination" or "cancellation" as defined in Section 2-106.

The Statute of Frauds provisions of this Article are expressly applied to modifications by subsection (3). Under those provisions the "delivery and acceptance" test is limited to the goods which have been accepted, that is, to the past. "Modification" for the future cannot therefore be conjured up by oral testimony if the price involved is $500.00 or more since such modification must be shown at least by an authenticated memo. And since a memo is limited in its effect to the quantity of goods set forth in it there is safeguard against oral evidence.

Subsection (2) permits the parties in effect to make their own Statute of Frauds as regards any future modification of the contract by giving effect to a clause in a signed agreement which expressly requires any modification to be by signed writing. But note that if a consumer is to be held to such a clause on a form supplied by a merchant it must be separately signed.

4. Subsection (4) is intended, despite the provisions of subsections (2) and (3), to prevent contractual provisions excluding modification except by a signed writing from limiting in other respects the legal effect of the parties' actual later conduct. The effect of such conduct as a waiver is further regulated in subsection (5).

Cross References:

Point 1: Section 1-203.

Point 2: Sections 1-201, 1-203, 2-615 and 2-616.

Point 3: Sections 2-106, 2-201 and 2-202.

Point 4: Sections 2-202 and 2-208.

Definitional Cross References:

"Agreement". Section 1-201.

"Between merchants". Section 2-104.

"Contract". Section 1-201.

"Notification". Section 1-201.

"Signed". Section 1-201.

"Term". Section 1-201.

"Writing". Section 1-201.

§ 2-210. Delegation of Performance; Assignment of Rights

(1) A party may perform his duty through a delegate unless otherwise agreed or unless the other party has a substantial interest in having his original promisor perform or control the acts required by the contract. No delegation of performance relieves the party delegating of any duty to perform or any liability for breach.

(2) Unless otherwise agreed all rights of either seller or buyer can be assigned except where the assignment would materially change the duty of the other party, or increase materially the burden or risk imposed on him by his contract, or impair materially his chance of obtaining return performance. A right to dam-

ages for breach of the whole contract or a right arising out of the assignor's due performance of his entire obligation can be assigned despite agreement otherwise.

(3) Unless the circumstances indicate the contrary a prohibition of assignment of "the contract" is to be construed as barring only the delegation to the assignee of the assignor's performance.

(4) An assignment of "the contract" or of "all my rights under the contract" or an assignment in similar general terms is an assignment of rights and unless the language or the circumstances (as in an assignment for security) indicate the contrary, it is a delegation of performance of the duties of the assignor and its acceptance by the assignee constitutes a promise by him to perform those duties. This promise is enforceable by either the assignor or the other party to the original contract.

(5) The other party may treat any assignment which delegates performance as creating reasonable grounds for insecurity and may without prejudice to his rights against the assignor demand assurances from the assignee (Section 2-609).

Official Comments

Prior Uniform Statutory Provision: None.

Purposes:

1. Generally, this section recognizes both delegation of performance and assignability as normal and permissible incidents of a contract for the sale of goods.

2. Delegation of performance, either in conjunction with an assignment or otherwise, is provided for by subsection (1) where no substantial reason can be shown as to why the delegated performance will not be as satisfactory as personal performance.

3. Under subsection (2) rights which are no longer executory such as a right to damages for breach or a right to payment of an "account" as defined in the Article on Secured Transactions (Article 9) may be assigned although the agreement prohibits assignment. In such cases no question of delegation of any performance is involved. The assignment of a "contract right" as defined in the Article on Secured Transactions (Article 9) is not covered by this subsection.

4. The nature of the contract or the circumstances of the case, however, may bar assignment of the contract even where delegation of performance is not involved. This Article and this section are intended to clarify this problem, particularly in cases dealing with output requirement and exclusive dealing contracts. In the first place the section on requirements and exclusive dealing removes from the construction of the original contract most of the "personal discretion" element by substituting the reasonably objective standard of good faith operation of the plant or business to be supplied. Secondly, the section on insecurity and assurances, which is specifically referred to in subsection (5) of this section, frees the other party from the doubts and uncertainty

which may afflict him under an assignment of the character in question by permit-ting him to demand adequate assurance of due performance without which he may suspend his own performance. Subsection (5) is not in any way intended to limit the effect of the section on insecurity and assurances and the word "performance" includes the giving of orders under a requirements contract. Of course, in any case where a material personal discretion is sought to be transferred, effective assignment is barred by subsection (2).

5. Subsection (4) lays down a general rule of construction distinguishing between a normal commercial assignment, which substitutes the assignee for the assignor both as to rights and duties, and a financing assignment in which only the assignor's rights are transferred.

This Article takes no position on the possibility of extending some recognition or power to the original parties to work out normal commercial readjustments of the contract in the case of financing assignments even after the original obligor has been notified of the assignment. This question is dealt with in the Article on Secured Trans-actions (Article 9).

6. Subsection (5) recognizes that the non-assigning original party has a stake in the reliability of the person with whom he has closed the original contract, and is, therefore, entitled to due assurance that any delegated performance will be properly forthcoming.

7. This section is not intended as a complete statement of the law of delegation and assignment but is limited to clarifying a few points doubtful under the case law. Particularly, neither this section nor this Article touches directly on such questions as the need or effect of notice of the assignment, the rights of successive assignees, or any question of the form of an assignment, either as between the parties or as against any third parties. Some of these questions are dealt with in Article 9.

Cross References:

Point 3: Articles 5 and 9.

Point 4: Sections 2-306 and 2-609.

Point 5: Article 9, Sections 9-317 and 9-318.

Point 7: Article 9.

Definitional Cross References:

"Agreement". Section 1-201.

"Buyer". Section 2-103.

"Contract". Section 1-201.

"Party". Section 1-201.

"Rights". Section 1-201.

"Seller". Section 2-103.

"Term". Section 1-201.

PART 3. GENERAL OBLIGATION AND CONSTRUCTION OF CONTRACT

§ 2-301. General Obligations of Parties

The obligation of the seller is to transfer and deliver and that of the buyer is to accept and pay in accordance with the contract.

Official Comments

Prior Uniform Statutory Provision: Sections 11 and 41, Uniform Sales Act.

Changes: Rewritten.

Purposes of Changes:

This section uses the term "obligation" in contrast to the term "duty" in order to provide for the "condition" aspects of delivery and payment insofar as they are not modified by other sections of this Article such as those on cure of tender. It thus replaces not only the general provisions of the Uniform Sales Act on the parties' duties, but also the general provisions of that Act on the effect of conditions. In order to determine what is "in accordance with the contract" under this Article usage of trade, course of dealing and performance, and the general background of circumstances must be given due consideration in conjunction with the lay meaning of the words used to define the scope of the conditions and duties.

Cross References:

Section 1-106. See also Sections 1-205, 2-208, 2-209, 2-508 and 2-612.

Definitional Cross References:

"Buyer". Section 2-103.

"Contract". Section 1-201.

"Party". Section 1-201.

"Seller". Section 2-103.

§ 2-302. Unconscionable Contract or Clause

(1) If the court as a matter of law finds the contract or any clause of the contract to have been unconscionable at the time it was made the court may refuse to enforce the contract, or it may enforce the remainder of the contract without the unconscionable clause, or it may so limit the application of any unconscionable clause as to avoid any unconscionable result.

(2) When it is claimed or appears to the court that the contract or any clause thereof may be unconscionable the parties shall be afforded a reasonable opportunity to present evidence as to its commercial setting, purpose and effect to aid the court in making the determination.

Official Comments

Prior Uniform Statutory Provision: None.

Purposes:

1. This section is intended to make it possible for the courts to police explicitly against the contracts or clauses which they find to be unconscionable. In the past such policing has been accomplished by adverse construction of language, by manipulation of the rules of offer and acceptance or by determinations that the clause is contrary to public policy or to the dominant purpose of the contract. This section is intended to allow the court to pass directly on the unconscionability of the contract or particular clause therein and to make a conclusion of law as to its unconscionability. The basic test is whether, in the light of the general commercial background and the commercial needs of the particular trade or case, the clauses involved are so one-sided as to be unconscionable under the circumstances existing at the time of the making of the contract. Subsection (2) makes it clear that it is proper for the court to hear evidence upon these questions. The principle is one of the prevention of oppression and unfair surprise (Cf. Campbell Soup Co. v. Wentz, 172 F.2d 80, 3d Cir. 1948) and not of disturbance of allocation of risks because of superior bargaining power. The underlying basis of this section is illustrated by the results in cases such as the following:

Kansas City Wholesale Grocery Co. v. Weber Packing Corporation, 93 Utah 414, 73 P.2d 1272 (1937), where a clause limiting time for complaints was held inapplicable to latent defects in a shipment of catsup which could be discovered only by microscopic analysis; Hardy v. General Motors Acceptance Corporation, 38 Ga. App. 463, 144 S.E. 327 (1928), holding that a disclaimer of warranty clause applied only to express warranties, thus letting in a fair implied warranty; Andrews Bros. v. Singer & Co. (1934 CA) 1 K.B. 17, holding that where a car with substantial mileage was delivered instead of a "new" car, a disclaimer of warranties, including those "implied," left unaffected an "express obligation" on the description, even though the Sale of Goods Act called such an implied warranty; New Prague Flouring Mill Co. v. G. A. Spears, 194 Iowa 417, 189 N.W. 815 (1922), holding that a clause permitting the seller, upon the buyer's failure to supply shipping instructions, to cancel, ship, or allow delivery date to be indefinitely postponed 30 days at a time by the inaction, does not indefinitely postpone the date of measuring damages for the buyer's breach, to the seller's advantage; and Kansas Flour Mills Co. v. Dirks, 100 Kan. 376, 164 P. 273 (1917), where under a similar clause in a rising market the court permitted the buyer to measure his damages for non-delivery at the end of only one 30 day postponement; Green v. Arcos, Ltd. (1931 CA) 47 T.L.R. 336, where a blanket clause prohibiting rejection of shipments by the buyer was restricted to apply to shipments where discrepancies represented merely mercantile variations; Meyer v. Packard Cleveland Motor Co., 106 Ohio St. 328, 140 N.E. 118 (1922), in which the court held that a "waiver" of all agreements not specified did not preclude implied warranty of fitness of a rebuilt dump truck for ordinary use as a dump truck; Austin Co. v. J. H. Tillman Co., 104 Or. 541, 209 P. 131 (1922), where a clause limiting the buyer's remedy to return was held to be applicable only if the seller had delivered a machine needed for a construction job which reasonably met the contract description; Bekkevold v. Potts, 173 Minn. 87, 216 N.W. 790, 59 A.L.R. 1164 (1927), refusing to allow warranty of fitness for purpose imposed by law to be negated by clause excluding all warranties "made" by the seller; Robert A. Munroe & Co. v. Meyer (1930) 2 K.B. 312, holding that the warranty of description overrides a clause reading "with all faults and defects" where adulterated meat not up to the contract description was delivered.

2. Under this section the court, in its discretion, may refuse to enforce the contract as a whole if it is permeated by the unconscionability, or it may strike any single clause or group of clauses which are so tainted or which are contrary to the essential purpose of the agreement, or it may simply limit unconscionable clauses so as to avoid unconscionable results.

3. The present section is addressed to the court, and the decision is to be made by it. The commercial evidence referred to in subsection (2) is for the court's consideration, not the jury's. Only the agreement which results from the court's action on these matters is to be submitted to the general triers of the facts.

Definitional Cross Reference:

"Contract". Section 1-201.

§ 2-303. Allocation or Division of Risks

Where this Article allocates a risk or a burden as between the parties "unless otherwise agreed", the agreement may not only shift the allocation but may also divide the risk or burden.

Official Comments

Prior Uniform Statutory Provision: None.

Purposes:

1. This section is intended to make it clear that the parties may modify or allocate "unless otherwise agreed" risks or burdens imposed by this Article as they desire, always subject, of course, to the provisions on unconscionability.

Compare Section 1-102(4).

2. The risk or burden may be divided by the express terms of the agreement or by the attending circumstances, since under the definition of "agreement" in this Act the circumstances surrounding the transaction as well as the express language used by the parties enter into the meaning and substance of the agreement.

Cross References:

Point 1: Sections 1-102, 2-302.

Point 2: Section 1-201.

Definitional Cross References:

"Party". Section 1-201.

"Agreement". Section 1-201.

§ 2-304. Price Payable in Money, Goods, Realty, or Otherwise

(1) The price can be made payable in money or otherwise. If it is payable in whole or in part in goods each party is a seller of the goods which he is to transfer.

(2) Even though all or part of the price is payable in an interest in realty the transfer of the goods and the seller's obligations with reference to them are subject to this Article, but not the transfer of the interest in realty or the transferor's obligations in connection therewith.

Official Comments

Prior Uniform Statutory Provision: Subsections (2) and (3) of Section 9, Uniform Sales Act.

Changes: Rewritten.

Purposes of Changes:

1. This section corrects the phrasing of the Uniform Sales Act so as to avoid misconstruction and produce greater accuracy in commercial result. While it continues the essential intent and purpose of the Uniform Sales Act it rejects any purely verbalistic construction in disregard of the underlying reason of the provisions.

2. Under subsection (1) the provisions of this Article are applicable to transactions where the "price" of goods is payable in something other than money. This does not mean, however, that this whole Article applies automatically and in its entirety simply because an agreed transfer of title to goods is not a gift. The basic purposes and reasons of the Article must always be considered in determining the applicability of any of its provisions.

3. Subsection (2) lays down the general principle that when goods are to be exchanged for realty, the provisions of this Article apply only to those aspects of the transaction which concern the transfer of title to goods but do not affect the transfer of the realty since the detailed regulation of various particular contracts which fall outside the scope of this Article is left to the courts and other legislation. However, the complexities of these situations may be such that each must be analyzed in the light of the underlying reasons in order to determine the applicable principles. Local statutes dealing with realty are not to be lightly disregarded or altered by language of this Article. In contrast, this Article declares definite policies in regard to certain matters legitimately within its scope though concerned with real property situations, and in those instances the provisions of this Article control.

Cross References:

Point 1: Section 1-102.

Point 3: Sections 1-102, 1-103, 1-104 and 2-107.

Definitional Cross References:

"Goods". Section 2-105.

"Money". Section 1-201.

"Party". Section 1-201.

"Seller". Section 2-103.

§ 2-305. Open Price Term

(1) The parties if they so intend can conclude a contract for sale even though the price is not settled. In such a case the price is a reasonable price at the time for delivery if

    (a) nothing is said as to price; or

    (b) the price is left to be agreed by the parties and they fail to agree; or

    (c) the price is to be fixed in terms of some agreed market or other standard as set or recorded by a third person or agency and it is not so set or recorded.

(2) A price to be fixed by the seller or by the buyer means a price for him to fix in good faith.

(3) When a price left to be fixed otherwise than by agreement of the parties fails to be fixed through fault of one party the other may at his option treat the contract as cancelled or himself fix a reasonable price.

(4) Where, however, the parties intend not to be bound unless the price be fixed or agreed and it is not fixed or agreed there is no contract. In such a case the buyer must return any goods already received or if unable so to do must pay their reasonable value at the time of delivery and the seller must return any portion of the price paid on account.

Official Comments

Prior Uniform Statutory Provision: Sections 9 and 10, Uniform Sales Act.

Changes: Completely rewritten.

Purposes of Changes:

1. This section applies when the price term is left open on the making of an agreement which is nevertheless intended by the parties to be a binding agreement. This Article rejects in these instances the formula that "an agreement to agree is unenforceable" if the case falls within subsection (1) of this section, and rejects also defeating such agreements on the ground of "indefiniteness". Instead this Article recognizes the

dominant intention of the parties to have the deal continue to be binding upon both. As to future performance, since this Article recognizes remedies such as cover (Section 2-712), resale (Section 2-706) and specific performance (Section 2-716) which go beyond any mere arithmetic as between contract price and market price, there is usually a "reasonably certain basis for granting an appropriate remedy for breach" so that the contract need not fail for indefiniteness.

2. Under some circumstances the postponement of agreement on price will mean that no deal has really been concluded, and this is made express in the preamble of subsection (1) ("The parties if they so intend") and in subsection (4). Whether or not this is so is, in most cases, a question to be determined by the trier of fact.

3. Subsection (2), dealing with the situation where the price is to be fixed by one party rejects the uncommercial idea that an agreement that the seller may fix the price means that he may fix any price he may wish by the express qualification that the price so fixed must be fixed in good faith. Good faith includes observance of reasonable commercial standards of fair dealing in the trade if the party is a merchant. (Section 2-103). But in the normal case a "posted price" or a future seller's or buyer's "given price," "price in effect," "market price," or the like satisfies the good faith requirement.

4. The section recognizes that there may be cases in which a particular person's judgment is not chosen merely as a barometer or index of a fair price but is an essential condition to the parties' intent to make any contract at all. For example, the case where a known and trusted expert is to "value" a particular painting for which there is no market standard differs sharply from the situation where a named expert is to determine the grade of cotton, and the difference would support a finding that in the one the parties did not intend to make a binding agreement if that expert were unavailable whereas in the other they did so intend. Other circumstances would of course affect the validity of such a finding.

5. Under subsection (3), wrongful interference by one party with any agreed machinery for price fixing in the contract may be treated by the other party as a repudiation justifying cancellation, or merely as a failure to take cooperative action thus shifting to the aggrieved party the reasonable leeway in fixing the price.

6. Throughout the entire section, the purpose is to give effect to the agreement which has been made. That effect, however, is always conditioned by the requirement of good faith action which is made an inherent part of all contracts within this Act. (Section 1-203).

Cross References:

Point 1: Sections 2-204(3), 2-706, 2-712 and 2-716.

Point 3: Section 2-103.

Point 5: Sections 2-311 and 2-610.

Point 6: Section 1-203.

Definitional Cross References:

"Agreement". Section 1-201.

"Burden of establishing". Section 1-201.

"Buyer". Section 2-103.

"Cancellation". Section 2-106.

"Contract". Section 1-201.

"Contract for sale". Section 2-106.

"Fault". Section 1-201.

"Goods". Section 2-105.

"Party". Section 1-201.

"Receipt of goods". Section 2-103.

"Seller". Section 2-103.

"Term". Section 1-201.

§ 2-306. Output, Requirements and Exclusive Dealings

(1) A term which measures the quantity by the output of the seller or the requirements of the buyer means such actual output or requirements as may occur in good faith, except that no quantity unreasonably disproportionate to any stated estimate or in the absence of a stated estimate to any normal or otherwise comparable prior output or requirements may be tendered or demanded.

(2) A lawful agreement by either the seller or the buyer for exclusive dealing in the kind of goods concerned imposes unless otherwise agreed an obligation by the seller to use best efforts to supply the goods and by the buyer to use best efforts to promote their sale.

Official Comments

Prior Uniform Statutory Provision: None.

Purposes:

1. Subsection (1) of this section, in regard to output and requirements, applies to this specific problem the general approach of this Act which requires the reading of commercial background and intent into the language of any agreement and demands good faith in the performance of that agreement. It applies to such contracts of non-producing establishments such as dealers or distributors as well as to manufacturing concerns.

2. Under this Article, a contract for output or requirements is not too indefinite since it is held to mean the actual good faith output or requirements of the particular party. Nor does such a contract lack mutuality of obligation since, under this section,

the party who will determine quantity is required to operate his plant or conduct his business in good faith and according to commercial standards of fair dealing in the trade so that his output or requirements will approximate a reasonably foreseeable figure. Reasonable elasticity in the requirements is expressly envisaged by this section and good faith variations from prior requirements are permitted even when the variation may be such as to result in discontinuance. A shut-down by a requirements buyer for lack of orders might be permissible when a shut-down merely to curtail losses would not. The essential test is whether the party is acting in good faith. Similarly, a sudden expansion of the plant by which requirements are to be measured would not be included within the scope of the contract as made but normal expansion undertaken in good faith would be within the scope of this section. One of the factors in an expansion situation would be whether the market price had risen greatly in a case in which the requirements contract contained a fixed price. Reasonable variation of an extreme sort is exemplified in Southwest Natural Gas Co. v. Oklahoma Portland Cement Co., 102 F.2d 630 (C.C.A. 10, 1939). This Article takes no position as to whether a requirements contract is a provable claim in bankruptcy.

3. If an estimate of output or requirements is included in the agreement, no quantity unreasonably disproportionate to it may be tendered or demanded. Any minimum or maximum set by the agreement shows a clear limit on the intended elasticity. In similar fashion, the agreed estimate is to be regarded as a center around which the parties intend the variation to occur.

4. When an enterprise is sold, the question may arise whether the buyer is bound by an existing output or requirements contract. That question is outside the scope of this Article, and is to be determined on other principles of law. Assuming that the contract continues, the output or requirements in the hands of the new owner continue to be measured by the actual good faith output or requirements under the normal operation of the enterprise prior to sale. The sale itself is not grounds for sudden expansion or decrease.

5. Subsection (2), on exclusive dealing, makes explicit the commercial rule embodied in this Act under which the parties to such contracts are held to have impliedly, even when not expressly, bound themselves to use reasonable diligence as well as good faith in their performance of the contract. Under such contracts the exclusive agent is required, although no express commitment has been made, to use reasonable effort and due diligence in the expansion of the market or the promotion of the product, as the case may be. The principal is expected under such a contract to refrain from supplying any other dealer or agent within the exclusive territory. An exclusive dealing agreement brings into play all of the good faith aspects of the output and requirement problems of subsection (1). It also raises questions of insecurity and right to adequate assurance under this Article.

Cross References:

Point 4: Section 2-210.

Point 5: Sections 1-203 and 2-609.

Definitional Cross References:

"Agreement". Section 1-201.

"Buyer". Section 2-103.

"Contract for sale". Section 2-106.

"Good faith". Section 1-201.

"Goods". Section 2-105.

"Party". Section 1-201.

"Term". Section 1-201.

"Seller". Section 2-103.

§ 2-307. Delivery in Single Lot or Several Lots

Unless otherwise agreed all goods called for by a contract for sale must be tendered in a single delivery and payment is due only on such tender but where the circumstances give either party the right to make or demand delivery in lots the price if it can be apportioned may be demanded for each lot.

Official Comments

Prior Uniform Statutory Provision: Section 45(1), Uniform Sales Act.

Changes: Rewritten and expanded.

Purposes of Changes:

1. This section applies where the parties have not specifically agreed whether delivery and payment are to be by lots and generally continues the essential intent of original Act, Section 45(1) by assuming that the parties intended delivery to be in a single lot.

2. Where the actual agreement or the circumstances do not indicate otherwise, delivery in lots is not permitted under this section and the buyer is properly entitled to reject for a deficiency in the tender, subject to any privilege in the seller to cure the tender.

3. The "but" clause of this section goes to the case in which it is not commercially feasible to deliver or to receive the goods in a single lot as for example, where a contract calls for the shipment of ten carloads of coal and only three cars are available at a given time. Similarly, in a contract involving brick necessary to build a building the buyer's storage space may be limited so that it would be impossible to receive the entire amount of brick at once, or it may be necessary to assemble the goods as in the case of cattle on the range, or to mine them.

In such cases, a partial delivery is not subject to rejection for the defect in quantity alone, if the circumstances do not indicate a repudiation or default by the seller as to the expected balance or do not give the buyer ground for suspending his performance because of insecurity under the provisions of Section 2-609. However, in such cases the undelivered balance of goods under the contract must be forthcoming within a reasonable time and in a reasonable manner according to the policy of Section 2-503 on manner of tender of delivery. This is reinforced by the express provisions of Section 2-608 that if a lot has been accepted on the reasonable assumption that its nonconformity will be cured, the acceptance may be revoked if the cure does not seasonably occur. The section rejects the rule of Kelly Construction Co. v. Hackensack Brick Co., 91 N.J.L. 585, 103 A. 417, 2 A.L.R. 685 (1918) and approves the result in Lynn M. Ranger, Inc. v. Gildersleeve, 106 Conn. 372, 138 A. 142 (1927) in which a contract was made for six carloads of coal then rolling from the mines and consigned to the seller but the seller agreed to divert the carloads to the buyer as soon as the car numbers became known to him. He arranged a diversion of two cars and then notified the buyer who then repudiated the contract. The seller was held to be entitled to his full remedy for the two cars diverted because simultaneous delivery of all of the cars was not contemplated by either party.

4. Where the circumstances indicate that a party has a right to delivery in lots, the price may be demanded for each lot if it is apportionable.

Cross References:

Point 1: Section 1-201.

Point 2: Sections 2-508 and 2-601.

Point 3: Sections 2-503, 2-608 and 2-609.

Definitional Cross References:

"Contract for sale". Section 2-106.

"Goods". Section 2-105.

"Lot". Section 2-105.

"Party". Section 1-201.

"Rights". Section 1-201.

§ 2-308. Absence of Specified Place for Delivery Unless otherwise agreed

(a) the place for delivery of goods is the seller's place of business or if he has none his residence; but

(b) in a contract for sale of identified goods which to the knowledge of the parties at the time of contracting are in some other place, that place is the place for their delivery; and

(c) documents of title may be delivered through customary banking channels.

Official Comments

Prior Uniform Statutory Provision: Paragraphs (a) and (b) — Section 43(1), Uniform Sales Act; Paragraph (c) — none.

Changes: Slight modification in language.

Purposes of Changes and New Matter:

1. Paragraphs (a) and (b) provide for those noncommercial sales and for those occasional commercial sales where no place or means of delivery has been agreed upon by the parties. Where delivery by carrier is "required or authorized by the agreement", the seller's duties as to delivery of the goods are governed not by this section but by Section 2-504.

2. Under paragraph (b) when the identified goods contracted for are known to both parties to be in some location other than the seller's place of business or residence, the parties are presumed to have intended that place to be the place of delivery. This paragraph also applies (unless, as would be normal, the circumstances show that delivery by way of documents is intended) to a bulk of goods in the possession of a bailee. In such a case, however, the seller has the additional obligation to procure the acknowledgment by the bailee of the buyer's right to possession.

3. Where "customary banking channels" call only for due notification by the banker that the documents are on hand, leaving the buyer himself to see to the physical receipt of the goods, tender at the buyer's address is not required under paragraph (c). But that paragraph merely eliminates the possibility of a default by the seller if "customary banking channels" have been properly used in giving notice to the buyer. Where the bank has purchased a draft accompanied by documents or has undertaken its collection on behalf of the seller, Part 5 of Article 4 spells out its duties and relations to its customer. Where the documents move forward under a letter of credit the Article on Letters of Credit spells out the duties and relations between the bank, the seller and the buyer.

4. The rules of this section apply only "unless otherwise agreed." The surrounding circumstances, usage of trade, course of dealing and course of performance, as well as the express language of the parties, may constitute an "otherwise agreement".

Cross References:

Point 1: Sections 2-504 and 2-505.

Point 2: Section 2-503.

Point 3: Section 2-512, Articles 4, Part 5, and 5.

Definitional Cross References:

"Contract for sale". Section 2-106.

"Delivery". Section 1-201.

"Document of title". Section 1-201.

"Goods". Section 2-105.

"Party". Section 1-201.

"Seller". Section 2-103.

§ 2-309. Absence of Specific Time Provisions; Notice of Termination

(1) The time for shipment or delivery or any other action under a contract if not provided in this Article or agreed upon shall be a reasonable time.

(2) Where the contract provides for successive performances but is indefinite in duration it is valid for a reasonable time but unless otherwise agreed may be terminated at any time by either party.

(3) Termination of a contract by one party except on the happening of an agreed event requires that reasonable notification be received by the other party and an agreement dispensing with notification is invalid if its operation would be unconscionable.

Official Comments

Prior Uniform Statutory Provision: Subsection (1) — see Sections 43(2), 45(2), 47(1) and 48, Uniform Sales Act, for policy continued under this Article; Subsection (2) — none; Subsection (3) — none.

Changes: Completely different in scope.

Purposes of Changes and New Matter:

1. Subsection (1) requires that all actions taken under a sales contract must be taken within a reasonable time where no time has been agreed upon. The reasonable time under this provision turns on the criteria as to "reasonable time" and on good faith and commercial standards set forth in Sections 1-203, 1-204 and 2-103. It thus depends upon what constitutes acceptable commercial conduct in view of the nature, purpose and circumstances of the action to be taken. Agreement as to a definite time, however, may be found in a term implied from the contractual circumstances, usage of trade or course of dealing or performance as well as in an express term. Such cases fall outside of this subsection since in them the time for action is "agreed" by usage.

2. The time for payment, where not agreed upon, is related to the time for delivery; the particular problems which arise in connection with determining the appropriate time of payment and the time for any inspection before payment which is both allowed by law and demanded by the buyer are covered in Section 2-513.

3. The facts in regard to shipment and delivery differ so widely as to make detailed provision for them in the text of this Article impracticable. The applicable principles, however, make it clear that surprise is to be avoided, good faith judgment is to be protected, and notice or negotiation to reduce the uncertainty to certainty is to be favored.

4. When the time for delivery is left open, unreasonably early offers of or demands for delivery are intended to be read under this Article as expressions of desire or intention, requesting the assent or acquiescence of the other party, not as final positions which may amount without more to breach or to create breach by the other side. See Sections 2-207 and 2-609.

5. The obligation of good faith under this Act requires reasonable notification before a contract may be treated as breached because a reasonable time for delivery or demand has expired. This operates both in the case of a contract originally indefinite as to time and of one subsequently made indefinite by waiver.

When both parties let an originally reasonable time go by in silence, the course of conduct under the contract may be viewed as enlarging the reasonable time for tender or demand of performance. The contract may be terminated by abandonment.

6. Parties to a contract are not required in giving reasonable notification to fix, at peril of breach, a time which is in fact reasonable in the unforeseeable judgment of a later trier of fact. Effective communication of a proposed time limit calls for a response, so that failure to reply will make out acquiescence. Where objection is made, however, or if the demand is merely for information as to when goods will be delivered or will be ordered out, demand for assurances on the ground of insecurity may be made under this Article pending further negotiations. Only when a party insists on undue delay or on rejection of the other party's reasonable proposal is there a question of flat breach under the present section.

7. Subsection (2) applies a commercially reasonable view to resolve the conflict which has arisen in the cases as to contracts of indefinite duration. The "reasonable time" of duration appropriate to a given arrangement is limited by the circumstances. When the arrangement has been carried on by the parties over the years, the "reasonable time" can continue indefinitely and the contract will not terminate until notice.

8. Subsection (3) recognizes that the application of principles of good faith and sound commercial practice normally call for such notification of the termination of a going contract relationship as will give the other party reasonable time to seek a substitute arrangement. An agreement dispensing with notification or limiting the time for the seeking of a substitute arrangement is, of course, valid under this subsection unless the results of putting it into operation would be the creation of an unconscionable state of affairs.

9. Justifiable cancellation for breach is a remedy for breach and is not the kind of termination covered by the present subsection.

10. The requirement of notification is dispensed with where the contract provides for termination on the happening of an "agreed event." "Event" is a term chosen here to contrast with "option" or the like.

Cross References:

Point 1: Sections 1-203, 1-204 and 2-103.

Point 2: Sections 2-320, 2-321, 2-504, and 2-511 through 2-514.

Point 5: Section 1-203.

Point 6: Section 2-609.

Point 7: Section 2-204.

Point 9: Sections 2-106, 2-318, 2-610 and 2-703.

Definitional Cross References:

"Agreement". Section 1-201.

"Contract". Section 1-201.

"Notification". Section 1-201.

"Party". Section 1-201.

"Reasonable time". Section 1-204.

"Termination". Section 2-106.

§ 2-310. Open Time for Payment or Running of Credit; Authority to Ship Under Reservation Unless otherwise agreed

(a) payment is due at the time and place at which the buyer is to receive the goods even though the place of shipment is the place of delivery; and

(b) if the seller is authorized to send the goods he may ship them under reservation, and may tender the documents of title, but the buyer may inspect the goods after their arrival before payment is due unless such inspection is inconsistent with the terms of the contract (Section 2-513); and

(c) if delivery is authorized and made by way of documents of title otherwise than by subsection (b) then payment is due at the time and place at which the buyer is to receive the documents regardless of where the goods are to be received; and

(d) where the seller is required or authorized to ship the goods on credit the credit period runs from the time of shipment but post-dating the invoice or delaying its dispatch will correspondingly delay the starting of the credit period.

Official Comments

Prior Uniform Statutory Provision: Sections 42 and 47(2), Uniform Sales Act.

Changes: Completely rewritten in this and other sections.

Purposes of Changes: This section is drawn to reflect modern business methods of dealing at a distance rather than face to face. Thus:

1. Paragraph (a) provides that payment is due at the time and place "the buyer is to receive the goods" rather than at the point of delivery except in documentary shipment cases (paragraph (c)). This grants an opportunity for the exercise by the buyer of his preliminary right to inspection before paying even though under the delivery term the risk of loss may have previously passed to him or the running of the credit period has already started.

2. Paragraph (b) while providing for inspection by the buyer before he pays, protects the seller. He is not required to give up possession of the goods until he has received payment, where no credit has been contemplated by the parties. The seller may collect

through a bank by a sight draft against an order bill of lading "hold until arrival; inspection allowed." The obligations of the bank under such a provision are set forth in Part 5 of Article 4. In the absence of a credit term, the seller is permitted to ship under reservation and if he does payment is then due where and when the buyer is to receive the documents.

3. Unless otherwise agreed, the place for the receipt of the documents and payment is the buyer's city but the time for payment is only after arrival of the goods, since under paragraph (b), and Sections 2-512 and 2-513 the buyer is under no duty to pay prior to inspection.

4. Where the mode of shipment is such that goods must be unloaded immediately upon arrival, too rapidly to permit adequate inspection before receipt, the seller must be guided by the provisions of this Article on inspection which provide that if the seller wishes to demand payment before inspection, he must put an appropriate term into the contract. Even requiring payment against documents will not of itself have this desired result if the documents are to be held until the arrival of the goods. But under (b) and (c) if the terms are C.I.F., C.O.D., or cash against documents payment may be due before inspection.

5. Paragraph (d) states the common commercial understanding that an agreed credit period runs from the time of shipment or from that dating of the invoice which is commonly recognized as a representation of the time of shipment. The provision concerning any delay in sending forth the invoice is included because such conduct results in depriving the buyer of his full notice and warning as to when he must be prepared to pay.

Cross References:

Generally: Part 5.

Point 1: Section 2-509.

Point 2: Sections 2-505, 2-511, 2-512, 2-513 and Article 4.

Point 3: Sections 2-308(b), 2-512 and 2-513.

Point 4: Section 2-513(3)(b).

Definitional Cross References:

"Buyer". Section 2-103.

"Delivery". Section 1-201.

"Document of title". Section 1-201.

"Goods". Section 2-105.

"Receipt of goods". Section 2-103.

"Seller". Section 2-103.

"Send". Section 1-201.

"Term". Section 1-201.

§ 2-311. Options and Cooperation Respecting Performance

(1) An agreement for sale which is otherwise sufficiently definite (subsection (3) of Section 2-204) to be a contract is not made invalid by the fact that it leaves particulars of performance to be specified by one of the parties. Any such specification must be made in good faith and within limits set by commercial reasonableness.

(2) Unless otherwise agreed specifications relating to assortment of the goods are at the buyer's option and except as otherwise provided in subsections (1)(c) and (3) of Section 2-319 specifications or arrangements relating to shipment are at the seller's option.

(3) Where such specification would materially affect the other party's performance but is not seasonably made or where one party's cooperation is necessary to the agreed performance of the other but is not seasonably forthcoming, the other party in addition to all other remedies
   (a) is excused for any resulting delay in his own performance; and
   (b) may also either proceed to perform in any reasonable manner or after the time for a material part of his own performance treat the failure to specify or to cooperate as a breach by failure to deliver or accept the goods.

Official Comments

Prior Uniform Statutory Provision: None.

Purposes:

1. Subsection (1) permits the parties to leave certain detailed particulars of performance to be filled in by either of them without running the risk of having the contract invalidated for indefiniteness. The party to whom the agreement gives power to specify the missing details is required to exercise good faith and to act in accordance with commercial standards so that there is no surprise and the range of permissible variation is limited by what is commercially reasonable. The "agreement" which permits one party so to specify may be found as well in a course of dealing, usage of trade, or implication from circumstances as in explicit language used by the parties.

2. Options as to assortment of goods or shipping arrangements are specifically reserved to the buyer and seller respectively under subsection (2) where no other arrangement has been made. This section rejects the test which mechanically and without regard to usage or the purpose of the option gave the option to the party "first under a duty to move" and applies instead a standard commercial interpretation to these circumstances. The "unless otherwise agreed" provision of this subsection covers not only express terms but the background and circumstances which enter into the agreement.

3. Subsection (3) applies when the exercise of an option or cooperation by one party is necessary to or materially affects the other party's performance, but it is not seasonably forthcoming; the subsection relieves the other party from the necessity for perfor-

mance or excuses his delay in performance as the case may be. The contract-keeping party may at his option under this subsection proceed to perform in any commercially reasonable manner rather than wait. In addition to the special remedies provided, this subsection also reserves "all other remedies". The remedy of particular importance in this connection is that provided for insecurity. Request may also be made pursuant to the obligation of good faith for a reasonable indication of the time and manner of performance for which a party is to hold himself ready.

4. The remedy provided in subsection (3) is one which does not operate in the situation which falls within the scope of Section 2-614 on substituted performance. Where the failure to cooperate results from circumstances set forth in that Section, the other party is under a duty to proffer or demand (as the case may be) substitute performance as a condition to claiming rights against the noncooperating party.

Cross References:

Point 1: Sections 1-201, 2-204 and 1-203.

Point 3: Sections 1-203 and 2-609.

Point 4: Section 2-614.

Definitional Cross References:

"Agreement". Section 1-201.

"Buyer". Section 2-103.

"Contract for sale". Section 2-106.

"Goods". Section 2-105.

"Party". Section 1-201.

"Remedy". Section 1-201.

"Seasonably". Section 1-204.

"Seller". Section 2-103.

§ 2-312. Warranty of Title and Against Infringement; Buyer's Obligation Against Infringement

(1) Subject to subsection (2) there is in a contract for sale a warranty by the seller that
   (a) the title conveyed shall be good, and its transfer rightful; and
   (b) the goods shall be delivered free from any security interest or other lien or encumbrance of which the buyer at the time of contracting has no knowledge.

(2) A warranty under subsection (1) will be excluded or modified only by specific language or by circumstances which give the buyer reason to know that the person selling does not claim title in himself or that he is purporting to sell only such right or title as he or a third person may have.

(3) Unless otherwise agreed a seller who is a merchant regularly dealing in goods of the kind warrants that the goods shall be delivered free of the rightful claim of any third person by way of infringement or the like but a buyer who furnishes specifications to the seller must hold the seller harmless against any such claim which arises out of compliance with the specifications.

Official Comments

Prior Uniform Statutory Provision: Section 13, Uniform Sales Act.

Changes: Completely rewritten, the provisions concerning infringement being new.

Purposes of Changes:

1. Subsection (1) makes provision for a buyer's basic needs in respect to a title which he in good faith expects to acquire by his purchase, namely, that he receive a good, clean title transferred to him also in a rightful manner so that he will not be exposed to a lawsuit in order to protect it.

The warranty extends to a buyer whether or not the seller was in possession of the goods at the time the sale or contract to sell was made.

The warranty of quiet possession is abolished. Disturbance of quiet possession, although not mentioned specifically, is one way, among many, in which the breach of the warranty of title may be established.

The "knowledge" referred to in subsection 1(b) is actual knowledge as distinct from notice.

2. The provisions of this Article requiring notification to the seller within a reasonable time after the buyer's discovery of a breach apply to notice of a breach of the warranty of title, where the seller's breach was innocent. However, if the seller's breach was in bad faith he cannot be permitted to claim that he has been misled or prejudiced by the delay in giving notice. In such case the "reasonable" time for notice should receive a very liberal interpretation. Whether the breach by the seller is in good or bad faith Section 2-725 provides that the cause of action accrues when the breach occurs. Under the provisions of that section the breach of the warranty of good title occurs when tender of delivery is made since the warranty is not one which extends to "future performance of the goods."

3. When the goods are part of the seller's normal stock and are sold in his normal course of business, it is his duty to see that no claim of infringement of a patent or trademark by a third party will mar the buyer's title. A sale by a person other than a dealer, however, raises no implication in its circumstances of such a warranty. Nor is there such an implication when the buyer orders goods to be assembled, prepared or manufactured on his own specifications. If, in such a case, the resulting product infringes a patent or trademark, the liability will run from buyer to seller. There is, under such circumstances, a tacit representation on the part of the buyer that the seller will

be safe in manufacturing according to the specifications, and the buyer is under an obligation in good faith to indemnify him for any loss suffered.

4. This section rejects the cases which recognize the principle that infringements violate the warranty of title but deny the buyer a remedy unless he has been expressly prevented from using the goods. Under this Article "eviction" is not a necessary condition to the buyer's remedy since the buyer's remedy arises immediately upon receipt of notice of infringement; it is merely one way of establishing the fact of breach.

5. Subsection (2) recognizes that sales by sheriffs, executors, foreclosing lienors and persons similarly situated are so out of the ordinary commercial course that their peculiar character is immediately apparent to the buyer and therefore no personal obligation is imposed upon the seller who is purporting to sell only an unknown or limited right. This subsection does not touch upon and leaves open all questions of restitution arising in such cases, when a unique article so sold is reclaimed by a third party as the rightful owner.

6. The warranty of subsection (1) is not designated as an "implied" warranty, and hence is not subject to Section 2-316(3). Disclaimer of the warranty of title is governed instead by subsection (2), which requires either specific language or the described circumstances.

Cross References:

Point 1: Section 2-403.

Point 2: Sections 2-607 and 2-725.

Point 3: Section 1-203.

Point 4: Sections 2-609 and 2-725.

Point 6: Section 2-316.

Definitional Cross References:

"Buyer". Section 2-103.

"Contract for sale". Section 2-106.

"Goods". Section 2-105.

"Person". Section 1-201.

"Right". Section 1-201.

"Seller". Section 2-103.

§ 2-313. Express Warranties by Affirmation, Promise, Description, Sample

(1) Express warranties by the seller are created as follows:
   (a) Any affirmation of fact or promise made by the seller to the buyer which relates to the goods and becomes part of the basis of the bargain creates an express warranty that the goods shall conform to the affirmation or promise.

(b) Any description of the goods which is made part of the basis of the bargain creates an express warranty that the goods shall conform to the description.

(c) Any sample or model which is made part of the basis of the bargain creates an express warranty that the whole of the goods shall conform to the sample or model.

(2) It is not necessary to the creation of an express warranty that the seller use formal words such as "warrant" or "guarantee" or that he have a specific intention to make a warranty, but an affirmation merely of the value of the goods or a statement purporting to be merely the seller's opinion or commendation of the goods does not create a warranty.

Official Comments

Prior Uniform Statutory Provision: Sections 12, 14 and 16, Uniform Sales Act.

Changes: Rewritten.

Purposes of Changes: To consolidate and systematize basic principles with the result that:

1. "Express" warranties rest on "dickered" aspects of the individual bargain, and go so clearly to the essence of that bargain that words of disclaimer in a form are repugnant to the basic dickered terms. "Implied" warranties rest so clearly on a common factual situation or set of conditions that no particular language or action is necessary to evidence them and they will arise in such a situation unless unmistakably negated.

This section reverts to the older case law insofar as the warranties of description and sample are designated "express" rather than "implied".

2. Although this section is limited in its scope and direct purpose to warranties made by the seller to the buyer as part of a contract for sale, the warranty sections of this Article are not designed in any way to disturb those lines of case law growth which have recognized that warranties need not be confined either to sales contracts or to the direct parties to such a contract. They may arise in other appropriate circumstances such as in the case of bailments for hire, whether such bailment is itself the main contract or is merely a supplying of containers under a contract for the sale of their contents. The provisions of Section 2-318 on third party beneficiaries expressly recognize this case law development within one particular area. Beyond that, the matter is left to the case law with the intention that the policies of this Act may offer useful guidance in dealing with further cases as they arise.

3. The present section deals with affirmations of fact by the seller, descriptions of the goods or exhibitions of samples, exactly as any other part of a negotiation which ends in a contract is dealt with. No specific intention to make a warranty is necessary if any of these factors is made part of the basis of the bargain. In actual practice affirmations of fact made by the seller about the goods during a bargain are regarded as part of the description of those goods; hence no particular reliance on such statements need be shown in order to weave them into the fabric of the agreement. Rather, any fact which

is to take such affirmations, once made, out of the agreement requires clear affirmative proof. The issue normally is one of fact.

4. In view of the principle that the whole purpose of the law of warranty is to determine what it is that the seller has in essence agreed to sell, the policy is adopted of those cases which refuse except in unusual circumstances to recognize a material deletion of the seller's obligation. Thus, a contract is normally a contract for a sale of something describable and described. A clause generally disclaiming "all warranties, express or implied" cannot reduce the seller's obligation with respect to such description and therefore cannot be given literal effect under Section 2-316.

This is not intended to mean that the parties, if they consciously desire, cannot make their own bargain as they wish. But in determining what they have agreed upon good faith is a factor and consideration should be given to the fact that the probability is small that a real price is intended to be exchanged for a pseudo-obligation.

5. Paragraph (1)(b) makes specific some of the principles set forth above when a description of the goods is given by the seller.

A description need not be by words. Technical specifications, blueprints and the like can afford more exact description than mere language and if made part of the basis of the bargain goods must conform with them. Past deliveries may set the description of quality, either expressly or impliedly by course of dealing. Of course, all descriptions by merchants must be read against the applicable trade usages with the general rules as to merchantability resolving any doubts.

6. The basic situation as to statements affecting the true essence of the bargain is no different when a sample or model is involved in the transaction. This section includes both a "sample" actually drawn from the bulk of goods which is the subject matter of the sale, and a "model" which is offered for inspection when the subject matter is not at hand and which has not been drawn from the bulk of the goods.

Although the underlying principles are unchanged, the facts are often ambiguous when something is shown as illustrative, rather than as a straight sample. In general, the presumption is that any sample or model just as any affirmation of fact is intended to become a basis of the bargain. But there is no escape from the question of fact. When the seller exhibits a sample purporting to be drawn from an existing bulk, good faith of course requires that the sample be fairly drawn. But in mercantile experience the mere exhibition of a "sample" does not of itself show whether it is merely intended to "suggest" or to "be" the character of the subject-matter of the contract. The question is whether the seller has so acted with reference to the sample as to make him responsible that the whole shall have at least the values shown by it. The circumstances aid in answering this question. If the sample has been drawn from an existing bulk, it must be regarded as describing values of the goods contracted for unless it is accompanied by an unmistakable denial of such responsibility. If, on the other hand, a model of merchandise not on hand is offered, the mercantile presumption that it has become a literal description of the subject matter is not so strong, and particularly so if modification on the buyer's initiative impairs any feature of the model.

7. The precise time when words of description or affirmation are made or samples are shown is not material. The sole question is whether the language or samples or models are fairly to be regarded as part of the contract. If language is used after the closing of the deal (as when the buyer when taking delivery asks and receives an additional assurance), the warranty becomes a modification, and need not be supported by consideration if it is otherwise reasonable and in order (Section 2-209).

8. Concerning affirmations of value or a seller's opinion or commendation under subsection (2), the basic question remains the same: What statements of the seller have in the circumstances and in objective judgment become part of the basis of the bargain? As indicated above, all of the statements of the seller do so unless good reason is shown to the contrary. The provisions of subsection (2) are included, however, since common experience discloses that some statements or predictions cannot fairly be viewed as entering into the bargain. Even as to false statements of value, however, the possibility is left open that a remedy may be provided by the law relating to fraud or misrepresentation.

Cross References:

Point 1: Section 2-316.

Point 2: Sections 1-102(3) and 2-318.

Point 3: Section 2-316(2)(b).

Point 4: Section 2-316.

Point 5: Sections 1-205(4) and 2-314.

Point 6: Section 2-316.

Point 7: Section 2-209.

Point 8: Section 1-103.

Definitional Cross References:

"Buyer". Section 2-103.

"Conforming". Section 2-106.

"Goods". Section 2-105.

"Seller". Section 2-103.

§ 2-314. Implied Warranty: Merchantability; Usage of Trade

(1) Unless excluded or modified (Section 2-316), a warranty that the goods shall be merchantable is implied in a contract for their sale if the seller is a merchant with respect to goods of that kind. Under this section the serving for value of food or drink to be consumed either on the premises or elsewhere is a sale.

(2) Goods to be merchantable must be at least such as
   (a) pass without objection in the trade under the contract description; and
   (b) in the case of fungible goods, are of fair average quality within the description; and

(c) are fit for the ordinary purposes for which such goods are used; and

(d) run, within the variations permitted by the agreement, of even kind, quality and quantity within each unit and among all units involved; and

(e) are adequately contained, packaged, and labeled as the agreement may require; and

(f) conform to the promise or affirmations of fact made on the container or label if any.

(3) Unless excluded or modified (Section 2-316) other implied warranties may arise from course of dealing or usage of trade.

Official Comments

Prior Uniform Statutory Provision: Section 15(2), Uniform Sales Act.

Changes: Completely rewritten.

Purposes of Changes: This section, drawn in view of the steadily developing case law on the subject, is intended to make it clear that:

1. The seller's obligation applies to present sales as well as to contracts to sell subject to the effects of any examination of specific goods. (Subsection (2) of Section 2-316). Also, the warranty of merchantability applies to sales for use as well as to sales for resale.

2. The question when the warranty is imposed turns basically on the meaning of the terms of the agreement as recognized in the trade. Goods delivered under an agreement made by a merchant in a given line of trade must be of a quality comparable to that generally acceptable in that line of trade under the description or other designation of the goods used in the agreement. The responsibility imposed rests on any merchant-seller, and the absence of the words "grower or manufacturer or not" which appeared in Section 15(2) of the Uniform Sales Act does not restrict the applicability of this section.

3. A specific designation of goods by the buyer does not exclude the seller's obligation that they be fit for the general purposes appropriate to such goods. A contract for the sale of second-hand goods, however, involves only such obligation as is appropriate to such goods for that is their contract description. A person making an isolated sale of goods is not a "merchant" within the meaning of the full scope of this section and, thus, no warranty of merchantability would apply. His knowledge of any defects not apparent on inspection would, however, without need for express agreement and in keeping with the underlying reason of the present section and the provisions on good faith, impose an obligation that known material but hidden defects be fully disclosed.

4. Although a seller may not be a "merchant" as to the goods in question, if he states generally that they are "guaranteed" the provisions of this section may furnish a guide to the content of the resulting express warranty. This has particular significance in the case of second-hand sales, and has further significance in limiting the effect of fine-print disclaimer clauses where their effect would be inconsistent with large-print assertions of "guarantee".

5. The second sentence of subsection (1) covers the warranty with respect to food and drink. Serving food or drink for value is a sale, whether to be consumed on the premises or elsewhere. Cases to the contrary are rejected. The principal warranty is that stated in subsections (1) and (2)(c) of this section.

6. Subsection (2) does not purport to exhaust the meaning of "merchantable" nor to negate any of its attributes not specifically mentioned in the text of the statute, but arising by usage of trade or through case law. The language used is "must be at least such as…," and the intention is to leave open other possible attributes of merchantability.

7. Paragraphs (a) and (b) of subsection (2) are to be read together. Both refer, as indicated above, to the standards of that line of the trade which fits the transaction and the seller's business. "Fair average" is a term directly appropriate to agricultural bulk products and means goods centering around the middle belt of quality, not the least or the worst that can be understood in the particular trade by the designation, but such as can pass "without objection." Of course a fair percentage of the least is permissible but the goods are not "fair average" if they are all of the least or worst quality possible under the description. In cases of doubt as to what quality is intended, the price at which a merchant closes a contract is an excellent index of the nature and scope of his obligation under the present section.

8. Fitness for the ordinary purposes for which goods of the type are used is a fundamental concept of the present section and is covered in paragraph (c). As stated above, merchantability is also a part of the obligation owing to the purchaser for use. Correspondingly, protection, under this aspect of the warranty, of the person buying for resale to the ultimate consumer is equally necessary, and merchantable goods must therefore be "honestly" resalable in the normal course of business because they are what they purport to be.

9. Paragraph (d) on evenness of kind, quality and quantity follows case law. But precautionary language has been added as a remainder of the frequent usages of trade which permit substantial variations both with and without an allowance or an obligation to replace the varying units.

10. Paragraph (e) applies only where the nature of the goods and of the transaction require a certain type of container, package or label. Paragraph (f) applies, on the other hand, wherever there is a label or container on which representations are made, even though the original contract, either by express terms or usage of trade, may not have required either the labelling or the representation. This follows from the general obligation of good faith which requires that a buyer should not be placed in the position of reselling or using goods delivered under false representations appearing on the package or container. No problem of extra consideration arises in this connection since, under this Article, an obligation is imposed by the original contract not to deliver mislabeled articles, and the obligation is imposed where mercantile good faith so requires and without reference to the doctrine of consideration.

11. Exclusion or modification of the warranty of merchantability, or of any part of it, is dealt with in the section to which the text of the present section makes explicit precautionary references. That section must be read with particular reference to its subsection (4) on limitation of remedies. The warranty of merchantability, wherever it is normal, is so commonly taken for granted that its exclusion from the contract is a matter threatening surprise and therefore requiring special precaution.

12. Subsection (3) is to make explicit that usage of trade and course of dealing can create warranties and that they are implied rather than express warranties and thus subject to exclusion or modification under Section 2-316. A typical instance would be the obligation to provide pedigree papers to evidence conformity of the animal to the contract in the case of a pedigreed dog or blooded bull.

13. In an action based on breach of warranty, it is of course necessary to show not only the existence of the warranty but the fact that the warranty was broken and that the breach of the warranty was the proximate cause of the loss sustained. In such an action an affirmative showing by the seller that the loss resulted from some action or event following his own delivery of the goods can operate as a defense. Equally, evidence indicating that the seller exercised care in the manufacture, processing or selection of the goods is relevant to the issue of whether the warranty was in fact broken. Action by the buyer following an examination of the goods which ought to have indicated the defect complained of can be shown as matter bearing on whether the breach itself was the cause of the injury.

Cross References:

Point 1: Section 2-316.

Point 3: Sections 1-203 and 2-104.

Point 5: Section 2-315.

Point 11: Section 2-316.

Point 12: Sections 1-201, 1-205 and 2-316.

Definitional Cross References:

"Agreement". Section 1-201.

"Contract". Section 1-201.

"Contract for sale". Section 2-106.

"Goods". Section 2-105.

"Merchant". Section 2-104.

"Seller". Section 2-103.

§ 2-315. Implied Warranty: Fitness for Particular Purpose

Where the seller at the time of contracting has reason to know any particular purpose for which the goods are required and that the buyer is relying on the seller's skill or judgment to select or furnish suitable goods, there is unless excluded or modified under the next section an implied warranty that the goods shall be fit for such purpose.

Official Comments

Prior Uniform Statutory Provision: Section 15(1), (4), (5), Uniform Sales Act.

Changes: Rewritten.

Purposes of Changes:

1. Whether or not this warranty arises in any individual case is basically a question of fact to be determined by the circumstances of the contracting. Under this section the buyer need not bring home to the seller actual knowledge of the particular purpose for which the goods are intended or of his reliance on the seller's skill and judgment, if the circumstances are such that the seller has reason to realize the purpose intended or that the reliance exists. The buyer, of course, must actually be relying on the seller.

2. A "particular purpose" differs from the ordinary purpose for which the goods are used in that it envisages a specific use by the buyer which is peculiar to the nature of his business whereas the ordinary purposes for which goods are used are those envisaged in the concept of merchantability and go to uses which are customarily made of the goods in question. For example, shoes are generally used for the purpose of walking upon ordinary ground, but a seller may know that a particular pair was selected to be used for climbing mountains.

A contract may of course include both a warranty of merchantability and one of fitness for a particular purpose.

The provisions of this Article on the cumulation and conflict of express and implied warranties must be considered on the question of inconsistency between or among warranties. In such a case any question of fact as to which warranty was intended by the parties to apply must be resolved in favor of the warranty of fitness for a particular purpose as against all other warranties except where the buyer has taken upon himself the responsibility of furnishing the technical specifications.

3. In connection with the warranty of fitness for a particular purpose the provisions of this Article on the allocation or division of risks are particularly applicable in any transaction in which the purpose for which the goods are to be used combines requirements both as to the quality of the goods themselves and compliance with certain laws or regulations. How the risks are divided is a question of fact to be determined, where not expressly contained in the agreement, from the circumstances of contracting, usage of trade, course of performance and the like, matters which may constitute the "otherwise agreement" of the parties by which they may divide the risk or burden.

4. The absence from this section of the language used in the Uniform Sales Act in referring to the seller, "whether he be the grower or manufacturer or not," is not intended to impose any requirement that the seller be a grower or manufacturer. Although normally the warranty will arise only where the seller is a merchant with the appropriate "skill or judgment," it can arise as to non-merchants where this is justified by the particular circumstances.

5. The elimination of the "patent or other trade name" exception constitutes the major extension of the warranty of fitness which has been made by the cases and continued in this Article. Under the present section the existence of a patent or other trade name and the designation of the article by that name, or indeed in any other definite manner, is only one of the facts to be considered on the question of whether the buyer actually relied on the seller, but it is not of itself decisive of the issue. If the buyer himself is insisting on a particular brand he is not relying on the seller's skill and judgment and so no warranty results. But the mere fact that the article purchased has a particular patent or trade name is not sufficient to indicate nonreliance if the article has been recommended by the seller as adequate for the buyer's purposes.

6. The specific reference forward in the present section to the following section on exclusion or modification of warranties is to call attention to the possibility of eliminating the warranty in any given case. However it must be noted that under the following section the warranty of fitness for a particular purpose must be excluded or modified by a conspicuous writing.

Cross References:

Point 2: Sections 2-314 and 2-317.

Point 3: Section 2-303.

Point 6: Section 2-316.

Definitional Cross References:

"Buyer". Section 2-103.

"Goods". Section 2-105.

"Seller". Section 2-103.

§ 2-316. Exclusion or Modification of Warranties

(1) Words or conduct relevant to the creation of an express warranty and words or conduct tending to negate or limit warranty shall be construed wherever reasonable as consistent with each other; but subject to the provisions of this Article on parol or extrinsic evidence (Section 2-202) negation or limitation is inoperative to the extent that such construction is unreasonable.

(2) Subject to subsection (3), to exclude or modify the implied warranty of merchantability or any part of it the language must mention merchantability and in case of a writing must be conspicuous, and to exclude or modify any implied

warranty of fitness the exclusion must be by a writing and conspicuous. Language to exclude all implied warranties of fitness is sufficient if it states, for example, that "There are no warranties which extend beyond the description on the face hereof."

(3) Notwithstanding subsection (2)

    (a) unless the circumstances indicate otherwise, all implied warranties are excluded by expressions like "as is", "with all faults" or other language which in common understanding calls the buyer's attention to the exclusion of warranties and makes plain that there is no implied warranty; and

    (b) when the buyer before entering into the contract has examined the goods or the sample or model as fully as he desired or has refused to examine the goods there is no implied warranty with regard to defects which an examination ought in the circumstances to have revealed to him; and

    (c) an implied warranty can also be excluded or modified by course of dealing or course of performance or usage of trade.

(4) Remedies for breach of warranty can be limited in accordance with the provisions of this Article on liquidation or limitation of damages and on contractual modification of remedy (Sections 2-718 and 2-719).

Official Comments

Prior Uniform Statutory Provision: None. See sections 15 and 71, Uniform Sales Act.

Purposes:

1. This section is designed principally to deal with those frequent clauses in sales contracts which seek to exclude "all warranties, express or implied." It seeks to protect a buyer from unexpected and unbargained language of disclaimer by denying effect to such language when inconsistent with language of express warranty and permitting the exclusion of implied warranties only by conspicuous language or other circumstances which protect the buyer from surprise.

2. The seller is protected under this Article against false allegations of oral warranties by its provisions on parol and extrinsic evidence and against unauthorized representations by the customary "lack of authority" clauses. This Article treats the limitation or avoidance of consequential damages as a matter of limiting remedies for breach, separate from the matter of creation of liability under a warranty. If no warranty exists, there is of course no problem of limiting remedies for breach of warranty. Under subsection (4) the question of limitation of remedy is governed by the sections referred to rather than by this section.

3. Disclaimer of the implied warranty of merchantability is permitted under subsection (2), but with the safeguard that such disclaimers must mention merchantability and in case of a writing must be conspicuous.

4. Unlike the implied warranty of merchantability, implied warranties of fitness for a particular purpose may be excluded by general language, but only if it is in writing and conspicuous.

5. Subsection (2) presupposes that the implied warranty in question exists unless excluded or modified. Whether or not language of disclaimer satisfies the requirements of this section, such language may be relevant under other sections to the question whether the warranty was ever in fact created. Thus, unless the provisions of this Article on parol and extrinsic evidence prevent, oral language of disclaimer may raise issues of fact as to whether reliance by the buyer occurred and whether the seller had "reason to know" under the section on implied warranty of fitness for a particular purpose.

6. The exceptions to the general rule set forth in paragraphs (a), (b) and (c) of subsection (3) are common factual situations in which the circumstances surrounding the transaction are in themselves sufficient to call the buyer's attention to the fact that no implied warranties are made or that a certain implied warranty is being excluded.

7. Paragraph (a) of subsection (3) deals with general terms such as "as is," "as they stand," "with all faults," and the like. Such terms in ordinary commercial usage are understood to mean that the buyer takes the entire risk as to the quality of the goods involved. The terms covered by paragraph (a) are in fact merely a particularization of paragraph (c) which provides for exclusion or modification of implied warranties by usage of trade.

8. Under paragraph (b) of subsection (3) warranties may be excluded or modified by the circumstances where the buyer examines the goods or a sample or model of them before entering into the contract. "Examination" as used in this paragraph is not synonymous with inspection before acceptance or at any other time after the contract has been made. It goes rather to the nature of the responsibility assumed by the seller at the time of the making of the contract. Of course if the buyer discovers the defect and uses the goods anyway, or if he unreasonably fails to examine the goods before he uses them, resulting injuries may be found to result from his own action rather than proximately from a breach of warranty. See Sections 2-314 and 2-715 and comments thereto.

In order to bring the transaction within the scope of "refused to examine" in paragraph (b), it is not sufficient that the goods are available for inspection. There must in addition be a demand by the seller that the buyer examine the goods fully. The seller by the demand puts the buyer on notice that he is assuming the risk of defects which the examination ought to reveal. The language "refused to examine" in this paragraph is intended to make clear the necessity for such demand.

Application of the doctrine of "caveat emptor" in all cases where the buyer examines the goods regardless of statements made by the seller is, however, rejected by this Article. Thus, if the offer of examination is accompanied by words as to their merchantability or specific attributes and the buyer indicates clearly that he is relying on those words rather than on his examination, they give rise to an "express" warranty. In such cases the question is one of fact as to whether a warranty of merchantability has been expressly incorporated in the agreement. Disclaimer of such an express warranty is governed by subsection (1) of the present section.

The particular buyer's skill and the normal method of examining goods in the circumstances determine what defects are excluded by the examination. A failure to notice defects which are obvious cannot excuse the buyer. However, an examination under circumstances which do not permit chemical or other testing of the goods would not exclude defects which could be ascertained only by such testing. Nor can latent defects be excluded by a simple examination. A professional buyer examining a product in his field will be held to have assumed the risk as to all defects which a professional in the field ought to observe, while a nonprofessional buyer will be held to have assumed the risk only for such defects as a layman might be expected to observe.

9. The situation in which the buyer gives precise and complete specifications to the seller is not explicitly covered in this section, but this is a frequent circumstance by which the implied warranties may be excluded. The warranty of fitness for a particular purpose would not normally arise since in such a situation there is usually no reliance on the seller by the buyer. The warranty of merchantability in such a transaction, however, must be considered in connection with the next section on the cumulation and conflict of warranties. Under paragraph (c) of that section in case of such an inconsistency the implied warranty of merchantability is displaced by the express warranty that the goods will comply with the specifications. Thus, where the buyer gives detailed specifications as to the goods, neither of the implied warranties as to quality will normally apply to the transaction unless consistent with the specifications.

Cross References:

Point 2: Sections 2-202, 2-718 and 2-719.

Point 7: Sections 1-205 and 2-208.

Definitional Cross References:

"Agreement". Section 1-201.

"Buyer". Section 2-103.

"Contract". Section 1-201.

"Course of dealing". Section 1-205.

"Goods". Section 2-105.

"Remedy". Section 1-201.

"Seller". Section 2-103.

"Usage of trade". Section 1-205.

§ 2-317. Cumulation and Conflict of Warranties Express or Implied

Warranties whether express or implied shall be construed as consistent with each other and as cumulative, but if such construction is unreasonable the intention of the parties shall determine which warranty is dominant. In ascertaining that intention the following rules apply:

(a) Exact or technical specifications displace an inconsistent sample or model or general language of description.

(b) A sample from an existing bulk displaces inconsistent general language of description.

(c) Express warranties displace inconsistent implied warranties other than an implied warranty of fitness for a particular purpose.

Official Comments

Prior Uniform Statutory Provision: On cumulation of warranties see Sections 14, 15, and 16, Uniform Sales Act.

Changes: Completely rewritten into one section.

Purposes of Changes:

1. The present section rests on the basic policy of this Article that no warranty is created except by some conduct (either affirmative action or failure to disclose) on the part of the seller. Therefore, all warranties are made cumulative unless this construction of the contract is impossible or unreasonable.

This Article thus follows the general policy of the Uniform Sales Act except that in case of the sale of an article by its patent or trade name the elimination of the warranty of fitness depends solely on whether the buyer has relied on the seller's skill and judgment; the use of the patent or trade name is but one factor in making this determination.

2. The rules of this section are designed to aid in determining the intention of the parties as to which of inconsistent warranties which have arisen from the circumstances of their transaction shall prevail. These rules of intention are to be applied only where factors making for an equitable estoppel of the seller do not exist and where he has in perfect good faith made warranties which later turn out to be inconsistent. To the extent that the seller has led the buyer to believe that all of the warranties can be performed, he is estopped from setting up any essential inconsistency as a defense.

3. The rules in subsections (a), (b) and (c) are designed to ascertain the intention of the parties by reference to the factor which probably claimed the attention of the parties in the first instance. These rules are not absolute but may be changed by evidence showing that the conditions which existed at the time of contracting make the construction called for by the section inconsistent or unreasonable.

Cross Reference:

Point 1: Section 2-315.

Definitional Cross Reference:

"Party". Section 1-201.

§ 2-318. Third Party Beneficiaries of Warranties Express or Implied

If this Act is introduced in the Congress of the United States this section should be omitted. (States to select one alternative.)

Alternative A

A seller's warranty whether express or implied extends to any natural person who is in the family or household of his buyer or who is a guest in his home if it is reasonable to expect that such person may use, consume or be affected by the goods and who is injured in person by breach of the warranty. A seller may not exclude or limit the operation of this section.

Alternative B

A seller's warranty whether express or implied extends to any natural person who may reasonably be expected to use, consume or be affected by the goods and who is injured in person by breach of the warranty. A seller may not exclude or limit the operation of this section.

Alternative C

A seller's warranty whether express or implied extends to any person who may reasonably be expected to use, consume or be affected by the goods and who is injured by breach of the warranty. A seller may not exclude or limit the operation of this section with respect to injury to the person of an individual to whom the warranty extends.

As amended in 1966.

Official Comments

Prior Uniform Statutory Provision: None.

Purposes:

1. The last sentence of this section does not mean that a seller is precluded from excluding or disclaiming a warranty which might otherwise arise in connection with the sale provided such exclusion or modification is permitted by Section 2-316. Nor does that sentence preclude the seller from limiting the remedies of his own buyer and of any beneficiaries, in any manner provided in Sections 2-718 or 2-719. To the extent that the contract of sale contains provisions under which warranties are excluded or modified, or remedies for breach are limited, such provisions are equally operative against beneficiaries of warranties under this section. What this last sentence forbids is exclusion of liability by the seller to the persons to whom the warranties which he has made to his buyer would extend under this section.

2. The purpose of this section is to give certain beneficiaries the benefit of the same warranty which the buyer received in the contract of sale, thereby freeing any such beneficiaries from any technical rules as to "privity." It seeks to accomplish this purpose without any derogation of any right or remedy resting on negligence. It rests primarily upon the merchant-seller's warranty under this Article that the goods sold are merchantable and fit for the ordinary purposes for which such goods are used rather than the warranty of fitness for a particular purpose. Implicit in the section is that any beneficiary of a warranty may bring a direct action for breach of warranty against the seller whose warranty extends to him [As amended in 1966].

3. The first alternative expressly includes as beneficiaries within its provisions the family, household and guests of the purchaser. Beyond this, the section in this form is neutral and is not intended to enlarge or restrict the developing case law on whether the seller's warranties, given to his buyer who resells, extend to other persons in the distributive chain.

The second alternative is designed for states where the case law has already developed further and for those that desire to expand the class of beneficiaries. The third alternative goes further, following the trend of modern decisions as indicated by Restatement of Torts 2d § 402A (Tentative Draft No. 10, 1965) in extending the rule beyond injuries to the person [As amended in 1966].

Cross References:

Point 1: Sections 2-316, 2-718 and 2-719.

Point 2: Section 2-314.

Definitional Cross References:

"Buyer". Section 2-103.

"Goods". Section 2-105.

"Seller". Section 2-103.

§ 2-319. F.O.B. and F.A.S. Terms

(1) Unless otherwise agreed the term F.O.B. (which means "free on board") at a named place, even though used only in connection with the stated price, is a delivery term under which

    (a) when the term is F.O.B. the place of shipment, the seller must at that place ship the goods in the manner provided in this Article (Section 2-504) and bear the expense and risk of putting them into the possession of the carrier; or

    (b) when the term is F.O.B. the place of destination, the seller must at his own expense and risk transport the goods to that place and there tender delivery of them in the manner provided in this Article (Section 2-503);

    (c) when under either (a) or (b) the term is also F.O.B. vessel, car or other vehicle, the seller must in addition at his own expense and risk load the goods on board. If the term is F.O.B. vessel the buyer must name the vessel and in an appropriate case the seller must comply with the provisions of this Article on the form of bill of lading (Section 2-323).

(2) Unless otherwise agreed the term F.A.S. vessel (which means "free alongside") at a named port, even though used only in connection with the stated price, is a delivery term under which the seller must

   (a) at his own expense and risk deliver the goods alongside the vessel in the manner usual in that port or on a dock designated and provided by the buyer; and

   (b) obtain and tender a receipt for the goods in exchange for which the carrier is under a duty to issue a bill of lading.

(3) Unless otherwise agreed in any case falling within subsection (1)(a) or (c) or subsection (2) the buyer must seasonably give any needed instructions for making delivery, including when the term is F.A.S. or F.O.B. the loading berth of the vessel and in an appropriate case its name and sailing date. The seller may treat the failure of needed instructions as a failure of cooperation under this Article (Section 2-311). He may also at his option move the goods in any reasonable manner preparatory to delivery or shipment.

(4) Under the term F.O.B. vessel or F.A.S. unless otherwise agreed the buyer must make payment against tender of the required documents and the seller may not tender nor the buyer demand delivery of the goods in substitution for the documents.

Official Comments

Prior Uniform Statutory Provision: None.

Purposes:

1. This section is intended to negate the uncommercial line of decision which treats an "F.O.B." term as "merely a price term." The distinctions taken in subsection (1) handle most of the issues which have on occasion led to the unfortunate judicial language just referred to. Other matters which have led to sound results being based on unhappy language in regard to F.O.B. clauses are dealt with in this Act by Section 2-311(2) (seller's option re arrangements relating to shipment) and Sections 2-614 and 615 (substituted performance and seller's excuse).

2. Subsection (1)(c) not only specifies the duties of a seller who engages to deliver "F.O.B. vessel," or the like, but ought to make clear that no agreement is soundly drawn when it looks to reshipment from San Francisco or New York, but speaks merely of "F.O.B." the place.

3. The buyer's obligations stated in subsection (1)(c) and subsection (3) are, as shown in the text, obligations of cooperation. The last sentence of subsection (3) expressly, though perhaps unnecessarily, authorizes the seller, pending instructions, to go ahead with such preparatory moves as shipment from the interior to the named

point of delivery. The sentence presupposes the usual case in which instructions "fail"; a prior repudiation by the buyer, giving notice that breach was intended, would remove the reason for the sentence, and would normally bring into play, instead, the second sentence of Section 2-704, which duly calls for lessening damages.

4. The treatment of "F.O.B. vessel" in conjunction with F.A.S. fits, in regard to the need for payment against documents, with standard practice and case-law; but "F.O.B. vessel" is a term which by its very language makes express the need for an "on board" document. In this respect, that term is stricter than the ordinary overseas "shipment" contract (C.I.F., etc., Section 2-320).

Cross References:

Sections 2-311(3), 2-323, 2-503 and 2-504.

Definitional Cross References:

"Agreed". Section 1-201.

"Bill of lading". Section 1-201.

"Buyer". Section 2-103.

"Goods". Section 2-105.

"Seasonably". Section 1-204.

"Seller". Section 2-103.

"Term". Section 1-201.

§ 2-320. C.I.F. and C. & F. Terms

(1) The term C.I.F. means that the price includes in a lump sum the cost of the goods and the insurance and freight to the named destination. The term C. & F. or C.F. means that the price so includes cost and freight to the named destination.

(2) Unless otherwise agreed and even though used only in connection with the stated price and destination, the term C.I.F. destination or its equivalent requires the seller at his own expense and risk to

    (a) put the goods into the possession of a carrier at the port for shipment and obtain a negotiable bill or bills of lading covering the entire transportation to the named destination; and

    (b) load the goods and obtain a receipt from the carrier (which may be contained in the bill of lading) showing that the freight has been paid or provided for; and

    (c) obtain a policy or certificate of insurance, including any war risk insurance, of a kind and on terms then current at the port of shipment in the usual amount, in the currency of the contract, shown to cover the same goods covered by the bill of lading and providing for payment of loss to the order of the buyer or for the account of whom it may concern; but the seller may add to the price the amount of the premium for any such war risk insurance; and

(d) prepare an invoice of the goods and procure any other documents required to effect shipment or to comply with the contract; and

(e) forward and tender with commercial promptness all the documents in due form and with any indorsement necessary to perfect the buyer's rights.

(3) Unless otherwise agreed the term C. & F. or its equivalent has the same effect and imposes upon the seller the same obligations and risks as a C.I.F. term except the obligation as to insurance.

(4) Under the term C.I.F. or C. & F. unless otherwise agreed the buyer must make payment against tender of the required documents and the seller may not tender nor the buyer demand delivery of the goods in substitution for the documents.

Official Comments

Prior Uniform Statutory Provisions: None.

Purposes: To make it clear that:

1. The C.I.F. contract is not a destination but a shipment contract with risk of subsequent loss or damage to the goods passing to the buyer upon shipment if the seller has properly performed all his obligations with respect to the goods. Delivery to the carrier is delivery to the buyer for purposes of risk and "title". Delivery of possession of the goods is accomplished by delivery of the bill of lading, and upon tender of the required documents the buyer must pay the agreed price without awaiting the arrival of the goods and if they have been lost or damaged after proper shipment he must seek his remedy against the carrier or insurer. The buyer has no right of inspection prior to payment or acceptance of the documents.

2. The seller's obligations remain the same even though the C.I.F. term is "used only in connection with the stated price and destination".

3. The insurance stipulated by the C.I.F. term is for the buyer's benefit, to protect him against the risk of loss or damage to the goods in transit. A clause in a C.I.F. contract "insurance-for the account of sellers" should be viewed in its ordinary mercantile meaning that the sellers must pay for the insurance and not that it is intended to run to the seller's benefit.

4. A bill of lading covering the entire transportation from the port of shipment is explicitly required but the provision on this point must be read in the light of its reason to assure the buyer of as full protection as the conditions of shipment reasonably permit, remembering always that this type of contract is designed to move the goods in the channels commercially available. To enable the buyer to deal with the goods while they are afloat the bill of lading must be one that covers only the quantity of goods called for by the contract. The buyer is not required to accept his part of the goods without a bill of lading because the latter covers a larger quantity, nor is he required to accept a bill of lading for the whole quantity under a stipulation to hold the excess for the owner. Although the buyer is not compelled to accept either goods or documents

under such circumstances he may of course claim his rights in any goods which have been identified to his contract.

5. The seller is given the option of paying or providing for the payment of freight. He has no option to ship "freight collect" unless the agreement so provides. The rule of the common law that the buyer need not pay the freight if the goods do not arrive is preserved.

Unless the shipment has been sent "freight collect" the buyer is entitled to receive documentary evidence that he is not obligated to pay the freight; the seller is therefore required to obtain a receipt "showing that the freight has been paid or provided for." The usual notation in the appropriate space on the bill of lading that the freight has been prepaid is a sufficient receipt, as at common law. The phrase "provided for" is intended to cover the frequent situation in which the carrier extends credit to a shipper for the freight on successive shipments and receives periodical payments of the accrued freight charges from him.

6. The requirement that unless otherwise agreed the seller must procure insurance "of a kind and on terms then current at the port for shipment in the usual amount, in the currency of the contract, sufficiently shown to cover the same goods covered by the bill of lading", applies to both marine and war risk insurance. As applied to marine insurance, it means such insurance as is usual or customary at the port for shipment with reference to the particular kind of goods involved, the character and equipment of the vessel, the route of the voyage, the port of destination and any other considerations that affect the risk. It is the substantial equivalent of the ordinary insurance in the particular trade and on the particular voyage and is subject to agreed specifications of type or extent of coverage. The language does not mean that the insurance must be adequate to cover all risks to which the goods may be subject in transit. There are some types of loss or damage that are not covered by the usual marine insurance and are excepted in bills of lading or in applicable statutes from the causes of loss or damage for which the carrier or the vessel is liable. Such risks must be borne by the buyer under this Article.

Insurance secured in compliance with a C.I.F. term must cover the entire transportation of the goods to the named destination.

7. An additional obligation is imposed upon the seller in requiring him to procure customary war risk insurance at the buyer's expense. This changes the common law on the point. The seller is not required to assume the risk of including in the C.I.F. price the cost of such insurance, since it often fluctuates rapidly, but is required to treat it simply as a necessary for the buyer's account. What war risk insurance is "current" or usual turns on the standard forms of policy or rider in common use.

8. The C.I.F. contract calls for insurance covering the value of the goods at the time and place of shipment and does not include any increase in market value during transit or any anticipated profit to the buyer on a sale by him.

The contract contemplates that before the goods arrive at their destination they may be sold again and again on C.I.F. terms and that the original policy of insurance and bill of lading will run with the interest in the goods by being transferred to each successive buyer. A buyer who becomes the seller in such an intermediate contract for sale does not thereby, if his sub-buyer knows the circumstances, undertake to insure the goods again at an increased price fixed in the new contract or to cover the increase in price by additional insurance, and his buyer may not reject the documents on the ground that the original policy does not cover such higher price. If such a sub-buyer desires additional insurance he must procure it for himself.

Where the seller exercises an option to ship "freight collect" and to credit the buyer with the freight against the C.I.F. price, the insurance need not cover the freight since the freight is not at the buyer's risk. On the other hand, where the seller prepays the freight upon shipping under a bill of lading requiring prepayment and providing that the freight shall be deemed earned and shall be retained by the carrier "ship and/or cargo lost or not lost," or using words of similar import, he must procure insurance that will cover the freight, because notwithstanding that the goods are lost in transit the buyer is bound to pay the freight as part of the C.I.F. price and will be unable to recover it back from the carrier.

9. Insurance "for the account of whom it may concern" is usual and sufficient. However, for a valid tender the policy of insurance must be one which can be disposed of together with the bill of lading and so must be "sufficiently shown to cover the same goods covered by the bill of lading". It must cover separately the quantity of goods called for by the buyer's contract and not merely insure his goods as part of a larger quantity in which others are interested, a case provided for in American mercantile practice by the use of negotiable certificates of insurance which are expressly authorized by this section. By usage these certificates are treated as the equivalent of separate policies and are good tender under C.I.F. contracts. The term "certificate of insurance", however, does not of itself include certificates or "cover notes" issued by the insurance broker and stating that the goods are covered by a policy. Their sufficiency as substitutes for policies will depend upon proof of an established usage or course of dealing. The present section rejects the English rule that not only brokers' certificates and "cover notes" but also certain forms of American insurance certificates are not the equivalent of policies and are not good tender under a C.I.F. contract.

The seller's failure to tender a proper insurance document is waived if the buyer refuses to make payment on other and untenable grounds at a time when proper insurance could have been obtained and tendered by the seller if timely objection had been made. Even a failure to insure on shipment may be cured by seasonable tender of a policy retroactive in effect; e.g., one insuring the goods "lost or not lost." The provisions of this Article on cure of improper tender and on waiver of buyer's objections by silence are applicable to insurance tenders under a C.I.F. term. Where there is no waiver by the buyer as described above, however, the fact that the goods arrive safely does not cure the seller's breach of his obligations to insure them and tender to the buyer a proper insurance document.

10. The seller's invoice of the goods shipped under a C.I.F. contract is regarded as a usual and necessary document upon which reliance may properly be placed. It is the document which evidences points of description, quality and the like which do not readily appear in other documents. This Article rejects those statements to the effect that the invoice is a usual but not a necessary document under a C.I.F. term.

11. The buyer needs all of the documents required under a C.I.F. contract, in due form and with necessary endorsements, so that before the goods arrive he may deal with them by negotiating the documents or may obtain prompt possession of the goods after their arrival. If the goods are lost or damaged in transit the documents are necessary to enable him promptly to assert his remedy against the carrier or insurer. The seller is therefore obligated to do what is mercantilely reasonable in the circumstances and should make every reasonable exertion to send forward the documents as soon as possible after the shipment. The requirement that the documents be forwarded with "commercial promptness" expresses a more urgent need for action than that suggested by the phrase "reasonable time".

12. Under a C.I.F. contract the buyer, as under the common law, must pay the price upon tender of the required documents without first inspecting the goods, but his payment in these circumstances does not constitute an acceptance of the goods nor does it impair his right of subsequent inspection or his options and remedies in the case of improper delivery. All remedies and rights for the seller's breach are reserved to him. The buyer must pay before inspection and assert his remedy against the seller afterward unless the nonconformity of the goods amounts to a real failure of consideration, since the purpose of choosing this form of contract is to give the seller protection against the buyer's unjustifiable rejection of the goods at a distant port of destination which would necessitate taking possession of the goods and suing the buyer there.

13. A valid C.I.F. contract may be made which requires part of the transportation to be made on land and part on the sea, as where the goods are to be brought by rail from an inland point to a seaport and thence transported by vessel to the named destination under a "through" or combination bill of lading issued by the railroad company. In such a case shipment by rail from the inland point within the contract period is a timely shipment notwithstanding that the loading of the goods on the vessel is delayed by causes beyond the seller's control.

14. Although subsection (2) stating the legal effects of the C.I.F. term is an "unless otherwise agreed" provision, the express language used in an agreement is frequently a precautionary, fuller statement of the normal C.I.F. terms and hence not intended as a departure or variation from them. Moreover, the dominant outlines of the C.I.F. term are so well understood commercially that any variation should, whenever reasonably possible, be read as falling within those dominant outlines rather than as destroying the whole meaning of a term which essentially indicates a contract for proper shipment rather than one for delivery at destination. Particularly careful consideration is necessary before a printed form or clause is construed to mean agreement otherwise and

where a C.I.F. contract is prepared on a printed form designed for some other type of contract, the C.I.F. terms must prevail over printed clauses repugnant to them.

15. Under subsection (4) the fact that the seller knows at the time of the tender of the documents that the goods have been lost in transit does not affect his rights if he has performed his contractual obligations. Similarly, the seller cannot perform under a C.I.F. term by purchasing and tendering landed goods.

16. Under the C. & F. term, as under the C.I.F. term, title and risk of loss are intended to pass to the buyer on shipment. A stipulation in a C. & F. contract that the seller shall effect insurance on the goods and charge the buyer with the premium (in effect that he shall act as the buyer's agent for that purpose) is entirely in keeping with the pattern. On the other hand, it often happens that the buyer is in a more advantageous position than the seller to effect insurance on the goods or that he has in force an "open" or "floating" policy covering all shipments made by him or to him, in either of which events the C. & F. term is adequate without mention of insurance.

17. It is to be remembered that in a French contract the term "C.A.F." does not mean "Cost and Freight" but has exactly the same meaning as the term "C.I.F." since it is merely the French equivalent of that term. The "A" does not stand for "and" but for "assurance" which means insurance.

Cross References:

Point 4: Section 2-323.

Point 6: Section 2-509(1)(a).

Point 9: Sections 2-508 and 2-605(1)(a).

Point 12: Sections 2-321(3), 2-512 and 2-513(3) and Article 5.

Definitional Cross References:

"Bill of lading". Section 1-201.

"Buyer". Section 2-103.

"Contract". Section 1-201.

"Goods". Section 2-105.

"Rights". Section 1-201.

"Seller". Section 2-103.

"Term". Section 1-201.

§ 2-321. C.I.F. or C. & F.: "Net Landed Weights"; "Payment on Arrival"; Warranty of Condition on Arrival

Under a contract containing a term C.I.F. or C. & F.

(1) Where the price is based on or is to be adjusted according to "net landed weights", "delivered weights", "out turn" quantity or quality or the like, unless otherwise agreed the seller must reasonably estimate the price. The payment

due on tender of the documents called for by the contract is the amount so estimated, but after final adjustment of the price a settlement must be made with commercial promptness.

(2) An agreement described in subsection (1) or any warranty of quality or condition of the goods on arrival places upon the seller the risk of ordinary deterioration, shrinkage and the like in transportation but has no effect on the place or time of identification to the contract for sale or delivery or on the passing of the risk of loss.

(3) Unless otherwise agreed where the contract provides for payment on or after arrival of the goods the seller must before payment allow such preliminary inspection as is feasible; but if the goods are lost delivery of the documents and payment are due when the goods should have arrived.

Official Comments

Prior Uniform Statutory Provision: None.

Purposes:

This section deals with two variations of the C.I.F. contract which have evolved in mercantile practice but are entirely consistent with the basic C.I.F. pattern. Subsections (1) and (2), which provide for a shift to the seller of the risk of quality and weight deterioration during shipment, are designed to conform the law to the best mercantile practice and usage without changing the legal consequences of the C.I.F. or C. & F. term as to the passing of marine risks to the buyer at the point of shipment. Subsection (3) provides that where under the contract documents are to be presented for payment after arrival of the goods, this amounts merely to a postponement of the payment under the C.I.F. contract and is not to be confused with the "no arrival, no sale" contract. If the goods are lost, delivery of the documents and payment against them are due when the goods should have arrived. The clause for payment on or after arrival is not to be construed as such a condition precedent to payment that if the goods are lost in transit the buyer need never pay and the seller must bear the loss.

Cross Reference:

Section 2-324.

Definitional Cross References:

"Agreement". Section 1-201.

"Contract". Section 1-201.

"Delivery". Section 1-201.

"Goods". Section 2-105.

"Seller". Section 2-103.

"Term". Section 1-201.

§ 2-322. Delivery "Ex-Ship"

(1) Unless otherwise agreed a term for delivery of goods "ex-ship" (which means from the carrying vessel) or in equivalent language is not restricted to a particular ship and requires delivery from a ship which has reached a place at the named port of destination where goods of the kind are usually discharged.

(2) Under such a term unless otherwise agreed
  (a) the seller must discharge all liens arising out of the carriage and furnish the buyer with a direction which puts the carrier under a duty to deliver the goods; and
  (b) the risk of loss does not pass to the buyer until the goods leave the ship's tackle or are otherwise properly unloaded.

Official Comments

Prior Uniform Statutory Provision: None.

Purposes:

1. The delivery term, "ex-ship", as between seller and buyer, is the reverse of the f.a.s. term covered.

2. Delivery need not be made from any particular vessel under a clause calling for delivery "ex-ship", even though a vessel on which shipment is to be made originally is named in the contract, unless the agreement by appropriate language, restricts the clause to delivery from a named vessel.

3. The appropriate place and manner of unloading at the port of destination depend upon the nature of the goods and the facilities and usages of the port.

4. A contract fixing a price "ex-ship" with payment "cash against documents" calls only for such documents as are appropriate to the contract. Tender of a delivery order and of a receipt for the freight after the arrival of the carrying vessel is adequate. The seller is not required to tender a bill of lading as a document of title nor is he required to insure the goods for the buyer's benefit, as the goods are not at the buyer's risk during the voyage.

Cross Reference:

Point 1: Section 2-319(2).

Definitional Cross References:

"Buyer". Section 2-103.

"Goods". Section 2-105.

"Seller". Section 2-103.

"Term". Section 1-201.

§ 2-323. Form of Bill of Lading Required in Overseas Shipment; "Overseas"

(1) Where the contract contemplates overseas shipment and contains a term C.I.F. or C. & F. or F.O.B. vessel, the seller unless otherwise agreed must obtain a negotiable bill of lading stating that the goods have been loaded in board or, in the case of a term C.I.F. or C. & F., received for shipment.

(2) Where in a case within subsection (1) a bill of lading has been issued in a set of parts, unless otherwise agreed if the documents are not to be sent from abroad the buyer may demand tender of the full set; otherwise only one part of the bill of lading need be tendered. Even if the agreement expressly requires a full set

    (a) due tender of a single part is acceptable within the provisions of this Article on cure of improper delivery (subsection (1) of Section 2-508); and

    (b) even though the full set is demanded, if the documents are sent from abroad the person tendering an incomplete set may nevertheless require payment upon furnishing an indemnity which the buyer in good faith deems adequate.

(3) A shipment by water or by air or a contract contemplating such shipment is "overseas" insofar as by usage of trade or agreement it is subject to the commercial, financing or shipping practices characteristic of international deep water commerce.

Official Comments

Prior Uniform Statutory Provision: None.

Purposes:

1. Subsection (1) follows the "American" rule that a regular bill of lading indicating delivery of the goods at the dock for shipment is sufficient, except under a term "F.O.B. vessel." See Section 2-319 and comment thereto.

2. Subsection (2) deals with the problem of bills of lading covering deep water shipments, issued not as a single bill of lading but in a set of parts, each part referring to the other parts and the entire set constituting in commercial practice and at law a single bill of lading. Commercial practice in international commerce is to accept and pay against presentation of the first part of a set if the part is sent from overseas even though the contract of the buyer requires presentation of a full set of bills of lading provided adequate indemnity for the missing parts is forthcoming.

This subsection codifies that practice as between buyer and seller. Article 5 (Section 5-113) authorizes banks presenting drafts under letters of credit to give indemnities against the missing parts, and this subsection means that the buyer must accept and act on such indemnities if he in good faith deems them adequate. But neither this subsection nor Article 5 decides whether a bank which has issued a letter of credit is similarly bound. The issuing bank's obligation under a letter of credit is independent and depends on its own terms. See Article 5.

Cross References:

Sections 2-508(2), 5-113.

Definitional Cross References:

"Bill of lading". Section 1-201.

"Buyer". Section 2-103.

"Contract". Section 1-201.

"Delivery". Section 1-201.

"Financing agency". Section 2-104.

"Person". Section 1-201.

"Seller". Section 2-103.

"Send". Section 1-201.

"Term". Section 1-201.

§ 2-324. "No Arrival, No Sale" Term

Under a term "no arrival, no sale" or terms of like meaning, unless otherwise agreed,

(a)   the seller must properly ship conforming goods and if they arrive by any means he must tender them on arrival but he assumes no obligation that the goods will arrive unless he has caused the non-arrival; and

(b)   where without fault of the seller the goods are in part lost or have so deteriorated as no longer to conform to the contract or arrive after the contract time, the buyer may proceed as if there had been casualty to identified goods (Section 2-613).

Official Comments

Prior Uniform Statutory Provision: None.

Purposes:

1. The "no arrival, no sale" term in a "destination" overseas contract leaves risk of loss on the seller but gives him an exemption from liability for non-delivery. Both the nature of the case and the duty of good faith require that the seller must not interfere with the arrival of the goods in any way. If the circumstances impose upon him the responsibility for making or arranging the shipment, he must have a shipment made despite the exemption clause. Further, the shipment made must be a conforming one, for the exemption under a "no arrival, no sale" term applies only to the hazards of transportation and the goods must be proper in all other respects.

The reason of this section is that where the seller is reselling goods bought by him as shipped by another and this fact is known to the buyer, so that the seller is not under any obligation to make the shipment himself, the seller is entitled under the "no arrival, no sale" clause to exemption from payment of damages for non-delivery if the goods do not arrive or if the goods which actually arrive are non-conforming. This does not extend to sellers who arrange shipment by their own agents, in which case the clause is limited to casualty due to marine hazards. But sellers who make known that they are contracting only with respect to what will be delivered to them by parties over whom they assume no control are entitled to the full quantum of the exemption.

2. The provisions of this Article on identification must be read together with the present section in order to bring the exemption into application. Until there is some designation of the goods in a particular shipment or on a particular ship as being those to which the contract refers there can be no application of an exemption for their non-arrival.

3. The seller's duty to tender the agreed or declared goods if they do arrive is not impaired because of their delay in arrival or by their arrival after transshipment.

4. The phrase "to arrive" is often employed in the same sense as "no arrival, no sale" and may then be given the same effect. But a "to arrive" term, added to a C.I.F. or C. & F. contract, does not have the full meaning given by this section to "no arrival, no sale". Such a "to arrive" term is usually intended to operate only to the extent that the risks are not covered by the agreed insurance and the loss or casualty is due to such uncovered hazards. In some instances the "to arrive" term may be regarded as a time of payment term, or, in the case of the reselling seller discussed in point 1 above, as negating responsibility for conformity of the goods, if they arrive, to any description which was based on his good faith belief of the quality. Whether this is the intention of the parties is a question of fact based on all the circumstances surrounding the resale and in case of ambiguity the rules of Sections 2-316 and 2-317 apply to preclude dishonor.

5. Paragraph (b) applies where goods arrive impaired by damage or partial loss during transportation and makes the policy of this Article on casualty to identified goods applicable to such a situation. For the term cannot be regarded as intending to give the seller an unforeseen profit through casualty; it is intended only to protect him from loss due to causes beyond his control.

Cross References:

Point 1: Section 1-203.

Point 2: Section 2-501(a) and (c).

Point 5: Section 2-613.

Definitional Cross References:

"Buyer". Section 2-103.

"Conforming". Section 2-106.

"Contract". Section 1-201.

"Fault". Section 1-201.

"Goods". Section 2-105.

"Sale". Section 2-106.

"Seller". Section 2-103.

"Term". Section 1-201.

§ 2-325. "Letter of Credit" Term; "Confirmed Credit"

(1) Failure of the buyer seasonably to furnish an agreed letter of credit is a breach of the contract for sale.

(2) The delivery to seller of a proper letter of credit suspends the buyer's obligation to pay. If the letter of credit is dishonored, the seller may on seasonable notification to the buyer require payment directly from him.

(3) Unless otherwise agreed the term "letter of credit" or "banker's credit" in a contract for sale means an irrevocable credit issued by a financing agency of good repute and, where the shipment is overseas, of good international repute. The term "confirmed credit" means that the credit must also carry the direct obligation of such an agency which does business in the seller's financial market.

Official Comments

Prior Uniform Statutory Provision: None.

Purposes: To express the established commercial and banking understanding as to the meaning and effects of terms calling for "letters of credit" or "confirmed credit":

1. Subsection (2) follows the general policy of this Article and Article 3 (Section 3-802) on conditional payment, under which payment by check or other short-term instrument is not ordinarily final as between the parties if the recipient duly presents the instrument and honor is refused. Thus the furnishing of a letter of credit does not substitute the financing agency's obligation for the buyer's, but the seller must first give the buyer reasonable notice of his intention to demand direct payment from him.

2. Subsection (2) requires that the credit be irrevocable and be a prime credit as determined by the standing of the issuer. It is not necessary, unless otherwise agreed, that the credit be a negotiation credit; the seller can finance himself by an assignment of the proceeds under Section 5-116(2).

3. The definition of "confirmed credit" is drawn on the supposition that the credit is issued by a bank which is not doing direct business in the seller's financial market; there is no intention to require the obligation of two banks both local to the seller.

Cross References:

Sections 2-403, 2-511(3) and 3-802 and Article 5.

Definitional Cross References:

"Buyer". Section 2-103.

"Contract for sale". Section 2-106.

"Draft". Section 3-104.

"Financing agency". Section 2-104.

"Notifies". Section 1-201.

"Overseas". Section 2-323.

"Purchaser". Section 1-201.

"Seasonably". Section 1-204.

"Seller". Section 2-103.

"Term". Section 1-201.

§ 2-326. Sale on Approval and Sale or Return; Consignment Sales and Rights of Creditors

(1) Unless otherwise agreed, if delivered goods may be returned by the buyer even though they conform to the contract, the transaction is
    (a) a "sale on approval" if the goods are delivered primarily for use, and
    (b) a "sale or return" if the goods are delivered primarily for resale.

(2) Except as provided in subsection (3), goods held on approval are not subject to the claims of the buyer's creditors until acceptance; goods held on sale or return are subject to such claims while in the buyer's possession.

(3) Where goods are delivered to a person for sale and such person maintains a place of business at which he deals in goods of the kind involved, under a name other than the name of the person making delivery, then with respect to claims of creditors of the person conducting the business the goods are deemed to be on sale or return. The provisions of this subsection are applicable even though an agreement purports to reserve title to the person making delivery until payment or resale or uses such words as "on consignment" or "on memorandum". However, this subsection is not applicable if the person making delivery
    (a) complies with an applicable law providing for a consignor's interest or the like to be evidenced by a sign, or
    (b) establishes that the person conducting the business is generally known by his creditors to be substantially engaged in selling the goods of others, or (c) complies with the filing provisions of the Article on Secured Transactions (Article 9).

(4) Any "or return" term of a contract for sale is to be treated as a separate contract for sale within the statute of frauds section of this Article (Section 2-201) and as contradicting the sale aspect of the contract within the provisions of this Article on parol or extrinsic evidence (Section 2-202).

Official Comments

Prior Uniform Statutory Provision: Section 19(3), Uniform Sales Act.

Changes: Completely rewritten in this and the succeeding section.

Purposes of Changes: To make it clear that:

1. A "sale on approval" or "sale or return" is distinct from other types of transactions with which they have frequently been confused. The type of "sale on approval," "on trial" or "on satisfaction" dealt with involves a contract under which the seller undertakes a particular business risk to satisfy his prospective buyer with the appearance or performance of the goods in question. The goods are delivered to the proposed purchaser but they remain the property of the seller until the buyer accepts them. The price has already been agreed. The buyer's willingness to receive and test the goods is the consideration for the seller's engagement to deliver and sell. The type of "sale or return" involved herein is a sale to a merchant whose unwillingness to buy is overcome only by the seller's engagement to take back the goods (or any commercial unit of goods) in lieu of payment if they fail to be resold. These two transactions are so strongly delineated in practice and in general understanding that every presumption runs against a delivery to a consumer being a "sale or return" and against a delivery to a merchant for resale being a "sale on approval."

The right to return the goods for failure to conform to the contract does not make the transaction a "sale on approval" or "sale or return" and has nothing to do with this and the following section. The present section is not concerned with remedies for breach of contract. It deals instead with a power given by the contract to turn back the goods even though they are wholly as warranted.

This section nevertheless presupposes that a contract for sale is contemplated by the parties although that contract may be of the peculiar character here described.

Where the buyer's obligation as a buyer is conditioned not on his personal approval but on the article's passing a described objective test, the risk of loss by casualty pending the test is properly the seller's and proper return is at his expense. On the point of "satisfaction" as meaning "reasonable satisfaction" where an industrial machine is involved, this Article takes no position.

2. Pursuant to the general policies of this Act which require good faith not only between the parties to the sales contract, but as against interested third parties, subsection (3) resolves all reasonable doubts as to the nature of the transaction in favor of the general creditors of the buyer. As against such creditors words such as "on consignment" or "on memorandum", with or without words of reservation of title in the seller, are disregarded when the buyer has a place of business at which he deals in goods of the kind involved. A necessary exception is made where the buyer is known to be engaged primarily in selling the goods of others or is selling under a relevant sign law, or the seller complies with the filing provisions of Article 9 as if his interest were a security interest. However, there is no intent in this Section to narrow the protection afforded

to third parties in any jurisdiction which has a selling Factors Act. The purpose of the exception is merely to limit the effect of the present subsection itself, in the absence of any such Factors Act, to cases in which creditors of the buyer may reasonably be deemed to have been misled by the secret reservation.

3. Subsection (4) resolves a conflict in the pre-existing case law by recognition that an "or return" provision is so definitely at odds with any ordinary contract for sale of goods that where written agreements are involved it must be contained in a written memorandum. The "or return" aspect of a sales contract must be treated as a separate contract under the Statute of Frauds section and as contradicting the sale insofar as questions of parol or extrinsic evidence are concerned.

Cross References:

Point 2: Article 9.

Point 3: Sections 2-201 and 2-202.

Definitional Cross References:

"Between merchants". Section 2-104.

"Buyer". Section 2-103.

"Conform". Section 2-106.

"Contract for sale". Section 2-106.

"Creditor". Section 1-201.

"Goods". Section 2-105.

"Sale". Section 2-106.

"Seller". Section 2-103.

§ 2-327. Special Incidents of Sale on Approval and Sale or Return

(1) Under a sale on approval unless otherwise agreed
    (a) although the goods are identified to the contract the risk of loss and the title do not pass to the buyer until acceptance; and
    (b) use of the goods consistent with the purpose of trial is not acceptance but failure seasonably to notify the seller of election to return the goods is acceptance, and if the goods conform to the contract acceptance of any part is acceptance of the whole; and
    (c) after due notification of election to return, the return is at the seller's risk and expense but a merchant buyer must follow any reasonable instructions.

(2) Under a sale or return unless otherwise agreed
    (a) the option to return extends to the whole or any commercial unit of the goods while in substantially their original condition, but must be exercised seasonably; and
    (b) the return is at the buyer's risk and expense.

Official Comments

Prior Uniform Statutory Provision: Section 19(3), Uniform Sales Act.

Changes: Completely rewritten in preceding and this section.

Purposes of Changes: To make it clear that:

1. In the case of a sale on approval:

If all of the goods involved conform to the contract, the buyer's acceptance of part of the goods constitutes acceptance of the whole. Acceptance of part falls outside the normal intent of the parties in the "on approval" situation and the policy of this Article allowing partial acceptance of a defective delivery has no application here. A case where a buyer takes home two dresses to select one commonly involves two distinct contracts; if not, it is covered by the words "unless otherwise agreed".

2. In the case of a sale or return, the return of any unsold unit merely because it is unsold is the normal intent of the "sale or return" provision, and therefore the right to return for this reason alone is independent of any other action under the contract which would turn on wholly different considerations. On the other hand, where the return of goods is for breach, including return of items resold by the buyer and returned by the ultimate purchasers because of defects, the return procedure is governed not by the present section but by the provisions on the effects and revocation of acceptance.

3. In the case of a sale on approval the risk rests on the seller until acceptance of the goods by the buyer, while in a sale or return the risk remains throughout on the buyer.

4. Notice of election to return given by the buyer in a sale on approval is sufficient to relieve him of any further liability. Actual return by the buyer to the seller is required in the case of a sale or return contract. What constitutes due "giving" of notice, as required in "on approval" sales, is governed by the provisions on good faith and notice. "Seasonable" is used here as defined in Section 1-204. Nevertheless, the provisions of both this Article and of the contract on this point must be read with commercial reason and with full attention to good faith.

Cross References:

Point 1: Sections 2-501, 2-601 and 2-603.

Point 2: Sections 2-607 and 2-608.

Point 4: Sections 1-201 and 1-204.

Definitional Cross References:

"Agreed". Section 1-201.

"Buyer". Section 2-103.

"Commercial unit". Section 2-105.

"Conform". Section 2-106.

"Contract". Section 1-201.

"Goods". Section 2-105.

"Merchant". Section 2-104.

"Notifies". Section 1-201.

"Notification". Section 1-201.

"Sale on approval". Section 2-326.

"Sale or return". Section 2-326.

"Seasonably". Section 1-204.

"Seller". Section 2-103.

§ 2-328. Sale by Auction

(1) In a sale by auction if goods are put up in lots each lot is the subject of a separate sale.

(2) A sale by auction is complete when the auctioneer so announces by the fall of the hammer or in other customary manner. Where a bid is made while the hammer is falling in acceptance of a prior bid the auctioneer may in his discretion reopen the bidding or declare the goods sold under the bid on which the hammer was falling.

(3) Such a sale is with reserve unless the goods are in explicit terms put up without reserve. In an auction with reserve the auctioneer may withdraw the goods at any time until he announces completion of the sale. In an auction without reserve, after the auctioneer calls for bids on an article or lot, that article or lot cannot be withdrawn unless no bid is made within a reasonable time. In either case a bidder may retract his bid until the auctioneer's announcement of completion of the sale, but a bidder's retraction does not revive any previous bid.

(4) If the auctioneer knowingly receives a bid on the seller's behalf or the seller makes or procures such a bid, and notice has not been given that liberty for such bidding is reserved, the buyer may at his option avoid the sale or take the goods at the price of the last good faith bid prior to the completion of the sale. This subsection shall not apply to any bid at a forced sale.

Official Comments

Prior Uniform Statutory Provision: Section 21, Uniform Sales Act.

Changes: Completely rewritten.

Purposes of Changes: To make it clear that:

1. The auctioneer may in his discretion either reopen the bidding or close the sale on the bid on which the hammer was falling when a bid is made at that moment. The recognition of a bid of this kind by the auctioneer in his discretion does not mean a closing in favor of such a bidder, but only that the bid has been accepted as a continuation of the bidding. If recognized, such a bid discharges the bid on which the hammer was falling when it was made.

2. An auction "with reserve" is the normal procedure. The crucial point, however, for determining the nature of an auction is the "putting up" of the goods. This Article accepts the view that the goods may be withdrawn before they are actually "put up," regardless of whether the auction is advertised as one without reserve, without liability on the part of the auction announcer to persons who are present. This is subject to any peculiar facts which might bring the case within the "firm offer" principle of this Article, but an offer to persons generally would require unmistakable language in order to fall within that section. The prior announcement of the nature of the auction either as with reserve or without reserve will, however, enter as an "explicit term" in the "putting up" of the goods and conduct thereafter must be governed accordingly. The present section continues the prior rule permitting withdrawal of bids in auctions both with and without reserve; and the rule is made explicit that the retraction of a bid does not revive a prior bid.

Cross Reference:

Point 2: Section 2-205.

Definitional Cross References:

"Buyer". Section 2-103.

"Good faith". Section 1-201.

"Goods". Section 2-105.

"Lot". Section 2-105.

"Notice". Section 1-201.

"Sale". Section 2-106.

"Seller". Section 2-103.

PART 4. TITLE, CREDITORS AND GOOD FAITH PURCHASERS

§ 2-401. Passing of Title; Reservation for Security; Limited Application of This Section

Each provision of this Article with regard to the rights, obligations and remedies of the seller, the buyer, purchasers or other third parties applies irrespective of title to the goods except where the provision refers to such title. Insofar as situations are not covered by the other provisions of this Article and matters concerning title become material the following rules apply:

(1) Title to goods cannot pass under a contract for sale prior to their identification to the contract (Section 2-501), and unless otherwise explicitly agreed the buyer acquires by their identification a special property as limited by this Act. Any retention or reservation by the seller of the title (property) in goods shipped or delivered to the buyer is limited in effect to a reservation of a security interest. Subject to these provisions and to the provisions of the Article on Secured Transactions (Article 9), title to goods passes from the seller to the buyer in any manner and on any conditions explicitly agreed on by the parties.

(2) Unless otherwise explicitly agreed title passes to the buyer at the time and place at which the seller completes his performance with reference to the physical delivery of the goods, despite any reservation of a security interest and even though a document of title is to be delivered at a different time or place; and in particular and despite any reservation of a security interest by the bill of lading

    (a) if the contract requires or authorizes the seller to send the goods to the buyer but does not require him to deliver them at destination, title passes to the buyer at the time and place of shipment; but

    (b) if the contract requires delivery at destination, title passes on tender there.

(3) Unless otherwise explicitly agreed where delivery is to be made without moving the goods,

    (a) if the seller is to deliver a document of title, title passes at the time when and the place where he delivers such documents; or

    (b) if the goods are at the time of contracting already identified and no documents are to be delivered, title passes at the time and place of contracting.

(4) A rejection or other refusal by the buyer to receive or retain the goods, whether or not justified, or a justified revocation of acceptance revests title to the goods in the seller. Such revesting occurs by operation of law and is not a "sale".

Official Comments

Prior Uniform Statutory Provision: See generally, Sections 17, 18, 19 and 20, Uniform Sales Act.

Purposes: To make it clear that:

1. This Article deals with the issues between seller and buyer in terms of step by step performance or non-performance under the contract for sale and not in terms of whether or not "title" to the goods has passed. That the rules of this section in no way alter the rights of either the buyer, seller or third parties declared elsewhere in the Article is made clear by the preamble of this section. This section, however, in no way intends to indicate which line of interpretation should be followed in cases where the applicability of "public" regulation depends upon a "sale" or upon location of "title" without further definition. The basic policy of this Article that known purpose and reason should govern interpretation cannot extend beyond the scope of its own provisions. It is therefore necessary to state what a "sale" is and when title passes under this Article in case the courts deem any public regulation to incorporate the defined term of the "private" law.

2. "Future" goods cannot be the subject of a present sale. Before title can pass the goods must be identified in the manner set forth in Section 2-501. The parties, however, have full liberty to arrange by specific terms for the passing of title to goods which are existing.

3. The "special property" of the buyer in goods identified to the contract is excluded from the definition of "security interest"; its incidents are defined in provisions of this Article such as those on the rights of the seller's creditors, on good faith purchase, on

the buyer's right to goods on the seller's insolvency, and on the buyer's right to specific performance or replevin.

4. The factual situations in subsections (2) and (3) upon which passage of title turn actually base the test upon the time when the seller has finally committed himself in regard to specific goods. Thus in a "shipment" contract he commits himself by the act of making the shipment. If shipment is not contemplated subsection (3) turns on the seller's final commitment, i.e. the delivery of documents or the making of the contract.

Cross References:

Point 2: Sections 2-102, 2-501 and 2-502.

Point 3: Sections 1-201, 2-402, 2-403, 2-502 and 2-716.

Definitional Cross References:

"Agreement". Section 1-201.

"Bill of lading". Section 1-201.

"Buyer". Section 2-103.

"Contract". Section 1-201.

"Contract for sale". Section 2-106.

"Delivery". Section 1-201.

"Document of title". Section 1-201.

"Good faith". Section 2-103.

"Goods". Section 2-105.

"Party". Section 1-201.

"Purchaser". Section 1-201.

"Receipt" of goods. Section 2-103.

"Remedy". Section 1-201.

"Rights". Section 1-201.

"Sale". Section 2-106.

"Security interest". Section 1-201.

"Seller". Section 2-103.

"Send". Section 1-201.

§ 2-402. Rights of Seller's Creditors Against Sold Goods

(1) Except as provided in subsections (2) and (3), rights of unsecured creditors of the seller with respect to goods which have been identified to a contract for sale are subject to the buyer's rights to recover the goods under this Article (Sections 2-502 and 2-716).

(2) A creditor of the seller may treat a sale or an identification of goods to a contract for sale as void if as against him a retention of possession by the seller is fraud-

ulent under any rule of law of the state where the goods are situated, except that retention of possession in good faith and current course of trade by a merchant-seller for a commercially reasonable time after a sale or identification is not fraudulent.

(3) Nothing in this Article shall be deemed to impair the rights of creditors of the seller

(a) under the provisions of the Article on Secured Transactions (Article 9); or

(b) where identification to the contract or delivery is made not in current course of trade but in satisfaction of or as security for a pre-existing claim for money, security or the like and is made under circumstances which under any rule of law of the state where the goods are situated would apart from this Article constitute the transaction a fraudulent transfer or voidable preference.

Official Comments

Prior Uniform Statutory Provision: Subsection (2) — Section 26, Uniform Sales Act; Subsections (1) and (3) — none.

Changes: Rephrased.

Purposes of Changes and New Matter: To avoid confusion on ordinary issues between current sellers and buyers and issues in the field of preference and hindrance by making it clear that:

1. Local law on questions of hindrance of creditors by the seller's retention of possession of the goods are outside the scope of this Article, but retention of possession in the current course of trade is legitimate. Transactions which fall within the law's policy against improper preferences are reserved from the protection of this Article.

2. The retention of possession of the goods by a merchant seller for a commercially reasonable time after a sale or identification in current course is exempted from attack as fraudulent. Similarly, the provisions of subsection (3) have no application to identification or delivery made in the current course of trade, as measured against general commercial understanding of what a "current" transaction is.

Definitional Cross References:

"Contract for sale". Section 2-106.

"Creditor". Section 1-201.

"Good faith". Section 2-103.

"Goods". Section 2-105.

"Merchant". Section 2-104.

"Money". Section 1-201.

"Reasonable time". Section 1-204.

"Rights". Section 1-201.

"Sale". Section 2-106.

"Seller". Section 2-103.

§ 2-403. Power to Transfer; Good Faith Purchase of Goods; "Entrusting"

(1) A purchaser of goods acquires all title which his transferor had or had power to transfer except that a purchaser of a limited interest acquires rights only to the extent of the interest purchased. A person with voidable title has power to transfer a good title to a good faith purchaser for value. When goods have been delivered under a transaction of purchase the purchaser has such power even though

    (a) the transferor was deceived as to the identity of the purchaser, or

    (b) the delivery was in exchange for a check which is later dishonored, or

    (c) it was agreed that the transaction was to be a "cash sale", or

    (d) the delivery was procured through fraud punishable as larcenous under the criminal law.

(2) Any entrusting of possession of goods to a merchant who deals in goods of that kind gives him power to transfer all rights of the entruster to a buyer in ordinary course of business.

(3) "Entrusting" includes any delivery and any acquiescence in retention of possession regardless of any condition expressed between the parties to the delivery or acquiescence and regardless of whether the procurement of the entrusting or the possessor's disposition of the goods have been such as to be larcenous under the criminal law.

[Publisher's Editorial Note: If a state adopts the repealer of Article 6-Bulk Transfers (Alternative A), subsec. (4) should read as follows:]

(4) The rights of other purchasers of goods and of lien creditors are governed by the Articles on Secured Transactions (Article 9) and Documents of Title (Article 7).

[Publisher's Editorial Note: If a state adopts Revised Article 6-Bulk Sales (Alternative B), subsec. (4) should read as follows:]

(4) The rights of other purchasers of goods and of lien creditors are governed by the Articles on Secured Transactions (Article 9), Bulk Sales (Article 6) and Documents of Title (Article 7).

As amended in 1988.

For material relating to the changes made in text in 1988, see section 3 of Alternative A (Repealer of Article 6-Bulk Transfers) and Conforming Amendment to Section 2-403 following end of Alternative B (Revised Article 6-Bulk Sales).

Official Comments

Prior Uniform Statutory Provision: Sections 20(4), 23, 24, 25, Uniform Sales Act; Section 9, especially 9(2), Uniform Trust Receipts Act; Section 9, Uniform Conditional Sales Act.

Changes: Consolidated and rewritten.

Purposes of Changes: To gather together a series of prior uniform statutory provisions and the case-law thereunder and to state a unified and simplified policy on good faith purchase of goods.

1. The basic policy of our law allowing transfer of such title as the transferor has is generally continued and expanded under subsection (1). In this respect the provisions of the section are applicable to a person taking by any form of "purchase" as defined by this Act. Moreover the policy of this Act expressly providing for the application of supplementary general principles of law to sales transactions wherever appropriate joins with the present section to continue unimpaired all rights acquired under the law of agency or of apparent agency or ownership or other estoppel, whether based on statutory provisions or on case law principles. The section also leaves unimpaired the powers given to selling factors under the earlier Factors Acts. In addition subsection (1) provides specifically for the protection of the good faith purchaser for value in a number of specific situations which have been troublesome under prior law.

On the other hand, the contract of purchase is of course limited by its own terms as in a case of pledge for a limited amount or of sale of a fractional interest in goods.

2. The many particular situations in which a buyer in ordinary course of business from a dealer has been protected against reservation of property or other hidden interest are gathered by subsections (2)-(4) into a single principle protecting persons who buy in ordinary course out of inventory. Consignors have no reason to complain, nor have lenders who hold a security interest in the inventory, since the very purpose of goods in inventory is to be turned into cash by sale.

The principle is extended in subsection (3) to fit with the abolition of the old law of "cash sale" by subsection (1)(c). It is also freed from any technicalities depending on the extended law of larceny; such extension of the concept of theft to include trick, particular types of fraud, and the like is for the purpose of helping conviction of the offender; it has no proper application to the long-standing policy of civil protection of buyers from persons guilty of such trick or fraud. Finally, the policy is extended, in the interest of simplicity and sense, to any entrusting by a bailor; this is in consonance with the explicit provisions of Section 7-205 on the powers of a warehouseman who is also in the business of buying and selling fungible goods of the kind he warehouses. As to entrusting by a secured party, subsection (2) is limited by the more specific provisions of Section 9-307(1), which deny protection to a person buying farm products from a person engaged in farming operations.

3. The definition of "buyer in ordinary course of business" (Section 1-201) is effective here and preserves the essence of the healthy limitations engrafted by the case-law on the older statutes. The older loose concept of good faith and wide definition of value combined to create apparent good faith purchasers in many situations in which the result outraged common sense; the court's solution was to protect the original title especially by use of "cash sale" or of over-technical construction of the enabling clauses of the statutes. But such rulings then turned into limitations on the proper protection of buyers in the ordinary market. Section 1-201(9) cuts down the category of buyer in

ordinary course in such fashion as to take care of the results of the cases, but with no price either in confusion or in injustice to proper dealings in the normal market.

4. Except as provided in subsection (1), the rights of purchasers other than buyers in ordinary course are left to the Articles on Secured Transactions, Documents of Title, and Bulk Sales.

Cross References:

Point 1: Sections 1-103 and 1-201.

Point 2: Sections 1-201, 2-402, 7-205 and 9-307(1).

Points 3 and 4: Sections 1-102, 1-201, 2-104, 2-707 and Articles 6, 7 and 9.

Definitional Cross References:

"Buyer in ordinary course of business". Section 1-201.

"Good faith". Sections 1-201 and 2-103.

"Goods". Section 2-105.

"Person". Section 1-201.

"Purchaser". Section 1-201.

"Signed". Section 1-201.

"Term". Section 1-201.

"Value". Section 1-201.

PART 5. PERFORMANCE

§ 2-501. Insurable Interest in Goods; Manner of Identification of Goods

(1) The buyer obtains a special property and an insurable interest in goods by identification of existing goods as goods to which the contract refers even though the goods so identified are non-conforming and he has an option to return or reject them. Such identification can be made at any time and in any manner explicitly agreed to by the parties. In the absence of explicit agreement identification occurs

    (a) when the contract is made if it is for the sale of goods already existing and identified;

    (b) if the contract is for the sale of future goods other than those described in paragraph (c), when goods are shipped, marked or otherwise designated by the seller as goods to which the contract refers;

    (c) when the crops are planted or otherwise become growing crops or the young are conceived if the contract is for the sale of unborn young to be born within twelve months after contracting or for the sale of crops to be harvested within twelve months or the next normal harvest season after contracting whichever is longer.

(2) The seller retains an insurable interest in goods so long as title to or any security interest in the goods remains in him and where the identification is by the seller alone he may until default or insolvency or notification to the buyer that the identification is final substitute other goods for those identified.

(3) Nothing in this section impairs any insurable interest recognized under any other statute or rule of law.

Official Comments

Prior Uniform Statutory Provision: See Sections 17 and 19, Uniform Sales Act.

Purposes:

1. The present section deals with the manner of identifying goods to the contract so that an insurable interest in the buyer and the rights set forth in the next section will accrue. Generally speaking, identification may be made in any manner "explicitly agreed to" by the parties. The rules of paragraphs (a), (b) and (c) apply only in the absence of such "explicit agreement".

2. In the ordinary case identification of particular existing goods as goods to which the contract refers is unambiguous and may occur in one of many ways. It is possible, however, for the identification to be tentative or contingent. In view of the limited effect given to identification by this Article, the general policy is to resolve all doubts in favor of identification.

3. The provision of this section as to "explicit agreement" clarifies the present confusion in the law of sales which has arisen from the fact that under prior uniform legislation all rules of presumption with reference to the passing of title or to appropriation (which in turn depended upon identification) were regarded as subject to the contrary intention of the parties or of the party appropriating. Such uncertainty is reduced to a minimum under this section by requiring "explicit agreement" of the parties before the rules of paragraphs (a), (b) and (c) are displaced-as they would be by a term giving the buyer power to select the goods. An "explicit" agreement, however, need not necessarily be found in the terms used in the particular transaction. Thus, where a usage of the trade has previously been made explicit by reduction to a standard set of "rules and regulations" currently incorporated by reference into the contracts of the parties, a relevant provision of those "rules and regulations" is "explicit" within the meaning of this section.

4. In view of the limited function of identification there is no requirement in this section that the goods be in deliverable state or that all of the seller's duties with respect to the processing of the goods be completed in order that identification occur. For example, despite identification the risk of loss remains on the seller under the risk of loss provisions until completion of his duties as to the goods and all of his remedies remain dependent upon his not defaulting under the contract.

5. Undivided shares in an identified fungible bulk, such as grain in an elevator or oil in a storage tank, can be sold. The mere making of the contract with reference to an undivided share in an identified fungible bulk is enough under subsection (a) to effect an identification if there is no explicit agreement otherwise. The seller's duty, however, to segregate and deliver according to the contract is not affected by such an identification but is controlled by other provisions of this Article.

6. Identification of crops under paragraph (c) is made upon planting only if they are to be harvested within the year or within the next normal harvest season. The phrase "next normal harvest season" fairly includes nursery stock raised for normally quick "harvest," but plainly excludes a "timber" crop to which the concept of a harvest "season" is inapplicable.

Paragraph (c) is also applicable to a crop of wool or the young of animals to be born within twelve months after contracting. The product of a lumbering, mining or fishing operation, though seasonal, is not within the concept of "growing". Identification under a contract for all or part of the output of such an operation can be effected early in the operation.

Cross References:

Point 1: Section 2-502.

Point 4: Sections 2-509, 2-510 and 2-703.

Point 5: Sections 2-105, 2-308, 2-503 and 2-509.

Point 6: Sections 2-105(1), 2-107(1) and 2-402.

Definitional Cross References:

"Agreement". Section 1-201.

"Contract". Section 1-201.

"Contract for sale". Section 2-106.

"Future goods". Section 2-105.

"Goods". Section 2-105.

"Notification". Section 1-201.

"Party". Section 1-201.

"Sale". Section 2-106.

"Security interest". Section 1-201.

"Seller". Section 2-103.

§ 2-502. Buyer's Right to Goods on Seller's Insolvency

(1) Subject to subsection (2) and even though the goods have not been shipped a buyer who has paid a part or all of the price of goods in which he has a special property under the provisions of the immediately preceding section may on making and keeping good a tender of any unpaid portion of their price recover

them from the seller if the seller becomes insolvent within ten days after receipt of the first installment on their price.

(2) If the identification creating his special property has been made by the buyer he acquires the right to recover the goods only if they conform to the contract for sale.

Official Comments

Prior Uniform Statutory Provision: Compare Sections 17, 18 and 19, Uniform Sales Act.

Purposes:

1. This section gives an additional right to the buyer as a result of identification of the goods to the contract in the manner provided in Section 2-501. The buyer is given a right to the goods on the seller's insolvency occurring within 10 days after he receives the first installment on their price.

2. The question of whether the buyer also acquires a security interest in identified goods and has rights to the goods when insolvency takes place after the ten-day period provided in this section depends upon compliance with the provisions of the Article on Secured Transactions (Article 9).

3. Subsection (2) is included to preclude the possibility of unjust enrichment which exists if the buyer were permitted to recover goods even though they were greatly superior in quality or quantity to that called for by the contract for sale.

Cross References:

Point 1: Sections 1-201 and 2-702.

Point 2: Article 9.

Definitional Cross References:

"Buyer". Section 2-103.

"Conform". Section 2-106.

"Contract for sale". Section 2-106.

"Goods". Section 2-105.

"Insolvent". Section 1-201.

"Rights". Section 1-201.

"Seller". Section 2-103.

§ 2-503. Manner of Seller's Tender of Delivery

(1) Tender of delivery requires that the seller put and hold conforming goods at the buyer's disposition and give the buyer any notification reasonably necessary to enable him to take delivery. The manner, time and place for tender are determined by the agreement and this Article, and in particular

    (a) tender must be at a reasonable hour, and if it is of goods they must be kept available for the period reasonably necessary to enable the buyer to take possession; but

    (b) unless otherwise agreed the buyer must furnish facilities reasonably suited to the receipt of the goods.

(2) Where the case is within the next section respecting shipment tender requires that the seller comply with its provisions.

(3) Where the seller is required to deliver at a particular destination tender requires that he comply with subsection (1) and also in any appropriate case tender documents as described in subsections (4) and (5) of this section.

(4) Where goods are in the possession of a bailee and are to be delivered without being moved

    (a) tender requires that the seller either tender a negotiable document of title covering such goods or procure acknowledgment by the bailee of the buyer's right to possession of the goods; but

    (b) tender to the buyer of a non-negotiable document of title or of a written direction to the bailee to deliver is sufficient tender unless the buyer seasonably objects, and receipt by the bailee of notification of the buyer's rights fixes those rights as against the bailee and all third persons; but risk of loss of the goods and of any failure by the bailee to honor the non-negotiable document of title or to obey the direction remains on the seller until the buyer has had a reasonable time to present the document or direction, and a refusal by the bailee to honor the document or to obey the direction defeats the tender.

(5) Where the contract requires the seller to deliver documents

    (a) he must tender all such documents in correct form, except as provided in this Article with respect to bills of lading in a set (subsection (2) of Section 2-323); and

    (b) tender through customary banking channels is sufficient and dishonor of a draft accompanying the documents constitutes non-acceptance or rejection.

Official Comments

Prior Uniform Statutory Provision: See Sections 11, 19, 20, 43(3) and (4), 46 and 51, Uniform Sales Act.

Changes: The general policy of the above sections is continued and supplemented but subsection (3) changes the rule of prior section 19(5) as to what constitutes a "destination" contract and subsection (4) incorporates a minor correction as to tender of delivery of goods in the possession of a bailee.

Purposes of Changes:

1. The major general rules governing the manner of proper or due tender of delivery are gathered in this section. The term "tender" is used in this Article in two different

senses. In one sense it refers to "due tender" which contemplates an offer coupled with a present ability to fulfill all the conditions resting on the tendering party and must be followed by actual performance if the other party shows himself ready to proceed. Unless the context unmistakably indicates otherwise this is the meaning of "tender" in this Article and the occasional addition of the word "due" is only for clarity and emphasis. At other times it is used to refer to an offer of goods or documents under a contract as if in fulfillment of its conditions even though there is a defect when measured against the contract obligation. Used in either sense, however, "tender" connotes such performance by the tendering party as puts the other party in default if he fails to proceed in some manner.

2. The seller's general duty to tender and deliver is laid down in Section 2-301 and more particularly in Section 2-507. The seller's right to a receipt if he demands one and receipts are customary is governed by Section 1-205. Subsection (1) of the present section proceeds to set forth two primary requirements of tender: first, that the seller "put and hold conforming goods at the buyer's disposition" and, second, that he "give the buyer any notice reasonably necessary to enable him to take delivery."

In cases in which payment is due and demanded upon delivery the "buyer's disposition" is qualified by the seller's right to retain control of the goods until payment by the provision of this Article on delivery on condition. However, where the seller is demanding payment on delivery he must first allow the buyer to inspect the goods in order to avoid impairing his tender unless the contract for sale is on C.I.F., C.O.D., cash against documents or similar terms negating the privilege of inspection before payment.

In the case of contracts involving documents the seller can "put and hold conforming goods at the buyer's disposition" under subsection (1) by tendering documents which give the buyer complete control of the goods under the provisions of Article 7 on due negotiation.

3. Under paragraph (a) of subsection (1) usage of the trade and the circumstances of the particular case determine what is a reasonable hour for tender and what constitutes a reasonable period of holding the goods available.

4. The buyer must furnish reasonable facilities for the receipt of the goods tendered by the seller under subsection (1), paragraph (b). This obligation of the buyer is no part of the seller's tender.

5. For the purposes of subsections (2) and (3) there is omitted from this Article the rule under prior uniform legislation that a term requiring the seller to pay the freight or cost of transportation to the buyer is equivalent to an agreement by the seller to deliver to the buyer or at an agreed destination. This omission is with the specific intention of negating the rule, for under this Article the "shipment" contract is regarded as the normal one and the "destination" contract as the variant type. The seller is not obligated to deliver at a named destination and bear the concurrent risk of loss until arrival, unless he has specifically agreed so to deliver or the commercial understanding of the terms used by the parties contemplates such delivery.

6. Paragraph (a) of subsection (4) continues the rule of the prior uniform legislation as to acknowledgment by the bailee. Paragraph (b) of subsection (4) adopts the rule that between the buyer and the seller the risk of loss remains on the seller during a period reasonable for securing acknowledgment of the transfer from the bailee, while as against all other parties the buyer's rights are fixed as of the time the bailee receives notice of the transfer.

7. Under subsection (5) documents are never "required" except where there is an express contract term or it is plainly implicit in the peculiar circumstances of the case or in a usage of trade. Documents may, of course, be "authorized" although not required, but such cases are not within the scope of this subsection. When documents are required, there are three main requirements of this subsection: (1) "All": each required document is essential to a proper tender; (2) "Such": the documents must be the ones actually required by the contract in terms of source and substance; (3) "Correct form": All documents must be in correct form.

When a prescribed document cannot be procured, a question of fact arises under the provision of this Article on substituted performance as to whether the agreed manner of delivery is actually commercially impracticable and whether the substitute is commercially reasonable.

Cross References:

Point 2: Sections 1-205, 2-301, 2-310, 2-507 and 2-513 and Article 7.

Point 5: Sections 2-308, 2-310 and 2-509.

Point 7: Section 2-614(1).

Specific matters involving tender are covered in many additional sections of this Article. See Sections 1-205, 2-301, 2-306 to 2-319, 2-321(3), 2-504, 2-507(2), 2-511(1), 2-513, 2-612 and 2-614.

Definitional Cross References:

"Agreement". Section 1-201.

"Bill of lading". Section 1-201.

"Buyer". Section 2-103.

"Conforming". Section 2-106.

"Contract". Section 1-201.

"Delivery". Section 1-201.

"Dishonor". Section 3-508.

"Document of title". Section 1-201.

"Draft". Section 3-104.

"Goods". Section 2-105.

"Notification". Section 1-201.

"Reasonable time". Section 1-204.

"Receipt" of goods. Section 2-103.

"Rights". Section 1-201.

"Seasonably". Section 1-204.

"Seller". Section 2-103.

"Written". Section 1-201.

§ 2-504. Shipment by Seller

Where the seller is required or authorized to send the goods to the buyer and the contract does not require him to deliver them at a particular destination, then unless otherwise agreed he must

(a) put the goods in the possession of such a carrier and make such a contract for their transportation as may be reasonable having regard to the nature of the goods and other circumstances of the case; and

(b) obtain and promptly deliver or tender in due form any document necessary to enable the buyer to obtain possession of the goods or otherwise required by the agreement or by usage of trade; and

(c) promptly notify the buyer of the shipment.

Failure to notify the buyer under paragraph (c) or to make a proper contract under paragraph (a) is a ground for rejection only if material delay or loss ensues.

Official Comments

Prior Uniform Statutory Provision: Section 46, Uniform Sales Act.

Changes: Rewritten.

Purposes of Changes: To continue the general policy of the prior uniform statutory provision while incorporating certain modifications with respect to the requirement that the contract with the carrier be made expressly on behalf of the buyer and as to the necessity of giving notice of the shipment to the buyer, so that:

1. The section is limited to "shipment" contracts as contrasted with "destination" contracts or contracts for delivery at the place where the goods are located. The general principles embodied in this section cover the special cases of F.O.B. point of shipment contracts and C.I.F. and C. & F. contracts. Under the preceding section on manner of tender of delivery, due tender by the seller requires that he comply with the requirements of this section in appropriate cases.

2. The contract to be made with the carrier under paragraph (a) must conform to all express terms of the agreement, subject to any substitution necessary because of failure of agreed facilities as provided in the later provision on substituted performance. However, under the policies of this Article on good faith and commercial standards and on buyer's rights on improper delivery, the requirements of explicit provisions must be read in terms of their commercial and not their literal meaning. This policy is made

express with respect to bills of lading in a set in the provision of this Article on form of bills of lading required in overseas shipment.

3. In the absence of agreement, the provision of this Article on options and cooperation respecting performance gives the seller the choice of any reasonable carrier, routing and other arrangements. Whether or not the shipment is at the buyer's expense the seller must see to any arrangements, reasonable in the circumstances, such as refrigeration, watering of live stock, protection against cold, the sending along of any necessary help, selection of specialized cars and the like for paragraph (a) is intended to cover all necessary arrangements whether made by contract with the carrier or otherwise. There is, however, a proper relaxation of such requirements if the buyer is himself in a position to make the appropriate arrangements and the seller gives him reasonable notice of the need to do so. It is an improper contract under paragraph (a) for the seller to agree with the carrier to a limited valuation below the true value and thus cut off the buyer's opportunity to recover from the carrier in the event of loss, when the risk of shipment is placed on the buyer by his contract with the seller.

4. Both the language of paragraph (b) and the nature of the situation it concerns indicate that the requirement that the seller must obtain and deliver promptly to the buyer in due form any document necessary to enable him to obtain possession of the goods is intended to cumulate with the other duties of the seller such as those covered in paragraph (a).

In this connection, in the case of pool car shipments a delivery order furnished by the seller on the pool car consignee, or on the carrier for delivery out of a larger quantity, satisfies the requirements of paragraph (b) unless the contract requires some other form of document.

5. This Article, unlike the prior uniform statutory provision, makes it the seller's duty to notify the buyer of shipment in all cases. The consequences of his failure to do so, however, are limited in that the buyer may reject on this ground only where material delay or loss ensues.

A standard and acceptable manner of notification in open credit shipments is the sending of an invoice and in the case of documentary contracts is the prompt forwarding of the documents as under paragraph (b) of this section. It is also usual to send on a straight bill of lading but this is not necessary to the required notification. However, should such a document prove necessary or convenient to the buyer, as in the case of loss and claim against the carrier, good faith would require the seller to send it on request.

Frequently the agreement expressly requires prompt notification as by wire or cable. Such a term may be of the essence and the final clause of paragraph (c) does not prevent the parties from making this a particular ground for rejection. To have this vital and irreparable effect upon the seller's duties, such a term should be part of the "dickered" terms written in any "form," or should otherwise be called seasonally and sharply to the seller's attention.

6. Generally, under the final sentence of the section, rejection by the buyer is justified only when the seller's dereliction as to any of the requirements of this section in fact is followed by material delay or damage. It rests on the seller, so far as concerns matters not within the peculiar knowledge of the buyer, to establish that his error has not been followed by events which justify rejection.

Cross References:

Point 1: Sections 2-319, 2-320 and 2-503(2).

Point 2: Sections 1-203, 2-323(2), 2-601 and 2-614(1).

Point 3: Section 2-311(2).

Point 5: Section 1-203.

Definitional Cross References:

"Agreement". Section 1-201.

"Buyer". Section 2-103.

"Contract". Section 1-201.

"Delivery". Section 1-201.

"Goods". Section 2-105.

"Notifies". Section 1-201.

"Seller". Section 2-103.

"Send". Section 1-201.

"Usage of trade". Section 1-205.

§ 2-505. Seller's Shipment Under Reservation

(1) Where the seller has identified goods to the contract by or before shipment:

    (a) his procurement of a negotiable bill of lading to his own order or otherwise reserves in him a security interest in the goods. His procurement of the bill to the order of a financing agency or of the buyer indicates in addition only the seller's expectation of transferring that interest to the person named.

    (b) a non-negotiable bill of lading to himself or his nominee reserves possession of the goods as security but except in a case of conditional delivery (subsection (2) of Section 2-507) a non-negotiable bill of lading naming the buyer as consignee reserves no security interest even though the seller retains possession of the bill of lading.

(2) When shipment by the seller with reservation of a security interest is in violation of the contract for sale it constitutes an improper contract for transportation within the preceding section but impairs neither the rights given to the buyer by shipment and identification of the goods to the contract nor the seller's powers as a holder of a negotiable document.

Official Comments

Prior Uniform Statutory Provision: Section 20(2), (3), (4), Uniform Sales Act.

Changes: Completely rephrased, the "powers" of the parties in cases of reservation being emphasized primarily rather than the "rightfulness" of reservation.

Purposes of Changes: To continue in general the policy of the prior uniform statutory provision with certain modifications of emphasis and language, so that:

1. The security interest reserved to the seller under subsection (1) is restricted to securing payment or performance by the buyer and the seller is strictly limited in his disposition and control of the goods as against the buyer and third parties. Under this Article, the provision as to the passing of interest expressly applies "despite any reservation of security title" and also provides that the "rights, obligations and remedies" of the parties are not altered by the incidence of title generally. The security interest, therefore, must be regarded as a means given to the seller to enforce his rights against the buyer which is unaffected by and in turn does not affect the location of title generally. The rules set forth in subsection (1) are not to be altered by any apparent "contrary intent" of the parties as to passing of title, since the rights and remedies of the parties to the contract of sale, as defined in this Article, rest on the contract and its performance or breach and not on stereotyped presumptions as to the location of title.

This Article does not attempt to regulate local procedure in regard to the effective maintenance of the seller's security interest when the action is in replevin by the buyer against the carrier.

2. Every shipment of identified goods under a negotiable bill of lading reserves a security interest in the seller under subsection (1) paragraph (a).

It is frequently convenient for the seller to make the bill of lading to the order of a nominee such as his agent at destination, the financing agency to which he expects to negotiate the document or the bank issuing a credit to him. In many instances, also, the buyer is made the order party. This Article does not deal directly with the question as to whether a bill of lading made out by the seller to the order of a nominee gives the carrier notice of any rights which the nominee may have so as to limit its freedom or obligation to honor the bill of lading in the hands of the seller as the original shipper if the expected negotiation fails. This is dealt with in the Article on Documents of Title (Article 7).

3. A non-negotiable bill of lading taken to a party other than the buyer under subsection (1) paragraph (b) reserves possession of the goods as security in the seller but if he seeks to withhold the goods improperly the buyer can tender payment and recover them.

4. In the case of a shipment by non-negotiable bill of lading taken to a buyer, the seller, under subsection (1) retains no security interest or possession as against the buyer and by the shipment he de facto loses control as against the carrier except where he rightfully and effectively stops delivery in transit. In cases in which the contract gives the seller the right to payment against delivery, the seller, by making an imme-

diate demand for payment, can show that his delivery is conditional, but this does not prevent the buyer's power to transfer full title to a sub-buyer in ordinary course or other purchaser under Section 2-403.

5. Under subsection (2) an improper reservation by the seller which would constitute a breach in no way impairs such of the buyer's rights as result from identification of the goods. The security title reserved by the seller under subsection (1) does not protect his holding of the document or the goods for the purpose of exacting more than is due him under the contract.

Cross References:

Point 1: Section 1-201.

Point 2: Article 7.

Point 3: Sections 2-501(2) and 2-504.

Point 4: Sections 2-403, 2-507(2) and 2-705.

Point 5: Sections 2-310, 2-319(4), 2-320(4), 2-501 and 2-502 and Article 7.

Definitional Cross References:

"Bill of lading". Section 1-201.

"Buyer". Section 2-103.

"Consignee". Section 7-102.

"Contract". Section 1-201.

"Contract for sale". Section 2-106.

"Delivery". Section 1-201.

"Financing agency". Section 2-104.

"Goods". Section 2-105.

"Holder". Section 1-201.

"Person". Section 1-201.

"Security interest". Section 1-201.

"Seller". Section 2-103.

§ 2-506. Rights of Financing Agency

(1) A financing agency by paying or purchasing for value a draft which relates to a shipment of goods acquires to the extent of the payment or purchase and in addition to its own rights under the draft and any document of title securing it any rights of the shipper in the goods including the right to stop delivery and the shipper's right to have the draft honored by the buyer.

(2) The right to reimbursement of a financing agency which has in good faith honored or purchased the draft under commitment to or authority from the buyer is not impaired by subsequent discovery of defects with reference to any relevant document which was apparently regular on its face.

Official Comments

Prior Uniform Statutory Provision: None.

Purposes:

1. "Financing agency" is broadly defined in this Article to cover every normal instance in which a party aids or intervenes in the financing of a sales transaction. The term as used in subsection (1) is not in any sense intended as a limitation and covers any other appropriate situation which may arise outside the scope of the definition.

2. "Paying" as used in subsection (1) is typified by the letter of credit, or "authority to pay" situation in which a banker, by arrangement with the buyer or other consignee, pays on his behalf a draft for the price of the goods. It is immaterial whether the draft is formally drawn on the party paying or his principal, whether it is a sight draft paid in cash or a time draft "paid" in the first instance by acceptance, or whether the payment is viewed as absolute or conditional. All of these cases constitute "payment" under this subsection. Similarly, "purchasing for value" is used to indicate the whole area of financing by the seller's banker, and the principle of subsection (1) is applicable without any niceties of distinction between "purchase," "discount," "advance against collection" or the like. But it is important to notice that the only right to have the draft honored that is acquired is that against the buyer; if any right against any one else is claimed it will have to be under some separate obligation of that other person. A letter of credit does not necessarily protect purchasers of drafts. See Article 5. And for the relations of the parties to documentary drafts see Part 5 of Article 4.

3. Subsection (1) is made applicable to payments or advances against a draft which "relates to" a shipment of goods and this has been chosen as a term of maximum breadth. In particular the term is intended to cover the case of a draft against an invoice or against a delivery order. Further, it is unnecessary that there be an explicit assignment of the invoice attached to the draft to bring the transaction within the reason of this subsection.

4. After shipment, "the rights of the shipper in the goods" are merely security rights and are subject to the buyer's right to force delivery upon tender of the price. The rights acquired by the financing agency are similarly limited and, moreover, if the agency fails to procure any outstanding negotiable document of title, it may find its exercise of these rights hampered or even defeated by the seller's disposition of the document to a third party. This section does not attempt to create any new rights in the financing agency against the carrier which would force the latter to honor a stop order from the agency, a stranger to the shipment, or any new rights against a holder to whom a document of title has been duly negotiated under Article 7.

Cross References:

Point 1: Section 2-104(2) and Article 4.

Point 2: Part 5 of Article 4, and Article 5.

Point 4: Sections 2-501 and 2-502(1) and Article 7.

Definitional Cross References:

"Buyer". Section 2-103.

"Document of title". Section 1-201.

"Draft". Section 3-104.

"Financing agency". Section 2-104.

"Good faith". Section 2-103.

"Goods". Section 2-105.

"Honor". Section 1-201.

"Purchase". Section 1-201.

"Rights". Section 1-201.

"Value". Section 1-201.

§ 2-507. Effect of Seller's Tender; Delivery on Condition

(1) Tender of delivery is a condition to the buyer's duty to accept the goods and, unless otherwise agreed, to his duty to pay for them. Tender entitles the seller to acceptance of the goods and to payment according to the contract.

(2) Where payment is due and demanded on the delivery to the buyer of goods or documents of title, his right as against the seller to retain or dispose of them is conditional upon his making the payment due.

Official Comments

Prior Uniform Statutory Provision: See Sections 11, 41, 42 and 69, Uniform Sales Act.

Purposes:

1. Subsection (1) continues the policies of the prior uniform statutory provisions with respect to tender and delivery by the seller. Under this Article the same rules in these matters are applied to present sales and to contracts for sale. But the provisions of this subsection must be read within the framework of the other sections of this Article which bear upon the question of delivery and payment.

2. The "unless otherwise agreed" provision of subsection (1) is directed primarily to cases in which payment in advance has been promised or a letter of credit term has been included. Payment "according to the contract" contemplates immediate payment, payment at the end of an agreed credit term, payment by a time acceptance or the like. Under this Act, "contract" means the total obligation in law which results from the parties' agreement including the effect of this Article. In this context, therefore, there must be considered the effect in law of such provisions as those on means and manner of payment and on failure of agreed means and manner of payment.

3. Subsection (2) deals with the effect of a conditional delivery by the seller and in such a situation makes the buyer's "right as against the seller" conditional upon payment. These words are used as words of limitation to conform with the policy set forth in the bona fide purchase sections of this Article. Should the seller after making such a conditional delivery fail to follow up his rights, the condition is waived. This subsection (2) codifies the cash seller's right of reclamation which is in the nature of a lien. There is no specific time limit for a cash seller to exercise the right of reclamation. However, the right will be defeated by delay causing prejudice to the buyer, waiver, estoppel, or ratification of the buyer's right to retain possession. Common law rules and precedents governing such principles are applicable (Section 1-103). If third parties are involved, Section 2-403(1) protects good faith purchasers. See PEB Commentary No. 1, dated March 10, 1990 [Appendix V, infra].

Cross References:

Point 1: Sections 2-310, 2-503, 2-511, 2-601 and 2-711 to 2-713.

Point 2: Sections 1-201, 2-511 and 2-614.

Point 3: Sections 2-401, 2-403, and 2-702(1)(b).

Definitional Cross References:

"Buyer". Section 2-103.

"Contract". Section 1-201.

"Delivery". Section 1-201.

"Document of title". Section 1-201.

"Goods". Section 2-105.

"Rights". Section 1-201.

"Seller". Section 2-103.

§ 2-508. Cure by Seller of Improper Tender or Delivery; Replacement

(1) Where any tender or delivery by the seller is rejected because non-conforming and the time for performance has not yet expired, the seller may seasonably notify the buyer of his intention to cure and may then within the contract time make a conforming delivery.

(2) Where the buyer rejects a non-conforming tender which the seller had reasonable grounds to believe would be acceptable with or without money allowance the seller may if he seasonably notifies the buyer have a further reasonable time to substitute a conforming tender.

Official Comments

Prior Uniform Statutory Provision: None.

Purposes:

1. Subsection (1) permits a seller who has made a non-conforming tender in any case to make a conforming delivery within the contract time upon seasonable notification to the buyer. It applies even where the seller has taken back the non-conforming goods and refunded the purchase price. He may still make a good tender within the contract period. The closer, however, it is to the contract date, the greater is the necessity for extreme promptness on the seller's part in notifying of his intention to cure, if such notification is to be "seasonable" under this subsection.

The rule of this subsection, moreover, is qualified by its underlying reasons. Thus if, after contracting for June delivery, a buyer later makes known to the seller his need for shipment early in the month and the seller ships accordingly, the "contract time" has been cut down by the supervening modification and the time for cure of tender must be referred to this modified time term.

2. Subsection (2) seeks to avoid injustice to the seller by reason of a surprise rejection by the buyer. However, the seller is not protected unless he had "reasonable grounds to believe" that the tender would be acceptable. Such reasonable grounds can lie in prior course of dealing, course of performance or usage of trade as well as in the particular circumstances surrounding the making of the contract. The seller is charged with commercial knowledge of any factors in a particular sales situation which require him to comply strictly with his obligations under the contract as, for example, strict conformity of documents in an overseas shipment or the sale of precision parts or chemicals for use in manufacture. Further, if the buyer gives notice either implicitly, as by a prior course of dealing involving rigorous inspections, or expressly, as by the deliberate inclusion of a "no replacement" clause in the contract, the seller is to be held to rigid compliance. If the clause appears in a "form" contract evidence that it is out of line with trade usage or the prior course of dealing and was not called to the seller's attention may be sufficient to show that the seller had reasonable grounds to believe that the tender would be acceptable.

3. The words "a further reasonable time to substitute a conforming tender" are intended as words of limitation to protect the buyer. What is a "reasonable time" depends upon the attending circumstances. Compare Section 2-511 on the comparable case of a seller's surprise demand for legal tender.

4. Existing trade usages permitting variations without rejection but with price allowance enter into the agreement itself as contractual limitations of remedy and are not covered by this section.

Cross References:

Point 2: Section 2-302.

Point 3: Section 2-511.

Point 4: Sections 1-205 and 2-721.

Definitional Cross References:

"Buyer". Section 2-103.

"Conforming". Section 2-106.

"Contract". Section 1-201.

"Money". Section 1-201.

"Notifies". Section 1-201.

"Reasonable time". Section 1-204.

"Seasonably". Section 1-204.

"Seller". Section 2-103.

§ 2-509. Risk of Loss in the Absence of Breach

(1) Where the contract requires or authorizes the seller to ship the goods by carrier

    (a) if it does not require him to deliver them at a particular destination, the risk of loss passes to the buyer when the goods are duly delivered to the carrier even though the shipment is under reservation (Section 2-505); but

    (b) if it does require him to deliver them at a particular destination and the goods are there duly tendered while in the possession of the carrier, the risk of loss passes to the buyer when the goods are there duly so tendered as to enable the buyer to take delivery.

(2) Where the goods are held by a bailee to be delivered without being moved, the risk of loss passes to the buyer

    (a) on his receipt of a negotiable document of title covering the goods; or

    (b) on acknowledgment by the bailee of the buyer's right to possession of the goods; or

    (c) after his receipt of a non-negotiable document of title or other written direction to deliver, as provided in subsection (4)(b) of Section 2-503.

(3) In any case not within subsection (1) or (2), the risk of loss passes to the buyer on his receipt of the goods if the seller is a merchant; otherwise the risk passes to the buyer on tender of delivery.

(4) The provisions of this section are subject to contrary agreement of the parties and to the provisions of this Article on sale on approval (Section 2-327) and on effect of breach on risk of loss (Section 2-510).

Official Comments

Prior Uniform Statutory Provision: Section 22, Uniform Sales Act.

Changes: Rewritten, subsection (3) of this section modifying prior law.

Purposes of Changes: To make it clear that:

1. The underlying theory of these sections on risk of loss is the adoption of the contractual approach rather than an arbitrary shifting of the risk with the "property" in the goods. The scope of the present section, therefore, is limited strictly to those cases where there has been no breach by the seller. Where for any reason his delivery or tender fails to conform to the contract, the present section does not apply and the situation is governed by the provisions on effect of breach on risk of loss.

2. The provisions of subsection (1) apply where the contract "requires or authorizes" shipment of the goods. This language is intended to be construed parallel to comparable language in the section on shipment by seller. In order that the goods be "duly delivered to the carrier" under paragraph (a) a contract must be entered into with the carrier which will satisfy the requirements of the section on shipment by the seller and the delivery must be made under circumstances which will enable the seller to take any further steps necessary to a due tender. The underlying reason of this subsection does not require that the shipment be made after contracting, but where, for example, the seller buys the goods afloat and later diverts the shipment to the buyer, he must identify the goods to the contract before the risk of loss can pass. To transfer the risk it is enough that a proper shipment and a proper identification come to apply to the same goods although, aside from special agreement, the risk will not pass retroactively to the time of shipment in such a case.

3. Whether the contract involves delivery at the seller's place of business or at the situs of the goods, a merchant seller cannot transfer risk of loss and it remains upon him until actual receipt by the buyer, even though full payment has been made and the buyer has been notified that the goods are at his disposal. Protection is afforded him, in the event of breach by the buyer, under the next section.

The underlying theory of this rule is that a merchant who is to make physical delivery at his own place continues meanwhile to control the goods and can be expected to insure his interest in them. The buyer, on the other hand, has no control of the goods and it is extremely unlikely that he will carry insurance on goods not yet in his possession.

4. Where the agreement provides for delivery of the goods as between the buyer and seller without removal from the physical possession of a bailee, the provisions on manner of tender of delivery apply on the point of transfer of risk. Due delivery of a negotiable document of title covering the goods or acknowledgment by the bailee that he holds for the buyer completes the "delivery" and passes the risk.

5. The provisions of this section are made subject by subsection (4) to the "contrary agreement" of the parties. This language is intended as the equivalent of the phrase "unless otherwise agreed" used more frequently throughout this Act. "Contrary" is in no way used as a word of limitation and the buyer and seller are left free to readjust their rights and risks as declared by this section in any manner agreeable to them. Contrary agreement can also be found in the circumstances of the case, a trade usage or practice, or a course of dealing or performance.

Cross References:

Point 1: Section 2-510(1).

Point 2: Sections 2-503 and 2-504.

Point 3: Sections 2-104, 2-503 and 2-510.

Point 4: Section 2-503(4).

Point 5: Section 1-201.

Definitional Cross References:

"Agreement". Section 1-201.

"Buyer". Section 2-103.

"Contract". Section 1-201.

"Delivery". Section 1-201.

"Document of title". Section 1-201.

"Goods". Section 2-105.

"Merchant". Section 2-104.

"Party". Section 1-201.

"Receipt" of goods. Section 2-103.

"Sale on approval". Section 2-326.

"Seller". Section 2-103.

§ 2-510. Effect of Breach on Risk of Loss

(1) Where a tender or delivery of goods so fails to conform to the contract as to give a right of rejection the risk of their loss remains on the seller until cure or acceptance.

(2) Where the buyer rightfully revokes acceptance he may to the extent of any deficiency in his effective insurance coverage treat the risk of loss as having rested on the seller from the beginning.

(3) Where the buyer as to conforming goods already identified to the contract for sale repudiates or is otherwise in breach before risk of their loss has passed to him, the seller may to the extent of any deficiency in his effective insurance coverage treat the risk of loss as resting on the buyer for a commercially reasonable time.

Official Comments

Prior Uniform Statutory Provision: None.

Purposes: To make clear that:

1. Under subsection (1) the seller by his individual action cannot shift the risk of loss to the buyer unless his action conforms with all the conditions resting on him under the contract.

2. The "cure" of defective tenders contemplated by subsection (1) applies only to those situations in which the seller makes changes in goods already tendered, such as repair, partial substitution, sorting out from an improper mixture and the like since "cure" by repossession and new tender has no effect on the risk of loss of the goods originally tendered. The seller's privilege of cure does not shift the risk, however, until the cure is completed.

Where defective documents are involved a cure of the defect by the seller or a waiver of the defects by the buyer will operate to shift the risk under this section. However, if the goods have been destroyed prior to the cure or the buyer is unaware of their destruction at the time he waives the defect in the documents, the risk of the loss must still be borne by the seller, for the risk shifts only at the time of cure, waiver of documentary defects or acceptance of the goods.

3. In cases where there has been a breach of the contract, if the one in control of the goods is the aggrieved party, whatever loss or damage may prove to be uncovered by his insurance falls upon the contract breaker under subsections (2) and (3) rather than upon him. The word "effective" as applied to insurance coverage in those subsections is used to meet the case of supervening insolvency of the insurer. The "deficiency" referred to in the text means such deficiency in the insurance coverage as exists without subrogation. This section merely distributes the risk of loss as stated and is not intended to be disturbed by any subrogation of an insurer.

Cross Reference:

Section 2-509.

Definitional Cross References:

"Buyer". Section 2-103.

"Conform". Section 2-106.

"Contract for sale". Section 2-106.

"Goods". Section 2-105.

"Seller". Section 2-103.

§ 2-511. Tender of Payment by Buyer; Payment by Check

(1) Unless otherwise agreed tender of payment is a condition to the seller's duty to tender and complete any delivery.

(2) Tender of payment is sufficient when made by any means or in any manner current in the ordinary course of business unless the seller demands payment in legal tender and gives any extension of time reasonably necessary to procure it.

(3) Subject to the provisions of this Act on the effect of an instrument on an obligation (Section 3-310), payment by check is conditional and is defeated as between the parties by dishonor of the check on due presentment.

As amended in 1994.

Official Comments

Prior Uniform Statutory Provision: Section 42, Uniform Sales Act.

Changes: Rewritten by this section and Section 2-507.

Purposes of Changes:

1. The requirement of payment against delivery in subsection (1) is applicable to non-commercial sales generally and to ordinary sales at retail although it has no application to the great body of commercial contracts which carry credit terms. Subsection (1) applies also to documentary contracts in general and to contracts which look to shipment by the seller but contain no term on time and manner of payment, in which situations the payment may, in proper case, be demanded against delivery of appropriate documents.

In the case of specific transactions such as C.O.D. sales or agreements providing for payment against documents, the provisions of this subsection must be considered in conjunction with the special sections of the Article dealing with such terms. The provision that tender of payment is a condition to the seller's duty to tender and complete "any delivery" integrates this section with the language and policy of the section on delivery in several lots which call for separate payment. Finally, attention should be directed to the provision on right to adequate assurance of performance which recognizes, even before the time for tender, an obligation on the buyer not to impair the seller's expectation of receiving payment in due course.

2. Unless there is agreement otherwise the concurrence of the conditions as to tender of payment and tender of delivery requires their performance at a single place or time. This Article determines that place and time by determining in various other sections the place and time for tender of delivery under various circumstances and in particular types of transactions. The sections dealing with time and place of delivery together with the section on right to inspection of goods answer the subsidiary question as to when payment may be demanded before inspection by the buyer.

3. The essence of the principle involved in subsection (2) is avoidance of commercial surprise at the time of performance. The section on substituted performance covers the peculiar case in which legal tender is not available to the commercial community.

4. Subsection (3) is concerned with the rights and obligations as between the parties to a sales transaction when payment is made by check. This Article recognizes that the taking of a seemingly solvent party's check is commercially normal and proper and, if due diligence is exercised in collection, is not to be penalized in any way. The conditional character of the payment under this section refers only to the effect of the transaction "as between the parties" thereto and does not purport to cut into the law of "absolute" and "conditional" payment as applied to such other problems as the discharge of sureties or the responsibilities of a drawee bank which is at the same time an agent for collection.

The phrase "by check" includes not only the buyer's own but any check which does not effect a discharge under Article 3 (Section 3-802). Similarly the reason of this subsection should apply and the same result should be reached where the buyer "pays" by sight draft on a commercial firm which is financing him.

5. Under subsection (3) payment by check is defeated if it is not honored upon due presentment. This corresponds to the provisions of article on Commercial Paper. (Section 3-802). But if the seller procures certification of the check instead of cashing it, the buyer is discharged. (Section 3-411).

6. Where the instrument offered by the buyer is not a payment but a credit instrument such as a note or a check post-dated by even one day, the seller's acceptance of the instrument insofar as third parties are concerned, amounts to a delivery on credit and his remedies are set forth in the section on buyer's insolvency. As between the buyer and the seller, however, the matter turns on the present subsection and the section on conditional delivery and subsequent dishonor of the instrument gives the seller rights on it as well as for breach of the contract for sale.

Cross References:

Point 1: Sections 2-307, 2-310, 2-320, 2-325, 2-503, 2-513 and 2-609.

Point 2: Sections 2-307, 2-310, 2-319, 2-322, 2-503, 2-504 and 2-513.

Point 3: Section 2-614.

Point 5: Article 3, esp. Sections 3-802 and 3-411.

Point 6: Sections 2-507, 2-702, and Article 3.

Definitional Cross References:

"Buyer". Section 2-103.

"Check". Section 3-104.

"Dishonor". Section 3-508.

"Party". Section 1-201.

"Reasonable time". Section 1-204.

"Seller". Section 2-103.

§ 2-512. Payment by Buyer Before Inspection

[1995 Amendments to text indicated by strikeout and underline.]

(1) Where the contract requires payment before inspection non-conformity of the goods does not excuse the buyer from so making payment unless
    (a) the non-conformity appears without inspection; or
    (b) despite tender of the required documents the circumstances would justify injunction against honor under ~~the provisions of~~ this Act (Section ~~5-114~~ 5-109(b)).

(2) Payment pursuant to subsection (1) does not constitute an acceptance of goods or impair the buyer's right to inspect or any of his remedies.

As amended in 1995.

Official Comments

Prior Uniform Statutory Provision: None, but see Sections 47 and 49, Uniform Sales Act.

Purposes:

1. Subsection (1) of the present section recognizes that the essence of a contract providing for payment before inspection is the intention of the parties to shift to the buyer the risks which would usually rest upon the seller. The basic nature of the transaction is thus preserved and the buyer is in most cases required to pay first and litigate as to any defects later.

2. "Inspection" under this section is an inspection in a manner reasonable for detecting defects in goods whose surface appearance is satisfactory.

3. Clause (a) of this subsection states an exception to the general rule based on common sense and normal commercial practice. The apparent non-conformity referred to is one which is evident in the mere process of taking delivery.

4. Clause (b) is concerned with contracts for payment against documents and incorporates the general clarification and modification of the case law contained in the section on excuse of a financing agency. Section 5-114.

5. Subsection (2) makes explicit the general policy of the Uniform Sales Act that the payment required before inspection in no way impairs the buyer's remedies or rights in the event of a default by the seller. The remedies preserved to the buyer are all of his remedies, which include as a matter of reason the remedy for total non-delivery after payment in advance.

The provision on performance or acceptance under reservation of rights does not apply to the situations contemplated here in which payment is made in due course under the contract and the buyer need not pay "under protest" or the like in order to preserve his rights as to defects discovered upon inspection.

6. This section applies to cases in which the contract requires payment before inspection either by the express agreement of the parties or by reason of the effect in law of that contract. The present section must therefore be considered in conjunction with the provision on right to inspection of goods which sets forth the instances in which the buyer is not entitled to inspection before payment.

Cross References:

Point 4: Article 5.

Point 5: Section 1-207.

Point 6: Section 2-513(3).

Definitional Cross References:

"Buyer". Section 2-103.

"Conform". Section 2-106.

"Contract". Section 1-201.

"Financing agency". Section 2-104.

"Goods". Section 2-105.

"Remedy". Section 1-201.

"Rights". Section 1-201.

§ 2-513. Buyer's Right to Inspection of Goods

(1) Unless otherwise agreed and subject to subsection (3), where goods are tendered or delivered or identified to the contract for sale, the buyer has a right before payment or acceptance to inspect them at any reasonable place and time and in any reasonable manner. When the seller is required or authorized to send the goods to the buyer, the inspection may be after their arrival.

(2) Expenses of inspection must be borne by the buyer but may be recovered from the seller if the goods do not conform and are rejected.

(3) Unless otherwise agreed and subject to the provisions of this Article on C.I.F. contracts (subsection (3) of Section 2-321), the buyer is not entitled to inspect the goods before payment of the price when the contract provides
   (a) for delivery "C.O.D." or on other like terms; or
   (b) for payment against documents of title, except where such payment is due only after the goods are to become available for inspection.

(4) A place or method of inspection fixed by the parties is presumed to be exclusive but unless otherwise expressly agreed it does not postpone identification or shift the place for delivery or for passing the risk of loss. If compliance becomes impossible, inspection shall be as provided in this section unless the place or method fixed was clearly intended as an indispensable condition failure of which avoids the contract.

Official Comments

Prior Uniform Statutory Provisions: Section 47(2), (3), Uniform Sales Act.

Changes: Rewritten, Subsections (2) and (3) being new.

Purposes of Changes and New Matter: To correspond in substance with the prior uniform statutory provision and to incorporate in addition some of the results of the better case law so that:

1. The buyer is entitled to inspect goods as provided in subsection (1) unless it has been otherwise agreed by the parties. The phrase "unless otherwise agreed" is intended principally to cover such situations as those outlined in subsections (3) and (4) and those in which the agreement of the parties negates inspection before tender of delivery. However, no agreement by the parties can displace the entire right of inspection except where the contract is simply for the sale of "this thing." Even in a sale of boxed goods "as is" inspection is a right of the buyer, since if the boxes prove to contain some other merchandise altogether the price can be recovered back; nor do the limitations of the provision on effect of acceptance apply in such a case.

2. The buyer's right of inspection is available to him upon tender, delivery or appropriation of the goods with notice to him. Since inspection is available to him on tender, where payment is due against delivery he may, unless otherwise agreed, make his inspection before payment of the price. It is also available to him after receipt of the goods and so may be postponed after receipt for a reasonable time. Failure to inspect before payment does not impair the right to inspect after receipt of the goods unless the case falls within subsection (4) on agreed and exclusive inspection provisions. The right to inspect goods which have been appropriated with notice to the buyer holds whether or not the sale was by sample.

3. The buyer may exercise his right of inspection at any reasonable time or place and in any reasonable manner. It is not necessary that he select the most appropriate time, place or manner to inspect or that his selection be the customary one in the trade or locality. Any reasonable time, place or manner is available to him and the reasonableness will be determined by trade usages, past practices between the parties and the other circumstances of the case.

The last sentence of subsection (1) makes it clear that the place of arrival of shipped goods is a reasonable place for their inspection.

4. Expenses of an inspection made to satisfy the buyer of the seller's performance must be assumed by the buyer in the first instance. Since the rule provides merely for an allocation of expense there is no policy to prevent the parties from providing otherwise in the agreement. Where the buyer would normally bear the expenses of the inspection but the goods are rightly rejected because of what the inspection reveals, demonstrable and reasonable costs of the inspection are part of his incidental damage caused by the seller's breach.

5. In the case of payment against documents, subsection (3) requires payment before inspection, since shipping documents against which payment is to be made will

commonly arrive and be tendered while the goods are still in transit. This Article recognizes no exception in any peculiar case in which the goods happen to arrive before the documents. However, where by the agreement payment is to await the arrival of the goods, inspection before payment becomes proper since the goods are then "available for inspection."

Where by the agreement the documents are to be held until arrival the buyer is entitled to inspect before payment since the goods are then "available for inspection". Proof of usage is not necessary to establish this right, but if inspection before payment is disputed the contrary must be established by usage or by an explicit contract term to that effect.

For the same reason, that the goods are available for inspection, a term calling for payment against storage documents or a delivery order does not normally bar the buyer's right to inspection before payment under subsection (3)(b). This result is reinforced by the buyer's right under subsection (1) to inspect goods which have been appropriated with notice to him.

6. Under subsection (4) an agreed place or method of inspection is generally held to be intended as exclusive. However, where compliance with such an agreed inspection term becomes impossible, the question is basically one of intention. If the parties clearly intend that the method of inspection named is to be a necessary condition without which the entire deal is to fail, the contract is at an end if that method becomes impossible. On the other hand, if the parties merely seek to indicate a convenient and reliable method but do not intend to give up the deal in the event of its failure, any reasonable method of inspection may be substituted under this Article.

Since the purpose of an agreed place of inspection is only to make sure at that point whether or not the goods will be thrown back, the "exclusive" feature of the named place is satisfied under this Article if the buyer's failure to inspect there is held to be an acceptance with the knowledge of such defects as inspection would have revealed within the section on waiver of buyer's objections by failure to particularize. Revocation of the acceptance is limited to the situations stated in the section pertaining to that subject. The reasonable time within which to give notice of defects within the section on notice of breach begins to run from the point of the "acceptance."

7. Clauses on time of inspection are commonly clauses which limit the time in which the buyer must inspect and give notice of defects. Such clauses are therefore governed by the section of this Article which requires that such a time limitation must be reasonable.

8. Inspection under this Article is not to be regarded as a "condition precedent to the passing of title" so that risk until inspection remains on the seller. Under subsection (4) such an approach cannot be sustained. Issues between the buyer and seller are settled in this Article almost wholly by special provisions and not by the technical determination of the locus of the title. Thus "inspection as a condition to the passing of title" becomes a concept almost without meaning. However, in peculiar circumstances inspection may still have some of the consequences hitherto sought and obtained under that concept.

9. "Inspection" under this section has to do with the buyer's check-up on whether the seller's performance is in accordance with a contract previously made and is not to be confused with the "examination" of the goods or of a sample or model of them at the time of contracting which may affect the warranties involved in the contract.

Cross References:

Generally: Sections 2-310(b), 2-321(3) and 2-606(1)(b).

Point 1: Section 2-607.

Point 2: Sections 2-501 and 2-502.

Point 4: Section 2-715.

Point 5: Section 2-321(3).

Point 6: Sections 2-606 to 2-608.

Point 7: Section 1-204.

Point 8: Comment to Section 2-401.

Point 9: Section 2-316(3)(b).

Definitional Cross References:

"Buyer". Section 2-103.

"Conform". Section 2-106.

"Contract". Section 1-201.

"Contract for sale". Section 2-106.

"Document of title". Section 1-201.

"Goods". Section 2-105.

"Party". Section 1-201.

"Presumed". Section 1-201.

"Reasonable time". Section 1-204.

"Rights". Section 1-201.

"Seller". Section 2-103.

"Send". Section 1-201.

"Term". Section 1-201.

§ 2-514. When Documents Deliverable on Acceptance; When on Payment

Unless otherwise agreed documents against which a draft is drawn are to be delivered to the drawee on acceptance of the draft if it is payable more than three days after presentment; otherwise, only on payment.

Official Comments

Prior Uniform Statutory Provision: Section 41, Uniform Bills of Lading Act.

Changes: Rewritten.

Purposes of Changes: To make the provision one of general application so that:

1. It covers any document against which a draft may be drawn, whatever may be the form of the document, and applies to interpret the action of a seller or consignor insofar as it may affect the rights and duties of any buyer, consignee or financing agency concerned with the paper. Supplementary or corresponding provisions are found in Sections 4-503 and 5-112.

2. An "arrival" draft is a sight draft within the purpose of this section.

Cross References:

Point 1: See Sections 2-502, 2-505(2), 2-507(2), 2-512, 2-513, 2-607 concerning protection of rights of buyer and seller, and 4-503 and 5-112 on delivery of documents.

Definitional Cross References:

"Delivery". Section 1-201.

"Draft". Section 3-104.

§ 2-515. Preserving Evidence of Goods in Dispute

In furtherance of the adjustment of any claim or dispute

(a) either party on reasonable notification to the other and for the purpose of ascertaining the facts and preserving evidence has the right to inspect, test and sample the goods including such of them as may be in the possession or control of the other; and

(b) the parties may agree to a third party inspection or survey to determine the conformity or condition of the goods and may agree that the findings shall be binding upon them in any subsequent litigation or adjustment.

Official Comments

Prior Uniform Statutory Provision: None.

Purposes:

1. To meet certain serious problems which arise when there is a dispute as to the quality of the goods and thereby perhaps to aid the parties in reaching a settlement, and to further the use of devices which will promote certainty as to the condition of the goods, or at least aid in preserving evidence of their condition.

2. Under paragraph (a), to afford either party an opportunity for preserving evidence, whether or not agreement has been reached, and thereby to reduce uncertainty in any litigation and, in turn perhaps, to promote agreement.

Paragraph (a) does not conflict with the provisions on the seller's right to resell rejected goods or the buyer's similar right. Apparent conflict between these provisions which will be suggested in certain circumstances is to be resolved by requiring prompt action by the parties. Nor does paragraph (a) impair the effect of a term for payment before inspection.

Short of such defects as amount to fraud or substantial failure of consideration, non-conformity is neither an excuse nor a defense to an action for non-acceptance of documents. Normally, therefore, until the buyer has made payment, inspected and rejected the goods, there is no occasion or use for the rights under paragraph (a).

3. Under paragraph (b), to provide for third party inspection upon the agreement of the parties, thereby opening the door to amicable adjustments based upon the findings of such third parties.

The use of the phrase "conformity or condition" makes it clear that the parties' agreement may range from a complete settlement of all aspects of the dispute by a third party to the use of a third party merely to determine and record the condition of the goods so that they can be resold or used to reduce the stake in controversy. "Conformity", at one end of the scale of possible issues, includes the whole question of interpretation of the agreement and its legal effect, the state of the goods in regard to quality and condition, whether any defects are due to factors which operate at the risk of the buyer, and the degree of non-conformity where that may be material. "Condition", at the other end of the scale, includes nothing but the degree of damage or deterioration which the goods show. Paragraph (b) is intended to reach any point in the gamut which the parties may agree upon.

The principle of the section on reservation of rights reinforces this paragraph in simplifying such adjustments as the parties wish to make in partial settlement while reserving their rights as to any further points. Paragraph (b) also suggests the use of arbitration, where desired, of any points left open, but nothing in this section is intended to repeal or amend any statute governing arbitration. Where any question arises as to the extent of the parties' agreement under the paragraph, the presumption should be that it was meant to extend only to the relation between the contract description and the goods as delivered, since that is what a craftsman in the trade would normally be expected to report upon. Finally, a written and authenticated report of inspection or tests by a third party, whether or not sampling has been practicable, is entitled to be admitted as evidence under this Act, for it is a third party document.

Cross References:

Point 2: Sections 2-513(3), 2-706 and 2-711(2) and Article 5.

Point 3: Sections 1-202 and 1-207.

Definitional Cross References:

"Conform". Section 2-106.

"Goods". Section 2-105.

"Notification". Section 1-201.

"Party". Section 1-201.

PART 6. BREACH, REPUDIATION AND EXCUSE

§ 2-601. Buyer's Rights on Improper Delivery

Subject to the provisions of this Article on breach in installment contracts (Section 2-612) and unless otherwise agreed under the sections on contractual limitations of remedy (Sections 2-718 and 2-719), if the goods or the tender of delivery fail in any respect to conform to the contract, the buyer may

(a) reject the whole; or

(b) accept the whole; or

(c) accept any commercial unit or units and reject the rest.

Official Comments

Prior Uniform Statutory Provision: No one general equivalent provision but numerous provisions, dealing with situations of non-conformity where buyer may accept or reject, including Sections 11, 44 and 69(1), Uniform Sales Act.

Changes: Partial acceptance in good faith is recognized and the buyer's remedies on the contract for breach of warranty and the like, where the buyer has returned the goods after transfer of title, are no longer barred.

Purposes of Changes: To make it clear that:

1. A buyer accepting a non-conforming tender is not penalized by the loss of any remedy otherwise open to him. This policy extends to cover and regulate the acceptance of a part of any lot improperly tendered in any case where the price can reasonably be apportioned. Partial acceptance is permitted whether the part of the goods accepted conforms or not. The only limitation on partial acceptance is that good faith and commercial reasonableness must be used to avoid undue impairment of the value of the remaining portion of the goods. This is the reason for the insistence on the "commercial unit" in paragraph (c). In this respect, the test is not only what unit has been the basis of contract, but whether the partial acceptance produces so materially adverse an effect on the remainder as to constitute bad faith.

2. Acceptance made with the knowledge of the other party is final. An original refusal to accept may be withdrawn by a later acceptance if the seller has indicated that he is holding the tender open. However, if the buyer attempts to accept, either in whole or in part, after his original rejection has caused the seller to arrange for other disposition of the goods, the buyer must answer for any ensuing damage since the next section provides that any exercise of ownership after rejection is wrongful as against the seller. Further, he is liable even though the seller may choose to treat his action as acceptance rather than conversion, since the damage flows from the misleading

notice. Such arrangements for resale or other disposition of the goods by the seller must be viewed as within the normal contemplation of a buyer who has given notice of rejection. However, the buyer's attempts in good faith to dispose of defective goods where the seller has failed to give instructions within a reasonable time are not to be regarded as an acceptance.

Cross References:

Sections 2-602(2)(a), 2-612, 2-718 and 2-719.

Definitional Cross References:

"Buyer". Section 2-103.

"Commercial unit". Section 2-105.

"Conform". Section 2-106.

"Contract". Section 1-201.

"Goods". Section 2-105.

"Installment contract". Section 2-612.

"Rights". Section 1-201.

§ 2-602. Manner and Effect of Rightful Rejection

(1) Rejection of goods must be within a reasonable time after their delivery or tender. It is ineffective unless the buyer seasonably notifies the seller.

(2) Subject to the provisions of the two following sections on rejected goods (Sections 2-603 and 2-604),

    (a) after rejection any exercise of ownership by the buyer with respect to any commercial unit is wrongful as against the seller; and

    (b) if the buyer has before rejection taken physical possession of goods in which he does not have a security interest under the provisions of this Article (subsection (3) of Section 2-711), he is under a duty after rejection to hold them with reasonable care at the seller's disposition for a time sufficient to permit the seller to remove them; but

    (c) the buyer has no further obligations with regard to goods rightfully rejected.

(3) The seller's rights with respect to goods wrongfully rejected are governed by the provisions of this Article on Seller's remedies in general (Section 2-703).

Official Comments

Prior Uniform Statutory Provision: Section 50, Uniform Sales Act.

Changes: Rewritten.

Purposes of Changes: To make it clear that:

1. A tender or delivery of goods made pursuant to a contract of sale, even though wholly non-conforming, requires affirmative action by the buyer to avoid acceptance.

Under subsection (1), therefore, the buyer is given a reasonable time to notify the seller of his rejection, but without such seasonable notification his rejection is ineffective. The sections of this Article dealing with inspection of goods must be read in connection with the buyer's reasonable time for action under this subsection. Contract provisions limiting the time for rejection fall within the rule of the section on "Time" and are effective if the time set gives the buyer a reasonable time for discovery of defects. What constitutes a due "notifying" of rejection by the buyer to the seller is defined in Section 1-201.

2. Subsection (2) lays down the normal duties of the buyer upon rejection, which flow from the relationship of the parties. Beyond his duty to hold the goods with reasonable care for the buyer's [seller's] disposition, this section continues the policy of prior uniform legislation in generally relieving the buyer from any duties with respect to them, except when the circumstances impose the limited obligation of salvage upon him under the next section.

3. The present section applies only to rightful rejection by the buyer. If the seller has made a tender which in all respects conforms to the contract, the buyer has a positive duty to accept and his failure to do so constitutes a "wrongful rejection" which gives the seller immediate remedies for breach. Subsection (3) is included here to emphasize the sharp distinction between the rejection of an improper tender and the non-acceptance which is a breach by the buyer.

4. The provisions of this section are to be appropriately limited or modified when a negotiation is in process.

Cross References:

Point 1: Sections 1-201, 1-204(1) and (3), 2-512(2), 2-513(1) and 2-606(1)(b).

Point 2: Section 2-603(1).

Point 3: Section 2-703.

Definitional Cross References:

"Buyer". Section 2-103.

"Commercial unit". Section 2-105.

"Goods". Section 2-105.

"Merchant". Section 2-104.

"Notifies". Section 1-201.

"Reasonable time". Section 1-204.

"Remedy". Section 1-201.

"Rights". Section 1-201.

"Seasonably". Section 1-204.

"Security interest". Section 1-201.

"Seller". Section 2-103.

§ 2-603. Merchant Buyer's Duties as to Rightfully Rejected Goods

(1) Subject to any security interest in the buyer (subsection (3) of Section 2-711), when the seller has no agent or place of business at the market of rejection a merchant buyer is under a duty after rejection of goods in his possession or control to follow any reasonable instructions received from the seller with respect to the goods and in the absence of such instructions to make reasonable efforts to sell them for the seller's account if they are perishable or threaten to decline in value speedily. Instructions are not reasonable if on demand indemnity for expenses is not forthcoming.

(2) When the buyer sells goods under subsection (1), he is entitled to reimbursement from the seller or out of the proceeds for reasonable expenses of caring for and selling them, and if the expenses include no selling commission then to such commission as is usual in the trade or if there is none to a reasonable sum not exceeding ten per cent on the gross proceeds.

(3) In complying with this section the buyer is held only to good faith and good faith conduct hereunder is neither acceptance nor conversion nor the basis of an action for damages.

Official Comments

Prior Uniform Statutory Provision: None.

Purposes:

1. This section recognizes the duty imposed upon the merchant buyer by good faith and commercial practice to follow any reasonable instructions of the seller as to reshipping, storing, delivery to a third party, reselling or the like. Subsection (1) goes further and extends the duty to include the making of reasonable efforts to effect a salvage sale where the value of the goods is threatened and the seller's instructions do not arrive in time to prevent serious loss.

2. The limitations on the buyer's duty to resell under subsection (1) are to be liberally construed. The buyer's duty to resell under this section arises from commercial necessity and thus is present only when the seller has "no agent or place of business at the market of rejection". A financing agency which is acting in behalf of the seller in handling the documents rejected by the buyer is sufficiently the seller's agent to lift the burden of salvage resale from the buyer. (See provisions of Sections 4-503 and 5-112 on bank's duties with respect to rejected documents.) The buyer's duty to resell is extended only to goods in his "possession or control", but these are intended as words of wide, rather than narrow, import. In effect, the measure of the buyer's "control" is whether he can practicably effect control without undue commercial burden.

3. The explicit provisions for reimbursement and compensation to the buyer in subsection (2) are applicable and necessary only where he is not acting under instructions from the seller. As provided in subsection (1) the seller's instructions to be "reasonable" must on demand of the buyer include indemnity for expenses.

4. Since this section makes the resale of perishable goods an affirmative duty in contrast to a mere right to sell as under the case law, subsection (3) makes it clear that the buyer is liable only for the exercise of good faith in determining whether the value of the goods is sufficiently threatened to justify a quick resale or whether he has waited a sufficient length of time for instructions, or what a reasonable means and place of resale is.

5. A buyer who fails to make a salvage sale when his duty to do so under this section has arisen is subject to damages pursuant to the section on liberal administration of remedies.

Cross References:

Point 2: Sections 4-503 and 5-112.

Point 5: Section 1-106. Compare generally section 2-706.

Definitional Cross References:

"Buyer". Section 2-103.

"Good faith". Section 1-201.

"Goods". Section 2-105.

"Merchant". Section 2-104.

"Security interest". Section 1-201.

"Seller". Section 2-103.

§ 2-604. Buyer's Options as to Salvage of Rightfully Rejected Goods

Subject to the provisions of the immediately preceding section on perishables if the seller gives no instructions within a reasonable time after notification of rejection the buyer may store the rejected goods for the seller's account or reship them to him or resell them for the seller's account with reimbursement as provided in the preceding section. Such action is not acceptance or conversion.

Official Comments

Prior Uniform Statutory Provision: None.

Purposes:

The basic purpose of this section is twofold: on the one hand it aims at reducing the stake in dispute and on the other at avoiding the pinning of a technical "acceptance" on a buyer who has taken steps towards realization on or preservation of the goods in good faith. This section is essentially a salvage section and the buyer's right to act under it is conditioned upon (1) non-conformity of the goods, (2) due notification of rejection to the seller under the section on manner of rejection, and (3) the absence of any instructions from the seller which the merchant-buyer has a duty to follow under the preceding section.

This section is designed to accord all reasonable leeway to a rightfully rejecting buyer acting in good faith. The listing of what the buyer may do in the absence of instructions from the seller is intended to be not exhaustive but merely illustrative. This is not a "merchant's" section and the options are pure options given to merchant and nonmerchant buyers alike. The merchant-buyer, however, may in some instances be under a duty rather than an option to resell under the provisions of the preceding section.

Cross References:

Sections 2-602(1), and 2-603(1) and 2-706.

Definitional Cross References:

"Buyer". Section 2-103.

"Notification". Section 1-201.

"Reasonable time". Section 1-204.

"Seller". Section 2-103.

§ 2-605. Waiver of Buyer's Objections by Failure to Particularize

(1) The buyer's failure to state in connection with rejection a particular defect which is ascertainable by reasonable inspection precludes him from relying on the unstated defect to justify rejection or to establish breach

    (a) where the seller could have cured it if stated seasonably; or

    (b) between merchants when the seller has after rejection made a request in writing for a full and final written statement of all defects on which the buyer proposes to rely.

(2) Payment against documents made without reservation of rights precludes recovery of the payment for defects apparent on the face of the documents.

Official Comments

Prior Uniform Statutory Provision: None.

Purposes:

1. The present section rests upon a policy of permitting the buyer to give a quick and informal notice of defects in a tender without penalizing him for omissions in his statement, while at the same time protecting a seller who is reasonably misled by the buyer's failure to state curable defects.

2. Where the defect in a tender is one which could have been cured by the seller, a buyer who merely rejects the delivery without stating his objections to it is probably acting in commercial bad faith and seeking to get out of a deal which has become unprofitable. Subsection (1)(a), following the general policy of this Article which looks to preserving the deal wherever possible, therefore insists that the seller's right to correct his tender in such circumstances be protected.

3. When the time for cure is past, subsection (1)(b) makes it plain that a seller is entitled upon request to a final statement of objections upon which he can rely. What

is needed is that he make clear to the buyer exactly what is being sought. A formal demand under paragraph (b) will be sufficient in the case of a merchant-buyer.

4. Subsection (2) applies to the particular case of documents the same principle which the section on effects of acceptance applies to the case of goods. The matter is dealt with in this section in terms of "waiver" of objections rather than of right to revoke acceptance, partly to avoid any confusion with the problems of acceptance of goods and partly because defects in documents which are not taken as grounds for rejection are generally minor ones. The only defects concerned in the present subsection are defects in the documents which are apparent on their face. Where payment is required against the documents they must be inspected before payment, and the payment then constitutes acceptance of the documents. Under the section dealing with this problem, such acceptance of the documents does not constitute an acceptance of the goods or impair any options or remedies of the buyer for their improper delivery. Where the documents are delivered without requiring such contemporary action as payment from the buyer, the reason of the next section on what constitutes acceptance of goods, applies. Their acceptance by non-objection is therefore postponed until after a reasonable time for their inspection. In either situation, however, the buyer "waives" only what is apparent on the face of the documents.

Cross References:

Point 2: Section 2-508.

Point 4: Sections 2-512(2), 2-606(1)(b), 2-607(2).

Definitional Cross References:

"Between merchants". Section 2-104.

"Buyer". Section 2-103.

"Seasonably". Section 1-204.

"Seller". Section 2-103.

"Writing" and "written". Section 1-201.

§ 2-606. What Constitutes Acceptance of Goods

(1) Acceptance of goods occurs when the buyer
  (a) after a reasonable opportunity to inspect the goods signifies to the seller that the goods are conforming or that he will take or retain them in spite of their non-conformity; or
  (b) fails to make an effective rejection (subsection (1) of Section 2-602), but such acceptance does not occur until the buyer has had a reasonable opportunity to inspect them; or
  (c) does any act inconsistent with the seller's ownership; but if such act is wrongful as against the seller it is an acceptance only if ratified by him.

(2) Acceptance of a part of any commercial unit is acceptance of that entire unit.

Official Comments

Prior Uniform Statutory Provision: Section 48, Uniform Sales Act.

Changes: Rewritten, the qualification in paragraph (c) and subsection (2) being new; otherwise the general policy of the prior legislation is continued.

Purposes of Changes and New Matter: To make it clear that:

1. Under this Article "acceptance" as applied to goods means that the buyer, pursuant to the contract, takes particular goods which have been appropriated to the contract as his own, whether or not he is obligated to do so, and whether he does so by words, action, or silence when it is time to speak. If the goods conform to the contract, acceptance amounts only to the performance by the buyer of one part of his legal obligation.

2. Under this Article acceptance of goods is always acceptance of identified goods which have been appropriated to the contract or are appropriated by the contract. There is no provision for "acceptance of title" apart from acceptance in general, since acceptance of title is not material under this Article to the detailed rights and duties of the parties. (See Section 2-401). The refinements of the older law between acceptance of goods and of title become unnecessary in view of the provisions of the sections on effect and revocation of acceptance, on effects of identification and on risk of loss, and those sections which free the seller's and buyer's remedies from the complications and confusions caused by the question of whether title has or has not passed to the buyer before breach.

3. Under paragraph (a), payment made after tender is always one circumstance tending to signify acceptance of the goods but in itself it can never be more than one circumstance and is not conclusive. Also, a conditional communication of acceptance always remains subject to its expressed conditions.

4. Under paragraph (c), any action taken by the buyer, which is inconsistent with his claim that he has rejected the goods, constitutes an acceptance. However, the provisions of paragraph (c) are subject to the sections dealing with rejection by the buyer which permit the buyer to take certain actions with respect to the goods pursuant to his options and duties imposed by those sections, without effecting an acceptance of the goods. The second clause of paragraph (c) modifies some of the prior case law and makes it clear that "acceptance" in law based on the wrongful act of the acceptor is acceptance only as against the wrongdoer and then only at the option of the party wronged.

In the same manner in which a buyer can bind himself, despite his insistence that he is rejecting or has rejected the goods, by an act inconsistent with the seller's ownership under paragraph (c), he can obligate himself by a communication of acceptance despite a prior rejection under paragraph (a). However, the sections on buyer's rights on improper delivery and on the effect of rightful rejection, make it clear that after he once rejects a tender, paragraph (a) does not operate in favor of the buyer unless the seller has re-tendered the goods or has taken affirmative action indicating that he is holding the tender open. See also Comment 2 to Section 2-601.

5. Subsection (2) supplements the policy of the section on buyer's rights on improper delivery, recognizing the validity of a partial acceptance but insisting that the buyer exercise this right only as to whole commercial units.

Cross References:

Point 2: Sections 2-401, 2-509, 2-510, 2-607, 2-608 and Part 7.

Point 4: Sections 2-601 through 2-604.

Point 5: Section 2-601.

Definitional Cross References:

"Buyer". Section 2-103.

"Commercial unit". Section 2-105.

"Goods". Section 2-105.

"Seller". Section 2-103.

§ 2-607. Effect of Acceptance; Notice of Breach; Burden of Establishing Breach After Acceptance; Notice of Claim or Litigation to Person Answerable Over

(1) The buyer must pay at the contract rate for any goods accepted.

(2) Acceptance of goods by the buyer precludes rejection of the goods accepted and if made with knowledge of a non-conformity cannot be revoked because of it unless the acceptance was on the reasonable assumption that the non-conformity would be seasonably cured but acceptance does not of itself impair any other remedy provided by this Article for non-conformity.

(3) Where a tender has been accepted
   (a) the buyer must within a reasonable time after he discovers or should have discovered any breach notify the seller of breach or be barred from any remedy; and
   (b) if the claim is one for infringement or the like (subsection (3) of Section 2-312) and the buyer is sued as a result of such a breach he must so notify the seller within a reasonable time after he receives notice of the litigation or be barred from any remedy over for liability established by the litigation.

(4) The burden is on the buyer to establish any breach with respect to the goods accepted.

(5) Where the buyer is sued for breach of a warranty or other obligation for which his seller is answerable over
   (a) he may give his seller written notice of the litigation. If the notice states that the seller may come in and defend and that if the seller does not do so he will be bound in any action against him by his buyer by any determination of fact common to the two litigations, then unless the seller after seasonable receipt of the notice does come in and defend he is so bound.

(b) if the claim is one for infringement or the like (subsection (3) of Section 2-312) the original seller may demand in writing that his buyer turn over to him control of the litigation including settlement or else be barred from any remedy over and if he also agrees to bear all expense and to satisfy any adverse judgment, then unless the buyer after seasonable receipt of the demand does turn over control the buyer is so barred.

(6) The provisions of subsections (3), (4) and (5) apply to any obligation of a buyer to hold the seller harmless against infringement or the like (subsection (3) of Section 2-312).

Official Comments

Prior Uniform Statutory Provision: Subsection (1)-Section 41, Uniform Sales Act; Subsections (2) and (3)-Sections 49 and 69, Uniform Sales Act.

Changes: Rewritten.

Purposes of Changes: To continue the prior basic policies with respect to acceptance of goods while making a number of minor though material changes in the interest of simplicity and commercial convenience so that:

1. Under subsection (1), once the buyer accepts a tender the seller acquires a right to its price on the contract terms. In cases of partial acceptance, the price of any part accepted is, if possible, to be reasonably apportioned, using the type of apportionment familiar to the courts in quantum valebant cases, to be determined in terms of "the contract rate," which is the rate determined from the bargain in fact (the agreement) after the rules and policies of this Article have been brought to bear.

2. Under subsection (2) acceptance of goods precludes their subsequent rejection. Any return of the goods thereafter must be by way of revocation of acceptance under the next section. Revocation is unavailable for a non-conformity known to the buyer at the time of acceptance, except where the buyer has accepted on the reasonable assumption that the non-conformity would be seasonably cured.

3. All other remedies of the buyer remain unimpaired under subsection (2). This is intended to include the buyer's full rights with respect to future installments despite his acceptance of any earlier non-conforming installment.

4. The time of notification is to be determined by applying commercial standards to a merchant buyer. "A reasonable time" for notification from a retail consumer is to be judged by different standards so that in his case it will be extended, for the rule of requiring notification is designed to defeat commercial bad faith, not to deprive a good faith consumer of his remedy.

The content of the notification need merely be sufficient to let the seller know that the transaction is still troublesome and must be watched. There is no reason to require that the notification which saves the buyer's rights under this section must include a clear statement of all the objections that will be relied on by the buyer, as under the section covering statements of defects upon rejection (Section 2-605). Nor is there reason for requiring the notification to be a claim for damages or of any threatened litigation or other resort to a remedy. The notification which saves the buyer's rights under this Article need only be such as informs the seller that the transaction is claimed to involve a breach, and thus opens the way for normal settlement through negotiation.

5. Under this Article various beneficiaries are given rights for injuries sustained by them because of the seller's breach of warranty. Such a beneficiary does not fall within the reason of the present section in regard to discovery of defects and the giving of notice within a reasonable time after acceptance, since he has nothing to do with acceptance. However, the reason of this section does extend to requiring the beneficiary to notify the seller that an injury has occurred. What is said above, with regard to the extended time for reasonable notification from the lay consumer after the injury is also applicable here; but even a beneficiary can be properly held to the use of good faith in notifying, once he has had time to become aware of the legal situation.

6. Subsection (4) unambiguously places the burden of proof to establish breach on the buyer after acceptance. However, this rule becomes one purely of procedure when the tender accepted was non-conforming and the buyer has given the seller notice of breach under subsection (3). For subsection (2) makes it clear that acceptance leaves unimpaired the buyer's right to be made whole, and that right can be exercised by the buyer not only by way of cross-claim for damages, but also by way of recoupment in diminution or extinction of the price.

7. Subsections (3)(b) and (5)(b) give a warrantor against infringement an opportunity to defend or compromise third-party claims or be relieved of his liability. Subsection (5)(a) codifies for all warranties the practice of voucher to defend. Compare Section 3-803. Subsection (6) makes these provisions applicable to the buyer's liability for infringement under Section 2-312.

8. All of the provisions of the present section are subject to any explicit reservation of rights.

Cross References:

Point 1: Section 1-201.

Point 2: Section 2-608.

Point 4: Sections 1-204 and 2-605.

Point 5: Section 2-318.

Point 6: Section 2-717.

Point 7: Sections 2-312 and 3-803.

Point 8: Section 1-207.

Definitional Cross References:

"Burden of establishing". Section 1-201.

"Buyer". Section 2-103.

"Conform". Section 2-106.

"Contract". Section 1-201.

"Goods". Section 2-105.

"Notifies". Section 1-201.

"Reasonable time". Section 1-204.

"Remedy". Section 1-201.

"Seasonably". Section 1-204.

§ 2-608. Revocation of Acceptance in Whole or in Part

(1) The buyer may revoke his acceptance of a lot or commercial unit whose non-conformity substantially impairs its value to him if he has accepted it

    (a) on the reasonable assumption that its non-conformity would be cured and it has not been seasonably cured; or

    (b) without discovery of such non-conformity if his acceptance was reasonably induced either by the difficulty of discovery before acceptance or by the seller's assurances.

(2) Revocation of acceptance must occur within a reasonable time after the buyer discovers or should have discovered the ground for it and before any substantial change in condition of the goods which is not caused by their own defects. It is not effective until the buyer notifies the seller of it.

(3) A buyer who so revokes has the same rights and duties with regard to the goods involved as if he had rejected them.

Official Comments

Prior Uniform Statutory Provision: Section 69(1)(d), (3), (4) and (5), Uniform Sales Act.

Changes: Rewritten.

Purposes of Changes: To make it clear that:

1. Although the prior basic policy is continued, the buyer is no longer required to elect between revocation of acceptance and recovery of damages for breach. Both are now available to him. The non-alternative character of the two remedies is stressed by the terms used in the present section. The section no longer speaks of "rescission," a term capable of ambiguous application either to transfer of title to the goods or to the contract of sale and susceptible also of confusion with cancellation for cause of an executed or executory portion of the contract. The remedy under this section is instead referred to simply as "revocation of acceptance" of goods tendered under a contract for sale and involves no suggestion of "election" of any sort.

2. Revocation of acceptance is possible only where the non-conformity substantially impairs the value of the goods to the buyer. For this purpose the test is not what

the seller had reason to know at the time of contracting; the question is whether the non-conformity is such as will in fact cause a substantial impairment of value to the buyer though the seller had no advance knowledge as to the buyer's particular circumstances.

3. "Assurances" by the seller under paragraph (b) of subsection (1) can rest as well in the circumstances or in the contract as in explicit language used at the time of delivery. The reason for recognizing such assurances is that they induce the buyer to delay discovery. These are the only assurances involved in paragraph (b). Explicit assurances may be made either in good faith or bad faith. In either case any remedy accorded by this Article is available to the buyer under the section on remedies for fraud.

4. Subsection (2) requires notification of revocation of acceptance within a reasonable time after discovery of the grounds for such revocation. Since this remedy will be generally resorted to only after attempts at adjustment have failed, the reasonable time period should extend in most cases beyond the time in which notification of breach must be given, beyond the time for discovery of non-conformity after acceptance and beyond the time for rejection after tender. The parties may by their agreement limit the time for notification under this section, but the same sanctions and considerations apply to such agreements as are discussed in the comment on manner and effect of rightful rejection.

5. The content of the notice under subsection (2) is to be determined in this case as in others by considerations of good faith, prevention of surprise, and reasonable adjustment. More will generally be necessary than the mere notification of breach required under the preceding section. On the other hand the requirements of the section on waiver of buyer's objections do not apply here. The fact that quick notification of trouble is desirable affords good ground for being slow to bind a buyer by his first statement. Following the general policy of this Article, the requirements of the content of notification are less stringent in the case of a non-merchant buyer.

6. Under subsection (2) the prior policy is continued of seeking substantial justice in regard to the condition of goods restored to the seller. Thus the buyer may not revoke his acceptance if the goods have materially deteriorated except by reason of their own defects. Worthless goods, however, need not be offered back and minor defects in the articles reoffered are to be disregarded.

7. The policy of the section allowing partial acceptance is carried over into the present section and the buyer may revoke his acceptance, in appropriate cases, as to the entire lot or any commercial unit thereof.

Cross References:

Point 3: Section 2-721.

Point 4: Sections 1-204, 2-602 and 2-607.

Point 5: Sections 2-605 and 2-607.

Point 7: Section 2-601.

Definitional Cross References:

"Buyer". Section 2-103.

"Commercial unit". Section 2-105.

"Conform". Section 2-106.

"Goods". Section 2-105.

"Lot". Section 2-105.

"Notifies". Section 1-201.

"Reasonable time". Section 1-204.

"Rights". Section 1-201.

"Seasonably". Section 1-204.

"Seller". Section 2-103.

§ 2-609. Right to Adequate Assurance of Performance

(1) A contract for sale imposes an obligation on each party that the other's expectation of receiving due performance will not be impaired. When reasonable grounds for insecurity arise with respect to the performance of either party the other may in writing demand adequate assurance of due performance and until he receives such assurance may if commercially reasonable suspend any performance for which he has not already received the agreed return.

(2) Between merchants the reasonableness of grounds for insecurity and the adequacy of any assurance offered shall be determined according to commercial standards.

(3) Acceptance of any improper delivery or payment does not prejudice the aggrieved party's right to demand adequate assurance of future performance.

(4) After receipt of a justified demand failure to provide within a reasonable time not exceeding thirty days such assurance of due performance as is adequate under the circumstances of the particular case is a repudiation of the contract.

Official Comments

Prior Uniform Statutory Provision: See Sections 53, 54(1)(b), 55 and 63(2), Uniform Sales Act.

Purposes:

1. The section rests on the recognition of the fact that the essential purpose of a contract between commercial men is actual performance and they do not bargain merely for a promise, or for a promise plus the right to win a lawsuit and that a continuing sense of reliance and security that the promised performance will be forthcoming when due, is an important feature of the bargain. If either the willingness or the ability of a party to perform declines materially between the time of contracting and the time

for performance, the other party is threatened with the loss of a substantial part of what he has bargained for. A seller needs protection not merely against having to deliver on credit to a shaky buyer, but also against having to procure and manufacture the goods, perhaps turning down other customers. Once he has been given reason to believe that the buyer's performance has become uncertain, it is an undue hardship to force him to continue his own performance. Similarly, a buyer who believes that the seller's deliveries have become uncertain cannot safely wait for the due date of performance when he has been buying to assure himself of materials for his current manufacturing or to replenish his stock of merchandise.

2. Three measures have been adopted to meet the needs of commercial men in such situations. First, the aggrieved party is permitted to suspend his own performance and any preparation therefor, with excuse for any resulting necessary delay, until the situation has been clarified. "Suspend performance" under this section means to hold up performance pending the outcome of the demand, and includes also the holding up of any preparatory action. This is the same principle which governs the ancient law of stoppage and seller's lien, and also of excuse of a buyer from prepayment if the seller's actions manifest that he cannot or will not perform. (Original Act, Section 63(2).)

Secondly, the aggrieved party is given the right to require adequate assurance that the other party's performance will be duly forthcoming. This principle is reflected in the familiar clauses permitting the seller to curtail deliveries if the buyer's credit becomes impaired, which when held within the limits of reasonableness and good faith actually express no more than the fair business meaning of any commercial contract.

Third, and finally, this section provides the means by which the aggrieved party may treat the contract as broken if his reasonable grounds for insecurity are not cleared up within a reasonable time. This is the principle underlying the law of anticipatory breach, whether by way of defective part performance or by repudiation. The present section merges these three principles of law and commercial practice into a single theory of general application to all sales agreements looking to future performance.

3. Subsection (2) of the present section requires that "reasonable" grounds and "adequate" assurance as used in subsection (1) be defined by commercial rather than legal standards. The express reference to commercial standards carries no connotation that the obligation of good faith is not equally applicable here.

Under commercial standards and in accord with commercial practice, a ground for insecurity need not arise from or be directly related to the contract in question. The law as to "dependence" or "independence" of promises within a single contract does not control the application of the present section.

Thus a buyer who falls behind in "his account" with the seller, even though the items involved have to do with separate and legally distinct contracts, impairs the seller's expectation of due performance. Again, under the same test, a buyer who requires precision parts which he intends to use immediately upon delivery, may have reasonable grounds for insecurity if he discovers that his seller is making defective deliveries of such parts to other buyers with similar needs. Thus, too, in a situation such as arose in Jay Dreher Corporation v. Delco Appliance Corporation, 93 F.2d 275 (C.C.A. 2, 1937), where a manufacturer gave a dealer an exclusive franchise for the sale of his product but on two or three occasions breached the exclusive dealing clause, although there was no default in orders, deliveries or payments under the separate sales contract between the parties, the aggrieved dealer would be entitled to suspend his performance of the contract for sale under the present section and to demand assurance that the exclusive dealing contract would be lived up to. There is no need for an explicit clause tying the exclusive franchise into the contract for the sale of goods since the situation itself ties the agreements together.

The nature of the sales contract enters also into the question of reasonableness. For example, a report from an apparently trustworthy source that the seller had shipped defective goods or was planning to ship them would normally give the buyer reasonable grounds for insecurity. But when the buyer has assumed the risk of payment before inspection of the goods, as in a sales contract on C.I.F. or similar cash against documents terms, that risk is not to be evaded by a demand for assurance. Therefore no ground for insecurity would exist under this section unless the report went to a ground which would excuse payment by the buyer.

4. What constitutes "adequate" assurance of due performance is subject to the same test of factual conditions. For example, where the buyer can make use of a defective delivery, a mere promise by a seller of good repute that he is giving the matter his attention and that the defect will not be repeated, is normally sufficient. Under the same circumstances, however, a similar statement by a known corner-cutter might well be considered insufficient without the posting of a guaranty or, if so demanded by the buyer, a speedy replacement of the delivery involved. By the same token where a delivery has defects, even though easily curable, which interfere with easy use by the buyer, no verbal assurance can be deemed adequate which is not accompanied by replacement, repair, money-allowance, or other commercially reasonable cure.

A fact situation such as arose in Corn Products Refining Co. v. Fasola, 94 N.J.L. 181, 109 A. 505 (1920) offers illustration both of reasonable grounds for insecurity and "adequate" assurance. In that case a contract for the sale of oils on 30 days' credit, 2% off for payment within 10 days, provided that credit was to be extended to the buyer only if his financial responsibility was satisfactory to the seller. The buyer had been in the habit of taking advantage of the discount but at the same time that he failed to make his customary 10 day payment, the seller heard rumors, in fact false, that the buyer's financial condition was shaky. Thereupon, the seller demanded cash before shipment or security satisfactory to him. The buyer sent a good credit report from his banker, expressed willingness to make payments when due on the 30 day terms and insisted on further deliveries under the contract. Under this Article the rumors, although false, were enough to make the buyer's financial condition "unsatisfactory" to the seller under the contract clause. Moreover, the buyer's practice of taking the cash discounts is enough, apart from the contract clause, to lay a commercial foundation for suspicion when the practice is suddenly stopped. These matters, however, go only to the justification of the seller's demand for security, or his "reasonable grounds for insecurity".

The adequacy of the assurance given is not measured as in the type of "satisfaction" situation affected with intangibles, such as in personal service cases, cases involving a third party's judgment as final, or cases in which the whole contract is dependent on one party's satisfaction, as in a sale on approval. Here, the seller must exercise good faith and observe commercial standards. This Article thus approves the statement of the court in James B. Berry's Sons Co. of Illinois v. Monark Gasoline & Oil Co., Inc., 32 F.2d 74 (C.C.A. 8, 1929), that the seller's satisfaction under such a clause must be based upon reason and must not be arbitrary or capricious; and rejects the purely personal "good faith" test of the Corn Products Refining Co. case, which held that in the seller's sole judgment, if for any reason he was dissatisfied, he was entitled to revoke the credit. In the absence of the buyer's failure to take the 2% discount as was his custom, the banker's report given in that case would have been "adequate" assurance under this Act, regardless of the language of the "satisfaction" clause. However, the seller is reasonably entitled to feel insecure at a sudden expansion of the buyer's use of a credit term, and should be entitled either to security or to a satisfactory explanation.

The entire foregoing discussion as to adequacy of assurance by way of explanation is subject to qualification when repeated occasions for the application of this section arise. This Act recognizes that repeated delinquencies must be viewed as cumulative. On the other hand, commercial sense also requires that if repeated claims for assurance are made under this section, the basis for these claims must be increasingly obvious.

5. A failure to provide adequate assurance of performance and thereby to re-establish the security of expectation, results in a breach only "by repudiation" under subsection (4). Therefore, the possibility is continued of retraction of the repudiation under the section dealing with that problem, unless the aggrieved party has acted on the breach in some manner.

The thirty day limit on the time to provide assurance is laid down to free the question of reasonable time from uncertainty in later litigation.

6. Clauses seeking to give the protected party exceedingly wide powers to cancel or readjust the contract when ground for insecurity arises must be read against the fact that good faith is a part of the obligation of the contract and not subject to modification by agreement and includes, in the case of a merchant, the reasonable observance of commercial standards of fair dealing in the trade. Such clauses can thus be effective to enlarge the protection given by the present section to a certain extent, to fix the reasonable time within which requested assurance must be given, or to define adequacy of the assurance in any commercially reasonable fashion. But any clause seeking to set up arbitrary standards for action is ineffective under this Article. Acceleration clauses are treated similarly in the Articles on Commercial Paper and Secured Transactions.

Cross References:

Point 3: Section 1-203.

Point 5: Section 2-611.

Point 6: Sections 1-203 and 1-208 and Articles 3 and 9.

Definitional Cross References:

"Aggrieved party". Section 1-201.

"Between merchants". Section 2-104.

"Contract". Section 1-201.

"Contract for sale". Section 2-106.

"Party". Section 1-201.

"Reasonable time". Section 1-204.

"Rights". Section 1-201.

"Writing". Section 1-201.

§ 2-610. Anticipatory Repudiation

When either party repudiates the contract with respect to a performance not yet due the loss of which will substantially impair the value of the contract to the other, the aggrieved party may

(a) for a commercially reasonable time await performance by the repudiating party; or

(b) resort to any remedy for breach (Section 2-703 or Section 2-711), even though he has notified the repudiating party that he would await the latter's performance and has urged retraction; and

(c) in either case suspend his own performance or proceed in accordance with the provisions of this Article on the seller's right to identify goods to the contract notwithstanding breach or to salvage unfinished goods (Section 2-704).

Official Comments

Prior Uniform Statutory Provision: See Sections 63(2) and 65, Uniform Sales Act.

Purposes: To make it clear that:

1. With the problem of insecurity taken care of by the preceding section and with provision being made in this Article as to the effect of a defective delivery under an installment contract, anticipatory repudiation centers upon an overt communication of intention or an action which renders performance impossible or demonstrates a clear determination not to continue with performance.

Under the present section when such a repudiation substantially impairs the value of the contract, the aggrieved party may at any time resort to his remedies for breach, or he may suspend his own performance while he negotiates with, or awaits performance by, the other party. But if he awaits performance beyond a commercially reasonable time he cannot recover resulting damages which he should have avoided.

2. It is not necessary for repudiation that performance be made literally and utterly impossible. Repudiation can result from action which reasonably indicates a rejection of the continuing obligation. And, a repudiation automatically results under the preceding section on insecurity when a party fails to provide adequate assurance of due future performance within thirty days after a justifiable demand therefor has been made. Under the language of this section, a demand by one or both parties for more than the contract calls for in the way of counter-performance is not in itself a repudiation nor does it invalidate a plain expression of desire for future performance. However, when under a fair reading it amounts to a statement of intention not to perform except on conditions which go beyond the contract, it becomes a repudiation.

3. The test chosen to justify an aggrieved party's action under this section is the same as that in the section on breach in installment contracts-namely the substantial value of the contract. The most useful test of substantial value is to determine whether material inconvenience or injustice will result if the aggrieved party is forced to wait and receive an ultimate tender minus the part or aspect repudiated.

4. After repudiation, the aggrieved party may immediately resort to any remedy he chooses provided he moves in good faith (see Section 1-203). Inaction and silence by the aggrieved party may leave the matter open but it cannot be regarded as misleading the repudiating party. Therefore the aggrieved party is left free to proceed at any time with his options under this section, unless he has taken some positive action which in good faith requires notification to the other party before the remedy is pursued.

Cross References:

Point 1: Sections 2-609 and 2-612.

Point 2: Section 2-609.

Point 3: Section 2-612.

Point 4: Section 1-203.

Definitional Cross References:

"Aggrieved party". Section 1-201.

"Contract". Section 1-201.

"Party". Section 1-201.

"Remedy". Section 1-201.

§ 2-611. Retraction of Anticipatory Repudiation

(1) Until the repudiating party's next performance is due he can retract his repudiation unless the aggrieved party has since the repudiation cancelled or materially changed his position or otherwise indicated that he considers the repudiation final.

(2) Retraction may be by any method which clearly indicates to the aggrieved party that the repudiating party intends to perform, but must include any assurance justifiably demanded under the provisions of this Article (Section 2-609).

(3) Retraction reinstates the repudiating party's rights under the contract with due excuse and allowance to the aggrieved party for any delay occasioned by the repudiation.

Official Comments

Prior Uniform Statutory Provision: None.

Purposes: To make it clear that:

1. The repudiating party's right to reinstate the contract is entirely dependent upon the action taken by the aggrieved party. If the latter has cancelled the contract or materially changed his position at any time after the repudiation, there can be no retraction under this section.

2. Under subsection (2) an effective retraction must be accompanied by any assurances demanded under the section dealing with right to adequate assurance. A repudiation is of course sufficient to give reasonable ground for insecurity and to warrant a request for assurance as an essential condition of the retraction. However, after a timely and unambiguous expression of retraction, a reasonable time for the assurance to be worked out should be allowed by the aggrieved party before cancellation.

Cross Reference:

Point 2: Section 2-609.

Definitional Cross References:

"Aggrieved party". Section 1-201.

"Cancellation". Section 2-106.

"Contract". Section 1-201.

"Party". Section 1-201.

"Rights". Section 1-201.

§ 2-612. "Installment Contract"; Breach

(1) An "installment contract" is one which requires or authorizes the delivery of goods in separate lots to be separately accepted, even though the contract contains a clause "each delivery is a separate contract" or its equivalent.

(2) The buyer may reject any installment which is non-conforming if the non-conformity substantially impairs the value of that installment and cannot be cured or if the non-conformity is a defect in the required documents; but if the non-conformity does not fall within subsection (3) and the seller gives adequate assurance of its cure the buyer must accept that installment.

(3) Whenever non-conformity or default with respect to one or more installments substantially impairs the value of the whole contract there is a breach of the whole. But the aggrieved party reinstates the contract if he accepts a non-conforming installment without seasonably notifying of cancellation or if he brings an action with respect only to past installments or demands performance as to future installments.

Official Comments

Prior Uniform Statutory Provision: Section 45(2), Uniform Sales Act.

Changes: Rewritten.

Purposes of Changes: To continue prior law but to make explicit the more mercantile interpretation of many of the rules involved, so that:

1. The definition of an installment contract is phrased more broadly in this Article so as to cover installment deliveries tacitly authorized by the circumstances or by the option of either party.

2. In regard to the apportionment of the price for separate payment this Article applies the more liberal test of what can be apportioned rather than the test of what is clearly apportioned by the agreement. This Article also recognizes approximate calculation or apportionment of price subject to subsequent adjustment. A provision for separate payment for each lot delivered ordinarily means that the price is at least roughly calculable by units of quantity, but such a provision is not essential to an "installment contract." If separate acceptance of separate deliveries is contemplated, no generalized contrast between wholly "entire" and wholly "divisible" contracts has any standing under this Article.

3. This Article rejects any approach which gives clauses such as "each delivery is a separate contract" their legalistically literal effect. Such contracts nonetheless call for installment deliveries. Even where a clause speaks of "a separate contract for all purposes", a commercial reading of the language under the section on good faith and commercial standards requires that the singleness of the document and the negotiation, together with the sense of the situation, prevail over any uncommercial and legalistic interpretation.

4. One of the requirements for rejection under subsection (2) is non-conformity substantially impairing the value of the installment in question. However, an installment agreement may require accurate conformity in quality as a condition to the right to acceptance if the need for such conformity is made clear either by express provision or by the circumstances. In such a case the effect of the agreement is to define ex-

plicitly what amounts to substantial impairment of value impossible to cure. A clause requiring accurate compliance as a condition to the right to acceptance must, however, have some basis in reason, must avoid imposing hardship by surprise and is subject to waiver or to displacement by practical construction.

Substantial impairment of the value of an installment can turn not only on the quality of the goods but also on such factors as time, quantity, assortment, and the like. It must be judged in terms of the normal or specifically known purposes of the contract. The defect in required documents refers to such matters as the absence of insurance documents under a C.I.F. contract, falsity of a bill of lading, or one failing to show shipment within the contract period or to the contract destination. Even in such cases, however, the provisions on cure of tender apply if appropriate documents are readily procurable.

5. Under subsection (2) an installment delivery must be accepted if the non-conformity is curable and the seller gives adequate assurance of cure. Cure of non-conformity of an installment in the first instance can usually be afforded by an allowance against the price, or in the case of reasonable discrepancies in quantity either by a further delivery or a partial rejection. This Article requires reasonable action by a buyer in regard to discrepant delivery and good faith requires that the buyer make any reasonable minor outlay of time or money necessary to cure an overshipment by severing out an acceptable percentage thereof. The seller must take over a cure which involves any material burden; the buyer's obligation reaches only to cooperation. Adequate assurance for purposes of subsection (2) is measured by the same standards as under the section on right to adequate assurance of performance.

6. Subsection (3) is designed to further the continuance of the contract in the absence of an overt cancellation. The question arising when an action is brought as to a single installment only is resolved by making such action waive the right to cancellation. This involves merely a defect in one or more installments, as contrasted with the situation where there is a true repudiation within the section on anticipatory repudiation. Whether the non-conformity in any given installment justifies cancellation as to the future depends, not on whether such non-conformity indicates an intent or likelihood that the future deliveries will also be defective, but whether the non-conformity substantially impairs the value of the whole contract. If only the seller's security in regard to future installments is impaired, he has the right to demand adequate assurances of proper future performance but has not an immediate right to cancel the entire contract. It is clear under this Article, however, that defects in prior installments are cumulative in effect, so that acceptance does not wash out the defect "waived." Prior policy is continued, putting the rule as to buyer's default on the same footing as that in regard to seller's default.

7. Under the requirement of seasonable notification of cancellation under subsection (3), a buyer who accepts a non-conforming installment which substantially impairs the value of the entire contract should properly be permitted to withhold his decision as to

whether or not to cancel pending a response from the seller as to his claim for cure or adjustment. Similarly, a seller may withhold a delivery pending payment for prior ones, at the same time delaying his decision as to cancellation. A reasonable time for notifying of cancellation, judged by commercial standard under the section on good faith, extends of course to include the time covered by any reasonable negotiation in good faith. However, during this period the defaulting party is entitled, on request, to know whether the contract is still in effect, before he can be required to perform further.

Cross References:

Point 2: Sections 2-307 and 2-607.

Point 3: Section 1-203.

Point 5: Sections 2-208 and 2-609.

Point 6: Section 2-610.

Definitional Cross References:

"Action". Section 1-201.

"Aggrieved party". Section 1-201.

"Buyer". Section 2-103.

"Cancellation". Section 2-106.

"Conform". Section 2-106.

"Contract". Section 1-201.

"Lot". Section 2-105.

"Notifies". Section 1-201.

"Seasonably". Section 1-204.

"Seller". Section 2-103.

§ 2-613. Casualty to Identified Goods

Where the contract requires for its performance goods identified when the contract is made, and the goods suffer casualty without fault of either party before the risk of loss passes to the buyer, or in a proper case under a "no arrival, no sale" term (Section 2-324) then

(a) if the loss is total the contract is avoided; and

(b) if the loss is partial or the goods have so deteriorated as no longer to conform to the contract the buyer may nevertheless demand inspection and at his option either treat the contract as avoided or accept the goods with due allowance from the contract price for the deterioration or the deficiency in quantity but without further right against the seller.

Official Comments

Prior Uniform Statutory Provision: Sections 7 and 8, Uniform Sales Act.

Changes: Rewritten, the basic policy being continued but the test of a "divisible" or "indivisible" sale or contract being abandoned in favor of adjustment in business terms.

Purposes of Changes:

1. Where goods whose continued existence is presupposed by the agreement are destroyed without fault of either party, the buyer is relieved from his obligation but may at his option take the surviving goods at a fair adjustment. "Fault" is intended to include negligence and not merely wilful wrong. The buyer is expressly given the right to inspect the goods in order to determine whether he wishes to avoid the contract entirely or to take the goods with a price adjustment.

2. The section applies whether the goods were already destroyed at the time of contracting without the knowledge of either party or whether they are destroyed subsequently but before the risk of loss passes to the buyer. Where under the agreement, including of course usage of trade, the risk has passed to the buyer before the casualty, the section has no application. Beyond this, the essential question in determining whether the rules of this section are to be applied is whether the seller has or has not undertaken the responsibility for the continued existence of the goods in proper condition through the time of agreed or expected delivery.

3. The section on the term "no arrival, no sale" makes clear that delay in arrival, quite as much as physical change in the goods, gives the buyer the options set forth in this section.

Cross Reference:

Point 3: Section 2-324.

Definitional Cross References:

"Buyer". Section 2-103.

"Conform". Section 2-106.

"Contract". Section 1-201.

"Fault". Section 1-201.

"Goods". Section 2-105.

"Party". Section 1-201.

"Rights". Section 1-201.

"Seller". Section 2-103.

§ 2-614. Substituted Performance

(1) Where without fault of either party the agreed berthing, loading, or unloading facilities fail or an agreed type of carrier becomes unavailable or the agreed manner of delivery otherwise becomes commercially impracticable but a commercially reasonable substitute is available, such substitute performance must be tendered and accepted.

(2) If the agreed means or manner of payment fails because of domestic or foreign governmental regulation, the seller may withhold or stop delivery unless the buyer provides a means or manner of payment which is commercially a substantial equivalent. If delivery has already been taken, payment by the means or in the manner provided by the regulation discharges the buyer's obligation unless the regulation is discriminatory, oppressive or predatory.

Official Comments

Prior Uniform Statutory Provision: None.

Purposes:

1. Subsection (1) requires the tender of a commercially reasonable substituted performance where agreed to facilities have failed or become commercially impracticable. Under this Article, in the absence of specific agreement, the normal or usual facilities enter into the agreement either through the circumstances, usage of trade or prior course of dealing.

This section appears between Section 2-613 on casualty to identified goods and the next section on excuse by failure of presupposed conditions, both of which deal with excuse and complete avoidance of the contract where the occurrence or non-occurrence of a contingency which was a basic assumption of the contract makes the expected performance impossible. The distinction between the present section and those sections lies in whether the failure or impossibility of performance arises in connection with an incidental matter or goes to the very heart of the agreement. The differing lines of solution are contrasted in a comparison of International Paper Co. v. Rockefeller, 161 App.Div. 180, 146 N.Y.S. 371 (1914) and Meyer v. Sullivan, 40 Cal.App. 723, 181 P. 847 (1919). In the former case a contract for the sale of spruce to be cut from a particular tract of land was involved. When a fire destroyed the trees growing on that tract the seller was held excused since performance was impossible. In the latter case the contract called for delivery of wheat "f.o.b. Kosmos Steamer at Seattle." The war led to cancellation of that line's sailing schedule after space had been duly engaged and the buyer was held entitled to demand substituted delivery at the warehouse on the line's loading dock. Under this Article, of course, the seller would also be entitled, had the market gone the other way, to make a substituted tender in that manner.

There must, however, be a true commercial impracticability to excuse the agreed to performance and justify a substituted performance. When this is the case a reasonable substituted performance tendered by either party should excuse him from strict compliance with contract terms which do not go to the essence of the agreement.

2. The substitution provided in this section as between buyer and seller does not carry over into the obligation of a financing agency under a letter of credit, since such an agency is entitled to performance which is plainly adequate on its face and without need to look into commercial evidence outside of the documents. See Article 5, especially Sections 5-102, 5-103, 5-109, 5-110, 5-114.

3. Under subsection (2) where the contract is still executory on both sides, the seller is permitted to withdraw unless the buyer can provide him with a commercially equivalent return despite the governmental regulation. Where, however, only the debt for the price remains, a larger leeway is permitted. The buyer may pay in the manner provided by the regulation even though this may not be commercially equivalent provided that the regulation is not "discriminatory, oppressive or predatory."

Cross Reference:

Point 2: Article 5.

Definitional Cross References:

"Buyer". Section 2-103.

"Fault". Section 1-201.

"Party". Section 1-201.

"Seller". Section 2-103.

§ 2-615. Excuse by Failure of Presupposed Conditions

Except so far as a seller may have assumed a greater obligation and subject to the preceding section on substituted performance:

(a) Delay in delivery or non-delivery in whole or in part by a seller who complies with paragraphs (b) and (c) is not a breach of his duty under a contract for sale if performance as agreed has been made impracticable by the occurrence of a contingency the non-occurrence of which was a basic assumption on which the contract was made or by compliance in good faith with any applicable foreign or domestic governmental regulation or order whether or not it later proves to be invalid.

(b) Where the causes mentioned in paragraph (a) affect only a part of the seller's capacity to perform, he must allocate production and deliveries among his customers but may at his option include regular customers not then under contract as well as his own requirements for further manufacture. He may so allocate in any manner which is fair and reasonable.

(c) The seller must notify the buyer seasonably that there will be delay or non-delivery and, when allocation is required under paragraph (b), of the estimated quota thus made available for the buyer.

Official Comments

Prior Uniform Statutory Provision: None.

Purposes:

1. This section excuses a seller from timely delivery of goods contracted for, where his performance has become commercially impracticable because of unforeseen supervening circumstances not within the contemplation of the parties at the time of contracting. The destruction of specific goods and the problem of the use of substituted performance on points other than delay or quantity, treated elsewhere in this Article, must be distinguished from the matter covered by this section.

2. The present section deliberately refrains from any effort at an exhaustive expression of contingencies and is to be interpreted in all cases sought to be brought within its scope in terms of its underlying reason and purpose.

3. The first test for excuse under this Article in terms of basic assumption is a familiar one. The additional test of commercial impracticability (as contrasted with "impossibility," "frustration of performance" or "frustration of the venture") has been adopted in order to call attention to the commercial character of the criterion chosen by this Article.

4. Increased cost alone does not excuse performance unless the rise in cost is due to some unforeseen contingency which alters the essential nature of the performance. Neither is a rise or a collapse in the market in itself a justification, for that is exactly the type of business risk which business contracts made at fixed prices are intended to cover. But a severe shortage of raw materials or of supplies due to a contingency such as war, embargo, local crop failure, unforeseen shutdown of major sources of supply or the like, which either causes a marked increase in cost or altogether prevents the seller from securing supplies necessary to his performance, is within the contemplation of this section. (See Ford & Sons, Ltd. v. Henry Leetham & Sons, Ltd., 21 Com. Cas. 55 (1915, K.B.D.).)

5. Where a particular source of supply is exclusive under the agreement and fails through casualty, the present section applies rather than the provision on destruction or deterioration of specific goods. The same holds true where a particular source of supply is shown by the circumstances to have been contemplated or assumed by the parties at the time of contracting. (See Davis Co. v. Hoffmann-LaRoche Chemical Works, 178 App.Div. 855, 166 N.Y.S. 179 (1917) and International Paper Co. v. Rockefeller, 161 App.Div. 180, 146 N.Y.S. 371 (1914).) There is no excuse under this section, however, unless the seller has employed all due measures to assure himself that his source will not fail. (See Canadian Industrial Alcohol Co., Ltd., v. Dunbar Molasses

Co., 258 N.Y. 194, 179 N.E. 383, 80 A.L.R. 1173 (1932) and Washington Mfg. Co. v. Midland Lumber Co., 113 Wash. 593, 194 P. 777 (1921).)

In the case of failure of production by an agreed source for causes beyond the seller's control, the seller should, if possible, be excused since production by an agreed source is without more a basic assumption of the contract. Such excuse should not result in relieving the defaulting supplier from liability nor in dropping into the seller's lap an unearned bonus of damages over. The flexible adjustment machinery of this Article provides the solution under the provision on the obligation of good faith. A condition to his making good the claim of excuse is the turning over to the buyer of his rights against the defaulting source of supply to the extent of the buyer's contract in relation to which excuse is being claimed.

6. In situations in which neither sense nor justice is served by either answer when the issue is posed in flat terms of "excuse" or "no excuse," adjustment under the various provisions of this Article is necessary, especially the sections on good faith, on insecurity and assurance and on the reading of all provisions in the light of their purposes, and the general policy of this Act to use equitable principles in furtherance of commercial standards and good faith.

7. The failure of conditions which go to convenience or collateral values rather than to the commercial practicability of the main performance does not amount to a complete excuse. However, good faith and the reason of the present section and of the preceding one may properly be held to justify and even to require any needed delay involved in a good faith inquiry seeking a readjustment of the contract terms to meet the new conditions.

8. The provisions of this section are made subject to assumption of greater liability by agreement and such agreement is to be found not only in the expressed terms of the contract but in the circumstances surrounding the contracting, in trade usage and the like. Thus the exemptions of this section do not apply when the contingency in question is sufficiently foreshadowed at the time of contracting to be included among the business risks which are fairly to be regarded as part of the dickered terms, either consciously or as a matter of reasonable, commercial interpretation from the circumstances. (See Madeirense Do Brasil, S.A. v. Stulman-Emrick Lumber Co., 147 F.2d 399 (C.C.A., 2 Cir., 1945).) The exemption otherwise present through usage of trade under the present section may also be expressly negated by the language of the agreement. Generally, express agreements as to exemptions designed to enlarge upon or supplant the provisions of this section are to be read in the light of mercantile sense and reason, for this section itself sets up the commercial standard for normal and reasonable interpretation and provides a minimum beyond which agreement may not go.

Agreement can also be made in regard to the consequences of exemption as laid down in paragraphs (b) and (c) and the next section on procedure on notice claiming excuse.

9. The case of a farmer who has contracted to sell crops to be grown on designated land may be regarded as falling either within the section on casualty to identified goods or this section, and he may be excused, when there is a failure of the specific crop, either on the basis of the destruction of identified goods or because of the failure of a basic assumption of the contract.

Exemption of the buyer in the case of a "requirements" contract is covered by the "Output and Requirements" section both as to assumption and allocation of the relevant risks. But when a contract by a manufacturer to buy fuel or raw material makes no specific reference to a particular venture and no such reference may be drawn from the circumstances, commercial understanding views it as a general deal in the general market and not conditioned on any assumption of the continuing operation of the buyer's plant. Even when notice is given by the buyer that the supplies are needed to fill a specific contract of a normal commercial kind, commercial understanding does not see such a supply contract as conditioned on the continuance of the buyer's further contract for outlet. On the other hand, where the buyer's contract is in reasonable commercial understanding conditioned on a definite and specific venture or assumption as, for instance, a war procurement subcontract known to be based on a prime contract which is subject to termination, or a supply contract for a particular construction venture, the reason of the present section may well apply and entitle the buyer to the exemption.

10. Following its basic policy of using commercial practicability as a test for excuse, this section recognizes as of equal significance either a foreign or domestic regulation and disregards any technical distinctions between "law," "regulation," "order" and the like. Nor does it make the present action of the seller depend upon the eventual judicial determination of the legality of the particular governmental action. The seller's good faith belief in the validity of the regulation is the test under this Article and the best evidence of his good faith is the general commercial acceptance of the regulation. However, governmental interference cannot excuse unless it truly "supervenes" in such a manner as to be beyond the seller's assumption of risk. And any action by the party claiming excuse which causes or colludes in inducing the governmental action preventing his performance would be in breach of good faith and would destroy his exemption.

11. An excused seller must fulfill his contract to the extent which the supervening contingency permits, and if the situation is such that his customers are generally affected he must take account of all in supplying one. Subsections (a) and (b), therefore, explicitly permit in any proration a fair and reasonable attention to the needs of regular customers who are probably relying on spot orders for supplies. Customers at different stages of the manufacturing process may be fairly treated by including the seller's manufacturing requirements. A fortiori, the seller may also take account of contracts later in date than the one in question. The fact that such spot orders may be closed at an advanced price causes no difficulty, since any allocation which exceeds normal past requirements will not be reasonable.

However, good faith requires, when prices have advanced, that the seller exercise real care in making his allocations, and in case of doubt his contract customers should be favored and supplies prorated evenly among them regardless of price. Save for the extra care thus required by changes in the market, this section seeks to leave every reasonable business leeway to the seller.

Cross References:

Point 1: Sections 2-613 and 2-614.

Point 2: Section 1-102.

Point 5: Sections 1-203 and 2-613.

Point 6: Sections 1-102, 1-203 and 2-609.

Point 7: Section 2-614.

Point 8: Sections 1-201, 2-302 and 2-616.

Point 9: Sections 1-102, 2-306 and 2-613.

Definitional Cross References:

"Between merchants". Section 2-104.

"Buyer". Section 2-103.

"Contract". Section 1-201.

"Contract for sale". Section 2-106.

"Good faith". Section 1-201.

"Merchant". Section 2-104.

"Notifies". Section 1-201.

"Seasonably". Section 1-201.

"Seller". Section 2-103.

§ 2-616. Procedure on Notice Claiming Excuse

(1) Where the buyer receives notification of a material or indefinite delay or an allocation justified under the preceding section he may by written notification to the seller as to any delivery concerned, and where the prospective deficiency substantially impairs the value of the whole contract under the provisions of this Article relating to breach of installment contracts (Section 2-612), then also as to the whole,

    (a) terminate and thereby discharge any unexecuted portion of the contract; or

    (b) modify the contract by agreeing to take his available quota in substitution.

(2) If after receipt of such notification from the seller the buyer fails so to modify the contract within a reasonable time not exceeding thirty days the contract lapses with respect to any deliveries affected.

(3) The provisions of this section may not be negated by agreement except in so far as the seller has assumed a greater obligation under the preceding section.

Official Comments

Prior Uniform Statutory Provision: None.

Purposes:

This section seeks to establish simple and workable machinery for providing certainty as to when a supervening and excusing contingency "excuses" the delay, "discharges" the contract, or may result in a waiver of the delay by the buyer. When the seller notifies, in accordance with the preceding section, claiming excuse, the buyer may acquiesce, in which case the contract is so modified. No consideration is necessary in a case of this kind to support such a modification. If the buyer does not elect so to modify the contract, he may terminate it and under subsection (2) his silence after receiving the seller's claim of excuse operates as such a termination. Subsection (3) denies effect to any contract clause made in advance of trouble which would require the buyer to stand ready to take delivery whenever the seller is excused from delivery by unforeseen circumstances.

Cross References:

Point 1: Sections 2-209 and 2-615.

Definitional Cross References:

"Buyer". Section 2-103.

"Contract". Section 1-201.

"Installment contract". Section 2-612.

"Notification". Section 1-201.

"Reasonable time". Section 1-204.

"Seller". Section 2-103.

"Termination". Section 2-106.

"Written". Section 1-201.

PART 7. REMEDIES

§ 2-701. Remedies for Breach of Collateral Contracts Not Impaired

Remedies for breach of any obligation or promise collateral or ancillary to a contract for sale are not impaired by the provisions of this Article.

Official Comments

Prior Uniform Statutory Provision: None.

Purposes:

Whether a claim for breach of an obligation collateral to the contract for sale requires separate trial to avoid confusion of issues is beyond the scope of this Article;

but contractual arrangements which as a business matter enter vitally into the contract should be considered a part thereof in so far as cross-claims or defenses are concerned.

Definitional Cross References:

"Contract for sale". Section 2-106.

"Remedy". Section 1-201.

§ 2-702. Seller's Remedies on Discovery of Buyer's Insolvency

(1) Where the seller discovers the buyer to be insolvent he may refuse delivery except for cash including payment for all goods theretofore delivered under the contract, and stop delivery under this Article (Section 2-705).

(2) Where the seller discovers that the buyer has received goods on credit while insolvent he may reclaim the goods upon demand made within ten days after the receipt, but if misrepresentation of solvency has been made to the particular seller in writing within three months before delivery the ten day limitation does not apply. Except as provided in this subsection the seller may not base a right to reclaim goods on the buyer's fraudulent or innocent misrepresentation of solvency or of intent to pay.

(3) The seller's right to reclaim under subsection (2) is subject to the rights of a buyer in ordinary course or other good faith purchaser under this Article (Section 2-403). Successful reclamation of goods excludes all other remedies with respect to them.

As amended in 1966.

Official Comments

Prior Uniform Statutory Provision: Subsection (1) — Sections 53(1)(b), 54(1)(c) and 57, Uniform Sales Act; Subsection (2) — none; Subsection (3) — Section 76(3), Uniform Sales Act.

Changes: Rewritten, the protection given to a seller who has sold on credit and has delivered goods to the buyer immediately preceding his insolvency being extended.

Purposes of Changes and New Matter: To make it clear that:

1. The seller's right to withhold the goods or to stop delivery except for cash when he discovers the buyer's insolvency is made explicit in subsection (1) regardless of the passage of title, and the concept of stoppage has been extended to include goods in the possession of any bailee who has not yet attorned to the buyer.

2. Subsection (2) takes as its base line the proposition that any receipt of goods on credit by an insolvent buyer amounts to a tacit business misrepresentation of solvency and therefore is fraudulent as against the particular seller. This Article makes discovery of the buyer's insolvency and demand within a ten day period a condition of the right

to reclaim goods on this ground. The ten day limitation period operates from the time of receipt of the goods.

An exception to this time limitation is made when a written misrepresentation of solvency has been made to the particular seller within three months prior to the delivery. To fall within the exception the statement of solvency must be in writing, addressed to the particular seller and dated within three months of the delivery.

3. Because the right of the seller to reclaim goods under this section constitutes preferential treatment as against the buyer's other creditors, subsection (3) provides that such reclamation bars all his other remedies as to the goods involved. As amended 1966.

Cross References:

Point 1: Sections 2-401 and 2-705.

Compare Section 2-502.

Definitional Cross References:

"Buyer". Section 2-103.

"Buyer in ordinary course of business". Section 1-201.

"Contract". Section 1-201.

"Good faith". Section 1-201.

"Goods". Section 2-105.

"Insolvent". Section 1-201.

"Person". Section 1-201.

"Purchaser". Section 1-201.

"Receipt" of goods. Section 2-103.

"Remedy". Section 1-201.

"Rights". Section 1-201.

"Seller". Section 2-103.

"Writing". Section 1-201.

§ 2-703. Seller's Remedies in General

Where the buyer wrongfully rejects or revokes acceptance of goods or fails to make a payment due on or before delivery or repudiates with respect to a part or the whole, then with respect to any goods directly affected and, if the breach is of the whole contract (Section 2-612), then also with respect to the whole undelivered balance, the aggrieved seller may

(a) withhold delivery of such goods;

(b) stop delivery by any bailee as hereafter provided (Section 2-705);

(c) proceed under the next section respecting goods still unidentified to the contract;

(d) resell and recover damages as hereafter provided (Section 2-706);

(e) recover damages for non-acceptance (Section 2-708) or in a proper case the price (Section 2-709);

(f) cancel.

Official Comments

Prior Uniform Statutory Provision: No comparable index section. See Section 53, Uniform Sales Act.

Purposes:

1. This section is an index section which gathers together in one convenient place all of the various remedies open to a seller for any breach by the buyer. This Article rejects any doctrine of election of remedy as a fundamental policy and thus the remedies are essentially cumulative in nature and include all of the available remedies for breach. Whether the pursuit of one remedy bars another depends entirely on the facts of the individual case.

2. The buyer's breach which occasions the use of the remedies under this section may involve only one lot or delivery of goods, or may involve all of the goods which are the subject matter of the particular contract. The right of the seller to pursue a remedy as to all the goods when the breach is as to only one or more lots is covered by the section on breach in installment contracts. The present section deals only with the remedies available after the goods involved in the breach have been determined by that section.

3. In addition to the typical case of refusal to pay or default in payment, the language in the preamble, "fails to make a payment due," is intended to cover the dishonor of a check on due presentment, or the non-acceptance of a draft, and the failure to furnish an agreed letter of credit.

4. It should also be noted that this Act requires its remedies to be liberally administered and provides that any right or obligation which it declares is enforceable by action unless a different effect is specifically prescribed (Section 1-106).

Cross References:

Point 2: Section 2-612.

Point 3: Section 2-325.

Point 4: Section 1-106.

Definitional Cross References:

"Aggrieved party". Section 1-201.

"Buyer". Section 2-103.

"Cancellation". Section 2-106.

"Contract". Section 1-201.

"Goods". Section 2-105.

"Remedy". Section 1-201.

"Seller". Section 2-103.

§ 2-704. Seller's Right to Identify Goods to the Contract Notwithstanding Breach or to Salvage Unfinished Goods

(1) An aggrieved seller under the preceding section may
   (a) identify to the contract conforming goods not already identified if at the time he learned of the breach they are in his possession or control;
   (b) treat as the subject of resale goods which have demonstrably been intended for the particular contract even though those goods are unfinished.

(2) Where the goods are unfinished an aggrieved seller may in the exercise of reasonable commercial judgment for the purposes of avoiding loss and of effective realization either complete the manufacture and wholly identify the goods to the contract or cease manufacture and resell for scrap or salvage value or proceed in any other reasonable manner.

Official Comments

Prior Uniform Statutory Provision: Sections 63(3) and 64(4), Uniform Sales Act.

Changes: Rewritten, the seller's rights being broadened.

Purposes of Changes:

1. This section gives an aggrieved seller the right at the time of breach to identify to the contract any conforming finished goods, regardless of their resalability, and to use reasonable judgment as to completing unfinished goods. It thus makes the goods available for resale under the resale section, the seller's primary remedy, and in the special case in which resale is not practicable, allows the action for the price which would then be necessary to give the seller the value of his contract.

2. Under this Article the seller is given express power to complete manufacture or procurement of goods for the contract unless the exercise of reasonable commercial judgment as to the facts as they appear at the time he learns of the breach makes it clear that such action will result in a material increase in damages. The burden is on the buyer to show the commercially unreasonable nature of the seller's action in completing manufacture.

Cross References:

Sections 2-703 and 2-706.

Definitional Cross References:

"Aggrieved party". Section 1-201.

"Conforming". Section 2-106.

"Contract". Section 1-201.

"Goods". Section 2-105.

"Rights". Section 1-201.

"Seller". Section 2-103.

§ 2-705. Seller's Stoppage of Delivery in Transit or Otherwise

(1) The seller may stop delivery of goods in the possession of a carrier or other bailee when he discovers the buyer to be insolvent (Section 2-702) and may stop delivery of carload, truckload, planeload or larger shipments of express or freight when the buyer repudiates or fails to make a payment due before delivery or if for any other reason the seller has a right to withhold or reclaim the goods.

(2) As against such buyer the seller may stop delivery until

    (a) receipt of the goods by the buyer; or

    (b) acknowledgment to the buyer by any bailee of the goods except a carrier that the bailee holds the goods for the buyer; or

    (c) such acknowledgment to the buyer by a carrier by reshipment or as warehouseman; or

    (d) negotiation to the buyer of any negotiable document of title covering the goods.

(3) (a) To stop delivery the seller must so notify as to enable the bailee by reasonable diligence to prevent delivery of the goods.

    (b) After such notification the bailee must hold and deliver the goods according to the directions of the seller but the seller is liable to the bailee for any ensuing charges or damages.

    (c) If a negotiable document of title has been issued for goods the bailee is not obliged to obey a notification to stop until surrender of the document.

    (d) A carrier who has issued a non-negotiable bill of lading is not obliged to obey a notification to stop received from a person other than the consignor.

Official Comments

Prior Uniform Statutory Provision: Sections 57-59, Uniform Sales Act; see also Sections 12, 14 and 42, Uniform Bills of Lading Act and Sections 9, 11 and 49, Uniform Warehouse Receipts Act.

Changes: This section continues and develops the above sections of the Uniform Sales Act in the light of the other uniform statutory provisions noted.

Purposes: To make it clear that:

1. Subsection (1) applies the stoppage principle to other bailees as well as carriers.

It also expands the remedy to cover the situations, in addition to buyer's insolvency, specified in the subsection. But since stoppage is a burden in any case to carriers, and might be a very heavy burden to them if it covered all small shipments in all these situations, the right to stop for reasons other than insolvency is limited to carload, truckload, planeload or larger shipments. The seller shipping to a buyer of doubtful credit can protect himself by shipping C.O.D.

Where stoppage occurs for insecurity it is merely a suspension of performance, and if assurances are duly forthcoming from the buyer the seller is not entitled to resell or divert.

Improper stoppage is a breach by the seller if it effectively interferes with the buyer's right to due tender under the section on manner of tender of delivery. However, if the bailee obeys an unjustified order to stop he may also be liable to the buyer. The measure of his obligation is dependent on the provisions of the Documents of Title Article (Section 7-303). Subsection 3(b) therefore gives him a right of indemnity as against the seller in such a case.

2. "Receipt by the buyer" includes receipt by the buyer's designated representative, the subpurchaser, when shipment is made direct to him and the buyer himself never receives the goods. It is entirely proper under this Article that the seller, by making such direct shipment to the sub-purchaser, be regarded as acquiescing in the latter's purchase and as thus barred from stoppage of the goods as against him.

As between the buyer and the seller, the latter's right to stop the goods at any time until they reach the place of final delivery is recognized by this section.

Under subsection (3)(c) and (d), the carrier is under no duty to recognize the stop order of a person who is a stranger to the carrier's contract. But the seller's right as against the buyer to stop delivery remains, whether or not the carrier is obligated to recognize the stop order. If the carrier does obey it, the buyer cannot complain merely because of that circumstance; and the seller becomes obligated under subsection (3)(b) to pay the carrier any ensuing damages or charges.

3. A diversion of a shipment is not a "reshipment" under subsection (2)(c) when it is merely an incident to the original contract of transportation. Nor is the procurement of "exchange bills" of lading which change only the name of the consignee to that of the buyer's local agent but do not alter the destination of a reshipment.

Acknowledgment by the carrier as a "warehouseman" within the meaning of this Article requires a contract of a truly different character from the original shipment, a contract not in extension of transit but as a warehouseman.

4. Subsection (3)(c) makes the bailee's obedience of a notification to stop conditional upon the surrender of any outstanding negotiable document.

5. Any charges or losses incurred by the carrier in following the seller's orders, whether or not he was obligated to do so, fall to the seller's charge.

6. After an effective stoppage under this section the seller's rights in the goods are the same as if he had never made a delivery.

Cross References:

Sections 2-702 and 2-703.

Point 1: Sections 2-503 and 2-609, and Article 7.

Point 2: Section 2-103 and Article 7.

Definitional Cross References:

"Buyer". Section 2-103.

"Contract for sale". Section 2-106.

"Document of title". Section 1-201.

"Goods". Section 2-105.

"Insolvent". Section 1-201.

"Notification". Section 1-201.

"Receipt" of goods. Section 2-103.

"Rights". Section 1-201.

"Seller". Section 2-103.

§ 2-706. Seller's Resale Including Contract for Resale

(1) Under the conditions stated in Section 2-703 on seller's remedies, the seller may resell the goods concerned or the undelivered balance thereof. Where the resale is made in good faith and in a commercially reasonable manner the seller may recover the difference between the resale price and the contract price together with any incidental damages allowed under the provisions of this Article (Section 2-710), but less expenses saved in consequence of the buyer's breach.

(2) Except as otherwise provided in subsection (3) or unless otherwise agreed resale may be at public or private sale including sale by way of one or more contracts to sell or of identification to an existing contract of the seller. Sale may be as a unit or in parcels and at any time and place and on any terms but every aspect of the sale including the method, manner, time, place and terms must be commercially reasonable. The resale must be reasonably identified as referring to the broken contract, but it is not necessary that the goods be in existence or that any or all of them have been identified to the contract before the breach.

(3) Where the resale is at private sale the seller must give the buyer reasonable notification of his intention to resell.

(4) Where the resale is at public sale

    (a) only identified goods can be sold except where there is a recognized market for a public sale of futures in goods of the kind; and

(b) it must be made at a usual place or market for public sale if one is reasonably available and except in the case of goods which are perishable or threaten to decline in value speedily the seller must give the buyer reasonable notice of the time and place of the resale; and

(c) if the goods are not to be within the view of those attending the sale the notification of sale must state the place where the goods are located and provide for their reasonable inspection by prospective bidders; and

(d) the seller may buy.

(5) A purchaser who buys in good faith at a resale takes the goods free of any rights of the original buyer even though the seller fails to comply with one or more of the requirements of this section.

(6) The seller is not accountable to the buyer for any profit made on any resale. A person in the position of a seller (Section 2-707) or a buyer who has rightfully rejected or justifiably revoked acceptance must account for any excess over the amount of his security interest, as hereinafter defined (subsection (3) of Section 2-711).

Official Comments

Prior Uniform Statutory Provision: Section 60, Uniform Sales Act.

Changes: Rewritten.

Purposes of Changes: To simplify the prior statutory provision and to make it clear that:

1. The only condition precedent to the seller's right of resale under subsection (1) is a breach by the buyer within the section on the seller's remedies in general or insolvency. Other meticulous conditions and restrictions of the prior uniform statutory provision are disapproved by this Article and are replaced by standards of commercial reasonableness. Under this section the seller may resell the goods after any breach by the buyer. Thus, an anticipatory repudiation by the buyer gives rise to any of the seller's remedies for breach, and to the right of resale. This principle is supplemented by subsection (2) which authorizes a resale of goods which are not in existence or were not identified to the contract before the breach.

2. In order to recover the damages prescribed in subsection (1) the seller must act "in good faith and in a commercially reasonable manner" in making the resale. This standard is intended to be more comprehensive than that of "reasonable care and judgment" established by the prior uniform statutory provision. Failure to act properly under this section deprives the seller of the measure of damages here provided and relegates him to that provided in Section 2-708.

Under this Article the seller resells by authority of law, in his own behalf, for his own benefit and for the purpose of fixing his damages. The theory of a seller's agency is thus rejected.

3. If the seller complies with the prescribed standard of duty in making the resale, he may recover from the buyer the damages provided for in subsection (1). Evidence of

market or current prices at any particular time or place is relevant only on the question of whether the seller acted in a commercially reasonable manner in making the resale.

The distinction drawn by some courts between cases where the title had not passed to the buyer and the seller had resold as owner, and cases where the title had passed and the seller had resold by virtue of his lien on the goods, is rejected.

4. Subsection (2) frees the remedy of resale from legalistic restrictions and enables the seller to resell in accordance with reasonable commercial practices so as to realize as high a price as possible in the circumstances. By "public" sale is meant a sale by auction. A "private" sale may be effected by solicitation and negotiation conducted either directly or through a broker. In choosing between a public and private sale the character of the goods must be considered and relevant trade practices and usages must be observed.

5. Subsection (2) merely clarifies the common law rule that the time for resale is a reasonable time after the buyer's breach, by using the language "commercially reasonable." What is such a reasonable time depends upon the nature of the goods, the condition of the market and the other circumstances of the case; its length cannot be measured by any legal yardstick or divided into degrees. Where a seller contemplating resale receives a demand from the buyer for inspection under the section of preserving evidence of goods in dispute, the time for resale may be appropriately lengthened.

On the question of the place for resale, subsection (2) goes to the ultimate test, the commercial reasonableness of the seller's choice as to the place for an advantageous resale. This Article rejects the theory that the seller is required to resell at the agreed place for delivery and that a resale elsewhere can be permitted only in exceptional cases.

6. The purpose of subsection (2) being to enable the seller to dispose of the goods to the best advantage, he is permitted in making the resale to depart from the terms and conditions of the original contract for sale to any extent "commercially reasonable" in the circumstances.

7. The provision of subsection (2) that the goods need not be in existence to be resold applies when the buyer is guilty of anticipatory repudiation of a contract for future goods, before the goods or some of them have come into existence. In such a case the seller may exercise the right of resale and fix his damages by "one or more contracts to sell" the quantity of conforming future goods affected by the repudiation. The companion provision of subsection (2) that resale may be made although the goods were not identified to the contract prior to the buyer's breach, likewise contemplates an anticipatory repudiation by the buyer but occurring after the goods are in existence. If the goods so identified conform to the contract, their resale will fix the seller's damages quite as satisfactorily as if they had been identified before the breach.

8. Where the resale is to be by private sale, subsection (3) requires that reasonable notification of the seller's intention to resell must be given to the buyer. The length of notification of a private sale depends upon the urgency of the matter. Notification of the time and place of this type of sale is not required.

Subsection (4)(b) requires that the seller give the buyer reasonable notice of the time and place of a public resale so that he may have an opportunity to bid or to secure the attendance of other bidders. An exception is made in the case of goods "which are perishable or threaten to decline speedily in value."

9. Since there would be no reasonable prospect of competitive bidding elsewhere, subsection (4) requires that a public resale "must be made at a usual place or market for public sale if one is reasonably available;" i.e., a place or market which prospective bidders may reasonably be expected to attend. Such a market may still be "reasonably available" under this subsection, though at a considerable distance from the place where the goods are located. In such a case the expense of transporting the goods for resale is recoverable from the buyer as part of the seller's incidental damages under subsection (1). However, the question of availability is one of commercial reasonableness in the circumstances and if such "usual" place or market is not reasonably available, a duly advertised public resale may be held at another place if it is one which prospective bidders may reasonably be expected to attend, as distinguished from a place where there is no demand whatsoever for goods of the kind.

Paragraph (a) of subsection (4) qualifies the last sentence of subsection (2) with respect to resales of unidentified and future goods at public sale. If conforming goods are in existence the seller may identify them to the contract after the buyer's breach and then resell them at public sale. If the goods have not been identified, however, he may resell them at public sale only as "future" goods and only where there is a recognized market for public sale of futures in goods of the kind.

The provisions of paragraph (c) of subsection (4) are intended to permit intelligent bidding.

The provision of paragraph (d) of subsection (4) permitting the seller to bid and, of course, to become the purchaser, benefits the original buyer by tending to increase the resale price and thus decreasing the damages he will have to pay.

10. This Article departs in subsection (5) from the prior uniform statutory provision in permitting a good faith purchaser at resale to take a good title as against the buyer even though the seller fails to comply with the requirements of this section.

11. Under subsection (6), the seller retains profit, if any, without distinction based on whether or not he had a lien since this Article divorces the question of passage of title to the buyer from the seller's right of resale or the consequences of its exercise. On the other hand, where "a person in the position of a seller" or a buyer acting under the section on buyer's remedies, exercises his right of resale under the present section he does so only for the limited purpose of obtaining cash for his "security interest" in the goods. Once that purpose has been accomplished any excess in the resale price belongs to the seller to whom an accounting must be made as provided in the last sentence of subsection (6).

Cross References:

Point 1: Sections 2-610, 2-702 and 2-703.

Point 2: Section 1-201.

Point 3: Sections 2-708 and 2-710.

Point 4: Section 2-328.

Point 8: Section 2-104.

Point 9: Section 2-710.

Point 11: Sections 2-401, 2-707 and 2-711(3).

Definitional Cross References:

"Buyer". Section 2-103.

"Contract". Section 1-201.

"Contract for sale". Section 2-106.

"Good faith". Section 2-103.

"Goods". Section 2-105.

"Merchant". Section 2-104.

"Notification". Section 1-201.

"Person in position of seller". Section 2-707.

"Purchase". Section 1-201.

"Rights". Section 1-201.

"Sale". Section 2-106.

"Security interest". Section 1-201.

"Seller". Section 2-103.

§ 2-707. "Person in the Position of a Seller"

(1) A "person in the position of a seller" includes as against a principal an agent who has paid or become responsible for the price of goods on behalf of his principal or anyone who otherwise holds a security interest or other right in goods similar to that of a seller.

(2) A person in the position of a seller may as provided in this Article withhold or stop delivery (Section 2-705) and resell (Section 2-706) and recover incidental damages (Section 2-710).

Official Comments

Prior Uniform Statutory Provision: Section 52(2), Uniform Sales Act.

Changes: Rewritten.

Purposes of Changes: To make it clear that:

In addition to following in general the prior uniform statutory provision, the case of a financing agency which has acquired documents by honoring a letter of credit for the buyer or by discounting a draft for the seller has been included in the term "a person in the position of a seller."

Cross Reference:

Article 5, Section 2-506.

Definitional Cross References:

"Consignee". Section 7-102.

"Consignor". Section 7-102.

"Goods". Section 2-105.

"Security interest". Section 1-201.

"Seller". Section 2-103.

§ 2-708. Seller's Damages for Non-acceptance or Repudiation

(1) Subject to subsection (2) and to the provisions of this Article with respect to proof of market price (Section 2-723), the measure of damages for non-acceptance or repudiation by the buyer is the difference between the market price at the time and place for tender and the unpaid contract price together with any incidental damages provided in this Article (Section 2-710), but less expenses saved in consequence of the buyer's breach.

(2) If the measure of damages provided in subsection (1) is inadequate to put the seller in as good a position as performance would have done then the measure of damages is the profit (including reasonable overhead) which the seller would have made from full performance by the buyer, together with any incidental damages provided in this Article (Section 2-710), due allowance for costs reasonably incurred and due credit for payments or proceeds of resale.

Official Comments

Prior Uniform Statutory Provision: Section 64, Uniform Sales Act.

Changes: Rewritten.

Purposes of Changes: To make it clear that:

1. The prior uniform statutory provision is followed generally in setting the current market price at the time and place for tender as the standard by which damages for non-acceptance are to be determined. The time and place of tender is determined by reference to the section on manner of tender of delivery, and to the sections on the effect of such terms as FOB, FAS, CIF, C & F, Ex Ship and No Arrival, No Sale.

In the event that there is no evidence available of the current market price at the time and place of tender, proof of a substitute market may be made under the section on determination and proof of market price. Furthermore, the section on the admissibility of market quotations is intended to ease materially the problem of providing competent evidence.

2. The provision of this section permitting recovery of expected profit including reasonable overhead where the standard measure of damages is inadequate, together with the new requirement that price actions may be sustained only where resale is impractical, are designed to eliminate the unfair and economically wasteful results arising under the older law when fixed price articles were involved. This section permits the recovery of lost profits in all appropriate cases, which would include all standard priced goods. The normal measure there would be list price less cost to the dealer or list price less manufacturing cost to the manufacturer. It is not necessary to a recovery of "profit" to show a history of earnings, especially if a new venture is involved.

3. In all cases the seller may recover incidental damages.

Cross References:

Point 1: Sections 2-319 through 2-324, 2-503, 2-723 and 2-724.

Point 2: Section 2-709.

Point 3: Section 2-710.

Definitional Cross References:

"Buyer". Section 2-103.

"Contract". Section 1-201.

"Seller". Section 2-103.

§ 2-709. Action for the Price

(1) When the buyer fails to pay the price as it becomes due the seller may recover, together with any incidental damages under the next section, the price
    (a) of goods accepted or of conforming goods lost or damaged within a commercially reasonable time after risk of their loss has passed to the buyer; and
    (b) of goods identified to the contract if the seller is unable after reasonable effort to resell them at a reasonable price or the circumstances reasonably indicate that such effort will be unavailing.

(2) Where the seller sues for the price he must hold for the buyer any goods which have been identified to the contract and are still in his control except that if resale becomes possible he may resell them at any time prior to the collection of the judgment. The net proceeds of any such resale must be credited to the buyer and payment of the judgment entitles him to any goods not resold.

(3) After the buyer has wrongfully rejected or revoked acceptance of the goods or has failed to make a payment due or has repudiated (Section 2-610), a seller who is held not entitled to the price under this section shall nevertheless be awarded damages for non-acceptance under the preceding section.

Official Comments

Prior Uniform Statutory Provision: Section 63, Uniform Sales Act.

Changes: Rewritten, important commercially needed changes being incorporated.

Purposes of Changes: To make it clear that:

1. Neither the passing of title to the goods nor the appointment of a day certain for payment is now material to a price action.

2. The action for the price is now generally limited to those cases where resale of the goods is impracticable except where the buyer has accepted the goods or where they have been destroyed after risk of loss has passed to the buyer.

3. This section substitutes an objective test by action for the former "not readily resalable" standard. An action for the price under subsection (1)(b) can be sustained only after a "reasonable effort to resell" the goods "at reasonable price" has actually been made or where the circumstances "reasonably indicate" that such an effort will be unavailing.

4. If a buyer is in default not with respect to the price, but on an obligation to make an advance, the seller should recover not under this section for the price as such, but for the default in the collateral (though coincident) obligation to finance the seller. If the agreement between the parties contemplates that the buyer will acquire, on making the advance, a security interest in the goods, the buyer on making the advance has such an interest as soon as the seller has rights in the agreed collateral. See Section 9-204.

5. "Goods accepted" by the buyer under subsection (1)(a) include only goods as to which there has been no justified revocation of acceptance, for such a revocation means that there has been a default by the seller which bars his rights under this section. "Goods lost or damaged" are covered by the section on risk of loss. "Goods identified to the contract" under subsection (1)(b) are covered by the section on identification and the section on identification notwithstanding breach.

6. This section is intended to be exhaustive in its enumeration of cases where an action for the price lies.

7. If the action for the price fails, the seller may nonetheless have proved a case entitling him to damages for non-acceptance. In such a situation, subsection (3) permits recovery of those damages in the same action.

Cross References:

Point 4: Section 1-106.

Point 5: Sections 2-501, 2-509, 2-510 and 2-704.

Point 7: Section 2-708.

Definitional Cross References:

"Action". Section 1-201.

"Buyer". Section 2-103.

"Conforming". Section 2-106.

"Contract". Section 1-201.

"Goods". Section 2-105.

"Seller". Section 2-103.

§ 2-710. Seller's Incidental Damages

Incidental damages to an aggrieved seller include any commercially reasonable charges, expenses or commissions incurred in stopping delivery, in the transportation, care and custody of goods after the buyer's breach, in connection with return or resale of the goods or otherwise resulting from the breach.

Official Comments

Prior Uniform Statutory Provision: See Sections 64 and 70, Uniform Sales Act.

Purposes: To authorize reimbursement of the seller for expenses reasonably incurred by him as a result of the buyer's breach. The section sets forth the principal normal and necessary additional elements of damage flowing from the breach but intends to allow all commercially reasonable expenditures made by the seller.

Definitional Cross References:

"Aggrieved party". Section 1-201.

"Buyer". Section 2-103.

"Goods". Section 2-105.

"Seller". Section 2-103.

§ 2-711. Buyer's Remedies in General; Buyer's Security Interest in Rejected Goods

(1) Where the seller fails to make delivery or repudiates or the buyer rightfully rejects or justifiably revokes acceptance then with respect to any goods involved, and with respect to the whole if the breach goes to the whole contract (Section 2-612), the buyer may cancel and whether or not he has done so may in addition to recovering so much of the price as has been paid
    (a) "cover" and have damages under the next section as to all the goods affected whether or not they have been identified to the contract; or
    (b) recover damages for non-delivery as provided in this Article (Section 2-713).

(2) Where the seller fails to deliver or repudiates the buyer may also
    (a) if the goods have been identified recover them as provided in this Article (Section 2-502); or
    (b) in a proper case obtain specific performance or replevy the goods as provided in this Article (Section 2-716).

(3) On rightful rejection or justifiable revocation of acceptance a buyer has a security interest in goods in his possession or control for any payments made on their price and any expenses reasonably incurred in their inspection, receipt, transportation, care and custody and may hold such goods and resell them in like manner as an aggrieved seller (Section 2-706).

Official Comments

Prior Uniform Statutory Provision: No comparable index section; Subsection (3) — Section 69(5), Uniform Sales Act.

Changes: The prior uniform statutory provision is generally continued and expanded in Subsection (3).

Purposes of Changes and New Matter:

1. To index in this section the buyer's remedies, subsection (1) covering those remedies permitting the recovery of money damages, and subsection (2) covering those which permit reaching the goods themselves. The remedies listed here are those available to a buyer who has not accepted the goods or who has justifiably revoked his acceptance. The remedies available to a buyer with regard to goods finally accepted appear in the section dealing with breach in regard to accepted goods. The buyer's right to proceed as to all goods when the breach is as to only some of the goods is determined by the section on breach in installment contracts and by the section on partial acceptance.

Despite the seller's breach, proper retender of delivery under the section on cure of improper tender or replacement can effectively preclude the buyer's remedies under this section, except for any delay involved.

2. To make it clear in subsection (3) that the buyer may hold and resell rejected goods if he has paid a part of the price or incurred expenses of the type specified. "Paid" as used here includes acceptance of a draft or other time negotiable instrument or the signing of a negotiable note. His freedom of resale is coextensive with that of a seller under this Article except that the buyer may not keep any profit resulting from the resale and is limited to retaining only the amount of the price paid and the costs involved in the inspection and handling of the goods. The buyer's security interest in the goods is intended to be limited to the items listed in subsection (3), and the buyer is not permitted to retain such funds as he might believe adequate for his damages. The buyer's right to cover, or to have damages for non-delivery, is not impaired by his exercise of his right of resale.

3. It should also be noted that this Act requires its remedies to be liberally administered and provides that any right or obligation which it declares is enforceable by action unless a different effect is specifically prescribed (Section 1-106).

Cross References:

Point 1: Sections 2-508, 2-601(c), 2-608, 2-612 and 2-714.

Point 2: Section 2-706.

Point 3: Section 1-106.

Definitional Cross References:

"Aggrieved party". Section 1-201.

"Buyer". Section 2-103.

"Cancellation". Section 2-106.

"Contract". Section 1-201.

"Cover". Section 2-712.

"Goods". Section 2-105.

"Notifies". Section 1-201.

"Receipt" of goods. Section 2-103.

"Remedy". Section 1-201.

"Security interest". Section 1-201.

"Seller". Section 2-103.

§ 2-712. "Cover"; Buyer's Procurement of Substitute Goods

(1) After a breach within the preceding section the buyer may "cover" by making in good faith and without unreasonable delay any reasonable purchase of or contract to purchase goods in substitution for those due from the seller.

(2) The buyer may recover from the seller as damages the difference between the cost of cover and the contract price together with any incidental or consequential damages as hereinafter defined (Section 2-715), but less expenses saved in consequence of the seller's breach.

(3) Failure of the buyer to effect cover within this section does not bar him from any other remedy.

Official Comments

Prior Uniform Statutory Provision: None.

Purposes:

1. This section provides the buyer with a remedy aimed at enabling him to obtain the goods he needs thus meeting his essential need. This remedy is the buyer's equivalent of the seller's right to resell.

2. The definition of "cover" under subsection (1) envisages a series of contracts or sales, as well as a single contract or sale; goods not identical with those involved but commercially usable as reasonable substitutes under the circumstances of the particular case; and contracts on credit or delivery terms differing from the contract in breach, but again reasonable under the circumstances. The test of proper cover is whether at the time and place the buyer acted in good faith and in a reasonable manner, and it is immaterial that hindsight may later prove that the method of cover used was not the cheapest or most effective.

The requirement that the buyer must cover "without unreasonable delay" is not intended to limit the time necessary for him to look around and decide as to how he may best effect cover. The test here is similar to that generally used in this Article as to reasonable time and seasonable action.

3. Subsection (3) expresses the policy that cover is not a mandatory remedy for the buyer. The buyer is always free to choose between cover and damages for non-delivery under the next section.

However, this subsection must be read in conjunction with the section which limits the recovery of consequential damages to such as could not have been obviated by cover. Moreover, the operation of the section on specific performance of contracts for "unique" goods must be considered in this connection for availability of the goods to the particular buyer for his particular needs is the test for that remedy and inability to cover is made an express condition to the right of the buyer to replevy the goods.

4. This section does not limit cover to merchants, in the first instance. It is the vital and important remedy for the consumer buyer as well. Both are free to use cover: the domestic or non-merchant consumer is required only to act in normal good faith while the merchant buyer must also observe all reasonable commercial standards of fair dealing in the trade, since this falls within the definition of good faith on his part.

Cross References:

Point 1: Section 2-706.

Point 2: Section 1-204.

Point 3: Sections 2-713, 2-715 and 2-716.

Point 4: Section 1-203.

Definitional Cross References:

"Buyer". Section 2-103.

"Contract". Section 1-201.

"Good faith". Section 2-103.

"Goods". Section 2-105.

"Purchase". Section 1-201.

"Remedy". Section 1-201.

"Seller". Section 2-103.

§ 2-713. Buyer's Damages for Non-delivery or Repudiation

(1) Subject to the provisions of this Article with respect to proof of market price (Section 2-723), the measure of damages for non-delivery or repudiation by the seller is the difference between the market price at the time when the buyer learned of the breach and the contract price together with any incidental and consequential damages provided in this Article (Section 2-715), but less expenses saved in consequence of the seller's breach.

(2) Market price is to be determined as of the place for tender or, in cases of rejection after arrival or revocation of acceptance, as of the place of arrival.

Official Comments

Prior Uniform Statutory Provision: Section 67(3), Uniform Sales Act.

Changes: Rewritten.

Purposes of Changes: To clarify the former rule so that:

1. The general baseline adopted in this section uses as a yardstick the market in which the buyer would have obtained cover had he sought that relief. So the place for measuring damages is the place of tender (or the place of arrival if the goods are rejected or their acceptance is revoked after reaching their destination) and the crucial time is the time at which the buyer learns of the breach.

2. The market or current price to be used in comparison with the contract price under this section is the price for goods of the same kind and in the same branch of trade.

3. When the current market price under this section is difficult to prove the section on determination and proof of market price is available to permit a showing of a comparable market price or, where no market price is available, evidence of spot sale prices is proper. Where the unavailability of a market price is caused by a scarcity of goods of the type involved, a good case is normally made for specific performance under this Article. Such scarcity conditions, moreover, indicate that the price has risen and under the section providing for liberal administration of remedies, opinion evidence as to the value of the goods would be admissible in the absence of a market price and a liberal construction of allowable consequential damages should also result.

4. This section carries forward the standard rule that the buyer must deduct from his damages any expenses saved as a result of the breach.

5. The present section provides a remedy which is completely alternative to cover under the preceding section and applies only when and to the extent that the buyer has not covered.

Cross References:

Point 3: Sections 1-106, 2-716 and 2-723.

Point 5: Section 2-712.

Definitional Cross References:

"Buyer". Section 2-103.

"Contract". Section 1-201.

"Seller". Section 2-103.

§ 2-714. Buyer's Damages for Breach in Regard to Accepted Goods

(1) Where the buyer has accepted goods and given notification (subsection (3) of Section 2-607) he may recover as damages for any non-conformity of tender the loss resulting in the ordinary course of events from the seller's breach as determined in any manner which is reasonable.

(2) The measure of damages for breach of warranty is the difference at the time and place of acceptance between the value of the goods accepted and the value they would have had if they had been as warranted, unless special circumstances show proximate damages of a different amount.

(3) In a proper case any incidental and consequential damages under the next section may also be recovered.

Official Comments

Prior Uniform Statutory Provision: Section 69(6) and (7), Uniform Sales Act.

Changes: Rewritten.

Purposes of Changes:

1. This section deals with the remedies available to the buyer after the goods have been accepted and the time for revocation of acceptance has gone by. In general this section adopts the rule of the prior uniform statutory provision for measuring damages where there has been a breach of warranty as to goods accepted, but goes further to lay down an explicit provision as to the time and place for determining the loss.

The section on deduction of damages from price provides an additional remedy for a buyer who still owes part of the purchase price, and frequently the two remedies will be available concurrently. The buyer's failure to notify of his claim under the section on effects of acceptance, however, operates to bar his remedies under either that section or the present section.

2. The "non-conformity" referred to in subsection (1) includes not only breaches of warranties but also any failure of the seller to perform according to his obligations under the contract. In the case of such non-conformity, the buyer is permitted to recover for his loss "in any manner which is reasonable."

3. Subsection (2) describes the usual, standard and reasonable method of ascertaining damages in the case of breach of warranty but it is not intended as an exclusive measure. It departs from the measure of damages for non-delivery in utilizing the place of acceptance rather than the place of tender. In some cases the two may coincide, as where the buyer signifies his acceptance upon the tender. If, however, the non-conformity is such as would justify revocation of acceptance, the time and place of acceptance under this section is determined as of the buyer's decision not to revoke.

4. The incidental and consequential damages referred to in subsection (3), which will usually accompany an action brought under this section, are discussed in detail in the comment on the next section.

Cross References:

Point 1: Compare Section 2-711; Sections 2-607 and 2-717.

Point 2: Section 2-106.

Point 3: Sections 2-608 and 2-713.

Point 4: Section 2-715.

Definitional Cross References:

"Buyer". Section 2-103.

"Conform". Section 2-106.

"Goods". Section 1-201.

"Notification". Section 1-201.

"Seller". Section 2-103.

§ 2-715. Buyer's Incidental and Consequential Damages

(1) Incidental damages resulting from the seller's breach include expenses reasonably incurred in inspection, receipt, transportation and care and custody of goods rightfully rejected, any commercially reasonable charges, expenses or commissions in connection with effecting cover and any other reasonable expense incident to the delay or other breach.

(2) Consequential damages resulting from the seller's breach include

    (a) any loss resulting from general or particular requirements and needs of which the seller at the time of contracting had reason to know and which could not reasonably be prevented by cover or otherwise; and

    (b) injury to person or property proximately resulting from any breach of warranty.

Official Comments

Prior Uniform Statutory Provisions: Subsection (2)(b) — Sections 69(7) and 70, Uniform Sales Act.

Changes: Rewritten.

Purposes of Changes and New Matter:

1. Subsection (1) is intended to provide reimbursement for the buyer who incurs reasonable expenses in connection with the handling of rightfully rejected goods or goods whose acceptance may be justifiably revoked, or in connection with effecting cover where the breach of the contract lies in non-conformity or non-delivery of the goods. The incidental damages listed are not intended to be exhaustive but are merely illustrative of the typical kinds of incidental damage.

2. Subsection (2) operates to allow the buyer, in an appropriate case, any consequential damages which are the result of the seller's breach. The "tacit agreement" test for the recovery of consequential damages is rejected. Although the older rule at common law which made the seller liable for all consequential damages of which he had "reason to know" in advance is followed, the liberality of that rule is modified by refusing to permit recovery unless the buyer could not reasonably have prevented the loss by cover

or otherwise. Subparagraph (2) carries forward the provisions of the prior uniform statutory provision as to consequential damages resulting from breach of warranty, but modifies the rule by requiring first that the buyer attempt to minimize his damages in good faith, either by cover or otherwise.

3. In the absence of excuse under the section on merchant's excuse by failure of presupposed conditions, the seller is liable for consequential damages in all cases where he had reason to know of the buyer's general or particular requirements at the time of contracting. It is not necessary that there be a conscious acceptance of an insurer's liability on the seller's part, nor is his obligation for consequential damages limited to cases in which he fails to use due effort in good faith.

Particular needs of the buyer must generally be made known to the seller while general needs must rarely be made known to charge the seller with knowledge.

Any seller who does not wish to take the risk of consequential damages has available the section on contractual limitation of remedy.

4. The burden of proving the extent of loss incurred by way of consequential damage is on the buyer, but the section on liberal administration of remedies rejects any doctrine of certainty which requires almost mathematical precision in the proof of loss. Loss may be determined in any manner which is reasonable under the circumstances.

5. Subsection (2)(b) states the usual rule as to breach of warranty, allowing recovery for injuries "proximately" resulting from the breach.

Where the injury involved follows the use of goods without discovery of the defect causing the damage, the question of "proximate" cause turns on whether it was reasonable for the buyer to use the goods without such inspection as would have revealed the defects. If it was not reasonable for him to do so, or if he did in fact discover the defect prior to his use, the injury would not proximately result from the breach of warranty.

6. In the case of sale of wares to one in the business of reselling them, resale is one of the requirements of which the seller has reason to know within the meaning of subsection (2)(a).

Cross References:

Point 1: Section 2-608.

Point 3: Sections 1-203, 2-615 and 2-719.

Point 4: Section 1-106.

Definitional Cross References:

"Cover". Section 2-712.

"Goods". Section 1-201.

"Person". Section 1-201.

"Receipt" of goods. Section 2-103.

"Seller". Section 2-103.

§ 2-716. Buyer's Right to Specific Performance or Replevin

(1) Specific performance may be decreed where the goods are unique or in other proper circumstances.

(2) The decree for specific performance may include such terms and conditions as to payment of the price, damages, or other relief as the court may deem just.

(3) The buyer has a right of replevin for goods identified to the contract if after reasonable effort he is unable to effect cover for such goods or the circumstances reasonably indicate that such effort will be unavailing or if the goods have been shipped under reservation and satisfaction of the security interest in them has been made or tendered.

Official Comments

Prior Uniform Statutory Provision: Section 68, Uniform Sales Act.

Changes: Rephrased.

Purposes of Changes: To make it clear that:

1. The present section continues in general prior policy as to specific performance and injunction against breach. However, without intending to impair in any way the exercise of the court's sound discretion in the matter, this Article seeks to further a more liberal attitude than some courts have shown in connection with the specific performance of contracts of sale.

2. In view of this Article's emphasis on the commercial feasibility of replacement, a new concept of what are "unique" goods is introduced under this section. Specific performance is no longer limited to goods which are already specific or ascertained at the time of contracting. The test of uniqueness under this section must be made in terms of the total situation which characterizes the contract. Output and requirements contracts involving a particular or peculiarly available source or market present today the typical commercial specific performance situation, as contrasted with contracts for the sale of heirlooms or priceless works of art which were usually involved in the older cases. However, uniqueness is not the sole basis of the remedy under this section for the relief may also be granted "in other proper circumstances" and inability to cover is strong evidence of "other proper circumstances".

3. The legal remedy of replevin is given to the buyer in cases in which cover is reasonably unavailable and goods have been identified to the contract. This is in addition to the buyer's right to recover identified goods on the seller's insolvency (Section 2-502).

4. This section is intended to give the buyer rights to the goods comparable to the seller's rights to the price.

5. If a negotiable document of title is outstanding, the buyer's right of replevin relates of course to the document not directly to the goods. See Article 7, especially Section 7-602.

Cross References:

Point 3: Section 2-502.

Point 4: Section 2-709.

Point 5: Article 7.

Definitional Cross References:

"Buyer". Section 2-103.

"Goods". Section 1-201.

"Rights". Section 1-201.

§ 2-717. Deduction of Damages From the Price

The buyer on notifying the seller of his intention to do so may deduct all or any part of the damages resulting from any breach of the contract from any part of the price still due under the same contract.

Official Comments

Prior Uniform Statutory Provision: See Section 69(1)(a), Uniform Sales Act.

Purposes:

1. This section permits the buyer to deduct from the price damages resulting from any breach by the seller and does not limit the relief to cases of breach of warranty as did the prior uniform statutory provision. To bring this provision into application the breach involved must be of the same contract under which the price in question is claimed to have been earned.

2. The buyer, however, must give notice of his intention to withhold all or part of the price if he wishes to avoid a default within the meaning of the section on insecurity and right to assurances. In conformity with the general policies of this Article, no formality of notice is required and any language which reasonably indicates the buyer's reason for holding up his payment is sufficient.

Cross Reference:

Point 2: Section 2-609.

Definitional Cross References:

"Buyer". Section 2-103.

"Notifies". Section 1-201.

§ 2-718. Liquidation or Limitation of Damages; Deposits

(1) Damages for breach by either party may be liquidated in the agreement but only at an amount which is reasonable in the light of the anticipated or actual harm caused by the breach, the difficulties of proof of loss, and the inconvenience or

nonfeasibility of otherwise obtaining an adequate remedy. A term fixing unreasonably large liquidated damages is void as a penalty.

(2) Where the seller justifiably withholds delivery of goods because of the buyer's breach, the buyer is entitled to restitution of any amount by which the sum of his payments exceeds

(a) the amount to which the seller is entitled by virtue of terms liquidating the seller's damages in accordance with subsection (1), or

(b) in the absence of such terms, twenty per cent of the value of the total performance for which the buyer is obligated under the contract or $500, whichever is smaller.

(3) The buyer's right to restitution under subsection (2) is subject to offset to the extent that the seller establishes

(a) a right to recover damages under the provisions of this Article other than subsection (1), and

(b) the amount or value of any benefits received by the buyer directly or indirectly by reason of the contract.

(4) Where a seller has received payment in goods their reasonable value or the proceeds of their resale shall be treated as payments for the purposes of subsection (2); but if the seller has notice of the buyer's breach before reselling goods received in part performance, his resale is subject to the conditions laid down in this Article on resale by an aggrieved seller (Section 2-706).

Official Comments

Prior Uniform Statutory Provision: None.

Purposes:

1. Under subsection (1) liquidated damage clauses are allowed where the amount involved is reasonable in the light of the circumstances of the case. The subsection sets forth explicitly the elements to be considered in determining the reasonableness of a liquidated damage clause. A term fixing unreasonably large liquidated damages is expressly made void as a penalty. An unreasonably small amount would be subject to similar criticism and might be stricken under the section on unconscionable contracts or clauses.

2. Subsection (2) refuses to recognize a forfeiture unless the amount of the payment so forfeited represents a reasonable liquidation of damages as determined under subsection (1). A special exception is made in the case of small amounts (20% of the price or $500, whichever is smaller) deposited as security. No distinction is made between cases in which the payment is to be applied on the price and those in which it is intended as security for performance. Subsection (2) is applicable to any deposit or down or part payment. In the case of a deposit or turn in of goods resold before the breach, the

amount actually received on the resale is to be viewed as the deposit rather than the amount allowed the buyer for the trade in. However, if the seller knows of the breach prior to the resale of the goods turned in, he must make reasonable efforts to realize their true value, and this is assured by requiring him to comply with the conditions laid down in the section on resale by an aggrieved seller.

Cross References:

Point 1: Section 2-302.

Point 2: Section 2-706.

Definitional Cross References:

"Aggrieved party". Section 1-201.

"Agreement". Section 1-201.

"Buyer". Section 2-103.

"Goods". Section 2-105.

"Notice". Section 1-201.

"Party". Section 1-201.

"Remedy". Section 1-201.

"Seller". Section 2-103.

"Term". Section 1-201.

§ 2-719. Contractual Modification or Limitation of Remedy

(1) Subject to the provisions of subsections (2) and (3) of this section and of the preceding section on liquidation and limitation of damages,

    (a) the agreement may provide for remedies in addition to or in substitution for those provided in this Article and may limit or alter the measure of damages recoverable under this Article, as by limiting the buyer's remedies to return of the goods and repayment of the price or to repair and replacement of non-conforming goods or parts; and

    (b) resort to a remedy as provided is optional unless the remedy is expressly agreed to be exclusive, in which case it is the sole remedy.

(2) Where circumstances cause an exclusive or limited remedy to fail of its essential purpose, remedy may be had as provided in this Act.

(3) Consequential damages may be limited or excluded unless the limitation or exclusion is unconscionable. Limitation of consequential damages for injury to the person in the case of consumer goods is prima facie unconscionable but limitation of damages where the loss is commercial is not.

Official Comments

Prior Uniform Statutory Provision: None.

Purposes:

1. Under this section parties are left free to shape their remedies to their particular requirements and reasonable agreements limiting or modifying remedies are to be given effect.

However, it is of the very essence of a sales contract that at least minimum adequate remedies be available. If the parties intend to conclude a contract for sale within this Article they must accept the legal consequence that there be at least a fair quantum of remedy for breach of the obligations or duties outlined in the contract. Thus any clause purporting to modify or limit the remedial provisions of this Article in an unconscionable manner is subject to deletion and in that event the remedies made available by this Article are applicable as if the stricken clause had never existed. Similarly, under subsection (2), where an apparently fair and reasonable clause because of circumstances fails in its purpose or operates to deprive either party of the substantial value of the bargain, it must give way to the general remedy provisions of this Article.

2. Subsection (1)(b) creates a presumption that clauses prescribing remedies are cumulative rather than exclusive. If the parties intend the term to describe the sole remedy under the contract, this must be clearly expressed.

3. Subsection (3) recognizes the validity of clauses limiting or excluding consequential damages but makes it clear that they may not operate in an unconscionable manner. Actually such terms are merely an allocation of unknown or undeterminable risks. The seller in all cases is free to disclaim warranties in the manner provided in Section 2-316.

Cross References:

Point 1: Section 2-302.

Point 3: Section 2-316.

Definitional Cross References:

"Agreement". Section 1-201.

"Buyer". Section 2-103.

"Conforming". Section 2-106.

"Contract". Section 1-201.

"Goods". Section 2-105.

"Remedy". Section 1-201.

"Seller". Section 2-103.

§ 2-720. Effect of "Cancellation" or "Rescission" on Claims for Antecedent Breach

Unless the contrary intention clearly appears, expressions of "cancellation" or "rescission" of the contract or the like shall not be construed as a renunciation or discharge of any claim in damages for an antecedent breach.

Official Comments

Prior Uniform Statutory Provision: None.

Purpose:

This section is designed to safeguard a person holding a right of action from any unintentional loss of rights by the ill-advised use of such terms as "cancellation", "rescission", or the like. Once a party's rights have accrued they are not to be lightly impaired by concessions made in business decency and without intention to forego them. Therefore, unless the cancellation of a contract expressly declares that it is "without reservation of rights", or the like, it cannot be considered to be a renunciation under this section.

Cross Reference:

Section 1-107.

Definitional Cross References:

"Cancellation". Section 2-106.

"Contract". Section 1-201.

§ 2-721. Remedies for Fraud

Remedies for material misrepresentation or fraud include all remedies available under this Article for non-fraudulent breach. Neither rescission or a claim for rescission of the contract for sale nor rejection or return of the goods shall bar or be deemed inconsistent with a claim for damages or other remedy.

Official Comments

Prior Uniform Statutory Provision: None.

Purposes: To correct the situation by which remedies for fraud have been more circumscribed than the more modern and mercantile remedies for breach of warranty. Thus the remedies for fraud are extended by this section to coincide in scope with those for non-fraudulent breach. This section thus makes it clear that neither rescission of the contract for fraud nor rejection of the goods bars other remedies unless the circumstances of the case make the remedies incompatible.

Definitional Cross References:

"Contract for sale". Section 2-106.

"Goods". Section 1-201.

"Remedy". Section 1-201.

§ 2-722. Who Can Sue Third Parties for Injury to Goods

Where a third party so deals with goods which have been identified to a contract for sale as to cause actionable injury to a party to that contract

(a) a right of action against the third party is in either party to the contract for sale who has title to or a security interest or a special property or an insurable interest in the goods; and if the goods have been destroyed or converted a right of action is also in the party who either bore the risk of loss under the contract for sale or has since the injury assumed that risk as against the other;

(b) if at the time of the injury the party plaintiff did not bear the risk of loss as against the other party to the contract for sale and there is no arrangement between them for disposition of the recovery, his suit or settlement is, subject to his own interest, as a fiduciary for the other party to the contract;

(c) either party may with the consent of the other sue for the benefit of whom it may concern.

Official Comments

Prior Uniform Statutory Provision: None.

Purposes: To adopt and extend somewhat the principle of the statutes which provide for suit by the real party in interest. The provisions of this section apply only after identification of the goods. Prior to that time only the seller has a right of action. During the period between identification and final acceptance (except in the case of revocation of acceptance) it is possible for both parties to have the right of action. Even after final acceptance both parties may have the right of action if the seller retains possession or otherwise retains an interest.

Definitional Cross References:

"Action". Section 1-201.

"Buyer". Section 2-103.

"Contract for sale". Section 2-106.

"Goods". Section 2-105.

"Party". Section 1-201.

"Rights". Section 1-201.

"Security interest". Section 1-201.

§ 2-723. Proof of Market Price: Time and Place

(1) If an action based on anticipatory repudiation comes to trial before the time for performance with respect to some or all of the goods, any damages based on market price (Section 2-708 or Section 2-713) shall be determined according to the price of such goods prevailing at the time when the aggrieved party learned of the repudiation.

(2) If evidence of a price prevailing at the times or places described in this Article is not readily available the price prevailing within any reasonable time before or after the time described or at any other place which in commercial judgment or under usage of trade would serve as a reasonable substitute for the one de-scribed may be used, making any proper allowance for the cost of transporting the goods to or from such other place.

(3) Evidence of a relevant price prevailing at a time or place other than the one described in this Article offered by one party is not admissible unless and until he has given the other party such notice as the court finds sufficient to prevent unfair surprise.

Official Comments

Prior Uniform Statutory Provision: None.

Purposes: To eliminate the most obvious difficulties arising in connection with the determination of market price, when that is stipulated as a measure of damages by some provision of this Article. Where the appropriate market price is not readily available the court is here granted reasonable leeway in receiving evidence of prices current in other comparable markets or at other times comparable to the one in question. In accordance with the general principle of this Article against surprise, however, a party intending to offer evidence of such a substitute price must give suitable notice to the other party.

This section is not intended to exclude the use of any other reasonable method of determining market price or of measuring damages if the circumstances of the case make this necessary.

Definitional Cross References:

"Action". Section 1-201.

"Aggrieved party". Section 1-201.

"Goods". Section 2-105.

"Notifies". Section 1-201.

"Party". Section 1-201.

"Reasonable time". Section 1-204.

"Usage of trade". Section 1-205.

§ 2-724. Admissibility of Market Quotations

Whenever the prevailing price or value of any goods regularly bought and sold in any established commodity market is in issue, reports in official publications or trade journals or in newspapers or periodicals of general circulation published as the reports of such market shall be admissible in evidence. The circumstances of the preparation of such a report may be shown to affect its weight but not its admissibility.

Official Comments

Prior Uniform Statutory Provision: None.

Purposes: To make market quotations admissible in evidence while providing for a challenge of the material by showing the circumstances of its preparation.

No explicit provision as to the weight to be given to market quotations is contained in this section, but such quotations, in the absence of compelling challenge, offer an adequate basis for a verdict.

Market quotations are made admissible when the price or value of goods traded "in any established market" is in issue. The reason of the section does not require that the market be closely organized in the manner of a produce exchange. It is sufficient if transactions in the commodity are frequent and open enough to make a market established by usage in which one price can be expected to affect another and in which an informed report of the range and trend of prices can be assumed to be reasonably accurate.

This section does not in any way intend to limit or negate the application of similar rules of admissibility to other material, whether by action of the courts or by statute. The purpose of the present section is to assure a minimum of mercantile administration in this important situation and not to limit any liberalizing trend in modern law.

Definitional Cross Reference:

"Goods". Section 2-105.

§ 2-725. Statute of Limitations in Contracts for Sale

(1) An action for breach of any contract for sale must be commenced within four years after the cause of action has accrued. By the original agreement the parties may reduce the period of limitation to not less than one year but may not extend it.

(2) A cause of action accrues when the breach occurs, regardless of the aggrieved party's lack of knowledge of the breach. A breach of warranty occurs when tender of delivery is made, except that where a warranty explicitly extends to future performance of the goods and discovery of the breach must await the time of such performance the cause of action accrues when the breach is or should have been discovered.

(3) Where an action commenced within the time limited by subsection (1) is so terminated as to leave available a remedy by another action for the same breach

such other action may be commenced after the expiration of the time limited and within six months after the termination of the first action unless the termination resulted from voluntary discontinuance or from dismissal for failure or neglect to prosecute.

(4) This section does not alter the law on tolling of the statute of limitations nor does it apply to causes of action which have accrued before this Act becomes effective.

Official Comments

Prior Uniform Statutory Provision: None.

Purposes: To introduce a uniform statute of limitations for sales contracts, thus eliminating the jurisdictional variations and providing needed relief for concerns doing business on a nationwide scale whose contracts have heretofore been governed by several different periods of limitation depending upon the state in which the transaction occurred. This Article takes sales contracts out of the general laws limiting the time for commencing contractual actions and selects a four year period as the most appropriate to modern business practice. This is within the normal commercial record keeping period.

Subsection (1) permits the parties to reduce the period of limitation. The minimum period is set at one year. The parties may not, however, extend the statutory period.

Subsection (2), providing that the cause of action accrues when the breach occurs, states an exception where the warranty extends to future performance.

Subsection (3) states the saving provision included in many state statutes and permits an additional short period for bringing new actions, where suits begun within the four year period have been terminated so as to leave a remedy still available for the same breach.

Subsection (4) makes it clear that this Article does not purport to alter or modify in any respect the law on tolling of the Statute of Limitations as it now prevails in the various jurisdictions.

Definitional Cross References:

"Action". Section 1-201.

"Aggrieved party". Section 1-201.

"Agreement". Section 1-201.

"Contract for sale". Section 2-106.

"Goods". Section 2-105.

"Party". Section 1-201.

"Remedy". Section 1-201.

"Term". Section 1-201.

"Termination". Section 2-106.

UNITED NATIONS CONVENTION ON CONTRACTS FOR THE INTERNATIONAL SALE OF GOODS (CISG)

[Editors' Note: The United Nations Convention on Contracts for the International Sale of Goods (CISG) is a multilateral treaty that provides a uniform sales law governing sales between contracting states. The CISG was drafted and signed in Vienna in 1980 and came into force in 1988 after ratification by 11 countries. As of 2023, 95 countries have ratified the CISG, including the United States. Therefore, the CISG will govern sales between parties in the United States and parties located in other contracting states, unless the parties opt out of its provisions through a choice of law clause. The CISG supersedes state contract law under the Supremacy Clause of the Constitution.]

THE STATES PARTIES TO THIS CONVENTION,

BEARING IN MIND the broad objectives in the resolutions adopted by the sixth special session of the General Assembly of the United Nations on the establishment of a New International Economic Order,

CONSIDERING that the development of international trade on the basis of equality and mutual benefit is an important element in promoting friendly relations among States,

BEING OF THE OPINION that the adoption of uniform rules which govern contracts for the international sale of goods and take into account the different social, economic and legal systems would contribute to the removal of legal barriers in international trade and promote the development of international trade,

HAVE AGREED as follows:

PART I

SPHERE OF APPLICATION AND GENERAL PROVISIONS

Chapter I

SPHERE OF APPLICATION

Article 1

(1) This Convention applies to contracts of sale of goods between parties whose places of business are in different States:
  (a) when the States are Contracting States; or
  (b) when the rules of private international law lead to the application of the law of a Contracting State.

(2) The fact that the parties have their places of business in different States is to be disregarded whenever this fact does not appear either from the contract or from any dealings between, or from information disclosed by, the parties at any time before or at the conclusion of the contract.

(3) Neither the nationality of the parties nor the civil or commercial character of the parties or of the contract is to be taken into consideration in determining the application of this Convention.

Article 2

This Convention does not apply to sales:

(a) of goods bought for personal, family or household use, unless the seller, at any time before or at the conclusion of the contract, neither knew nor ought to have known that the goods were bought for any such use;

(b) by auction;

(c) on execution or otherwise by authority of law;

(d) of stocks, shares, investment securities, negotiable instruments or money;

(e) of ships, vessels, hovercraft or aircraft;

(f) of electricity.

Article 3

(1) Contracts for the supply of goods to be manufactured or produced are to be considered sales unless the party who orders the goods undertakes to supply a substantial part of the materials necessary for such manufacture or production.

(2) This Convention does not apply to contracts in which the preponderant part of the obligations of the party who furnishes the goods consists in the supply of labour or other services.

Article 4

This Convention governs only the formation of the contract of sale and the rights and obligations of the seller and the buyer arising from such a contract. In particular, except as otherwise expressly provided in this Convention, it is not concerned with:

(a) the validity of the contract or of any of its provisions or of any usage;

(b) the effect which the contract may have on the property in the goods sold.

Article 5

This Convention does not apply to the liability of the seller for death or personal injury caused by the goods to any person.

Article 6

The parties may exclude the application of this Convention or, subject to article 12, derogate from or vary the effect of any of its provisions.

Chapter II

GENERAL PROVISIONS

Article 7

(1) In the interpretation of this Convention, regard is to be had to its international character and to the need to promote uniformity in its application and the observance of good faith in international trade.

(2) Questions concerning matters governed by this Convention which are not expressly settled in it are to be settled in conformity with the general principles on which it is based or, in the absence of such principles, in conformity with the law applicable by virtue of the rules of private international law.

Article 8

(1) For the purposes of this Convention statements made by and other conduct of a party are to be interpreted according to his intent where the other party knew or could not have been unaware what that intent was.

(2) If the preceding paragraph is not applicable, statements made by and other conduct of a party are to be interpreted according to the understanding that a reasonable person of the same kind as the other party would have had in the same circumstances.

(3) In determining the intent of a party or the understanding a reasonable person would have had, due consideration is to be given to all relevant circumstances of the case including the negotiations, any practices which the parties have established between themselves, usages and any subsequent conduct of the parties.

Article 9

(1) The parties are bound by any usage to which they have agreed and by any practices which they have established between themselves.

(2) The parties are considered, unless otherwise agreed, to have impliedly made applicable to their contract or its formation a usage of which the parties knew or ought to have known and which in international trade is widely known to, and regularly observed by, parties to contracts of the type involved in the particular trade concerned.

Article 10

For the purposes of this Convention:

(a) if a party has more than one place of business, the place of business is that which has the closest relationship to the contract and its performance, having regard to the circumstances known to or contemplated by the parties at any time before or at the conclusion of the contract;

(b) if a party does not have a place of business, reference is to be made to his habitual residence.

Article 11

A contract of sale need not be concluded in or evidenced by writing and is not subject to any other requirement as to form. It may be proved by any means, including witnesses.

Article 12

Any provision of article 11, article 29 or Part II of this Convention that allows a contract of sale or its modification or termination by agreement or any offer, acceptance or other indication of intention to be made in any form other than in writing does not apply where any party has his place of business in a Contracting State which has made a declaration under article 96 of this Convention. The parties may not derogate from or vary the effect or this article.

Article 13

For the purposes of this Convention "writing" includes telegram and telex.

PART II

FORMATION OF THE CONTRACT

Article 14

(1) A proposal for concluding a contract addressed to one or more specific persons constitutes an offer if it is sufficiently definite and indicates the intention of the offeror to be bound in case of acceptance. A proposal is sufficiently definite if it indicates the goods and expressly or implicitly fixes or makes provision for determining the quantity and the price.

(2) A proposal other than one addressed to one or more specific persons is to be considered merely as an invitation to make offers, unless the contrary is clearly indicated by the person making the proposal.

Article 15

(1) An offer becomes effective when it reaches the offeree.

(2) An offer, even if it is irrevocable, may be withdrawn if the withdrawal reaches the offeree before or at the same time as the offer.

Article 16

(1) Until a contract is concluded an offer may be revoked if the revocation reaches the offeree before he has dispatched an acceptance.

(2) However, an offer cannot be revoked:
  (a) if it indicates, whether by stating a fixed time for acceptance or otherwise, that it is irrevocable; or
  (b) if it was reasonable for the offeree to rely on the offer as being irrevocable and the offeree has acted in reliance on the offer.

Article 17

An offer, even if it is irrevocable, is terminated when a rejection reaches the offeror.

Article 18

(1) A statement made by or other conduct of the offeree indicating assent to an offer is an acceptance. Silence or inactivity does not in itself amount to acceptance.

(2) An acceptance of an offer becomes effective at the moment the indication of assent reaches the offeror. An acceptance is not effective if the indication of assent does not reach the offeror within the time he has fixed or, if no time is fixed, within a reasonable time, due account being taken of the circumstances of the transaction, including the rapidity of the means of communication employed by the offeror. An oral offer must be accepted immediately unless the circumstances indicate otherwise.

(3) However, if, by virtue of the offer or as a result of practices which the parties have established between themselves or of usage, the offeree may indicate assent by performing an act, such as one relating to the dispatch of the goods or payment of the price, without notice to the offeror, the acceptance is effective at the moment the act is performed, provided that the act is performed within the period of time laid down in the preceding paragraph.

Article 19

(1) A reply to an offer which purports to be an acceptance but contains additions, limitations or other modifications is a rejection of the offer and constitutes a counter-offer.

(2) However, a reply to an offer which purports to be an acceptance but contains additional or different terms which do not materially alter the terms of the offer constitutes an acceptance, unless the offeror, without undue delay, objects orally to the discrepancy or dispatches a notice to that effect. If he does not so object, the terms of the contract are the terms of the offer with the modifications contained in the acceptance.

(3) Additional or different terms relating, among other things, to the price, payment, quality and quantity of the goods, place and time of delivery, extent of one party's liability to the other or the settlement of disputes are considered to alter the terms of the offer materially.

Article 20

(1) A period of time for acceptance fixed by the offeror in a telegram or a letter begins to run from the moment the telegram is handed in for dispatch or from the date shown on the letter or, if no such date is shown, from the date shown on the envelope. A period of time for acceptance fixed by the offeror by telephone, telex or other means of instantaneous communication, begins to run from the moment that the offer reaches the offeree.

(2) Official holidays or non-business days occurring during the period for acceptance are included in calculating the period. However, if a notice of acceptance cannot be delivered at the address of the offeror on the last day of the period because that day falls on an official holiday or a non-business day at the place of business of the offeror, the period is extended until the first business day which follows.

Article 21

(1) A late acceptance is nevertheless effective as an acceptance if without delay the offeror orally so informs the offeree or dispatches a notice to that effect.

(2) If a letter or other writing containing a late acceptance shows that it has been sent in such circumstances that if its transmission had been normal it would have reached the offeror in due time, the late acceptance is effective as an acceptance unless, without delay, the offeror orally informs the offeree that he considers his offer as having lapsed or dispatches a notice to that effect.

Article 22

An acceptance may be withdrawn if the withdrawal reaches the offeror before or at the same time as the acceptance would have become effective.

Article 23

A contract is concluded at the moment when an acceptance of an offer becomes effective in accordance with the provisions of this Convention.

Article 24

For the purposes of this Part of the Convention, an offer, declaration of acceptance or any other indication of intention "reaches" the addressee when it is made orally to him or delivered by any other means to him personally, to his place of business or mailing address or, if he does not have a place of business or mailing address, to his habitual residence.

PART III

SALE OF GOODS

Chapter I

GENERAL PROVISIONS

Article 25

A breach of contract committed by one of the parties is fundamental if it results in such detriment to the other party as substantially to deprive him of what he is entitled to expect under the contract, unless the party in breach did not foresee and a reasonable person of the same kind in the same circumstances would not have foreseen such a result.

Article 26

A declaration of avoidance of the contract is effective only if made by notice to the other party.

Article 27

Unless otherwise expressly provided in this Part of the Convention, if any notice, request or other communication is given or made by a party in accordance with this Part and by means appropriate in the circumstances, a delay or error in the transmission of the communication or its failure to arrive does not deprive that party of the right to rely on the communication.

Article 28

If, in accordance with the provisions of this Convention, one party is entitled to require performance of any obligation by the other party, a court is not bound to enter a judgement for specific performance unless the court would do so under its own law in respect of similar contracts of sale not governed by this Convention.

Article 29

(1) A contract may be modified or terminated by the mere agreement of the parties.

(2) A contract in writing which contains a provision requiring any modification or termination by agreement to be in writing may not be otherwise modified or terminated by agreement. However, a party may be precluded by his conduct from asserting such a provision to the extent that the other party has relied on that conduct.

Chapter II

OBLIGATIONS OF THE SELLER

Article 30

The seller must deliver the goods, hand over any documents relating to them and transfer the property in the goods, as required by the contract and this Convention.

Section I. Delivery of the goods and handing over of documents

Article 31

If the seller is not bound to deliver the goods at any other particular place, his obligation to deliver consists:

(a) if the contract of sale involves carriage of the goods — in handing the goods over to the first carrier for transmission to the buyer;

(b) if, in cases not within the preceding subparagraph, the contract relates to specific goods, or unidentified goods to be drawn from a specific stock or to be manufactured or produced, and at the time of the conclusion of the contract the parties knew that the goods were at, or were to be manufactured or produced at, a particular place — in placing the goods at the buyer's disposal at that place;

(c) in other cases — in placing the goods at the buyer's disposal at the place where the seller had his place of business at the time of the conclusion of the contract.

Article 32

(1) If the seller, in accordance with the contract or this Convention, hands the goods over to a carrier and if the goods are not clearly identified to the contract by markings on the goods, by shipping documents or otherwise, the seller must give the buyer notice of the consignment specifying the goods.

(2) If the seller is bound to arrange for carriage of the goods, he must make such contracts as are necessary for carriage to the place fixed by means of transportation appropriate in the circumstances and according to the usual terms for such transportation.

(3) If the seller is not bound to effect insurance in respect of the carriage of the goods, he must, at the buyer's request, provide him with all available information necessary to enable him to effect such insurance.

Article 33

The seller must deliver the goods:

(a) if a date is fixed by or determinable from the contract, on that date;

(b) if a period of time is fixed by or determinable from the contract, at any time within that period unless circumstances indicate that the buyer is to choose a date; or

(c) in any other case, within a reasonable time after the conclusion of the contract.

Article 34

If the seller is bound to hand over documents relating to the goods, he must hand them over at the time and place and in the form required by the contract. If the seller has handed over documents before that time, he may, up to that time, cure any lack of conformity in the documents, if the exercise of this right does not cause the buyer unreasonable inconvenience or unreasonable expense. However, the buyer retains any right to claim damages as provided for in this Convention.

Section II. Conformity of the goods and third party claims

Article 35

(1) The seller must deliver goods which are of the quantity, quality and description required by the contract and which are contained or packaged in the manner required by the contract.

(2) Except where the parties have agreed otherwise, the goods do not conform with the contract unless they:
   (a) are fit for the purposes for which goods of the same description would ordinarily be used;
   (b) are fit for any particular purpose expressly or impliedly made known to the seller at the time of the conclusion of the contract, except where the circumstances show that the buyer did not rely, or that it was unreasonable for him to rely, on the seller's skill and judgement;
   (c) possess the qualities of goods which the seller has held out to the buyer as a sample or model;
   (d) are contained or packaged in the manner usual for such goods or, where there is no such manner, in a manner adequate to preserve and protect the goods.

(3) The seller is not liable under subparagraphs (a) to (d) of the preceding paragraph for any lack of conformity of the goods if at the time of the conclusion of the contract the buyer knew or could not have been unaware of such lack of conformity.

Article 36

(1) The seller is liable in accordance with the contract and this Convention for any lack of conformity which exists at the time when the risk passes to the buyer, even though the lack of conformity becomes apparent only after that time.

(2) The seller is also liable for any lack of conformity which occurs after the time indicated in the preceding paragraph and which is due to a breach of any of his obligations, including a breach of any guarantee that for a period of time the goods will remain fit for their ordinary purpose or for some particular purpose or will retain specified qualities or characteristics.

Article 37

If the seller has delivered goods before the date for delivery, he may, up to that date, deliver any missing part or make up any deficiency in the quantity of the goods delivered, or deliver goods in replacement of any non-conforming goods delivered or remedy any lack of conformity in the goods delivered, provided that the exercise of this right does not cause the buyer unreasonable inconvenience or unreasonable expense. However, the buyer retains any right to claim damages as provided for in this Convention.

Article 38

(1) The buyer must examine the goods, or cause them to be examined, within as short a period as is practicable in the circumstances.

(2) If the contract involves carriage of the goods, examination may be deferred until after the goods have arrived at their destination.

(3) If the goods are redirected in transit or redispatched by the buyer without a reasonable opportunity for examination by him and at the time of the conclusion of the contract the seller knew or ought to have known of the possibility of such redirection or redispatch, examination may be deferred until after the goods have arrived at the new destination.

Article 39

(1) The buyer loses the right to rely on a lack of conformity of the goods if he does not give notice to the seller specifying the nature of the lack of conformity within a reasonable time after he has discovered it or ought to have discovered it.

(2) In any event, the buyer loses the right to rely on a lack of conformity of the goods if he does not give the seller notice thereof at the latest within a period of two years from the date on which the goods were actually handed over to the buyer, unless this time-limit is inconsistent with a contractual period of guarantee.

Article 40

The seller is not entitled to rely on the provisions of articles 38 and 39 if the lack of conformity relates to facts of which he knew or could not have been unaware and which he did not disclose to the buyer.

Article 41

The seller must deliver goods which are free from any right or claim of a third party, unless the buyer agreed to take the goods subject to that right or claim. However, if such right or claim is based on industrial property or other intellectual property, the seller's obligation is governed by article 42.

Article 42

(1) The seller must deliver goods which are free from any right or claim of a third party based on industrial property or other intellectual property, of which at the time of the conclusion of the contract the seller knew or could not have been unaware, provided that the right or claim is based on industrial property or other intellectual property:

    (a) under the law of the State where the goods will be resold or otherwise used, if it was contemplated by the parties at the time of the conclusion of the contract that the goods would be resold or otherwise used in that State; or

    (b) in any other case, under the law of the State where the buyer has his place of business.

(2) The obligation of the seller under the preceding paragraph does not extend to cases where:

    (a) at the time of the conclusion of the contract the buyer knew or could not have been unaware of the right or claim; or

    (b) the right or claim results from the seller's compliance with technical drawings, designs, formulae or other such specifications furnished by the buyer.

Article 43

(1) The buyer loses the right to rely on the provisions of article 41 or article 42 if he does not give notice to the seller specifying the nature of the right or claim of the third party within a reasonable time after he has become aware or ought to have become aware of the right or claim.

(2) The seller is not entitled to rely on the provisions of the preceding paragraph if he knew of the right or claim of the third party and the nature of it.

Article 44

Notwithstanding the provisions of paragraph (1) of article 39 and paragraph (1) of article 43, the buyer may reduce the price in accordance with article 50 or claim damages, except for loss of profit, if he has a reasonable excuse for his failure to give the required notice.

Section III. Remedies for breach of contract by the seller

Article 45

(1) If the seller fails to perform any of his obligations under the contract or this Convention, the buyer may:
   (a) exercise the rights provided in articles 46 to 52;
   (b) claim damages as provided in articles 74 to 77.

(2) The buyer is not deprived of any right he may have to claim damages by exercising his right to other remedies.

(3) No period of grace may be granted to the seller by a court or arbitral tribunal when the buyer resorts to a remedy for breach of contract.

Article 46

(1) The buyer may require performance by the seller of his obligations unless the buyer has resorted to a remedy which is inconsistent with this requirement.

(2) If the goods do not conform with the contract, the buyer may require delivery of substitute goods only if the lack of conformity constitutes a fundamental breach of contract and a request for substitute goods is made either in conjunction with notice given under article 39 or within a reasonable time thereafter.

(3) If the goods do not conform with the contract, the buyer may require the seller to remedy the lack of conformity by repair, unless this is unreasonable having regard to all the circumstances. A request for repair must be made either in conjunction with notice given under article 39 or within a reasonable time thereafter.

Article 47

(1) The buyer may fix an additional period of time of reasonable length for performance by the seller of his obligations.

(2) Unless the buyer has received notice from the seller that he will not perform within the period so fixed, the buyer may not, during that period, resort to any remedy for breach of contract. However, the buyer is not deprived thereby of any right he may have to claim damages for delay in performance.

Article 48

(1) Subject to article 49, the seller may, even after the date for delivery, remedy at his own expense any failure to perform his obligations, if he can do so without unreasonable delay and without causing the buyer unreasonable inconvenience or uncertainty of reimbursement by the seller of expenses advanced by the buyer. However, the buyer retains any right to claim damages as provided for in this Convention.

(2) If the seller requests the buyer to make known whether he will accept performance and the buyer does not comply with the request within a reasonable time, the seller may perform within the time indicated in his request. The buyer may not, during that period of time, resort to any remedy which is inconsistent with performance by the seller.

(3) A notice by the seller that he will perform within a specified period of time is assumed to include a request, under the preceding paragraph, that the buyer make known his decision.

(4) A request or notice by the seller under paragraph (2) or (3) of this article is not effective unless received by the buyer.

Article 49

(1) The buyer may declare the contract avoided:
   (a) if the failure by the seller to perform any of his obligations under the contract or this Convention amounts to a fundamental breach of contract; or
   (b) in case of non-delivery, if the seller does not deliver the goods within the additional period of time fixed by the buyer in accordance with paragraph (1) of article 47 or declares that he will not deliver within the period so fixed.

(2) However, in cases where the seller has delivered the goods, the buyer loses the right to declare the contract avoided unless he does so:
   (a) in respect of late delivery, within a reasonable time after he has become aware that delivery has been made;
   (b) in respect of any breach other than late delivery, within a reasonable time:
      (i) after he knew or ought to have known of the breach;
      (ii) after the expiration of any additional period of time fixed by the buyer in accordance with paragraph (1) of article 47, or after the seller has declared that he will not perform his obligations within such an additional period; or
      (iii) after the expiration of any additional period of time indicated by the seller in accordance with paragraph (2) of article 48, or after the buyer has declared that he will not accept performance.

Article 50

If the goods do not conform with the contract and whether or not the price has already been paid, the buyer may reduce the price in the same proportion as the value that the goods actually delivered had at the time of the delivery bears to the value that conforming goods would have had at that time. However, if the seller remedies any failure to perform his obligations in accordance with article 37 or article 48 or if the buyer refuses to accept performance by the seller in accordance with those articles, the buyer may not reduce the price.

Article 51

(1) If the seller delivers only a part of the goods or if only a part of the goods delivered is in conformity with the contract, articles 46 to 50 apply in respect of the part which is missing or which does not conform.

(2) The buyer may declare the contract avoided in its entirety only if the failure to make delivery completely or in conformity with the contract amounts to a fundamental breach of the contract.

Article 52

(1) If the seller delivers the goods before the date fixed, the buyer may take delivery or refuse to take delivery.

(2) If the seller delivers a quantity of goods greater than that provided for in the contract, the buyer may take delivery or refuse to take delivery of the excess quantity. If the buyer takes delivery of all or part of the excess quantity, he must pay for it at the contract rate.

Chapter III

OBLIGATIONS OF THE BUYER

Article 53

The buyer must pay the price for the goods and take delivery of them as required by the contract and this Convention.

Section I. Payment of the price

Article 54

The buyer's obligation to pay the price includes taking such steps and complying with such formalities as may be required under the contract or any laws and regulations to enable payment to be made.

Article 55

Where a contract has been validly concluded but does not expressly or implicitly fix or make provision for determining the price, the parties are considered, in the absence of any indication to the contrary, to have impliedly made reference to the price generally charged at the time of the conclusion of the contract for such goods sold under comparable circumstances in the trade concerned.

Article 56

If the price is fixed according to the weight of the goods, in case of doubt it is to be determined by the net weight.

Article 57

(1) If the buyer is not bound to pay the price at any other particular place, he must pay it to the seller:
   (a) at the seller's place of business; or
   (b) if the payment is to be made against the handing over of the goods or of documents, at the place where the handing over takes place.

(2) The seller must bear any increases in the expenses incidental to payment which is caused by a change in his place of business subsequent to the conclusion of the contract.

Article 58

(1) If the buyer is not bound to pay the price at any other specific time, he must pay it when the seller places either the goods or documents controlling their disposition at the buyer's disposal in accordance with the contract and this Convention. The seller may make such payment a condition for handing over the goods or documents.

(2) If the contract involves carriage of the goods, the seller may dispatch the goods on terms whereby the goods, or documents controlling their disposition, will not be handed over to the buyer except against payment of the price.

(3) The buyer is not bound to pay the price until he has had an opportunity to examine the goods, unless the procedures for delivery or payment agreed upon by the parties are inconsistent with his having such an opportunity.

Article 59

The buyer must pay the price on the date fixed by or determinable from the contract and this Convention without the need for any request or compliance with any formality on the part of the seller.

Section II. Taking delivery

Article 60

The buyer's obligation to take delivery consists:

(a) in doing all the acts which could reasonably be expected of him in order to enable the seller to make delivery; and

(b) in taking over the goods.

Section III. Remedies for breach of contract by the buyer

Article 61

(1) If the buyer fails to perform any of his obligations under the contract or this Convention, the seller may:
　(a) exercise the rights provided in articles 62 to 65;
　(b) claim damages as provided in articles 74 to 77.

(2) The seller is not deprived of any right he may have to claim damages by exercising his right to other remedies.

(3) No period of grace may be granted to the buyer by a court or arbitral tribunal when the seller resorts to a remedy for breach of contract.

Article 62

The seller may require the buyer to pay the price, take delivery or perform his other obligations, unless the seller has resorted to a remedy which is inconsistent with this requirement.

Article 63

(1) The seller may fix an additional period of time of reasonable length for performance by the buyer of his obligations.

(2) Unless the seller has received notice from the buyer that he will not perform within the period so fixed, the seller may not, during that period, resort to any remedy for breach of contract. However, the seller is not deprived thereby of any right he may have to claim damages for delay in performance.

Article 64

(1) The seller may declare the contract avoided:
　(a) if the failure by the buyer to perform any of his obligations under the contract or this Convention amounts to a fundamental breach of contract; or
　(b) if the buyer does not, within the additional period of time fixed by the seller in accordance with paragraph (1) of article 63, perform his obligation to pay the price or take delivery of the goods, or if he declares that he will not do so within the period so fixed.

(2) However, in cases where the buyer has paid the price, the seller loses the right to declare the contract avoided unless he does so:

   (a) in respect of late performance by the buyer, before the seller has become aware that performance has been rendered; or

   (b) in respect of any breach other than late performance by the buyer, within a reasonable time:

      (i) after the seller knew or ought to have known of the breach; or

      (ii) after the expiration of any additional period of time fixed by the seller in accordance with paragraph (1) of article 63, or after the buyer has declared that he will not perform his obligations within such an additional period.

Article 65

(1) If under the contract the buyer is to specify the form, measurement or other features of the goods and he fails to make such specification either on the date agreed upon or within a reasonable time after receipt of a request from the seller, the seller may, without prejudice to any other rights he may have, make the specification himself in accordance with the requirements of the buyer that may be known to him.

(2) If the seller makes the specification himself, he must inform the buyer of the details thereof and must fix a reasonable time within which the buyer may make a different specification. If, after receipt of such a communication, the buyer fails to do so within the time so fixed, the specification made by the seller is binding.

Chapter IV

PASSING OF RISK

Article 66

Loss of or damage to the goods after the risk has passed to the buyer does not discharge him from his obligation to pay the price, unless the loss or damage is due to an act or omission of the seller.

Article 67

(1) If the contract of sale involves carriage of the goods and the seller is not bound to hand them over at a particular place, the risk passes to the buyer when the goods are handed over to the first carrier for transmission to the buyer in accordance with the contract of sale. If the seller is bound to hand the goods over to a carrier at a particular place, the risk does not pass to the buyer until the goods are handed over to the carrier at that place. The fact that the seller is authorized

to retain documents controlling the disposition of the goods does not affect the passage of the risk.

(2) Nevertheless, the risk does not pass to the buyer until the goods are clearly identified to the contract, whether by markings on the goods, by shipping documents, by notice given to the buyer or otherwise.

Article 68

The risk in respect of goods sold in transit passes to the buyer from the time of the conclusion of the contract. However, if the circumstances so indicate, the risk is assumed by the buyer from the time the goods were handed over to the carrier who issued the documents embodying the contract of carriage. Nevertheless, if at the time of the conclusion of the contract of sale the seller knew or ought to have known that the goods had been lost or damaged and did not disclose this to the buyer, the loss or damage is at the risk of the seller.

Article 69

(1) In cases not within articles 67 and 68, the risk passes to the buyer when he takes over the goods or, if he does not do so in due time, from the time when the goods are placed at his disposal and he commits a breach of contract by failing to take delivery.

(2) However, if the buyer is bound to take over the goods at a place other than a place of business of the seller, the risk passes when delivery is due and the buyer is aware of the fact that the goods are placed at his disposal at that place.

(3) If the contract relates to goods not then identified, the goods are considered not to be placed at the disposal of the buyer until they are clearly identified to the contract.

Article 70

If the seller has committed a fundamental breach of contract, articles 67, 68 and 69 do not impair the remedies available to the buyer on account of the breach.

Chapter V

PROVISIONS COMMON TO THE OBLIGATIONS OF THE SELLER AND OF THE BUYER

Section I. Anticipatory breach and instalment contracts

Article 71

(1) A party may suspend the performance of his obligations if, after the conclusion of the contract, it becomes apparent that the other party will not perform a substantial part of his obligations as a result of:

(a) a serious deficiency in his ability to perform or in his creditworthiness; or

(b) his conduct in preparing to perform or in performing the contract.

(2) If the seller has already dispatched the goods before the grounds described in the preceding paragraph become evident, he may prevent the handing over of the goods to the buyer even though the buyer holds a document which entitles him to obtain them. The present paragraph relates only to the rights in the goods as between the buyer and the seller.

(3) A party suspending performance, whether before or after dispatch of the goods, must immediately give notice of the suspension to the other party and must continue with performance if the other party provides adequate assurance of his performance.

Article 72

(1) If prior to the date for performance of the contract it is clear that one of the parties will commit a fundamental breach of contract, the other party may declare the contract avoided.

(2) If time allows, the party intending to declare the contract avoided must give reasonable notice to the other party in order to permit him to provide adequate assurance of his performance.

(3) The requirements of the preceding paragraph do not apply if the other party has declared that he will not perform his obligations.

Article 73

(1) In the case of a contract for delivery of goods by instalments, if the failure of one party to perform any of his obligations in respect of any instalment constitutes a fundamental breach of contract with respect to that instalment, the other party may declare the contract avoided with respect to that instalment.

(2) If one party's failure to perform any of his obligations in respect of any instalment gives the other party good grounds to conclude that a fundamental breach of contract will occur with respect to future instalments, he may declare the contract avoided for the future, provided that he does so within a reasonable time.

(3) A buyer who declares the contract avoided in respect of any delivery may, at the same time, declare it avoided in respect of deliveries already made or of future deliveries if, by reason of their interdependence, those deliveries could not be used for the purpose contemplated by the parties at the time of the conclusion of the contract.

Section II. Damages

Article 74

Damages for breach of contract by one party consist of a sum equal to the loss, including loss of profit, suffered by the other party as a consequence of the breach. Such damages may not exceed the loss which the party in breach foresaw or ought to have foreseen at the time of the conclusion of the contract, in the light of the facts and matters of which he then knew or ought to have known, as a possible consequence of the breach of contract.

Article 75

If the contract is avoided and if, in a reasonable manner and within a reasonable time after avoidance, the buyer has bought goods in replacement or the seller has resold the goods, the party claiming damages may recover the difference between the contract price and the price in the substitute transaction as well as any further damages recoverable under article 74.

Article 76

(1) If the contract is avoided and there is a current price for the goods, the party claiming damages may, if he has not made a purchase or resale under article 75, recover the difference between the price fixed by the contract and the current price at the time of avoidance as well as any further damages recoverable under article 74. If, however, the party claiming damages has avoided the contract after taking over the goods, the current price at the time of such taking over shall be applied instead of the current price at the time of avoidance.

(2) For the purposes of the preceding paragraph, the current price is the price prevailing at the place where delivery of the goods should have been made or, if there is no current price at that place, the price at such other place as serves as a reasonable substitute, making due allowance for differences in the cost of transporting the goods.

Article 77

A party who relies on a breach of contract must take such measures as are reasonable in the circumstances to mitigate the loss, including loss of profit, resulting from the breach. If he fails to take such measures, the party in breach may claim a reduction in the damages in the amount by which the loss should have been mitigated.

Section III. Interest

Article 78

If a party fails to pay the price or any other sum that is in arrears, the other party is entitled to interest on it, without prejudice to any claim for damages recoverable under article 74.

Section IV. Exemptions

Article 79

(1) A party is not liable for a failure to perform any of his obligations if he proves that the failure was due to an impediment beyond his control and that he could not reasonably be expected to have taken the impediment into account at the time of the conclusion of the contract or to have avoided or overcome it or its consequences.

(2) If the party's failure is due to the failure by a third person whom he has engaged to perform the whole or a part of the contract, that party is exempt from liability only if:

    (a) he is exempt under the preceding paragraph; and

    (b) the person whom he has so engaged would be so exempt if the provisions of that paragraph were applied to him.

(3) The exemption provided by this article has effect for the period during which the impediment exists.

(4) The party who fails to perform must give notice to the other party of the impediment and its effect on his ability to perform. If the notice is not received by the other party within a reasonable time after the party who fails to perform knew or ought to have known of the impediment, he is liable for damages resulting from such non-receipt.

(5) Nothing in this article prevents either party from exercising any right other than to claim damages under this Convention.

Article 80

A party may not rely on a failure of the other party to perform, to the extent that such failure was caused by the first party's act or omission.

Section V. Effects of avoidance

Article 81

(1) Avoidance of the contract releases both parties from their obligations under it, subject to any damages which may be due. Avoidance does not affect any provision of the contract for the settlement of disputes or any other provision of the

contract governing the rights and obligations of the parties consequent upon the avoidance of the contract.

(2) A party who has performed the contract either wholly or in part may claim restitution from the other party of whatever the first party has supplied or paid under the contract. If both parties are bound to make restitution, they must do so concurrently.

Article 82

(1) The buyer loses the right to declare the contract avoided or to require the seller to deliver substitute goods if it is impossible for him to make restitution of the goods substantially in the condition in which he received them.

(2) The preceding paragraph does not apply:
    (a) if the impossibility of making restitution of the goods or of making restitution of the goods substantially in the condition in which the buyer received them is not due to his act or omission;
    (b) if the goods or part of the goods have perished or deteriorated as a result of the examination provided for in article 38; or
    (c) if the goods or part of the goods have been sold in the normal course of business or have been consumed or transformed by the buyer in the course of normal use before he discovered or ought to have discovered the lack of conformity.

Article 83

A buyer who has lost the right to declare the contract avoided or to require the seller to deliver substitute goods in accordance with article 82 retains all other remedies under the contract and this Convention.

Article 84

(1) If the seller is bound to refund the price, he must also pay interest on it, from the date on which the price was paid.

(2) The buyer must account to the seller for all benefits which he has derived from the goods or part of them:
    (a) if he must make restitution of the goods or part of them; or
    (b) if it is impossible for him to make restitution of all or part of the goods or to make restitution of all or part of the goods substantially in the condition in which he received them, but he has nevertheless declared the contract avoided or required the seller to deliver substitute goods.

Section VI. Preservation of the goods

Article 85

If the buyer is in delay in taking delivery of the goods or, where payment of the price and delivery of the goods are to be made concurrently, if he fails to pay the price, and the seller is either in possession of the goods or otherwise able to control their disposition, the seller must take such steps as are reasonable in the circumstances to preserve them. He is entitled to retain them until he has been reimbursed his reasonable expenses by the buyer.

Article 86

(1) If the buyer has received the goods and intends to exercise any right under the contract or this Convention to reject them, he must take such steps to preserve them as are reasonable in the circumstances. He is entitled to retain them until he has been reimbursed his reasonable expenses by the seller.

(2) If goods dispatched to the buyer have been placed at his disposal at their destination and he exercises the right to reject them, he must take possession of them on behalf of the seller, provided that this can be done without payment of the price and without unreasonable inconvenience or unreasonable expense. This provision does not apply if the seller or a person authorized to take charge of the goods on his behalf is present at the destination. If the buyer takes possession of the goods under this paragraph, his rights and obligations are governed by the preceding paragraph.

Article 87

A party who is bound to take steps to preserve the goods may deposit them in a warehouse of a third person at the expense of the other party provided that the expense incurred is not unreasonable.

Article 88

(1) A party who is bound to preserve the goods in accordance with article 85 or 86 may sell them by any appropriate means if there has been an unreasonable delay by the other party in taking possession of the goods or in taking them back or in paying the price or the cost of preservation, provided that reasonable notice of the intention to sell has been given to the other party.

(2) If the goods are subject to rapid deterioration or their preservation would invole unreasonable expense, a party who is bound to preserve the goods in accordance with article 85 or 86 must take reasonable measures to sell them. To the extent possible he must give notice to the other party of his intention to sell.

(3) A party selling the goods has the right to retain out of the proceeds of sale an amount equal to the reasonable expenses of preserving the goods and of selling them. He must account to the other party for the balance.

PART IV

FINAL PROVISIONS

Article 89

The Secretary-General of the United Nations is hereby designated as the depositary for this Convention.

Article 90

This Convention does not prevail over any international agreement which has already been or may be entered into and which contains provisions concerning the matters governed by this Convention, provided that the parties have their places of business in States parties to such agreement.

Article 91

(1) This Convention is open for signature at the concluding meeting of the United Nations Conference on Contracts for the International Sale of Goods and will remain open for signature by all States at the Headquarters of the United Nations, New York until 30 September 1981.

(2) This Convention is subject to ratification, acceptance or approval by the signatory States.

(3) This Convention is open for accession by all States which are not signatory States as from the date it is open for signature.

(4) Instruments of ratification, acceptance, approval and accession are to be deposited with the Secretary-General of the United Nations.

Article 92

(1) A Contracting State may declare at the time of signature, ratification, acceptance, approval or accession that it will not be bound by Part II of this Convention or that it will not be bound by Part III of this Convention.

(2) A Contracting State which makes a declaration in accordance with the preceding paragraph in respect of Part II or Part III of this Convention is not to be considered a Contracting State within paragraph (1) of article 1 of this Convention in respect of matters governed by the Part to which the declaration applies.

Article 93

(1) If a Contracting State has two or more territorial units in which, according to its constitution, different systems of law are applicable in relation to the matters dealt with in this Convention, it may, at the time of signature, ratification, acceptance, approval or accession, declare that this Convention is to extend to all its territorial units or only to one or more of them, and may amend its declaration by submitting another declaration at any time.

(2) These declarations are to be notified to the depositary and are to state expressly the territorial units to which the Convention extends.

(3) If, by virtue of a declaration under this article, this Convention extends to one or more but not all of the territorial units of a Contracting State, and if the place of business of a party is located in that State, this place of business, for the purposes of this Convention, is considered not to be in a Contracting State, unless it is in a territorial unit to which the Convention extends.

(4) If a Contracting State makes no declaration under paragraph (1) of this article, the Convention is to extend to all territorial units of that State.

Article 94

(1) Two or more Contracting States which have the same or closely related legal rules on matters governed by this Convention may at any time declare that the Convention is not to apply to contracts of sale or to their formation where the parties have their places of business in those States. Such declarations may be made jointly or by reciprocal unilateral declarations.

(2) A Contracting State which has the same or closely related legal rules on matters governed by this Convention as one or more non-Contracting States may at any time declare that the Convention is not to apply to contracts of sale or to their formation where the parties have their places of business in those States.

(3) If a State which is the object of a declaration under the preceding paragraph subsequently becomes a Contracting State, the declaration made will, as from the date on which the Convention enters into force in respect of the new Contracting State, have the effect of a declaration made under paragraph (1), provided that the new Contracting State joins in such declaration or makes a reciprocal unilateral declaration.

Article 95

Any State may declare at the time of the deposit of its instrument of ratification, acceptance, approval or accession that it will not be bound by subparagraph (1)(b) of article 1 of this Convention.

Article 96

A Contracting State whose legislation requires contracts of sale to be concluded in or evidenced by writing may at any time make a declaration in accordance with article 12 that any provision of article 11, article 29, or Part II of this Convention, that allows a contract of sale or its modification or termination by agreement or any offer, acceptance, or other indication of intention to be made in any form other than in writing, does not apply where any party has his place of business in that State.

Article 97

(1) Declarations made under this Convention at the time of signature are subject to confirmation upon ratification, acceptance or approval.

(2) Declarations and confirmations of declarations are to be in writing and be formally notified to the depositary.

(3) A declaration takes effect simultaneously with the entry into force of this Convention in respect of the State concerned. However, a declaration of which the depositary receives formal notification after such entry into force takes effect on the first day of the month following the expiration of six months after the date of its receipt by the depositary. Reciprocal unilateral declarations under article 94 take effect on the first day of the month following the expiration of six months after the receipt of the latest declaration by the depositary.

(4) Any State which makes a declaration under this Convention may withdraw it at any time by a formal notification in writing addressed to the depositary. Such withdrawal is to take effect on the first day of the month following the expiration of six months after the date of the receipt of the notification by the depositary.

(5) A withdrawal of a declaration made under article 94 renders inoperative, as from the date on which the withdrawal takes effect, any reciprocal declaration made by another State under that article.

Article 98

No reservations are permitted except those expressly authorized in this Convention.

Article 99

(1) This Convention enters into force, subject to the provisions of paragraph (6) of this article, on the first day of the month following the expiration of twelve months after the date of deposit of the tenth instrument of ratification, acceptance, approval or accession, including an instrument which contains a declaration made under article 92.

(2) When a State ratifies, accepts, approves or accedes to this Convention after the deposit of the tenth instrument of ratification, acceptance, approval or accession, this Convention, with the exception of the Part excluded, enters into force

in respect of that State, subject to the provisions of paragraph (6) of this article, on the first day of the month following the expiration of twelve months after the date of the deposit of its instrument of ratification, acceptance, approval or accession.

(3) A State which ratifies, accepts, approves or accedes to this Convention and is a party to either or both the Convention relating to a Uniform Law on the Formation of Contracts for the International Sale of Goods done at The Hague on 1 July 1964 § 1964 Hague Formation Convention) and the Convention relating to a Uniform Law on the International Sale of Goods done at The Hague on 1 July 1964 § 1964 Hague Sales Convention) shall at the same time denounce, as the case may be, either or both the 1964 Hague Sales Convention and the 1964 Hague Formation Convention by notifying the Government of the Netherlands to that effect.

(4) A State party to the 1964 Hague Sales Convention which ratifies, accepts, approves or accedes to the present Convention and declares or has declared under article 52 that it will not be bound by Part II of this Convention shall at the time of ratification, acceptance, approval or accession denounce the 1964 Hague Sales Convention by notifying the Government of the Netherlands to that effect.

(5) A State party to the 1964 Hague Formation Convention which ratifies, accepts, approves or accedes to the present Convention and declares or has declared under article 92 that it will not be bound by Part III of this Convention shall at the time of ratification, acceptance, approval or accession denounce the 1964 Hague Formation Convention by notifying the Government of the Netherlands to that effect.

(6) For the purpose of this article, ratifications, acceptances, approvals and accessions in respect of this Convention by States parties to the 1964 Hague Formation Convention or to the 1964 Hague Sales Convention shall not be effective until such denunciations as may be required on the part of those States in respect of the latter two Conventions have themselves become effective. The depositary of this Convention shall consult with the Government of the Netherlands, as the depositary of the 1964 Conventions, so as to ensure necessary co-ordination in this respect.

Article 100

(1) This Convention applies to the formation of a contract only when the proposal for concluding the contract is made on or after the date when the Convention enters into force in respect of the Contracting States referred to in subparagraph (1)(a) or the Contracting State referred to in subparagraph (1)(b) of article 1.

(2) This Convention applies only to contracts concluded on or after the date when the Convention enters into force in respect of the Contracting States referred to in subparagraph (1)(a) or the Contracting State referred to in subparagraph (1)(b) of article 1.

Article 101

(1) A Contracting State may denounce this Convention, or Part II or Part III of the Convention, by a formal notification in writing addressed to the depositary.

(2) The denunciation takes effect on the first day of the month following the expiration of twelve months after the notification is received by the depositary. Where a longer period for the denunciation to take effect is specified in the notification, the denunciation takes effect upon the expiration of such longer period after the notification is received by the depositary.

DONE at Vienna, this day of eleventh day of April, one thousand nine hundred and eighty, in a single original, of which the Arabic, Chinese, English, French, Russian and Spanish texts are equally authentic.

IN WITNESS WHEREOF the undersigned plenipotentiaries, being duly authorized by their respective Governments, have signed this Convention.